Moving to VB.NET: Strategies, Concepts, and Code

DAN APPLEMAN

Moving to VB.NET: Strategies, Concepts, and Code

Copyright ©2001 by Dan Appleman

ISBN (pbk): 1-893115-97-6

Printed and bound in the United States of America   45678910

Trademarked names may appear in this book. Rather than use a trademark symbol with every occurrence of a trademarked name, we use the names only in an editorial fashion and to the benefit of the trademark owner, with no intention of infringement of the trademark.

Editorial Directors: Dan Appleman, Gary Cornell, Karen Watterson

Assistant Editorial Director: Jason Gilmore

Managing Editor: Grace Wong

Technical Reviewer: Scott Stabbert

Editor: Kiersten Burke

Production Editor: Kari Brooks

Page Composition: Susan Glinert

Artist and Cover Designer: Karl Miyajima

Indexer: Julie Kawabata

Distributed to the book trade in the United States by Springer-Verlag New York, Inc., 175 Fifth Avenue, New York, NY, 10010

and outside the United States by Springer-Verlag GmbH & Co. KG, Tiergartenstr. 17, 69112 Heidelberg, Germany

In the United States, phone 1-800-SPRINGER; orders@springer-ny.com; http://www.springer-ny.com

Outside the United States, contact orders@springer.de; http://www.springer.de; fax +49 6221 345229

For information on translations, please contact Apress directly at 901 Grayson Street, Suite 204, Berkeley, CA, 94710

Phone: 510-549-5937; Fax: 510-549-5939; info@apress.com; http://www.apress.com

The information in this book is distributed on an "as is" basis, without warranty. Although every precaution has been taken in the preparation of this work, neither the author nor Apress shall have any liability to any person or entity with respect to any loss or damage caused or alleged to be caused directly or indirectly by the information contained in this work.

The code download is available online at http://www.apress.com and is for purchasers of this book only. Readers will need to have this book in hand in order to successfully answer questions that will provide access to the code.

Contents at a Glance

Contents

Part IV   The Wonderful World of .NET *341*

Introduction

YOU'VE PROBABLY BEEN HEARING ABOUT Microsoft's .NET Framework and the new features of Visual Basic.NET. Perhaps you've read articles about it in magazines. Perhaps you've read promotional material from Microsoft. Perhaps you've even played with one of the beta versions.

Regardless of how you've learned about it, you're probably feeling a bit overwhelmed. It's such a massive change both in language and approach that it's difficult to sort out the reality from the marketing and difficult to decide where one should actually start when approaching this new technology.

That's what this book is about.

- It's about the priorities you should use in learning .NET and the strategies you should use in deciding how and when to deploy .NET.

- It's about the concepts you need to know in order to understand the new features of Visual Basic.NET and how they will influence the way you write code under this new framework.

- And it's about the changes in the Visual Basic language itself.

Even though this is one of the earliest books on .NET, it is not intended to be a general survey of the framework or even a comprehensive reference to Visual Basic.NET—I'm sure there will be plenty of those books available later. Nor will you find here a rehash of the .NET documentation. The .NET Framework is so large and the changes to Visual Basic.NET so widespread that a comprehensive book would be huge and probably overwhelming (assuming it is even possible to fit one into a single volume). Entire subjects such as the development environment, debugging, and high-level services are deserving of books of their own and will be covered here barely or not at all.

This book is intended to be one of the first books you read on .NET—the one that will prepare you to understand the more comprehensive books, Microsoft's documentation, and the inevitable manual rehashes. It is intended to help you to think about this new technology in the context of your own development plans, and to get you up to speed quickly on concepts that will be new to most Visual Basic programmers. It is intended to be concise and easy read yet provide enough depth to make you an expert on the VB.NET language and to lay the foundation for you to become an expert in those areas of the .NET Framework that most interest you.

Who Are You?

I am assuming that you are an intermediate to advanced-level Visual Basic programmer. This book is emphatically *not* intended for people who are new to programming in general, though it should prove useful to non-Visual Basic programmers who are coming to VB.NET from other languages. It will also be valuable to team leaders and managers who are making deployment decisions—they'll find that Part One—Strategies directly addresses management and technology issues.

Unlike many similar books, this one is focused entirely on helping current VB6 programmers come up to speed on .NET in general and VB.NET in particular. Hence, the organization is quite unusual. I waste no time explaining basic concepts such as "What is a class?" or "How does a For...Next loop work?" or "What is a collection?" Believe me, there is plenty to teach without rehashing the things that every VB6 programmer beyond the beginner level knows.

Regarding Microsoft

The world seems to have recently divided itself into two camps: those who love and support Microsoft and those who hate and despise them. Personally, I fall into that somewhat unworldly group who refuses to see Microsoft as a major deity.[1] As a result, I sometimes find myself condemned by the non-Microsoft world as a "Microsoft supporter" and condemned by the Microsoft world as someone who "hates Microsoft."

The truth is that I have a lot of respect for Microsoft.[2] They have a great deal of good technology, quite a bit of great technology, and a depressing amount of bloated technology. They also have a very effective marketing department whose actions I often find incomprehensible. I know enough about them to know that they are a chaotic organization—and their decisions are sometimes influenced as much by internal politics as technological sophistication (which is true of any company but somehow people think saying this of Microsoft is an insult).

So, I like them. I also like to make fun of them—partly because they make a great target but partly because it's a natural and human reaction in dealing with an overwhelming force.[3]

For the record, I don't hate them. I like them.

However, that doesn't mean that I blindly agree with them or believe that they make the right choices on technology. I certainly don't believe everything they write about "the best way for you to write software" and neither should you. Why?

---

1. A minor deity perhaps. My point is that Microsoft has joined the ranks of keyboards, programmer's editors, and operating systems as a "religious" issue—one on which I am a confirmed atheist.

2. Some of my best friends work at Microsoft—it's a cliché but true.

3. And if you don't think they're an overwhelming force, just think for a moment about the impact .NET is going to have on your own career.

Because you know as well as I do that the best way for you to write software changes quickly—often in ways that Microsoft itself doesn't anticipate.

In this book, I will be sharing my opinions on the .NET Framework and the changes that have been made to the Visual Basic language. Some of those opinions will differ from what Microsoft says. Some will be controversial. Some will probably turn out to be wrong. But that's okay. My goal is not that you take everything I say as gospel, but that you think about the new technology in the context of your own situation—that you evaluate and judge it for yourself. I hope my perspective will broaden the way you look at Visual Basic.NET and ultimately help you in the process of adopting the technology to suit your own needs.

Regarding Prereleases

If you've followed my prior books and articles, you probably know that there are two types of books I hate: manual rehashes and books that are rushed and inaccurate because they're based on prerelease code.

So here I am writing a book based on prerelease code, which leads to three possibilities:

1. I have become a complete hypocrite.

2. I've sold out for the money because an early book sells well even if it's crap.

3. I have some good reason for doing this book that isn't obvious but you're at least willing to hear my side of the story.

I know what you're thinking. The answer is three, right?

Of course. But it's also two[4]—except that I sincerely hope and believe that this book isn't crap.

Even though the .NET Framework is not yet released, the overall architecture and approach of the framework is set, as are the vast majority of the namespaces. The Visual Basic.NET language definition is final and seems to work as specified in the documentation. Its architecture is also well defined. According to Microsoft there should be few language changes from Beta 2 until final release.

You don't need to wait until the final release to start learning about them and they are well enough defined at this point for me to write about them.

More important, I am very concerned that people will approach these technologies the wrong way…

- That they'll condemn the language changes to VB.NET unfairly just because they break compatibility with existing code.

---

4. Sometimes it's painful to be honest.

- That they'll condemn the Common Language Runtime just because it's a huge runtime and VB.NET no longer has native code support.

- That they'll cheerfully start using inheritance and multithreading in ways that will get them into trouble—with code that is unscalable, unsupportable, or hard to debug.

With this technology, more than any in recent memory, it is critical that you start out right—that you understand why Microsoft made the choices they did and why they are mostly good choices. You need to understand that inheritance is something you use only after a great deal of thought—almost as a last resort. You need to realize that consequences of a design mistake in a free-threaded environment can be incredibly expensive due to the difficulty of detecting obscure synchronization bugs.

That's the main reason that I wanted to get this book out early—because I want to help VB programmers get started off correctly. And I guess I'm confident enough in my own ability to think that what I have to say will help.

Regarding Source Code

There are quite a few sample programs included with this book. You can download them from the publisher's Web site at http://www.apress.com. The source code is organized by chapter so if you see a reference to a project named TwoInterfaces in Chapter 5, look under the Source\CH5\TwoInterfaces directory.

My assumption is that you will use the source code provided from the Web site and not attempt to type in the code printed in the book. There are two reasons for this. First, in many cases, I have not included all of the code needed to run the project—just enough to explain the concept under discussion. That way you don't have to wade through endless printed listings. Second, this edition of the book is based on prerelease code and I expect that some of the code will break as Microsoft makes changes. I'll update the code as often as I can to include these changes. Also, check out the book's Web site at http://www.desaware.com for lists of updates and corrections.

The code printed in the book was tested as a pre-Beta 2 build made available to authors. The code available on the Web site will be Beta 2 code (depending on what Microsoft ends up calling the forthcoming beta) and will include a revision sheet that lists any last minute changes from the printed book to final Beta 2 code (this approach is necessary given the time it takes to actually produce and print a book). The code on the Web site will be updated to be compatible with future public betas and the final release as soon as possible.

Regarding Desaware

I always mention Desaware in my books. I do so because I am first and foremost a software developer. I write real code that ships and is currently running on untold thousands of systems. I helped cofound Apress in order to find a good home for my books (and if you are a software developer who is interested in writing, you'll find no better home—send me an email if you're interested).

But Desaware is the home for my software—primarily component software designed to help Visual Basic (and now Visual Studio) developers. At this time, I don't know what kinds of products we'll have for VB.NET—but you can bet we'll have some, so I invite you to visit http://www.desaware.com and see what we're up to. More important, you'll also find the updates and corrections page for this book on that site—and given the early publication, I'm sure there will be updates as the .NET Framework progresses and is ultimately released.

With that, I invite you join me in this introduction to Visual Basic.NET and the .NET Framework.

Dan Appleman
May 2001
dan_appleman@apress.com

An Important Note Regarding Code in This Book

THE EDITION OF THE BOOK you are holding is a **Beta 2-compliant** book. There have been dramatic breaking changes between Beta 1 and Beta 2 of Visual Studio.NET.

Updates and corrections to both the source code and contents of this book will be available on the Web for both future beta releases and for the final release of Visual Studio. So, you can be confident that this book will not become obsolete as the release date gets closer.

All code listings in this book have been verified against the latest software build available to authors. Every effort has been made to make it accurate to the final Beta 2 gold release.

> **NOTE** *The code download is available online at* http://www.apress.com *and is for purchasers of this book only. Readers will need to have this book in hand in order to successfully answer questions that will provide access to the code.*

The source code available for download has been tested under the final Beta 2 release. Therefore you should *not* attempt to test code by typing it in from listings in the book but should download the source code from http://www.apress.com.

Be sure to check the Web site at http://www.apress.com or http://www.desaware.com for the latest updates and corrections.

Sample code for this book has been verified only under Windows 2000. Updates and corrections will be provided on the Web site for other operating systems before release of the final product. At the time of publication, Microsoft recommends doing all .NET development on Windows 2000.

Another Important Note Regarding Code in This Book

All of the code examples shown in this book have Option Strict set to *on* using the Project Properties dialog box (Build tab).

I *strongly* recommend that you always turn Option Strict *on* for all of your VB.NET projects.

I feel so strongly about this that the only place in this book where I will even acknowledge the possibility of turning this option off is in Chapter 8, where I will do my best to show you that not only should turning it on be the first thing you do in any program, but also that Microsoft's decision to leave it off by default should possibly be counted as their single greatest mistake with regards to VB.NET.

Acknowledgments

I HAVE SO MANY PEOPLE to thank for their help with this book that it's hard to know where to begin. The entire team at Apress has been fantastic. Grace Wong continues to work miracles as managing editor and put together a fantastic team for this book: Kari Brooks managed to stay flexible as the schedule kept changing. Kiersten Burke was exactly the kind of copyeditor I like—one with a light touch, yet imposing discipline and consistency so I don't have to. Thanks to Carol Burbo who helped on formatting (great to work with you again). Also thanks to Susan Glinert, Julie Kawabata, and Karl Miyajima for their contributions in composition, indexing, and art respectively. Also kudos to Stephanie Rodriguez for going above and beyond in helping with the early and ongoing promotion for the book; to Mason Smith and the rest of the Springer team on the sales side; and to Cherryl Schwinges on the scheduling and administrative side. Thanks to Karen Watterson, who somehow found time in her impossible schedule to look over many of the chapters and offer sage advice. To Jason Gilmore, who I'm glad to have on the team even though he had nothing to do with this particular book. And, of course, to Gary Cornell—the guy who really makes Apress work.

I can't even begin to express my gratitude to Scott Stabbert—one of the finest technical editors I've ever had the pleasure of working with. Aside from the obvious help in keeping the book accurate (especially considering the many changes that took place to VB.NET while the book was being written), he showed infinite patience on those occasions when I found it necessary to criticize Microsoft—more than I would normally expect from a Microsoft employee. And he provided additional insights into the minds and motivations of the developers. Thanks, Scott—I hope we can work together on something again soon. Also thanks to some others at Microsoft including Eric Andre, Drew Fletcher, Dave Mendlen, Ari Bixhorn, and Mike Iem, for reasons they know and I probably can't tell you without getting into trouble.

Thanks to Chris MacAskill, Maggie Cannon, and Judy Kirkpatrick at MightyWords. Their help in getting my Ebook comparing VB.NET and C# published also helped get the word out on this book.

As always, this book could not possibly have been published without the strong support of my family at Desaware. Karyn Duncan, Stjepan Pejic, Marian Kicklighter, Franky Wong, and the rest of the gang: Ariel, Gil, Igor, Oded, and Luke—thanks to you all.

And, of course, to my family outside of Desaware—to the guys in Dr. Seuss AZA who didn't gripe when my presence at their events consisted of me sitting in a corner writing on my laptop. And to Roan, Maya, and Kendra for helping me come up for air occasionally. Finally, thanks Mom, for forcing me to eat now and then; and Dad for everything—plus reviewing every chapter before it was submitted.

Part I

Strategies

"Technology is a queer thing. It brings you great gifts with one hand
and it stabs you in the back with the other."

—Charles Percy Snow

CHAPTER 1

Where Should You Begin?

FRANK HERBERT, IN HIS BOOK *Dune*, begins with the quote, "A beginning is the time for taking the most delicate care that the balances are correct."

I suppose that applies to books also. It certainly applies to learning a new technology.

First judgments, attitude, and the order in which material is introduced can have a huge impact on how well and how quickly one learns. A misconception instilled early on can become a huge obstacle to later understanding. The lack of a key concept can create a chasm that prevents progress in learning an advanced topic.

Beginnings are, indeed, dangerous times.

So it is with great care that I thought of how to begin.

I could begin as if this were one of the introductory sessions Microsoft has presented about .NET at conferences. I can picture it now....

You are sitting in a large auditorium. On a distant podium, a speaker is barely visible behind a monitor—the screen of which is blown up on several other screens that would not be out of place in an Imax theatre. He shows you Visual Basic.NET, drops some controls on a form, then runs it. In a separate browser—POW! Instant Web page! He goes a step further and creates what looks like a Visual Basic class on a separate server. He then goes back to the first program and, almost magically, the methods and properties of the new class are visible through the Web. The whole audience is astonished by the ease of development and by the idea of Web sites becoming not just providers of visible information or sources of XML-based data but complete application libraries that can be accessed easily from Visual Basic.

You even get some glimpses of the code that performs one of these amazing feats and it seems almost familiar....

Or, I could take the tutorial approach.

The whole first chapter could contain step-by-step instructions showing you the code to type in along with numerous screen shots. A few cryptic comments would describe the code, along with some vague promises of in-depth explanations to follow. Why, I could write the *whole* book in that format and you would be able to extend the sample applications I provide, and they would work—as long as what you needed to do happened to be one of the examples I came up with. And if your particular task didn't quite match my tutorial, well...there are always other books.

Or maybe I can take the approach that I believe is right even though it is unlike anything I've seen in a similar book. I'm going to break a few rules for these first few chapters.

I'm not going to show you any code.

In fact, I'm not really going to tell you much about the .NET Framework or Visual Basic.NET at all.

Instead, I'm going to talk about context. About marketing. About attitude. I'm going to do my best to help you see .NET in a way that will help you avoid frustration and false starts and adapt to what is coming as quickly as possible.

I realize that this is a tough approach to take. Code is fun. So I encourage you to take a break here, open your copy of Visual Studio.NET, and play with some code. Maybe experiment with some of the simple examples included in the documentation. Then return when you've gotten a feel for things.

Back already? Good, let us continue.

The Importance of Context (Keeping Things in Perspective)

I love MSDN. It's probably the best thing to come out of Microsoft ever—at least for professional software developers. Every programmer should have `http://msdn.microsoft.com` permanently bookmarked and should probably be an MSDN subscriber as well.

But, I confess, sometimes I find it a bit myopic. Every new technology I read about is (of course) the best possible solution to a problem. Every new technology should be learned and deployed as quickly as possible. Every new technology is easier to use and deploy than ever before (and comes with an increasing number of courses and certification exam guides to make certain of this).

Case in point:

I once needed an e-mail system for my company—it's a small company, and at any given time we only needed a dozen or so Email accounts. My first thought was to deploy Exchange Server. Since I write about Microsoft technology and develop products for it, it makes sense to use it as much as possible, the better to learn the technology I write about.

So, I installed Exchange Server and tried to figure out how to make it work. I even bought a book (a big thick book) and tried to understand enough to make it work. I didn't have much luck though—I started getting the blue screen of death on the NT system on which we installed it. I finally read that Exchange Server really needed it's own dedicated server to work properly and one with considerably more memory than we had on that one.

I solved the problem by formatting the hard drive and reinstalling NT—without Exchange Server.

I went to the local Fry's Electronics and bought Eudora's Worldmail server for $99, plus a bit more for an extra set of client licenses.

It installed in about ten minutes.

The configuration was trivial and largely intuitive.

And it has worked flawlessly ever since on a server that was busy doing many other things as well.

Now don't get me wrong—I have nothing against Exchange Server[1]—I'm sure it's a phenomenal product. I know some people who use it with great success in their larger businesses. But the truth is that it was a lousy solution for a small company like mine—and there was nothing in the material that I saw from Microsoft that shouted in big bold letters, "If you have a small company, in one location and only need Internet mail, DON'T USE THIS PRODUCT!!!"

Which brings me to my point.

Technology—any technology—only has value in the context of the problem that it is meant to solve. In other words, technology is good only if it solves your particular problem. If you accept this premise (and if you don't, you should probably return this book right away because I doubt you're going to like anything that follows), you'll see that it leads to some inevitable complications in a number of areas.

For example, it makes writing a book about a given technology very difficult. As an author, I can't possibly know your particular problem. I thus have two choices: I can propose generic solutions and hope that they will work reasonably well for you (or worse, pretend that my solutions are "right" and not warn you of the consequences of following them if they aren't). Or, I can try to teach you enough about the technology so you can evaluate it in the context of your own situation.

This latter approach is the harder one but one that I'll try to follow nonetheless. As a first step, I invite you to keep the following in mind throughout this book:

Take everything I (or any other writer, for that matter) say with skepticism. Evaluate it in the context of your own situation.

A second complication is even more significant. In providing their solutions, Microsoft tries to identify a need and a market, fill that need, and sell into that market. I believe that most Microsoft programmers do wish to provide excellent solutions for developers. But I also believe that Microsoft's goal is to sell software and make money.[2] While one can argue that, on average, they will sell the most software when they are solving the most problems, this does not mean that any particular software product represents the best solution to your particular problem. Thus, I invite you to keep the following in mind throughout this book as well:

Take everything Microsoft (or any business, for that matter) says with skepticism. Evaluate it in the context of your own situation.

Almost feels like blasphemy doesn't it?

With these rules in mind, let's take a look at .NET. Not the technology—no, we're not quite ready for that. But rather, the context.

---

1. Okay, maybe a little bit of resentment over the time wasted but not enough to matter.

2. Believe it or not, some people will actually take this as if I were insulting Microsoft. They are a business and if their primary goal isn't to make money, their shareholders have some serious grounds for complaint.

.NET—Is It Real or Is It Marketing?

I once took a course on problem solving. Curiously enough, the first step in problem solving was to determine whether the problem actually existed. It's amazing how many problems turn out to vanish after even one good night's sleep. The same question applies to new Microsoft technologies—do they actually exist?

As I see it, Microsoft actually creates two types of "product."

The first product is a real product—these are things that are clearly identifiable. You can buy them, you can use them. Visual Basic is a product. Windows 2000 is a product. Microsoft Transaction Server is a product. So is Microsoft Message Queue.[3]

If Microsoft only sold products, this section of this chapter wouldn't be necessary.

But you see, there's another kind of product that comes out of Microsoft, one that isn't created by programmers at all. These products come out of the marketing department.[4]

Consider what happened a few years back when Microsoft "discovered" the Internet. One day they seemed threatened to be left behind by the new wave from Netscape, Sun, and other Internet technology companies. Seemingly overnight they had a whole new technology, ActiveX, which appeared with great fanfare.

What was ActiveX?

It was OLE2—with a new name.

That's right. An entire new "Internet strategy," a major new technology shift was fundamentally a new name for something that was already shipping.

Not convinced?

Microsoft introduced a number of important services to help create scalable COM objects for multi-tiered applications: Microsoft Transaction Server and it's related parts handled transactioning, pooling, and sharing data. Microsoft Message Queue handled asynchronous reliable messaging. Then, one day almost like magic, COM+ appeared. And darn if it didn't do those same things (along with some other goodies).

And what exactly was Windows DNA?

Have you noticed how Windows DNA vanished remarkably overnight to be replaced nearly instantly with something called .NET Enterprise Services? Microsoft even put out a list to translate between DNA and .NET terms.

These terms seem to be generated by Microsoft's marketing folks to bring their various technologies together and present them as part of a unified strategy

---

3. MTS and MSMQ were products initially. Remember that as you read on.

4. Microsoft reorganizations are so frequent and of such complexity that it is virtually impossible for an outsider to understand exactly who does what to whom and when, or who (if anyone) actually writes code. In other words, my comments distinguishing between development and marketing is a vast oversimplification to make a point and does not reflect what really happens at Microsoft.

intended to provide complete solutions to most enterprise computing problems. Now, there's nothing wrong with that.

But the story and terms seem to change so often that it's hard to determine whether the latest "major strategic initiative" represents a real technology innovation, a repackaging of existing components, or an attempt to yet again rephrase the marketing message.

So any exploration of .NET must begin with the question: how much of it is real and how much of it is hype?

By the time you read this, you've probably read enough through other sources to know that .NET represents new technology and not just an exercise in marketing.

But even now you may not have realized how big of a change .NET represents. One of the consequences of Microsoft's marketing practices is that, like the boy who cried wolf once too often, they've long since run out of superlatives to identify truly unique technology.

So let me try:

- All of the hype you've read about .NET doesn't come close to describing how "real" .NET is—how different and new it is.

- .NET represents a major paradigm shift in Windows development.

- .NET will require a radical change in strategy and software design for most current Visual Basic programmers.

- .NET will require a major investment in education by all current Visual Basic programmers.

I could go on (and will later), but I hope you see my point. .NET represents for Visual Basic programmers a greater change than the transition from 16-bit to 32-bit Windows. In fact, I would suggest that it is a greater transition than the shift from DOS Basic to Visual Basic.

But .NET not only represents a huge change for Visual Basic programmers—it presents a huge opportunity as well:

- .NET places Visual Basic programmers on equal footing with their C++ counterparts in terms of the power of the language.[5]

- .NET turns Visual Basic programmers into Internet application developers almost without effort. Once you know how to develop VB.NET Windows applications, it's a short step to writing VB.NET Internet applications.

---

5. Visual Basic programmers have always been ahead of C++ programmers in terms of general software development efficiency.

- .NET provides Visual Basic programmers with a vast object library—a treasury of components to enable even more rapid and powerful software development.

When I first began to grasp what Microsoft was doing, I must confess I was stunned. I'm still not over it. And that fact alone makes clear that there are still more issues that must be addressed before we start looking at the technology itself.

CHAPTER 2

Facing VB.NET without Fear or Panic

AT THE END OF MY SENIOR YEAR studying computer science, I took a required course called (something along the lines of) "Individual and Organizational Aspects of Computer Science." At the time, I wondered what it was doing there. Now I realize it was one of the most important courses I took.

You can't talk about learning technology if you don't acknowledge the impact it has on people.

At the end of the last chapter, I described the .NET Framework as a major paradigm shift—a way of programming that will be very new to most Visual Basic programmers. While I'm not quite ready to go into the details of the technology yet, let me give you a brief overview of the kinds of changes I'm writing about.

Oh My God, They Broke VB!

The .NET Framework is built on a new runtime called the Common Language Runtime (or CLR). The subject of runtimes is one that is a bit sensitive to many VB programmers. For a while, VB programmers felt that there was something "wrong" with Visual Basic because it had this huge distribution runtime that supposedly was not needed with C++ programs. Then they learned that most C++ programmers actually required huge runtimes as well (such as MFC[1]). Only C++ programmers writing pure API (Application Programming Interface) code or those willing to study the intricacies of the ATL (Active Template Library) could get away with creating components and applications that didn't require runtimes. The CLR is considerably more ambitious than the old VB or MFC runtimes.[2] According to Microsoft, the CLR was created with a number of goals in mind:

---

1. Microsoft Foundation Classes

2. It is difficult to compare runtime sizes because these languages require not only the base runtime file, such as the 1.3MB VB6 runtime or the 1MB MFC runtime, but also a variety of dependent DLL's relating to OLE or the C runtime. We don't know how large the .NET runtime will be but it is expected to be considerably larger—tens of megabytes.

- To make it easy to create objects that can be shared among languages.

- To make it easy to create scalable and robust components and applications (with, for example, good handling of threading issues and no resource or memory leaks).

- To make it possible to create verifiably secure components and applications.

- To make it easy to create components and applications for Web-based applications as well as traditional Windows applications.

I'll be writing more about these goals and others[3] as we continue. For now, let's just consider the impact these goals would have on a language.

A language designed for .NET needs to support the these features, among others:

- Inheritance

- Free-threaded multithreading

- Support for all the CLR-defined variable types

- Attributes and metadata (don't worry, you'll find out what this is later)

These features are part of a new Common Language Specification (CLS) that all .NET languages should support.

Visual Basic 6 did not support any of these features.

This presented the developers at Microsoft with an interesting challenge—how to "fix" each of their languages to work with the new Common Language Runtime that is the foundation on which .NET is built:

- They could graft a set of extensions onto the language. This is the choice they made for Visual C++.[4]

- They could create a new language designed specifically for the CLR. This is the choice they made in creating the new C# language (pronounced "C sharp"), which I'll discuss a bit more later.

---

3. Microsoft also claimed that applications written for the runtime would be able to run on any platform that supports the CLR—leaving open the suggestion that the CLR will exist on other systems such as Apple, Linux, or even Palm handhelds. Apple, I can believe. The others? This I gotta see…

4. I've only briefly looked at the way managed extensions are implemented with VC++. I must confess, my first impression was not particularly favorable. It seems a bit awkward.

- They could revise the language to fit the needs of the CLR even at the risk of breaking backward compatibility with previous editions of the language. This is the choice they made with Visual Basic.NET.

Then the Microsoft developers made a rather courageous and certainly controversial decision. They decided that as long as they had to break backward compatibility anyway, they might as well clean up the language completely—and by clean up, I mean clean up the syntax and add the kinds of features like strict type checking that professional developers have been asking for for years. Let's face it, as much as we like VB, can anyone really say that the syntax of the Line command makes any sense? Part Three of this book will focus entirely on specifics of changes to the language and how to migrate software. For now, the important things to know are:

- VB.NET is "a Visual Basic" but it is not Visual Basic as it has evolved from VB1 to VB6. It is a different language.

- VB6 code will not load without conversion into VB.NET.

- Microsoft has a Migration Wizard that converts VB6 code to VB.NET when you load a VB6 project into Visual Studio.NET. How good it will be remains to be seen.[5]

- The forms engine has changed from the current "Ruby-based" forms engine to the new .NET windows forms engine. ("Ruby" was the code name for the forms engine developed by Alan Cooper that ultimately became the forms package for VB1). In addition to the expected programmatic changes, one should expect subtle behavior changes as well.

- The new features in VB.NET open the opportunity to new and improved software architectures.

Which brings us to our next subject.

Everything You Know Is Now Obsolete

I began this chapter discussing the human factors of technology. I expect that the typical reader of this book has been programming in Visual Basic 5 or 6 for anywhere from a few months to as long as I have.[6] How does a software developer

---

5. I'll have a lot more to say about the Migration Wizard in Part III. From what I've seen it's not bad, but I can't imagine it ever being so good that a major application or one that uses advanced techniques won't need substantial additional work and testing.

6. For the record, I started programming VB during the VB1 beta.

react upon learning that the language in which he or she has expertise is undergoing such a radical change? Consider the questions that one might ask:

- What about those certification exams you just took that are meaningless in the context of VB.NET?

- Will you still have a job when your company or clients switch over to .NET?

- How will you learn what is clearly a major shift in technology in the limited time you have, given that you're still working long hours with today's technology?

I've attended enough conferences, spoken to enough programmers, and spent enough time in front of a mirror to know full well how programmers react to this kind of technology shift.

- We are overwhelmed—by the inability to keep up with all the changes and by the fact that there isn't enough time to learn everything.

- We are afraid—that our careers will suffer because we can't learn everything we think we need to know. And that everybody else knows more than we do.

- We are excited—most of us got into this business in the first place because we do love the technology and enjoy learning and using it.

Now, I know some of you may be very uncomfortable reading this or even thinking about it. And you may feel I've gone off the deep end—what does this kind of psychological mumbo-jumbo have to do with learning VB.NET?

Everything.

Because the attitude and approach that you take when starting to learn a new technology has a major impact on how well and quickly you learn it.

If you approach VB.NET through fearful eyes, you will have a difficult time abandoning techniques and approaches that are obsolete. You will view many of the new features as mistakes or meaningless. Why, you may even join those who condemn Microsoft's changes—asking them for wholesale return of favorite language features. You may even join those who condemn the entire .NET approach.

Throughout this book, I will question some of Microsoft's decisions and I may even ask for the return of a language feature or two. But, overall, I am very excited by the possibilities of this new technology and I invite you to join me in conquering fear and approaching .NET with as positive a viewpoint as possible. Not uncritical and not without intellectual skepticism—but also not letting fear cause us to unfairly criticize what we do not yet understand.

Let me now tell you why you shouldn't be afraid of .NET. For the time being, take these statements on faith—I'll be making my case on these issues throughout the book:

1. You have time—.NET is a major paradigm shift. It will not be deployed overnight. It will not be learned overnight. That's one of the reasons Microsoft is doing widespread technology and beta previews—because they know that .NET has a steep learning curve. Everybody else is in the same situation as you are.

2. VB.NET is ultimately going to help you to be a better programmer. Your applications will be easier to test, debug, and support over the long term. You will be able to do things more easily and quickly than you can now.

3. .NET levels the playing field. If you are a beginning or intermediate VB programmer who has been wondering how you'll ever catch up with the experts, .NET is wonderful—everybody is now starting at pretty much the same level. Oh, some people have advantages—those with formal computer science training are going to pick up on the concepts quickly because they are familiar but, overall, it's a great opportunity to start and stay at the leading edge of technology.[7]

The Business of Software Development

In addition to human factors, there are business factors to consider when looking at .NET. I've already mentioned several times that technology should be evaluated in the context of how well it solves your particular problem. If you think about it, this statement really reflects a business criterion rather than a technical criterion. Many of you are (hopefully) nodding your head in agreement at this point but some of you may be wondering what business decisions have to do with learning a language?

I have a little secret to share…I do have formal training in computer science. But while I was picking up that degree, I also picked up a BS degree in electronic engineering.[8] And it turns out that one of the most important courses I took in that program was called "Engineering Economics."[9] This was a required course

---

7. Many current "experts" and "gurus" will, of course, not be so thrilled with this aspect of .NET since it means they need to work hard to become experts in this new field and may have all sorts of new competition. Personally, I resigned guru status the minute I saw .NET— but have been working hard to be worthy of the title again.

8. BSCS and BSEE from the University of California, Irvine.

9. Text for the course was *Engineering Economic*, by James L. Riggs et al., (McGraw-Hill, 4th ed. 1996). A good text—but very advanced as you would expect a college textbook to be.

for all Engineering freshmen. In it, I was taught that it is the responsibility of every engineering professional to understand and consider the economic implications of their decisions—the business behind the technology. I believe this applies to every software developer as well.[10]

The history of Visual Basic proves this point. How did Visual Basic become so successful even though for years programmers (especially C++ programmers) condemned it as a "toy language?" The answer is clear: because it is cheaper to develop most applications in Visual Basic than in any other language. Visual Basic ultimately became the most popular Windows development language for economic reasons. C++ programmers like myself switched to Visual Basic because even though the language lacked some features that we considered important (strict type checking for example), we could still write, debug, and test code an order of magnitude faster than we could in C++. The flood of widely available and reasonably priced software components in the form of VBX's[11] and then ActiveX controls (OCX) made it possible to incorporate substantial functionality into a Visual Basic application at a very low total cost of ownership.

Look at any product or technology from OS/2 to Windows, ASP (Active Server Pages) to WebClasses. The determining factor for the adoption and success of a technology is almost invariably human, political, and economic—not technological!

So, for those of you who are still wondering why this book did not start with code or discussions of VB.NET features, here is the crux of my argument. The success of VB.NET, your success at learning it, and your decisions of when to learn and adopt this technology will be driven largely by human, political, and economic issues. Most technical books focus on technology and leave you to muddle through these other issues on your own. In this book, my goal is to address these critical issues head-on from the beginning—before you've even looked at the technology, then continue to address them throughout the book as we delve into the technology itself. With this in mind, it is time to turn our attention to the strategic decisions you will be making with regards to VB.NET and the .NET Framework.

---

10. Perhaps excluding hobbyists, who have different criteria and priorities.

11. VBX = Visual Basic controls—the predecessor to today's ActiveX controls.

CHAPTER 3
Adoption Strategies

You'VE PROBABLY ALREADY STARTED reading about .NET. Perhaps in magazine articles, perhaps on Microsoft's site. You may have attended Developer Days or another conference. Even if this book is your first exposure to .NET, you've undoubtedly begun to ask some critical questions:

- How soon do I need to learn about this technology?

- Is it something our company should deploy right away or should we wait?

- Under what scenarios should we deploy this technology?

- How much will it cost to train our people on this new technology?

- How much of an improvement (if any) will it bring to our particular applications?

- Should I port my existing applications?

I won't attempt to answer these questions here. In fact, most of them will be so dependent on your particular situation that it's unlikely I would be able to answer them at all. The idea here is to expand upon these questions—discussing the factors that you'll need to consider to answer them. Then, as you actually begin to learn about the technological issues, I hope you will be able to apply your newfound knowledge and come up with your own answers to these questions.

Time Frames

When I wrote this chapter for the first time, the official first beta version of Visual Studio.NET was not yet available. Microsoft had already published a great deal of marketing information about .NET along with quite a few articles discussing the underlying technology and architecture and had released a widely distributed technology preview at their Professional Developer's Conference. Even now,[1] we don't know when Visual Studio.NET will actually be released. Winter of 2001 is the

---

1. The Beta 2 period.

earliest anyone expects it but I'll be pretty impressed if it shows up anytime in 2001. So, all of this exciting new technology, while far from vapor, is certainly "not ready for prime time."

The flip side of all of the early promotional activity on Microsoft's part is that it is easy for programmers to get the idea that VB6 is effectively obsolete already, that it is essential to learn VB.NET quickly, and that they should immediately start figuring out how to port existing applications to VB.NET. These ideas are basically nonsense.

Even after release, it's going to take some time for programmers to learn the technology and to write and deploy code using this technology. The magnitude of the change is such that the transition to VB.NET is likely to be measured in years rather than months—and for some applications, it may not make sense to switch at all.

What does this mean to you?

1. Don't throw out your current version of Visual Basic. You'll probably be using it for a while.

2. Don't panic! You have time to learn and adjust to this new technology.

3. Take time to read, study, and play with this technology before you dive in and start designing applications or writing code. This will increase the likelihood that your designs will be solid and take full advantage of the new .NET features.

Porting Code

One of the most important questions you will face is whether to port your existing code to VB.NET. In previous versions of Visual Basic, this was not really a difficult decision to make. The transition from VB1 to VB4 (16-bit edition) was smooth for most programmers, relatively few of whom had to delay their transition due to compatibility issues in the later versions. The transition to 32 bits was more substantial but the greatest delays came from waiting for ActiveX components to be available in their newer OCX versions (as compared to 16-bit VBX versions). The transition from 32-bit VB4 to VB6 was again smooth for most developers. Note that even though Microsoft made great efforts to ensure backward compatibility, some developers were still stymied in their efforts to upgrade due to subtle incompatibilities between versions or obscure bugs that appeared during the upgrade process. This is one reason that even today some development teams are still using Visual Basic 5.

Now, imagine what the process of porting will mean to a language in which compatibility was intentionally eliminated?

Again, let me stress that I am not criticizing Microsoft's decision to break compatibility here—I happen to agree with their reasons for doing so. But it does mean that porting existing code to VB.NET will involve a substantial investment.

How much will porting existing code cost? This depends both on how good the Migration Wizard turns out to be and on the quality of your code.

Even if the migration tool is 95% effective on a ten-thousand-line program, this leaves five hundred lines that need to be examined, evaluated, and updated manually. Not to mention the possibility of obscure bugs due to the change in architecture. Or, the possibility of obscure bugs resulting from the migration process itself. At the very least, each application and component ported will require extensive testing.

What does this mean to you as a developer? It means that you must weigh the cost of porting against the benefits to be gained from porting. It means that there will inevitably be situations where porting existing code to VB.NET is not economically sound. It means that Microsoft should continue to sell and support Visual Basic 6 for some time to come.[2]

Deployment Considerations

The motivation for moving to .NET is going to vary dramatically based on the types of applications and components you develop. Here are the key facts that will influence the deployment of .NET:

- The .NET Framework is excellent for development of new Web-based applications. The framework's ability to control memory and resource use and to scale upwards is a definite improvement over previous Visual Basic 6 and ASP technologies.

- The .NET Framework does require installation of the .NET runtime on all systems using components or applications written using the Common Language Runtime (including all VB.NET applications and components).

- VB.NET has enough differences from Visual Basic 6 to require a substantial learning effort on the part of current VB programmers.

- VB.NET offers potential performance improvements in cases where components can benefit from free threading. The faster code processing provided by the .NET languages (as compared to a scripting language) also contributes to improved performance in ASP applications.

---

2. I don't know whether Microsoft has officially commented on the future of VB6. However, based on my discussions with people at Microsoft, I do believe that they understand this issue and that at least some of them will be advocating internally that Microsoft continue to sell and support VB6 even after VB.NET appears.

- VB.NET is likely to offer no performance improvement and possibly some performance loss in cases that will not benefit from architectural changes, such as free threading or moving from a script to compiled language.[3]

- VB.NET applications and components can take advantage of all the substantial resources in the Common Language Runtime including libraries and components.

From these, we can make some good guesses in terms of where VB.NET is likely to be deployed and how quickly.

New Server-Based Applications

This one is almost a no-brainer. If you are starting a new server-based application, whether it is an ASP.NET Web application or server-side logic or middle-tier business logic, switching to VB.NET shortly after release (or even developing with a later beta or release candidate) is a logical move. The only real cost is the time and expense to train developers for the new environment. True, this can be significant but the benefits of stability and access to new .NET features make it likely that the cost can be quickly justified. Since the software is deployed only on servers (over which you presumably have tight control), the cost to install and deploy the runtime on the servers is negligible.

Old Server-Based Applications

The argument here is similar to the previous one except that you have the additional cost of porting. As mentioned, this cost can be substantial. The good news is that .NET is designed to work well with existing COM Framework and components (although, as you will soon see, .NET is not itself based on COM). This means that you should be able to selectively move individual components of your application to the .NET Framework in order to gain the benefits of new features, performance, or scalability while still using existing COM components for those parts of your solution that would not benefit or would be too costly to port.

Your best bet in this case is likely to begin the training process early and evaluate the various components in your system to see where it may be advantageous to port your existing components. I would encourage you to start with smaller or simpler components in order to gain experience. Better yet, consider starting with new components that are added to incorporate new features into your application.

---

3. Performance is an issue that will receive additional attention throughout this book.

While it is too early to say for sure, I would recommend focusing on components that do not have user interfaces. While it is certainly possible to mix COM and .NET user-interface components, the very complexity of the interfaces involved increases the chances of problems and subtle incompatibilities during porting. This means focusing primarily on the server, Web server, and middle tier. Let me stress, my concern about mixing COM and .NET user-interface components only applies to porting where subtle changes in behavior need to be dealt with. Using existing COM components in a new .NET project (and vice versa) is not a problem. Microsoft has put a great deal of effort into making COM and .NET components work well together.

Client Applications

The primary factor in determining whether you should use VB.NET to create client-side components (either stand-alone applications or browser-based components) is your confidence that your clients will either have the .NET runtime installed, be willing to install it, or have already upgraded to a version of Windows that includes the .NET runtime. We don't know what the final distribution size of the runtime will be but it will likely be large enough that a Zip drive, CD, or DSL modem would be the minimum requirement for transferring the runtime files to a client. Floppy disk and modem downloads are almost certainly out.

If you don't have the .NET runtime available, VB.NET applications and components simply won't run.

Once you do have it available, not only do you gain the benefits of new features, you also gain a vastly improved ability to safely deploy your application and its components without the DLL Hell issues so common using current technology.[4] You'll also have the ability to create verifiably secure components and applications—which will be increasingly important as the spread of computer viruses drive end users to be more and more security conscious.

Once the Common Language Runtime is included with the operating system (which is likely), VB.NET will become a compelling platform for client applications and browser-based components.[5] In fact, it wouldn't surprise me at all if .NET signals a move back to rich clients in many situations since it looks like it will be as easy to reliably deploy a rich client application under .NET as it is for a client to view a Web page.

---

4. DLL Hell, for those who aren't familiar with the term, refers to the situation that occurs when the installation of an upgraded component on a system causes one or more applications to fail. You'll read a lot more about this problem and deployment in general, later in this book.

5. There are even some cool capabilities that allow you to create applications that run on either a Web server or a local system with effectively the same user interface.

This transition should not be as bad as that from 16 to 32-bit applications since the CLR should be deployable on all current 32-bit Windows systems. However, end users being who they are and running the wide variety of systems that they do, it seems clear that VB.NET will not be a good platform for most client applications at first.

Initial client deployment will probably be to small businesses and enterprises that have good control and management of end-user desktops and the ability to roll out the runtime and support any problems that may occur in the process. Developers of shrink-wrap software will probably avoid .NET development until there is some history to judge whether the Common Language Runtime can be deployed safely to the wide variety of systems in use.

What about C#?

Many Visual Basic programmers have suffered from a slight inferiority complex about their language of choice (often encouraged by C++ programmers who criticize Visual Basic as a "toy language"). Some have gone on to learn C++. Others have switched to Java.[6]

With the arrival of VB.NET, it is inevitable to ask whether VB programmers should switch to C# or C++.

If you decide that you want no part of .NET, there is an argument to be made for moving to C++. C++ continues to provide excellent support for creating Windows applications and components that use either the MFC runtimes or (with a bit more effort) no runtime dependencies at all. It remains the language of choice for specialized applications such as ISAPI applications created with ATL Server. Though, as an experienced VB programmer, there is probably a stronger argument to stay with VB6.

If you decide that Microsoft's .NET strategy truly represents Microsoft's next-generation software development platform with the implication that it will not only be around for a long time but will continue to evolve and be supported as is the current Win32 API, then I strongly encourage you to choose C# or VB.NET over C++ with managed extensions.

C# was developed along with the Common Language Runtime to, in effect, be the "perfect" language for the .NET environment. The language was designed by default to create efficient verifiable code.

But what about VB.NET? Once it was clear that moving Visual Basic to .NET required breaking language compatibility with VB6, they decided to go all the way and make VB.NET a fully .NET-compatible language. Then they cleaned up the

---

6. I won't comment anymore on the choice of Java. I simply don't have enough experience with the language to evaluate the trade-offs of the choice between Java, VB6, VB.NET, and C#. You'll have to figure out this one on your own.

language, in the process removing or changing those very factors that led C++ programmers to criticize Visual Basic in the first place.

In other words, if you're going to use .NET, there is virtually no difference between C# and VB.NET either in terms of features or performance. C# gives you a greater ability to use "unsafe" code—a low-level feature that should be avoided and about which you will read more later in this book. But even this is not enough reason to choose C# over VB.NET because it is easy to mix languages in an application.[7]

There are some areas where I would argue that the VB.NET syntax is cleaner and more readable than the corresponding C# syntax. One could make the argument that C++ programmers should consider moving to VB.NET instead of C# for that reason.

Ultimately, you might as well stick with the syntax that you are most familiar with.[8] If you're a Visual Basic programmer, stick with VB.NET. If you're a C++ or Java programmer, stick with C#.[9]

What about Alternatives to .NET from Sources Other than Microsoft?

Some of you may look at the changes involved in learning .NET and wonder if it makes sense to look at non-Microsoft technologies and languages to solve your problems. I honestly wish I could offer guidance in that area but the truth is that I am not familiar enough with non-Microsoft alternatives to help you through the process of comparing alternate approaches. In fact, the available platforms and languages are changing so quickly that it would be rather pointless for me to do so even if I were an expert on them all. Let me give you two examples:

Many VB programmers look towards Java for its promise of cross-platform compatibility. Yet, much of that compatibility has remained just that—a promise. And that promise has been muddled by intercompany politics, legalities, and questionable performance in its implementations. Curiously, there's nothing to prevent someone from implementing Java on .NET but it seems to me that if you're using the .NET Framework, choosing Java over C# would be rather pointless unless the .NET version of Java turns out to be a better implementation than others.

Microsoft has emphasized both the .NET Framework support for standards such as SOAP (Simple Object Access Protocol) and XML (Extensible Markup Language) and that they are putting the C# language out for standardization as well. Yet,

---

7. That's one reason they created the Common Language Runtime in the first place—to make it easy for languages to use components and code from other languages. For example, a VB.NET class can not only use C# objects but can also inherit from them. At last count, I hear that there are eighteen .NET-compatible languages under development.

8. Economics again. Why waste expensive time learning a new syntax without good reason?

9. Visit http://www.desaware.com/vborcsharp.htm for links to an Ebook, *Visual Basic or C#: Which to Choose*, in which I perform a more in-depth comparison of VB.NET and C# if you are seriously considering switching from one to the other.

these standards are but promises too and the journey from today's state to final standardization is fraught with politics and controversy.

I'm not sure it's possible to choose the "best" platform for a particular application given the uncertainty of how things will develop. I think it is safe to say that .NET will represent a viable platform for some time to come[10] but I do encourage you to explore other possibilities even if it means wading through vast amounts of marketing hype to extract nuggets of real knowledge.

This book operates under the assumption that you have, for whatever reason, chosen Microsoft's technology to solve your problem. My job here is to help you navigate the transition from today's technology to .NET.[11] I encourage you to explore and evaluate other alternatives in the context of your own needs.

Moving On

I hope you've found these first three chapters thought provoking. And I hope they help you to focus in on your own needs as you read on. With this in mind, I invite you to turn to Part Two where you'll learn the fundamental concepts every VB.NET developer should know before they design their first real VB.NET component or application.

---

10. I once worked for a company that was among the first to adopt a GUI-based environment to test equipment. I had to choose at the time between Digital Research's GEM platform and Microsoft Windows 1. As you can probably guess, I made the right choice. But it was certainly not an obvious choice at the time as other companies had the misfortune to discover.

11. Although after reading this book, your understanding of .NET may help you to evaluate alternatives on your own.

Part II

Concepts

"The source of expertise is not in the memorization of the minute details of a subject but in the thorough understanding of the fundamental concepts on which it is based."

—Dan Appleman, opinionated author

.NET in Context

BY NOW, YOU MUST BE nearly desperate to see some actual code. Bear with me just a little longer—you'll start to see code shortly.

I've already mentioned that if this were a typical programming book intended for people learning Visual Basic.NET from scratch, the book would have been structured very differently. I would have started with language concepts and basic syntax.

But this book is designed for intermediate to advanced-level VB6 programmers. Frankly, I'm not particularly worried about your ability to handle the syntax of VB.NET. You already know about variables and For…Next loops. You already understand object libraries from your experience with ActiveX DLLs and ActiveX controls. And you know how to look up methods and properties and use them.

I won't insult your intelligence by covering those aspects of Visual Basic that are either common to the two languages or represent trivial differences.[1] In Part Three of this book, I'll be covering a myriad of specific language changes to help you quickly adjust to the new syntax.

No, those kinds of language changes don't worry me at all.

What worries me are the changes that represent paradigm shifts, changes that influence the way programs should be designed under .NET—the concepts that will be new to most VB.NET programmers. To be specific:

- I'm worried about VB programmers who don't fully understand the need for synchronization before they design their first multithreaded application or component because VB6 hides the complexity from them.

- I'm worried about VB programmers who are so excited by the appearance of true inheritance that they decide to actually use it.[2]

- I'm worried about VB programmers who are so used to solving problems using built-in intrinsic functions and API calls that they neglect to thoroughly explore the .NET Framework.

---

1. Hopefully I won't insult your intelligence any other way either but one never knows. If I have done so or do so in the future, I assure you it is unintentional.

2. My technical editor, Scott Stabbert, pointed out that this implies that I think inheritance is a bad thing. That is not quite accurate. You'll learn in Chapter 5 that inheritance is a feature to be neither adopted nor discarded lightly.

- I'm worried about VB programmers who are so biased against runtimes and P-Code that they'll form snap judgments about the .NET Intermediate Language (IL) rather than judge the approach on its own merits.

The purpose of this part of the book is to introduce you to the underlying concepts that every VB.NET programmer needs to know. Correction: perhaps not *every* VB.NET programmer—beginners can certainly use the language and write simple programs without a full understanding of these concepts. But this part of the book covers concepts that every experienced programmer moving from VB6 to VB.NET should know—and one should focus on these concepts before delving into the minute details of specific language changes.

The Virtual Machine

A virtual machine, from the perspective of a programmer, is a term used to describe the platform for which you are writing code.[3] This may sound a bit silly but think about it: your machine may be a Pentium III, Athlon, Pentium II, etc.—and may be configured with different amounts of memory and storage. But as a programmer, you don't care how the physical machine is configured. You're coding to a virtual machine that depends on the operating system and software environment.

For example, Figure 4-1 shows the virtual machine you may have used back in the days of MS-DOS (if you go back that far).

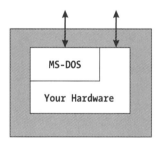

Figure 4-1. Virtual machine for MS-DOS programmers.

Programmers in those days had access to the relatively small set of functions built into the operating system along with whatever capability was included in their language. They would also sometimes need direct access to the hardware

---

3. Do not confuse the term virtual machine with a runtime environment. For example, Java's Virtual Machine is implemented using a runtime and classes. It is, indeed, a virtual machine because it defines a programming environment. But the term virtual machine refers to *any* programming environment. Even assembly programmers write to a virtual machine defined by the CPU's instruction set (which is, in turn, implemented by microcode within the processor itself).

since MS-DOS was not particularly capable when it came to areas like graphics and communications.

Today, as a VB6 programmer, you are accustomed to using a more sophisticated virtual machine such as that shown in Figure 4-2. It includes the Visual Basic runtime, the Win32 API, the COM subsystem, and a variety of subsystems that use COM. Direct hardware access is virtually impossible.

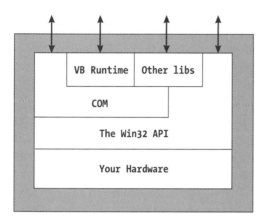

Figure 4-2. Virtual Machine for VB6 programmers.

The key concept to realize in looking at these two figures is that even though we are still using PC's in our coding, the virtual machine that we are targeting is radically different from the one used back in the days of MS-DOS and—though not shown here—even different from the one used in the days of VB3.

Now, take a look at Figure 4-3, which shows the virtual machine for VB.NET programmers.

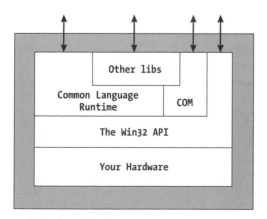

Figure 4-3. Virtual machine for VB.NET programmers.

What key facts can one see from this?

- There is no longer a VB-specific runtime—Visual Basic uses the .NET Common Language Runtime (CLR).[4]

- Visual Basic 6 and its runtime are COM-based. The CLR is not based on COM, though it is possible for .NET applications to use COM and vice versa.

In short, a VB.NET programmer writes code to a virtual machine that is radically different from the virtual machine used by a VB6 programmer. Learning VB.NET is comparable to learning to write code for a completely different operating system. In fact, a Common Language (one that follows the Common Language Specification defined by the .NET Frameworks) will theoretically be able to run unchanged and without recompilation on any platform or operating system that hosts the Common Language Runtime!

Why do we need such a radically different virtual machine for Visual Basic? And why did Microsoft effectively come up with something that seems (from a programmer's perspective) to be almost a new operating system? These are important issues to understand because most of the language changes to VB.NET from VB6 were driven by the requirements of the CLR, not the other way around.

What is broken in the current virtual machine that demands such a radical approach?

Figures 4-1 through 4-3 make it clear. What is broken in Windows is COM.

COM Is Dead. Long Live COM?

Honestly, I dread trying to explain what follows. What Microsoft's marketing folks have done in the process of naming COM, OLE, and COM+ (and almost tried with COM+ 2.0) is nearly unforgivable. Trying to straighten them out is going to be an adventure, to say the least, but I will do my best.

COM—Ideas versus Implementation

COM stands for the Component Object Model. It defines a way for objects to communicate with each other regardless of what language they are written in. COM makes it possible to create applications and components made up of objects written by different people in different languages. It makes it possible for objects

---

4. Purists will note that the CLR does, of course, include methods intended to be used primarily by Visual Basic.

to call methods, access properties, and raise events in other objects even if they are located on a different system across a network.

The ideas behind COM are relatively simple:

- An interface defines a contract: a list of methods and properties that are exposed by an object. Once defined, an interface may never change.

- Every COM object and interface has a GUID: a globally unique identifier that is associated with that object or interface and no other.

- A COM object may expose multiple interfaces. There must be a way to navigate from one interface to another and uniquely identify an object regardless of which interface you are using.

- There must exist a standard binary mechanism by which objects can call each other and which is independent of the language used.

- There must be a common mechanism for raising errors, so that errors raised by one object can be correctly detected and identified by another object.

The implementation behind COM addresses each of the ideas just listed:

- Interfaces are defined in type libraries: a block of data that holds the list of methods and properties of an interface and their parameters, parameter types, and return types. Interfaces are created automatically when you add methods and properties to a VB class or by using a language called IDL (Interface Description Language) in C++.

- In order to access a COM object, its GUID information is stored in the system registry.

- Each COM object exposes an interface called IUnknown. This interface contains three methods: AddRef, Release, and QueryInterface. The AddRef and Release methods implement reference counting so an object can keep track of how many references to the object exist—when the reference count is zero, the object can delete itself. QueryInterface is used to navigate from one interface to another.

- COM objects use virtual function tables (an array of function pointers) internally to call the methods and properties of an object's interface. This is hidden from VB6 programmers, except for the foolish few who insist on using the ObjPtr operator to rewrite virtual tables in VB.[5]

- COM objects return errors internally by returning a value called an HRESULT—a 32-bit value that has a standard format defined by COM. VB6 maps COM error results into raised error values.

When I suggest that COM is broken, I'm really referring to the implementation and not the idea. And when I say the implementation is broken, I must stress that the problem is not in the theoretical design of the implementation or even in the code behind the implementation but in the real world consequences of that design. In other words, the failing of COM is not that it doesn't work but that it does not adequately protect us from our own stupidity and that of our end users.[6]

The Problem with Interfaces

The rule behind COM interfaces is simple: once you define and release an interface, you must never, ever change it. Not only must you not change the interface but you must also make sure that the functionality behind that interface never changes.

Consider these scenarios. You release an object with a method:

```
Public Function Verify(CreditCardInfo As String) As Boolean
```

…and release version 1 of a component that uses this method to verify a credit card. You release version 1 of an E-commerce application that uses the version 1 component.

---

5. I've had a number of intense arguments with people who have used or advocated this approach. It has been widely publicized in magazines and an occasional book, though I'm glad to say many of the authors who have written about it have warned people that it should be looked at as an academic exercise rather than a recommended approach. I claimed that it was just bad code, unsupportable, and unlikely to survive into the next version of Visual Basic. Little did I know how right I would be.

6. In his book *The Dilbert Principle* (HarperBusiness, 1996), Scott Adams says that we are all idiots some of the time. I believe this is a great truth—I have no doubt that I will be an idiot many times even in this book. This principal lies at the root of COM's failing—it doesn't allow for that idiocy, which also goes back to what I said in Chapter 2: "The determining factor for the adoption and success of a technology is invariably human, political, and economic—not technological!"

Then, one of the following happens (or both):

- An ambitious programmer decides that the function really needs a new parameter, which includes the credit card type and then ignores the warning about binary compatibility when the component is recompiled.

Or

- A programmer forgets to set binary compatibility correctly when rebuilding the component.

You then release version 2 of the component with version 1 of the credit approval system.

Unfortunately, the version 2 component is no longer compatible with the version 1 E-commerce application, which promptly fails on any system on which the credit approval program (with the updated component) is installed.

Having suffered a major public relations disaster and unbelievable technical support costs, you rush to create a new version 2 E-commerce application that uses the version 2 credit approval component. In fact, you've found a way to improve performance considerably, so you go directly to a version 3 component. This time, you are careful to maintain binary compatibility with the version 2 component. Unfortunately, one of your programmers in the course of the performance improvement accidentally mangles one of the tables that determines card type so Discover card charges will be sent to American Express.

When the component is installed on systems with the credit approval program, the program works fine in that the interface is correct. However, the new component is not functionally backward compatible so you again face a flood of customer complaints.

In short, you are in DLL Hell.

You are in DLL Hell because COM components in DLLs are designed to be shared.

Now, DLL Hell should never occur. The COM rules are quite specific: you should never change an interface once it is defined. And you should never break backward compatibility.

Guess what? Programmers aren't perfect. In fact, Microsoft's programmers aren't perfect—they've probably created more DLL Hell problems than any other company (which makes sense since they've created more DLLs than any other company).

The Problem with the Registry

An obvious solution to DLL Hell is to let each application load and run its own versions of components. This is called side-by-side execution—where different versions of a component can be run by different applications at once. While Windows 2000 does support this, it's awkward because COM insists on registering only one of each version component at a time.

Worse, every component must be registered to work. This means that in order for an application to run, all of its components must be registered and each of their dependencies must be present on a system and registered.

If another application comes along and installs a different version of a DLL in their own directory, it blissfully overwrites the entries of the first one.

And, of course, if your registry becomes corrupt, everything must be reinstalled and re-registered from scratch.

The Problem with IUnknown

Under COM, every time you hold a reference to an object, a call must be made to the AddRef method of the object's IUnknown interface. Every time you release that reference, you must call the Release method. The object maintains an internal counter that keeps track of the number of outstanding references. When they hit zero, the object deletes itself.

This leads to two problems:

The first, which really applies to C++ more than Visual Basic, is that it is easy to forget to release an object. Forgetting to call AddRef in a program is fairly easy to detect—it usually triggers an exception when the program tries to access a deleted object. But forgetting to release an object results in an object that stays in memory until the program terminates. This can result in a memory leak that causes your application's memory footprint to grow until it takes up all of the resources in the system—a real problem for applications meant to run 24/7.

The second problem is well known to VB programmers and shown in the following demonstration.

Create a class namcd Class1 with the following code:

```
Public HoldingCollection As Collection
Private Sub Class_Terminate()
   Debug.Print "Object freed"
End Sub
```

And create a form with a Command button that invokes the following code:

```
Private Sub cmdExecute_Click()
    Dim col As New Collection
    Dim myobject As New Class1
    Dim counter As Long
    For counter = 1 To 1000
        Set myobject.HoldingCollection = col
        col.Add myobject
    Next counter
End Sub
```

Run the program and click the button a few times. Watch the Immediate window for messages that indicate that an object was deleted. You won't see one. You can also bring up the Task Manager and look at the application (or VB6 if you are running in the design environment) in the process list. Run the program, clicking on the button while watching the Mem Usage column.

Note how the memory use keeps increasing.

This is a circular reference problem. Each Class1 object is referenced by the collection. But each object also contains a reference to the collection (presumably in order to provide some sort of navigation to other Class1 objects). When you exit the function, the reference to the collection provided by the col variable is removed, but the collection is not deleted because its reference count is not zero. It is, in fact, equal to the number of Class1 objects in the collection.

This type of memory leak is equally harmful to both long-term application reliability and scalability.

Error Handling

The problem of error handling today isn't really so much a problem with COM as the fact that nobody can really agree on how error handling should be done. When you create a VB component, do you raise errors? Do you return error values as results of function calls? If you look at API functions, you will also find huge inconsistencies on how errors are returned.

And let's face it, Visual Basic's error handling is really a pain. On Error Goto? Nobody uses Goto—we've known it's evil for decades. The VB error syntax is a holdover from ancient BASIC days.

COM+

It's funny, even though I've dealt with all of the problems I've just described, it wasn't until I actually wrote this section that I truly realized how broken the current implementation of COM is. So, before showing you how .NET not only addresses these issues but actually solves them, let me briefly mention COM+.

COM+ is largely one of those technologies I mentioned in Chapter 1 that is more a result of marketing than real technology. Don't get me wrong—there is a lot of technology in COM+. It adds contexts, transactioning, object pooling, asynchronous features, and so on. But these already existed to some degree under different labels: primarily Microsoft Transaction Server and Microsoft Message Queue. Naming them COM+ didn't really add anything new—it just provided a new marketing label under which to hype these other technologies.[7]

As far as the ideas and implementation described earlier, COM+ is synonymous with COM.

COM+ 2.0

For a brief time, it looked as if Microsoft was about to do something that, frankly, I found hard to comprehend. They were actually considering calling the framework implemented by the Common Runtime Language, COM+ 2.0.

So let's make this clear for the record.

The .NET Frameworks do not use COM. They are not based on COM. Yes, they can interoperate with COM—use COM components and have COM components use them—but that's it.

I'm glad to report that it looks as if wiser heads prevailed and Microsoft has abandoned the idea of calling the .NET Framework, COM+ 2.0. Current references to COM+ 2.0 in MSDN simply offer a redirection to .NET Framework.

Does this mean COM is dead?

Yes and no.

Yes in that if Microsoft is successful in turning .NET into the dominant development platform in the Windows world (and others?), COM will become less and less important. If they integrate it into future operating systems and rebuild their other applications in the .NET Frameworks, COM will become an afterthought— a historical quirk that somehow lingers on.

But linger on it will. There is too much existing technology built on COM for it to actually die completely. Look, Windows today still supports DDE even though many programmers reading this may have no idea what that means.[8]

---

7. And no, I don't really want to get into DNA at this point. It's dead and it's not coming back.

8. DDE—Dynamic Data Exchange: An early Windows protocol for exchanging information between applications. Remembered with mixed feelings by your humble author who had the pleasure of implementing it in an application before the standard DDE libraries existed.

The Common Language Runtime

It is essential to learn about technology in its proper context. Floods of new features and hyped-up promises are fine for marketing briefs but when evaluating a new technology, there is nothing like understanding the context in which it exists and the problems it was intended to solve. This is especially important when you evaluate whether a certain technology is appropriate to solve your particular problems.

So, now that you know what is wrong with COM, it's time to take a look at how .NET addresses these issues.

Let's start by asking this question: what would it take to do the following?[9]

- Allow a program that uses a component to continue to work even if someone installs a later version of the component that is not backward compatible onto a system.

- Allow a program to detect if someone installs an incompatible version of a component over a working version of that component.

- Eliminate the need to register components.

- Eliminate the problem of circular references and associated memory leaks even in the case where a programmer neglects to free an object.

First, you would need the ability to run multiple versions of a component on a system at one time. That way, the presence of a newer or older copy of a component somewhere on a system would not interfere with a good copy that is available in the application directory. This is side-by-side execution.

Next, you'd need to build into the operating system a mechanism by which it could compare the methods and properties expected by a program with those actually present in a component and not allow the application to run at all if there is a problem. This test should be performed before the program runs rather than waiting for a runtime error or Memory exception to occur.

You'd need to modify the operating system to automatically find and "register" components without using the registry—typically by looking for them in the application's directory or other defined locations where shared components can reside.

Finally, you'd need a way for the operating system to keep track of every object used by an application as it is running and to automatically free those that are no longer in-use.

---

9. One can't help but wonder whether the .NET development team actually had these features on a list and in what order they may have placed them. All we can do is speculate based on the results.

These requirements cannot be met with Windows as it exists now. Nor are they compatible with COM in its current implementation. Meeting these requirements requires an entirely different architecture—a different virtual machine. That virtual machine is provided by the Common Language Runtime.

A Visual Basic DLL or EXE created with VB.NET is very different from those you've used in the past. Yes, it does use the PE (Portable Executable) format internally but if you try to run a VB.NET executable on a system without the CLR installed, you'll get a bunch of "DLL not found" errors.[10] That's because Windows needs the CLR to interpret new types of records that are stored in the executable file.

In the .NET world, rather than focusing on DLL's and EXE files, you'll hear the term assembly used. I'll discuss assemblies more later in this chapter. For now, just assume that there is a one-to-one correspondence—each DLL and EXE file you create will contain one assembly and every assembly will be made up of just one DLL or EXE.[11]

One of the new records stored in a .NET executable file is called a manifest. A manifest contains a huge amount of information about an assembly. It contains a list of all the components used by the assembly. It contains the version numbers of those components and hashed values that allow the runtime to determine if those components have changed. It contains a list of all of the objects exposed by the assembly as well as all of their methods, properties, associated parameters, and return types. It also includes a list of all of the objects required by the assembly and their methods, properties, associated parameters, and return types.

Another new type of record is an Intermediate Language record—or IL for short. I'll discuss this in more detail shortly.

Manifests

The manifest is the answer to the problems of versioning and deployment that exist under COM. Let's look at these issues one by one.

- The manifest allows a program that uses a component to continue to work even if someone installs a later version of the component that is not backward compatible onto a system.

---

10. In the prerelease version, that is. One would hope that they might come up with a more friendly way to detect and notify users that an application requires the .NET runtime before release.

11. In fact, it is possible for an assembly to be made up of multiple DLL and EXE files. However VB.NET does not support this capability in the current beta and there is no evidence that this will change for the final release of this version of VB.NET.

The CLR supports side-by-side execution. This means that if a component exists in the application directory, the CLR will load that component even if the same component exists (in the same or differing version) somewhere else on the system—and even if the other component is in one of the shared assembly directories.

Does this mean that developers will begin to install components in their own private directories instead of system32 or other shared directories in order to minimize component distribution problems?

You'd better believe it. It will still be possible to create shared components but it will undoubtedly become less common.

Doesn't this mean that systems will start becoming cluttered with multiple versions of the same component? Isn't that a terrible waste of disk space? And won't that also waste memory when components are loaded simultaneously when it isn't necessary? Wasn't the ability to share memory and reduce disk space use the whole idea behind dynamic link libraries in the first place?

Yes, this approach is potentially wasteful in terms of disk space and memory use. And yes, DLLs were originally created in order to reduce memory and disk requirements. But those features were created back in the days where a normal system had 640K of memory and a high-end system had maybe a few megabytes—and disk space cost ten dollars per megabyte or more.[12] These days, the minimum memory on a low-end system is 64MB and you have to work hard to spend more than a penny per megabyte of disk space. With those kinds of numbers, the amount of waste due to duplication of DLL files on a system or even in memory is negligible. Developers today try to avoid memory leaks that occur while an application is running, which can ultimately use up even these large amounts of memory (or disk space) in applications designed to run continuously for days or weeks on end. Developers also try to minimize changes to components in one application from interfering in any way with another application.

- The manifest allows a program to detect if someone installs an incompatible version of a component over a working version of that component.

But what if you actually overwrite an existing component with a newer one that is incompatible with the one your application needs?

In this case, what happens depends to some degree on how you've configured the application. You can, for example, require that your application always use a specific version of an assembly. If the correct version is not found, the application will fail to load. The manifest even contains hashed signatures for the dependent assemblies so it can detect if they were changed even if the developer forgot to update the version number!

---

12. I remember the thrill of having a whole 500MB on my machine and what a bargain it was to get it for only $1,000!

You can also allow your application to attempt to use newer versions of a component. In this case, the CLR is able to use the manifest to check the new version of the component and verify that it exposes all of the correct objects; and also that the methods and properties and their associated parameters exactly match those expected by your application. If they don't, the application won't be allowed to run.

- The manifest eliminates the need to register components.

The CLR obtains manifest information from your application and its dependency components at load time. None of this information is stored in the registry. It is able to load components from your application directory or the global assembly cache (depending on how the application is configured).

Curiously enough, this capability and others provided by use of a manifest make possible a radically new feature with regard to deploying applications. It will actually be possible to successfully deploy an application simply by copying files (or XCopy a directory structure) onto a system![13]

By the way, it should go without saying (but I'll mention it just in case), that as wonderful as these capabilities are, they aren't magic. In other words, if you use traditional COM components from your .NET application, all of the old rules still apply. You'll need to register them and watch out for the usual compatibility issues—but only for those traditional COM components.

I must also note that the long-term success of this approach will also depend a great deal on Microsoft's ability to keep the CLR itself backward compatible as they enhance it.[14]

Intermediate Language (IL)

You may be wondering how the CLR can do all of these amazing things with the manifest. Think about it—a compiled program basically contains a bunch of subroutine calls. COM works because once you've compiled your application that uses a COM component, that application will get a virtual function table to each object—an array of function pointers that it can call. At least that's how it works with early binding. With late binding, it's possible to call functions with a dynamic name but there is substantial overhead involved.

---

13. I'm sure I'm not the only one thoroughly entertained by the fact that after all these years of advanced Windows technology, we are finally able to do something that was an everyday occurrence under DOS.

14. However, I've heard rumors that it may be possible to deploy different versions of the CLR itself on a system, in which case it may be possible to avoid runtime-based incompatibilities.

And, of course, there remains our final requirement for solving COM's problems:

- The CLR eliminates the problem of circular references and associated memory leaks even in the case where a programmer neglects to free an object.

What kind of runtime can examine your compiled application and figure out exactly where it may be referencing an object and where it may be releasing it? Surely the effort required to do so would ruin the performance of any application.

The tasks of generating code for method or property calls and adding and freeing object references is traditionally that of the compiler—because the compiler has all of the information about the names and types of methods and their parameters. And a compiler can see where in the code you are allocating or freeing an object. By the time the compilation is done, that extra information is thrown away and it's too late to know where object references are occurring.

So, .NET solves these problems in an obvious way—it defers much of the compilation until the application is loaded.

When you compile a .NET assembly into a DLL or EXE file, the compilation process is not actually complete. Much of the information that would typically be used by a compiler is actually stored with the manifest. And the code that is produced is not native code but an Intermediate Language.

When you load a .NET application for the first time, a JIT (just-in-time) compiler is invoked. This compiler produces the actual native code needed to run the application. But along the way, it does some other things:

- It examines the code to make sure that all memory access takes place through correctly typed variables—thus, your application is not able to access memory locations outside of the objects and data structures that it defines.[15]

- It builds the necessary code and tables so that the CLR can find the root-level variables in your program. These are the global variables and all the local variables allocated on the stack or temporarily held by CPU registers.

- It only compiles code as needed.

IL code should not be confused with the P-Code familiar to most Visual Basic programmers. P-Code is, in fact, an Intermediate Language. But P-Code is interpreted by the runtime. The .NET Intermediate Language is compiled into native code, which is then cached. The result is a performance hit at load time but full

---

15. Most .NET documentation emphasizes the fact that .NET-managed code applications (more on this shortly) no longer suffer from uninitialized pointers that overwrite random memory or from stray pointers that access memory incorrectly, thus leading to Memory exceptions. This is, in fact, a great new feature—but one that is already familiar to VB programmers since we never really had pointers in the first place.

native code performance for subsequent execution of any given block of code. It is also possible to run an assembly through the JIT compiler as it is installed and save the resulting native code, which can improve performance the first time the application is run.[16]

The term managed code is used to describe IL code that can be verified by the JIT compiler as always accessing memory by way of a defined type. Managed code does not use direct memory pointers since those could be set to values that do not correspond to legal memory locations. VB.NET creates managed code. The C# language is designed primarily to create managed code but you do have the option to create unmanaged code. The C++ language is designed primarily to create unmanaged code but has been extended to allow the creation of managed code.

One of the potentially interesting side effects of IL-based managed code is this: since the actual generation of native code only occurs when the JIT compiler compiles the code on the target machine, it is theoretically possible that your .NET applications will be portable to any platform or operating system that supports the CLR. It will be fascinating to see which (if any) operating systems other than Windows will ultimately have the CLR available. Meanwhile, we can hope that .NET applications will at least be easy to deploy on the ever-increasing number of Windows permutations.

Goodbye Circular References

The combination of Intermediate Language with JIT compilation and the Common Language Runtime makes it possible for the CLR to discover at runtime a list of the root-level variables for an application or component:

- The CLR knows where the application's global variables are.

- The CLR knows how to walk the stack and check each stack frame for its local variables.

- The CLR knows which registers are temporarily holding variables.

- The CLR knows which variables contain object references.

---

16. When you precompile code at installation, you must still keep the original IL code and manifest around—this is because the CLR may need to recompile code if dependent assemblies change.

- The CLR knows which members (within objects themselves) hold object references.

- All objects are created by the runtime on behalf of assemblies so the CLR knows the location of every object in the memory heap or on the stack.

When a .NET application begins, a heap is created that consists of a large block of free memory. Normally, when an assembly asks the CLR for an object (and the CLR considers everything to be an object), it just allocates the object from the block of free memory under the top of the heap—without trying to fill any spaces that might exist due to previously freed objects.[17] When that block of free memory is used up, the CLR performs a task called garbage collection. Here is a simplified description of what happens:

- The CLR marks every object in the heap as unused.

- It checks each global variable in your application and marks the object it references as used, then performs a recursive search on any objects that are referenced by that first object and marks them as in-use. During this search process, if it finds that an object is already marked as in-use, it does not check further beyond that object—it knows that objects beyond that one have already been found.

- It walks the stack checking every object referenced by local variables in each stack frame, performing the same recursive search, and marking every object found as in-use.

- It checks any objects referenced by CPU registers and marks them in-use, again performing the recursive search.

- After this process is complete, any objects in the heap still marked as unused are deleted. All other objects are moved to the bottom of the heap and every memory reference to those objects is updated to refer to the new location.

Figures 4-4A through 4-4D illustrate this process.

---

17. Value type objects can also be allocated on the stack as you'll read later but, for now, let's focus on the heap.

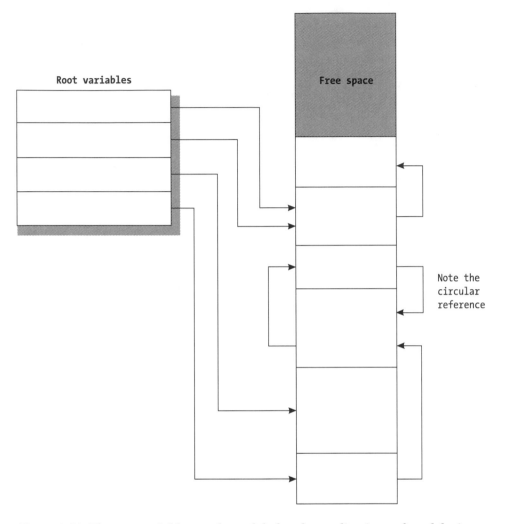

Figure 4-4A. The root variables are those global to the application or found during a stack trace. The pointers represent object references to the heap. Objects on the heap can point to other objects. Note the presence of a circular reference that would not be deleted under COM.

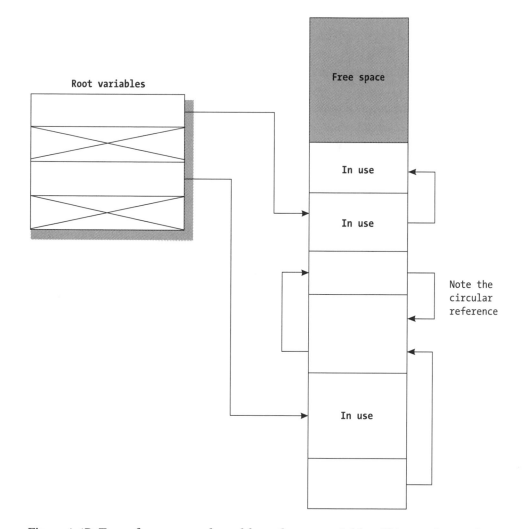

Figure 4-4B. Two references are cleared from the root variables. Objects referenced from the remaining variables are marked in-use, as are those objects referenced by the remaining variables.

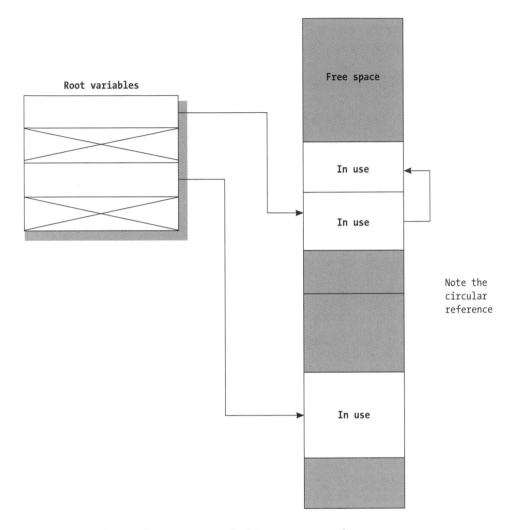

Figure 4-4C. Objects that are not marked in-use are now free.

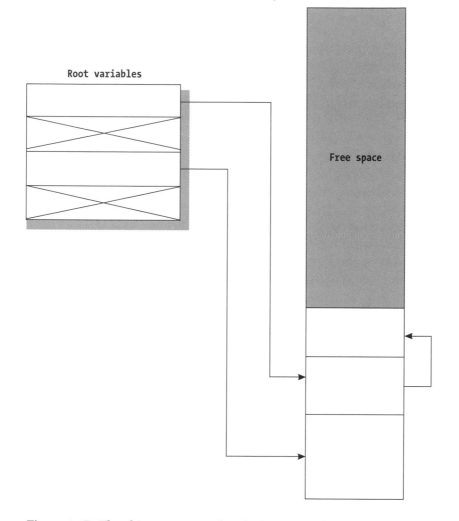

Figure 4-4D. The objects are moved to the bottom of the heap and all pointers are adjusted accordingly.

In Chapter 6, you'll learn that this description actually leaves out some very important aspects of garbage collection such as finalization and generations but it gives you an idea of the principles involved.

Naturally, this garbage collection process comes at a price. Your application will periodically be suspended to perform a garbage collection when insufficient memory is available to fill a request. The good news is that Microsoft has put a great deal of effort into minimizing the performance cost. Ultimately, it's a fair price to pay for the benefits gained.

Code at Last

The MemoryLeakNot sample project illustrates how the CLR eliminates the circular reference problem.

> **CAUTION**   *You are about to see a lot of code that you may not understand. Many of the concepts and most of the syntax behind this example have not yet been explained and won't be covered until much later in this book. I will include brief descriptions of most of the code that is likely to be unfamiliar but I encourage you to think of this as a quick preview rather than a code example that you are expected to fully understand.*

The original VB6 application consisted of the following class:

```
Public HoldingCollection As Collection
Private Sub Class_Terminate()
   Debug.Print "Object freed"
End Sub
```

…and a form with a Command button that invokes the following code:

```
Private Sub cmdExecute_Click()
   Dim col As New Collection
   Dim myobject As New Class1
   Dim counter As Long
   For counter = 1 To 1000
      Set myobject.HoldingCollection = col
      col.Add myobject
   Next counter
End Sub
```

The VB.NET class contains the code shown in Listing 4-1.

Listing 4-1. TestClass.vb module from the MemoryLeakNot project.

```
' No memory leak demonstrated
' Copyright ©2001 by Desaware Inc. All Rights Reserved
Public Class TestClassObject
    Shared m_classcount As Integer
    Dim m_ClassId As Integer
    Dim m_Collection As Collection
    Public Sub New(ByVal mycontainer As Collection)
        MyBase.New()
        mycontainer.Add(Me)
        m_Collection = mycontainer
        m_ClassId = m_classcount
        m_classcount = m_classcount + 1
    End Sub

    Protected Overrides Sub Finalize()
        System.Diagnostics.Debug.WriteLine("Destructed " + _
        m_ClassId.ToString())
    End Sub
End Class
```

And Listing 4-2 shows the form.

Listing 4-2. TestForm.vb form from the MemoryLeakNot project.

```
' No memory leak demonstrated
' Copyright ©2001 by Desaware Inc. All Rights Reserved
Public Class Form1
    Inherits System.Windows.Forms.Form

#Region " Windows Form Designer generated code "

    Public Sub New()
        MyBase.New()

        'This call is required by the Windows Form Designer.
        InitializeComponent()

        'Add any initialization after the InitializeComponent() call
    End Sub
```

```vbnet
'Form overrides dispose to clean up the component list.
Public Overloads Overrides Sub Dispose()
    MyBase.Dispose()
    If Not (components Is Nothing) Then
        components.Dispose()
    End If
End Sub
Private WithEvents button1 As System.Windows.Forms.Button

'Required by the Windows Form Designer
Private components As System.ComponentModel.Container

'NOTE: The following procedure is required by the Windows Form Designer
'It can be modified using the Windows Form Designer.
'Do not modify it using the code editor.
<System.Diagnostics.DebuggerStepThrough()> Private Sub _
 InitializeComponent()
    Me.button1 = New System.Windows.Forms.Button()
    Me.SuspendLayout()
    '
    'button1
    '
    Me.button1.Location = New System.Drawing.Point(104, 48)
    Me.button1.Name = "button1"
    Me.button1.TabIndex = 0
    Me.button1.Text = "Test"
    '
    'Form1
    '
    Me.AutoScaleBaseSize = New System.Drawing.Size(5, 13)
    Me.ClientSize = New System.Drawing.Size(275, 144)
    Me.Controls.AddRange(New System.Windows.Forms.Control() _
    {Me.button1})
    Me.Name = "Form1"
    Me.Text = "Memory Leak - Not"
    Me.ResumeLayout(False)

End Sub
```

```
Private Sub button1_Click(ByVal sender As System.Object, _
ByVal e As System.EventArgs) Handles button1.Click
    Dim x As Integer
    Dim col As New Collection()
    Dim obj As TestClassObject
    For x = 1 To 100
        obj = New TestClassObject(col)
    Next x
    debug.WriteLine("Collection contains " + col.Count.ToString() _
    + " objects")

    ' This would happen when we exit the function
    ' but is done here explicitly for illustrative purposes
    col = Nothing
    obj = Nothing

    ' Don't do this in real code
    ' It's here just to make it clear that the circular
    ' reference problem is gone.
    gc.Collect()
    gc.WaitForPendingFinalizers()

End Sub

#End Region

End Class
```

Please don't panic. It's not as bad as it looks.

The design of this sample takes a slightly different approach. In the VB6 example, the object held a reference to the collection—but that reference had to be set by the form using the object by way of a public property. In the MemoryLeakNot example, we take advantage of a feature new to VB.NET called parameterized constructors. This allows you to pass a parameter to the Initialize method of the object—in this case, we pass a reference to the collection.

Let's take another look at the class in Listing 4-1.

The class has three local member variables. Well, actually, only two of them are local to the object. The m_classcount member is marked as shared—which means that all of the objects created by this class in an application domain will share the same variable. This allows you in this example to keep track of the number of objects of this class type that were created, and to give each one an identifier number that is stored in the m_ClassId variable.

Don't worry about running out of identifiers quickly. Integers in VB.NET are 32-bit variables (equivalent to Long variables in VB6).

The m_Collection variable holds a reference to a Collection of objects.

The New method is the constructor. It receives a reference to the collection as its construction parameter and stores it in the variable. Note that there is no need to use the Set syntax from VB6 (good riddance). The first command is MyBase.New(), which calls the constructor for the base class. What's a base class? I'll discuss this later in Chapter 5 (it has something to do with inheritance). The constructor then increments the m_classcount member in preparation for the next time an object of this type is created.

The Finalize method is called when an object is about to be completely destroyed.[18] In this example, the Finalizer simply writes some debugging information to the Output window. The COM-based Debug object you are familiar with is gone, replaced by the considerably more powerful, though less familiar, Debug object in the System.Diagnostics namespace.

The parameter to the function may look rather odd. To display an object number in VB6, you might have done something like this:

```
"Destructed " & m_Classid
```

VB6 would see that you were trying to append an integer value to a string and automatically convert it to a string. Though convenient in this case, this kind of type coercion can lead to all sorts of bugs.[19] The VB.NET code:

```
"Destructed " m_Classid.Tostring()
```

explicitly uses the ToString method to convert the integer to a string.

Wait a minute—how can an integer have a method? It's an integer, right?

Yes and no. An integer is a numeric variable. But in .NET, it's also an object. In fact, every data type is an object (specifically, it inherits from a class named Object). And since the class Object has a method called ToString that provides some text representation of the object, every object that inherits from that class (including Integer) also has a ToString method. Pretty cool, eh? Don't worry if you find this confusing—you'll find out more about this later in this book.

---

18. This is a technically correct but potentially misleading statement. First, it doesn't address when an object is destroyed. Second, while the object is about to be destroyed, at this point, it's not certain that it actually *will* be destroyed. It is also possible for an object to be destroyed without this method being called. It's a long story and I ask you to wait until Chapter 6 where all will be explained.

19. The term evil type coercion describes VB6's habit of changing variables to whatever type it feels is best regardless of your particular design needs.

Let's take a look at the form module in Listing 4-3—but only the Button1_Click function.

Listing 4-3. The button1_Click method from the TestForm.vb module.

```
Private Sub button1_Click(ByVal sender As System.Object, _
    ByVal e As System.EventArgs) Handles button1.Click
    Dim x As Integer
    Dim col As New Collection()
    Dim obj As TestClassObject
    For x = 1 To 100
        obj = New TestClassObject(col)
    Next x
    debug.WriteLine("Collection contains " + col.Count.ToString() _
    + " objects")

    ' This would happen when we exit the function
    ' but is done here explicitly for illustrative purposes
    col = Nothing
    obj = Nothing

    ' Don't do this in real code
    ' It's here just to make it clear that the circular
    ' reference problem is gone.
    gc.Collect()
    gc.WaitForPendingFinalizers()

End Sub
```

Most VB6 programmers will find this code quite easy to follow. Don't worry about the parameters to the Button_Click event—the Button_Click event you're used to doesn't have any parameters anyway, right?

The event creates a collection object, then proceeds to create one hundred TestClassObject objects and add each one to the collection. Keep in mind that adding them to the collection in this example is accomplished by passing a reference to the collection as a parameter to the constructor (which is called when the object is created by the New operator). You know the objects have been added because the debug.Writeline method dumps the value of the collection's Count property to the Output window.

At the end of this method, you can see two bad examples of VB.NET code. First, I explicitly set the value of the col and obj variables to Nothing. This is totally unnecessary because they are automatically cleared when the object goes out of scope. There will be occasions when you will want to set objects to Nothing within a routine but there is no need to ever do so for local variables before a function exits.

Next, I run the garbage collector. You will rarely (if ever) need to do this explicitly.[20] The reason I do it in this example is that I want you to see that the objects are destroyed by the CLR. Remember, this is a case of circular reference—the collection references each object, which, in turn, references the collection. Under COM, those objects and the collection would not be freed until the application terminates. Under VB.NET, they are freed because they are not referenced by any root-level variable in the application. However, they aren't freed until the garbage collector runs and you can't be sure when it will run. So, in this example, I run the garbage collector explicitly so that you can see the object get destroyed by watching the debug messages in the Output window.

As exciting as it is to see the elimination of the circular reference problem, some of you may be thinking ahead and wondering how one deals with object termination if you don't know when it will actually terminate? In fact, the situation is worse because there are circumstances under which the Finalize method may never be called.

The truth is that we have just begun to discuss memory management under the Common Language Runtime. Bear with me, Chapter 6 will go into this in-depth.

The Code Controversy

You may also be wondering what all that extra code is in the form module. Take a quick look at it. Don't worry about the code you don't understand—you'll still find that a lot of the code makes sense. You can see that it is doing things like creating the form and the button control. There is also the interesting comment line:

```
'NOTE: The following procedure is required by the Win Form Designer
'It can be modified using the Win Form Designer.
'Do not modify it using the code editor.
```

Could it be that the VB.NET development environment is nothing more than a giant wizard that creates all of the code to implement a VB application? What happened to having that code encapsulated in the language itself and both hidden and unavailable to the user? Wasn't that one of the features that made Visual Basic so easy and accessible to so many programmers?

Here we are faced with one of the first controversies regarding VB.NET. Until now, even though Visual Basic and Visual C++ were both nominally part of Visual Studio, they really were different development environments.

Visual Basic hid all of the "glue" that made an application run from the programmer—effectively encapsulating it in the language and runtime environment. You didn't have to worry about where forms and buttons came from—you just

---

20. There may be esoteric examples where you might wish to do so but I can't think of any offhand.

used them. When you double-clicked on a control, the event code would magically appear and you would never know what was going on behind the scenes.

Visual C++ accomplished much of the same level of automation making it easy to add events (in some cases) by double-clicking on a control in a dialog box and allowing you to add methods and properties using a class browser. But, in each case, you were really interacting with a large and complex wizard. It would write code for you that you could see but would generally not modify.

What has happened in VB.NET depends upon your point of view.

Some would say that Visual Basic has finally been integrated as part of a unified development environment making it easy to create mixed language applications—in fact, making language choice dependent on personal style rather than differences in functionality.

Some would say that the Visual Basic language was effectively hijacked by the Visual Studio team bringing it to the wizard-based environment, which is not nearly as effective as that provided by the traditional VB environment and which many VB developers have intentionally done their best to avoid. They point out the lack of an Immediate window as an example of a great traditional VB feature that was sacrificed in the process of integrating VB into the new development environment.

Many who are saying these things are quite passionate and vocal in their views.[21]

Now, as you've probably noticed, I can also be quite passionate and vocal in my views on occasion[22]—but in this case, I'm afraid my view is one that will satisfy nobody.

You see, I really can't judge whether the approach Microsoft has taken was the right one or how VB programmers will find the adjustment. The problem is that while I do a lot of VB application and component development, I also do a lot of ATL-based COM development using Visual C++.[23] So, I'm quite used to the Visual Studio approach.

My current thought is that most Visual Basic programmers will not have much difficulty getting used to having wizard-based code in their projects—especially since the Visual Studio editor is able to hide most of it from them.

I'll tell you this though…I would have loved to be a fly on the wall listening in on the debates within Microsoft when they were making this decision.

---

21. I've followed some of the threads on developers' newsgroups. Let's just say that I don't recall seeing any specific death threats.

22. Definitely not to the point of death threats, though.

23. I haven't written a Visual C++ application with a user interface in ages. And I dumped MFC as soon as ATL came on the scene, even though ATL has a much steeper learning curve—but that's another story.

Recap: Why .NET?

Microsoft .NET represents such a huge change to developers that it's difficult to know where to begin. My intent is for you to gain a real understanding of .NET based not just on knowledge of a list of features but on an understanding of why those features exist and the problems they were intended to solve.

So far in this chapter you've read about virtual machines and the evolution of Windows programming. You've learned how, in a sense, Windows development reached an evolutionary dead end in COM—not due to any theoretical flaws in COM but due to its poor ability to deal with the flaws that exist in developers.

You've learned that .NET addresses those flaws with a new architecture based on a Common Language Runtime. That .NET applications and components are built from assemblies that are implemented by one or more DLL or EXE files. Each of these assemblies has a manifest that describes all of the components needed by the assembly and contains code in an Intermediate Language that is compiled into native code by a JIT (just-in-time) compiler when the assembly is loaded or installed on a system.

You've learned that this approach addressed two of the major flaws in COM: the versioning and deployment problem, and the problem of circular references and memory leaks that can occur when developers forget to free objects in their code.

You've also received a taste of VB.NET code. You've seen parameterized constructors that are called when an object is created. You've seen that there are significant changes to the syntax of the language—enough so that my claim that VB.NET is "a Visual Basic" (but not the Visual Basic you are familiar with) should begin to make sense. You've also seen inheritance, though only in the most rudimentary form (you may not have recognized it for what it was)—and that everything, even a numeric variable, is an object.

The concepts you've read about in this chapter are those that I felt most important for you to start with. But they are just a beginning. Some of the features you'll learn about in the chapters to come include:

- How inheritance and aggregation can be effectively combined.

- The use of multithreading to improve scalability—especially in Web applications and other enterprise applications (but it requires great care in design).

- The huge library of functions included with the Common Language Runtime.

- Exception-based error handling (a subject mentioned briefly in this chapter, then dropped—don't worry, it will be back with a vengeance).

- The ability to create code that is secure (in that you can tightly control what code from different sources is allowed to do on a system and create code that degrades gracefully depending on the privileges it is granted).

In the next chapter, you'll find out more about inheritance in VB.NET. It's a feature that has been requested by many and has received a great deal of hype. It is an important feature and fundamental to the architecture of the CLR—but in terms of your own application development, you may find the reality of inheritance has some surprises in store.

CHAPTER 5

Inheritance

DURING THE EARLY preview days of the .NET architecture, I would watch speakers from Microsoft stand up before Visual Basic programmers and announce some of the upcoming new features of what was then called VB7. One of the features that would always elicit loud cheers was inheritance.

And I never really understood why.

Well, actually, I do have a theory. I think Visual Basic programmers have been intimidated by the C++ crowds, who have a tendency to raise their noses and say, "Visual Basic is not a *real* object-oriented language. A *real* object-oriented language has true inheritance"—at which point, the poor VB programmer would slink into his cubicle and churn out in an hour as much code as the C++ programmer could generate in a week. But that didn't matter because C++ was a "modern, elegant, professional, object-oriented language" and VB was just a "holdover, toy, beginner's language" designed for those who couldn't handle C++.

In this context, why wouldn't a VB programmer cheer?

Now, I'm going to let you in on a little secret.

I've been a C++ programmer for longer than I've programmed in Visual Basic—and I still program actively in both languages. I've been a firm advocate of object-oriented programming since I first understood the concept of a class back in 1977; and I've programmed in frameworks like ATL that use inheritance extensively and successfully.

But in terms of using inheritance in one of my own applications or components, in all of those years, I can think of maybe half a dozen times, at most, where inheritance was the right choice.

So yes, .NET uses inheritance—it's built into the architecture. And yes, the code generated by the various designers will use inheritance to give you the framework on which you'll build your own code.

However, if you really understand inheritance, you may find yourself living the rest of your career without ever creating a single inheritable class or component.

This chapter will explain why.

The Mantra of Code Reuse

Inheritance, despite the hype that surrounds it, is really only about one thing— code reuse. In a nutshell, the idea of inheritance is that when one object inherits from another, it instantly implements all of the functionality of the other class, allowing you to build new capability on top of that functionality.

Sounds great, doesn't it?

But inheritance isn't the only way to reuse code.

There are code libraries where you literally copy source code from one project to another. There are components that provide objects and functionality that can be reused. And there are objects and programs that create instances of other objects and programs to gain access to their functionality.

Each of these approaches has its advantages and disadvantages.

To help understand these tradeoffs, I'm going to start out by showing you some bad code. In fact, this chapter is going to be full of bad code.

This may seem odd since one would hope that a book would contain lots of good code so you could learn the right way to do things. I think it's also important to look at the flip side—viewing bad code to learn to avoid doing things the wrong way.[1]

The example we will use is that of a simple linked list. A linked list is an extremely useful structure for maintaining lists of objects. It can be more efficient than an array because you can insert and remove entries without shifting data in the array. It can be more useful than a collection because it is easier to control the order of objects in a linked list and rearrange them as needed.

The principal of a linked list is simple: each object contains a pointer (or reference) to the next object in the list. A root variable points to the first object in the list.

A VB6 Linked List

Let's begin by considering a VB6 class that implements a linked list. I know this is a book about VB.NET but trust me, the best way for you to really learn and understand inheritance is through comparison to containment and interface inheritance as they are implemented in VB6. The LinkListVB6 project demonstrates a class designed to make it easy to add linked list functionality to another class. In other words, the goal is to be able to reuse this code as easily as possible.

The LinkList object has the following properties and methods:

- Property NextItem—used to obtain a reference to the next object in the list.

- Property PreviousItem—used to obtain a reference to the previous object in the list.

- Method Remove—Removes the current object from a list.

- Method Append—Appends the current object to a list.

---

1. I stress this because those of you who are familiar with this subject may look at a few of the examples and jump to the conclusion that I've completely lost my mind. I ask that you read through each example until I not only describe it but also describe what is wrong with it before you come to any firm conclusions about my judgment.

Under Visual Basic 6, you can achieve code reuse through containment. The class that you want to link can contain an instance of the LinkList class and can call its methods to perform the linking.

What type of object does the NextItem and PreviousItem properties refer to? Do they refer to a LinkList object or do they refer to the object that contains the LinkList object?

Figure 5-1 illustrates the first approach where each LinkList object can only point to another LinkList object. In this case, you need a way to obtain a reference to the container object, a hypothetical Customer object.

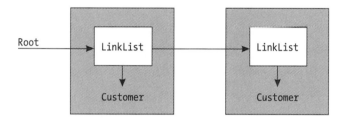

Figure 5-1. LinkList objects reference other LinkList objects. A Container property is used to obtain a reference to the container.

Figure 5-2 illustrates the latter approach where each LinkList object points to the actual Container object that holds the internal LinkList object.

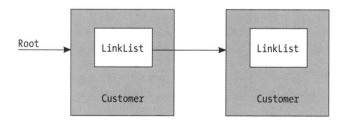

Figure 5-2. LinkList objects reference the Container objects.

Let's start with the latter approach, which is implemented by the LinkListVB6 project in the sample code for this book. The LinkList class is designed not only to be held by a container but also to provide the interface that the container can use to implement the linked list functionality. The Container object will use the Implements statement, which provides interface inheritance to quickly add linked list functionality to the object.

The LinkList object contains two Private variables. The m_Next variable is the reference to the next object in the list. The LinkList object will be pointing to the container but since the container implements the LinkList interface, the m_Next variable can be of type LinkList. The m_Container object holds a reference to the Container object. You'll soon see why it's needed. The LinkList object is defined as follows:

```
' LinkList VB6 example #1
' Copyright ©2000 by Desaware Inc.  All Rights Reserved

Option Explicit

' This version is designed to be embedded, so it links to the container
' object
Private m_Next As LinkList
' When adding to the list, it needs to know its container
Private m_Container As Object

' Container is set during initialization
' Would need to be public if you decided to componentize the class
Friend Property Set Container(ByVal ContainerObject As Object)
    Set m_Container = ContainerObject
End Property
```

The NextItem property simply returns a reference to the m_Next variable, which contains a reference to the next object in the list:

```
' Next is easy - just the next link.
Public Property Get NextItem() As LinkList
    Set NextItem = m_Next
End Property

Public Property Set NextItem(ByVal nextptr As LinkList)
    Set m_Next = nextptr
End Property
```

The PreviousItem property is a bit tricky. Since this is a singly linked list, the property needs a reference to the first object in the list so it can search forward for the current object or, rather, the object whose NextItem property is the current object. The tricky factor here is determining which object you are comparing to. You can't compare objects to "Me" because "Me" refers to the internal LinkList object, not the one referenced by the m_Next variable. No, the comparison must be to the Container objects; thus each LinkList object must hold a reference to its container as shown here:

```
' In a single linked list, Previous has to search forward from the root
Public Property Get PreviousItem(Root As LinkList) As LinkList
    Dim currentitem As LinkList
    ' Remember, all references are to the container object
    If (Root Is m_Container) Or (Root Is Nothing) Then
       Exit Property
    End If
    Set currentitem = Root
    Do
       If currentitem.NextItem Is m_Container Then
          Set PreviousItem = currentitem
          Exit Property
       Else
          Set currentitem = currentitem.NextItem
       End If
    Loop While Not currentitem Is Nothing
End Property
```

The Remove method uses the PreviousItem property to find the object that precedes the one being removed. If one exists, its m_Next variable is set to the current object's m_Next variable, effectively removing this entry from the linked list. If the object being removed is the first object in the list, the root variable must be set to reference the next object in the list. This is done by setting the root variable (which is called by reference) to the next object in the list. Don't be confused by the fact that it is set to a variable of type LinkList. Root references the container (that implements the LinkList interface) and not the internal object:

```
' Remove has to search from root to find the previous node.
' Root must be by reference so it can be cleared if this
' is the last object, or reset if the first object
Public Sub Remove(Root As LinkList)
    Dim previtem As LinkList

    Set previtem = PreviousItem(Root)

    If previtem Is Nothing Then
       Set Root = m_Next
    Else
       Set previtem.NextItem = m_Next
    End If
End Sub
```

The Append subroutine also uses the m_Container property in order to assign an object correctly into the list. The routine finds the last object in the list, then sets its m_Next variable to the container of the current object:

```
' Append searches from Root to the end of the list.
Public Sub Append(Root As LinkList)
    Dim currentitem As LinkList
    Set currentitem = Root
    If Root Is Nothing Then
        Set Root = m_Container
    Else
        While Not currentitem.NextItem Is Nothing
            Set currentitem = currentitem.NextItem
        Wend
        Set currentitem.NextItem = m_Container
    End If
End Sub
```

The Container class is defined in the Customer.cls file. It has a public CustomerName property that allows you to access the name of a customer. This class implements the LinkList object, thus inheriting the LinkList interface. It contains a private LinkList object called m_MyLinkList that is initialized during the Class_Initialize event. As you can see in Listing 5-1, each of the implemented functions simply calls into the contained LinkList object.

Listing 5-1. Customer.cls class for the LinkListVB6 project.

```
' LinkList VB6 example #1
' Copyright ©2000 by Desaware Inc.  All Rights Reserved

Option Explicit

' This version Implements the LinkList - making
' its methods accessible via LinkList objects
Implements LinkList

Public CustomerName As String

' The internal LinkList object provides the functionality
Private m_MyLinkList As LinkList

Private Sub Class_Initialize()
    Set m_MyLinkList = New LinkList
    Set m_MyLinkList.Container = Me
End Sub
```

```
' This will never be called. Read text for how
' to get around this problem
Private Sub Class_Terminate()
   Debug.Print "Terminating customer " & CustomerName
End Sub


' Methods & properties just map to the LinkList members & properties
Private Sub LinkList_Append(Root As LinkList)
   m_MyLinkList.Append Root
End Sub



Private Property Set LinkList_NextItem(ByVal nextobject As LinkList)
   Set m_MyLinkList.NextItem = nextobject
End Property

Private Property Get LinkList_NextItem() As LinkList
   Set LinkList_NextItem = m_MyLinkList.NextItem
End Property

Private Property Get LinkList_PreviousItem(Root As LinkList) As LinkList
   Set LinkList_PreviousItem = m_MyLinkList.PreviousItem(Root)
End Property

Private Sub LinkList_Remove(Root As LinkList)
   m_MyLinkList.Remove Root
End Sub
```

The TestForm.frm module contains a text box for new customer names, a Command button to add a new customer, a listbox to display the list of customers, and another Command button to remove the customer selected in the listbox. The module contains a variable m_List, which contains a reference to the first Customer object in the list. Again, even though the m_List variable is of the type LinkList, it references the Customer object itself (through its LinkList interface) and not the internal LinkList object:

```
' LinkList VB6 example #1
' Copyright ©2000 by Desaware Inc.  All Rights Reserved

Option Explicit Dim m_List As LinkList
```

Under VB6, you can access an interface's methods or properties using a variable that represents the interface you wish to use. To obtain a list of objects, you need two variables: a LinkList object that allows you to scan through the list using its

NextItem property and a Customer object that allows you to read the Customer-Name property. This idea—that each interface provides its own set of properties and that each object can expose multiple interfaces—is fundamental to COM. When you assign a variable of one type to another (as seen in the following Set currentcustomer = currentlist line), you are performing a QueryInterface operation that COM uses to navigate from one interface to another on an object. You'll soon understand why I stress this point. Here is the code for the Testfrm.frm form:

```
' Updates the list box
' Note the use of separate variables to access each interface
Private Sub UpdateList()
    lstCustomers.Clear
    Dim currentlist As LinkList
    Dim currentcustomer As Customer
    Set currentlist = m_List
    Do While Not currentlist Is Nothing
        Set currentcustomer = currentlist
        lstCustomers.AddItem currentcustomer.CustomerName
        Set currentlist = currentlist.NextItem
    Loop
End Sub
```

The cmdAdd_Click and cmdRemove_Click functions both show the same use of two types of variables to work with the object as you can see in Listing 5-2.

Listing 5-2. Code to add and remove link list entries.

```
Private Sub cmdAdd_Click()
    Dim newEntry As New Customer
    Dim newEntryll As LinkList
    newEntry.CustomerName = txtCustomerName.Text
    Set newEntryll = newEntry
    newEntryll.Append m_List
    UpdateList
End Sub

Private Sub cmdRemove_Click()
    Dim currentlist As LinkList
    Dim currentcustomer As Customer
```

```
    Set currentlist = m_List
    Do While Not currentlist Is Nothing
        Set currentcustomer = currentlist
        If currentcustomer.CustomerName = lstCustomers.Text Then
            currentlist.Remove m_List
            UpdateList
            Exit Sub
        End If
        Set currentlist = currentlist.NextItem
    Loop
    UpdateList
End Sub
```

What can we conclude from this example?

- It is possible using containment and interface inheritance to reuse function-ality with a minimal amount of coding. The amount of code needed to implement this type of containment in the container (Customer) object is minimal.

- Part of the awkwardness of interface inheritance comes from the fact that you must explicitly switch between interfaces to access the methods of each interface. This is reflected by the extra variables and assignments in the test form.

By the way, have you noticed the one truly fatal flaw in this example? If not, try running it and watch the Immediate window to see what happens when you remove objects from the list. Got it?

- The need for the Contained object to reference the Container object and for the Container object to reference the Contained object means that you automatically have a circular reference!

If you were to actually use this approach, you would need to find a way to eliminate this circular reference. The most common way to do this is to have the Contained object raise an event whose parameter is an Object variable passed by reference. When the container receives the event, it must set the object parameter to Me. This provides the LinkList object with a reference to its container. The LinkList object can then use the container reference directly for comparisons or return it as a value. The container reference should be released immediately to eliminate the circular reference. The flaw with this approach is twofold: it's awkward and it's slow. Events are not early bound, thus performance with this approach can be seriously impaired.

A Containment-Based Linked List Using VB.NET

> **NOTE** *All code examples shown in this book have Option Strict set to On using the Project Properties dialog box (Build tab). I strongly recommend that you always turn Option Strict on for all of your VB.NET projects. I will discuss the reasons for this in Chapter 8.*

Let's begin by looking at a direct port of the previous example from VB6 to VB.NET in solution LinkListNet2. Along the way, you will see how the syntax of VB.NET has changed. I think you'll see that while different, the code is not difficult to understand. But I also think you'll see additional confirmation that a major port from VB6 to VB.NET is not something to undertake lightly.

The first change you'll see with VB.NET is that the concept of interface has been separated from that of a class (implementation of an interface). With VB6, adding methods to an object automatically defines the interface of the object. With VB.NET, if you want to define an interface that can be implemented or shared, you must explicitly define it as an interface. The interface, called ILinkList,[2] is defined in the file LinkList.vb shown here:

```
' LinkList .Net example using aggregation
' Copyright © 2001 by Desaware Inc. All Rights Reserved

' We can't implement a class - only an interface.
' so here's the interface
Public Interface ILinkList
    WriteOnly Property Container() As Object

    Property NextItem() As ILinkList

    ReadOnly Property PreviousItem(ByVal Root As ILinkList) As ILinkList

    Sub Remove(ByRef Root As ILinkList)

    Sub Append(ByRef Root As ILinkList)
End Interface
```

---

2. Interfaces, by convention, always start with the letter I.

An interface is nice but we need an implementation for it (which can be used by the Customer object) as well. Thus, the LinkList object implements the ILinkList interface. The m_Next variable points to the ILinkList interface—not to the LinkList object. Why? Because we're going to want this variable to reference the Container object just as it did in the VB6 example. The Container object will implement the ILinkList interface—*not* the LinkList object:

```
Public Class LinkList
    Implements ILinkList

    ' This version is designed to be embedded, so it links to the _
      container object
    Private m_Next As ILinkList
    ' When adding to the list, it needs to know its container
    Private m_Container As Object
```

The syntax for implementing functions of an interface is different in VB.NET. Instead of a method name like ILinkList_Container, the method declaration explicitly says which method is being implemented. The method name used in the class can be completely different from the interface method name. It is even possible for one method to implement multiple interface methods. Instead of separate property Get and property Set/Let methods, the Get and Set blocks are part of the Property definition itself.

A property Get block returns the value of the property by assigning a value to the property name (as with VB6 or by using the Return statement.). The property Set block can access the value being set using the built-in Value variable. Since there is no Set statement for object assignment in VB.NET, there is only one way to set a property value. Don't let the fact that it's called a Set block confuse you—they basically took the functionality of both of the VB6 Set and the Let property methods, combined them, and put them into the Set block.

The property syntax has changed as well:

```
' Next is easy - just the next link.
' Note the syntax change. See text for discussion of the Implements
' statement as used here
Public Property NextItem() As ILinkList Implements ILinkList.NextItem
    Get
        NextItem = m_Next
    End Get
    Set(ByVal Value As ILinkList)
        m_Next = Value
    End Set
End Property
```

In VB6, a property is specified as read only or write only by the presence or absence of the corresponding Get or Set property methods. In VB.NET, the attribute WriteOnly or ReadOnly is used to control the property access. Only the necessary block is included in the property implementation:[3]

```
' Container is set during initialization
' Would need to be public if you decided to componentize the class
Friend WriteOnly Property Container() As Object Implements ILinkList.Container
    Set(ByVal Value As Object)
        m_Container = Value
    End Set
End Property
```

Aside from the syntax changes already mentioned, the code for the PreviousItem property and Remove methods are very similar to that in VB6:

```
' In a single linked list, Previous has to search forward from the root
Public ReadOnly Property PreviousItem(ByVal Root As ILinkList) As _
ILinkList Implements ILinkList.PreviousItem
    Get
        Dim currentitem As ILinkList
        ' Remember, all references are to the container object
        If (Root Is m_Container) Or (Root Is Nothing) Then
            Exit Property
        End If
        currentitem = Root
        Do
            If currentitem.NextItem Is m_Container Then
                PreviousItem = currentitem
                Exit Property
            Else
                currentitem = currentitem.NextItem
            End If
        Loop While Not currentitem Is Nothing
    End Get
End Property
```

---

3. Why do you need to specify ReadOnly or WriteOnly when the language should be able to figure this out based on whether you included Set or Get code? That's a good question. My best guess is that they could have figured it out from the code but the use of ReadOnly and WriteOnly fits better with the .NET architecture. The ReadOnly and WriteOnly keywords are actually attributes, which you'll learn about in great detail in Chapter 11.

```
' Remove has to search from root to find the previous node.
' Root must be by reference so it can be cleared if this
' is the last object, or reset if the first object
Public Sub Remove(ByRef Root As ILinkList) Implements ILinkList.Remove
    Dim previtem As ILinkList

    previtem = PreviousItem(Root)
    If previtem Is Nothing Then
        Root = m_Next
    Else
        previtem.NextItem = m_Next
    End If
End Sub
```

The Append method is very similar to the VB6 edition except for two things: assigning the Root parameter from the m_Container variable and assigning the NextItem property from the m_Container variable. In VB6, this is a simple assignment. Here, it is necessary to explicitly convert the m_Container object to an ILinkList type. Why is this?

At first glance, you might think that this is an example of the improved Strict Type Checking provided by VB.NET. And to some degree this is true. But in fact, there is more going on here than meets the eye. Hold this question for just a few more paragraphs and I promise you an answer that will hopefully lead to some fundamental insights as to the difference between VB6 and VB.NET:

```
' Append searches from Root to the end of the list.
Public Sub Append(ByRef Root As ILinkList) Implements ILinkList.Append
    Dim currentitem As ILinkList
    currentitem = Root
    If Root Is Nothing Then
        Root = CType(m_Container, ILinkList)
    Else
        While Not currentitem.NextItem Is Nothing
            currentitem = currentitem.NextItem
        End While
        currentitem.NextItem = CType(m_Container, ILinkList)
    End If
End Sub

End Class
```

The Customer object is in file Customer.vb and is shown in Listing 5-3. The Customer object implements the previously defined ILinkList interface and has a public CustomerName property as in the VB6 example. Other than the VB.NET syntax changes, this class is identical to the VB6 Customer object.

Listing 5-3. The Customer class is implemented in file Customer.vb.

```vb
' LinkList .Net example using aggregation
' Copyright © 2001 by Desaware Inc. All Rights Reserved
Public Class Customer
    ' This version Implements the LinkList - making
    ' its methods accessible via LinkList objects
    Implements ILinkList

    Public CustomerName As String

    ' The internal LinkList object provides the functionality
    Private m_MyLinkList As LinkList

    Public Sub New()
        MyBase.New()
        m_MyLinkList = New LinkList()
        m_MyLinkList.Container = Me
    End Sub

    ' Objects will terminate in VB.Net. See text for details.
    Protected Overrides Sub Finalize()
        system.diagnostics.Debug.WriteLine("Terminating customer " + CustomerName)
    End Sub

    ' Methods & properties just map to the LinkList members & properties
    Public Sub Append(ByRef Root As ILinkList) Implements ILinkList.Append
        m_MyLinkList.Append(Root)
    End Sub

    Public Property NextItem() As ILinkList Implements ILinkList.NextItem
        Set(ByVal Value As ILinkList)
            m_MyLinkList.NextItem = Value
        End Set
        Get
            NextItem = m_MyLinkList.NextItem
        End Get
    End Property

    Friend WriteOnly Property Container() As Object Implements ILinkList.Container
        Set(ByVal Value As Object)
            m_MyLinkList.Container = value
        End Set
    End Property
```

```
Public ReadOnly Property PreviousItem(ByVal Root As ILinkList) As ILinkList __
Implements ILinkList.previousitem
    Get
        PreviousItem = m_MyLinkList.PreviousItem(Root)
    End Get
End Property

Sub Remove(ByRef Root As ILinkList) Implements ILinkList.Remove
    m_MyLinkList.Remove(Root)
End Sub
```

```
End Class
```

Now let's look at the form code found in file TestForm.vb. I've excluded the code generated by the framework as it really isn't relevant to understanding the issue at hand. As with the VB6 example, a variable is defined to point to the first object in the list:

```
Public Class Form1

        Private m_List As ILinkList
```

The UpdateList subroutine loads the listbox with the list of current customers. There are a number of very important changes between the VB6 version and this one.

One change is small—listboxes don't work the way they used to. Instead of using an AddItem method, you must add the string to the Items collection of the listbox. Indeed, all of the Windows Forms controls[4] have syntactical and functional differences from their VB6 equivalents.

You can also see that this function has an explicit conversion of the m_List variable (which is of type ILinkList) to the currentcustomer object (which is of type Customer).

But the big change is that this function no longer has two different variables to access the object—one for the Customer interface and the other for the LinkList interface. The currentcustomer object can directly access the CustomerName property and the NextItem property as shown in Listing 5-4.[5]

---

4. Windows Forms controls are the .NET term for all controls in the .NET Framework. Think of them as the .NET equivalent of VB intrinsic controls or ActiveX controls.

5. You can, if you wish, use the Private attribute to hide the methods that implement the interface and allow access to the interface methods only through interface variables.

Listing 5-4. Update function in TestForm.vb.

```
' Updates the list box
' Note that there is no need for separate variables - the
' ILinkList interface is seamlessly added to the object
' Note also the change to the ListBox syntax
Private Sub UpdateList()
    lstCustomers.Items.Clear()
    Dim currentcustomer As Customer
    ' However, explicit type conversions are needed when promoting
    ' a reference to an interface to the object. Runtime errors will occur
    ' if the object type is not correct.
    currentcustomer = CType(m_List, Customer)
    Do While Not currentcustomer Is Nothing
        lstCustomers.Items.Add(currentcustomer.CustomerName)
        currentcustomer = CType(currentcustomer.NextItem, Customer)
    Loop
End Sub
```

So, let's consider both of these facts again:

- In VB6, a variable must match the interface being used to call methods on that interface. In VB.NET, an Object variable can access all methods of all of its interfaces directly.

- In VB6, when you assign a variable that references an interface on an object to that of another interface on an object, the assignment works directly. In VB.NET, you must explicitly convert the type from the implemented interface to that of the Container object or other implemented interface.

These are not minor language changes. They reflect a fundamental change in the underlying architecture that is essential to understand.

COM dictates the behavior of Visual Basic 6. Under COM, an interface pointer references an object. Each interface pointer exposes a set of methods. If you want to call a method on a different interface for an object, you must navigate to the other interface and call the method on that interface. Each interface corresponds to a Visual Basic type, thus you must assign an object to a variable of the correct type before you can call the methods for that type.

VB.NET is not based on COM so the old rules simply don't apply.

When you implement an interface in VB.NET, you are in effect inheriting an interface. That interface becomes part of the object—a subset of the object. If you assign an object reference to a variable with the type of the inherited interface, the assignment can be made directly. This is because VB.NET knows at compile time that the object implements the interface. For example, the following code is correct:

```
Dim il as ILinkList
Dim co as Customer
co = New Customer
il = co
```

The assignment works because VB.NET knows that the Customer object always implements the ILinkList interface.

But the reverse is not true. If you try to assign a Customer object from an ILinkList object reference, there is no way for VB.NET to know at compile time if the ILinkList object you assign is a Customer object. The ILinkList variable might point to a LinkList object or to some other arbitrary object that implements the ILinkList interface. The CLR will know at runtime what type of object is referenced by that variable so the assignment can be done at runtime—but since it is not guaranteed to work, the compiler will raise an error if you simply try an assignment such as this one directly:

```
Dim il as ILinkList
Dim co as Customer
il = New Customer
co = il
```

Instead, you must perform an explicit conversion using the generic CType conversion function as follows:

```
co = CType(il, Customer)
```

This tells the compiler that you think you actually know what you're doing in performing the conversion. The CLR will still raise a runtime error if 'il' does not reference a Customer object (the CLR will never let you assign an object reference to an incorrect Object type). You may wonder, if the CLR is going to perform a runtime check anyway, why require an explicit conversion? After all, VB6 is smart enough to do these conversions for you. This is actually a great new feature of VB.NET called Strict Type Checking. You can turn it off and have VB.NET perform these conversions for you without having to explicitly signal a conversion. However, this will be one of the many places in this book where I encourage you *not* to do so. Strict Type Checking is a wonderful new feature in VB.NET. It will improve your code. It will reduce bugs. And it will reduce the cost of bugs by helping you to find them more quickly. You should *turn on* Strict Type Checking as soon as you create any VB.NET project.[6]

Since the Customer object implements the ILinkList interface, all of the methods of that interface can be made directly available to the Customer object. The old

---

6. Because Microsoft blew it by leaving it off by default.

rules of COM are not applicable. Because the Customer object is a superset of the Object methods and properties and any implemented interfaces, it is able to expose all of its methods as well as those of the implemented interfaces.

The remaining functions in the form should be easy to follow. The code is again just like that of the VB6 example except for the syntax changes you've seen so far. There is also a new cmdGC Command button that performs a garbage collection. Try clicking on this button after removing an object from the list. You will see that it is deleted proving once again that VB.NET eliminates the circular reference problem:

```
Protected Sub cmdRemove_Click(ByVal sender As System.Object, _

ByVal e As System.EventArgs) Handles cmdRemove.Click
    Dim currentcustomer As Customer

    currentcustomer = CType(m_List, Customer)

    Do While Not currentcustomer Is Nothing
        If currentcustomer.CustomerName = CStr(lstCustomers().SelectedItem) Then
            currentcustomer.Remove(m_List)
            UpdateList()
            Exit Sub
        End If
        currentcustomer = CType(currentcustomer.NextItem, Customer)
    Loop
    UpdateList()

End Sub

Protected Sub cmdAdd_Click(ByVal sender As System.Object, _
ByVal e As System.EventArgs) Handles cmdAdd.Click
    Dim newEntry As New Customer()
    newEntry.CustomerName = txtCustomerName().Text
    newEntry.Append(m_List)
    UpdateList()
End Sub
```

```
' Click the GC button to force a garbage collection and see that
' abandoned objects are destroyed despite the circular reference.
Protected Sub cmdGC_Click(ByVal sender As System.Object, _
ByVal e As System.EventArgs) Handles cmdGC.Click
    gc.Collect()
    gc.WaitForPendingFinalizers()
End Sub

End Class
```

Let's take one last look at this example:

- VB.NET eliminates the circular reference problem present in the VB6 solution.

- By allowing direct access to all of the methods and properties of an object (including those on implemented interfaces), VB.NET dramatically simplifies coding when containment is used.

- The coding required in the Customer object to implement containment remains minimal.

In short, even without inheritance, VB.NET significantly improves the ease of code reuse through containment.

An Inheritance-Based Linked List Using VB.NET

In a sense, you have already seen inheritance. The Implements statement performs what is called interface inheritance—which exists in VB6 as well. Interface inheritance means that an object must implement all methods of an interface defined elsewhere (in an Interface definition in VB.NET or in a Class definition in VB6). With interface inheritance, an object can be referenced by a variable defined with the Interface type as well as one defined by the type of the object itself.

The LinkListNetInh project demonstrates the kind of inheritance everyone has been talking about for so long—true implementation inheritance.[7] With implementation inheritance, an object inherits the actual implementation of its base class. The object can override that implementation if you wish. Also, with implementation inheritance, an object can be referenced by a variable defined

---

7. You may have heard of something called visual inheritance as well—perhaps in some .NET marketing material. There is no such thing. What they call visual inheritance is just regular implementation inheritance applied to an object like a form or a control that has visual characteristics (for example, it can be displayed or printed, has a user interface, etc.).

with the base class type as well as one defined by the type of the object itself (the derived type).

In Listing 5-5, only the Customer object is changed as shown here in the Customer.vb file.

Listing 5-5. The LinkListNetInh Customer object.

```vb
' LinkList .Net example using inheritance
' Copyright © 2001 by Desaware Inc. All Rights Reserved
Public Class Customer
    Inherits LinkList

    Public CustomerName As String

    Public Sub New()
        MyBase.New()
        Me.Container = Me
    End Sub

    Protected Overrides Sub Finalize()
        system.diagnostics.Debug.WriteLine("Terminating customer " + CustomerName)
    End Sub
    ' There is no need to create a contained "LinkList" object -
    ' The customer object is a LinkList object as well.
    ' There is no need to implement the ILinkList interface, it's
    ' methods and properties are already implemented by the base class.

End Class
```

The private LinkList object is gone. So are all of the implemented functions. When the Customer object inherits the LinkList object, it becomes a LinkList object. We could, in fact, go back and modify the LinkList object so that it no longer used a Container variable—the LinkList object and the Customer object are now one and the same.

Pretty cool, isn't it?

Well, actually, it isn't.

Yes, this code works. Yes, it saves you a few lines of code, handling the aggregated object. But it doesn't change the client at all—and it doesn't make the Customer object any easier to use.

What really makes this code terrible is not so much technical as it is architectural. And it can be phrased thus:

> A customer is many things. A customer may be a person. A customer may be a corporation. A customer may be a government.
>
> But a customer is never a linked list.

Inheritance should only be used when you have a clear relationship in which the **inheriting object** *is an* **Inherited object**.

If this relationship does not exist, you should use interface inheritance and containment. The few extra lines of code to make this work are a small price to pay for the clarity of design (not to mention reduced support costs over the long term).

Curiously enough, this type of relationship is not very common in applications. It is common when building application frameworks that developers will use—thus (as you will soon see), the .NET framework itself uses inheritance extensively. You will be inheriting objects from the framework in every application and component you write. But you will rarely create objects intended to be inherited in turn.

The good news is that the elimination of the circular reference problem combined with the ease by which you can access methods of inherited interfaces makes containment an easy and effective way to reuse code.

A Dual Linked List Example

Here's a practical reason why inheritance is the wrong choice in this example. Linked lists are often used to place objects in order. What if you want to keep objects sorted two different ways at once? You might want the object to be present in two linked lists simultaneously. You can't inherit the same interface twice. You could define a new interface designed to support dual linked lists but you'll usually be better off with the approach shown in the LinkListNetDual project.

Listing 5-6 shows the revised LinkList class. It is similar to the previous one except that the container is a Public property. The architecture used here is also different from the previous example in that it follows the structure shown in Figure 5-1—the links reference the LinkList object itself rather than the Container object. The Container property can be used to navigate out to the actual object.

Listing 5-6. LinkList object revised to support dual use by a single object.

```
' LinkList .Net example showing dual lists
' Copyright ©2001 by Desaware Inc.  All Rights Reserved
Public Interface ILinkList

    ' This version is designed to link to the internal LinkList
    ' objects, using the public Container property to find the container
    Property NextItem() As ilinklist

    ' In this version all nodes are LinkList objects, so
    ' we need a public Container property to access the
    ' actual object
    Property Container() As Object

    ReadOnly Property PreviousItem(ByVal Root As ILinkList) As ILinkList

    Sub Remove(ByRef Root As ILinkList)

    Sub Append(ByRef Root As ILinkList)
End Interface

Public Class LinkList
    Implements ILinkList

    ' This version is designed to link to the internal LinkList
    ' objects, using the public Container property to find the container
    Private m_Next As ILinkList

    ' We need to be able to navigate to the container
    Private m_Container As Object

    Friend Property Container() As Object Implements ILinkList.Container
        Get
            Container = m_Container
        End Get
        Set(ByVal Value As Object)
            m_Container = Value
        End Set
    End Property
```

```
' Next is easy - just the next link.
Public Property NextItem() As ILinkList Implements ILinkList.NextItem
    Get
        NextItem = m_Next
    End Get
    Set(ByVal Value As ILinkList)
        m_Next = Value
    End Set
End Property


' In a single linked list, Previous has to search forward from the root
Public ReadOnly Property PreviousItem(ByVal Root As ILinkList) As ILinkList _
Implements ILinkList.PreviousItem
    Get
        Dim currentitem As ILinkList
        If (Root Is Me) Or (Root Is Nothing) Then
            Exit Property
        End If
        currentitem = Root
        Do
            If currentitem.NextItem Is Me Then
                PreviousItem = currentitem
                Exit Property
            Else
                currentitem = currentitem.NextItem
            End If
        Loop While Not currentitem Is Nothing
    End Get
End Property


' Remove has to search from root to find the previous node.
' Root must be by reference so it can be cleared if this
' is the last object, or reset if the first object
Public Sub Remove(ByRef Root As ILinkList) Implements ILinkList.Remove
    Dim previtem As ILinkList

    previtem = PreviousItem(Root)
    If previtem Is Nothing Then
        Root = m_Next
    Else
        previtem.NextItem = m_Next
    End If
End Sub
```

```
' Append searches from Root to the end of the list.
Public Sub Append(ByRef Root As ILinkList) Implements ILinkList.Append
    Dim currentitem As ILinkList
    currentitem = Root
    If Root Is Nothing Then
        Root = Me
    Else
        While Not currentitem.NextItem Is Nothing
            currentitem = currentitem.NextItem
        End While
        currentitem.NextItem = Me
    End If
End Sub
End Class
```

The Customer object shown in Listing 5-7 is considerably revised since it now supports linking the object into two lists at once. The object no longer inherits the ILinkList interface—an approach that limits you to a single linked list. Instead, it exposes its own methods for each list—for example, NextItem1 and NextItem2.

This approach requires more code to deal with the fact that the LinkList object only knows how to link objects that implement the ILinkList interface (like itself). The methods provided by the Customer object are references to other Customer objects.

Listing 5-7. The Customer object revised for use with multiple linked lists.

```
' LinkList .Net example showing dual lists
' Copyright ©2001 by Desaware Inc.  All Rights Reserved
Public Class Customer
    Public CustomerName As String

    ' This version shows how a node can be in two lists at once.
    ' Note that the object does NOT Implement the LinkList interface
    ' Even though the links are done internally between LinkList objects,
    ' the outside world sees only Customer objects - thus all parameters
    ' and return values on link methods are Customer and not LinkList
    Private m_MyLinkList1 As ILinkList
    Private m_MyLinkList2 As ILinkList

    Public Sub New()
        MyBase.New()
        m_MyLinkList1 = New LinkList()
        m_MyLinkList1.Container = Me
        m_MyLinkList2 = New LinkList()
        m_MyLinkList2.Container = Me
    End Sub
```

```vbnet
Protected Overrides Sub Finalize()
    system.diagnostics.Debug.WriteLine("Terminating customer " + CustomerName)
End Sub


' Because we link into the contained object, we need
' a way to get access to the contained object in other nodes
Friend ReadOnly Property LinkList1() As ILinkList
    Get
        LinkList1 = m_MyLinkList1
    End Get
End Property


Friend ReadOnly Property LinkList2() As ILinkList
    Get
        LinkList2 = m_MyLinkList2
    End Get
End Property



' Functions require a bit more work to detect
' boundary conditions such as an empty list.
Public Sub Append1(ByRef Root As Customer)
    If root Is Nothing Then
        root = Me
    Else
        ' This line would fail if Root is Nothing
        m_MyLinkList1.Append(Root.m_MyLinkList1)
    End If
End Sub


Public Sub Append2(ByRef Root As Customer)
    If root Is Nothing Then
        root = Me
    Else
        m_MyLinkList2.Append(Root.m_MyLinkList2)
    End If
End Sub
```

```vbnet
' Again note how the implementation uses the ILinkList interface,
' but people using the Customer object only see references to
' Customer objects
Public ReadOnly Property NextItem1() As Customer
    Get
        Dim nextref As ILinkList
        nextref = m_MyLinkList1.NextItem
        ' We have to check the Nothing condition explicitly,
        ' otherwise the call to nextref.Container will fail.
        If nextref Is Nothing Then
            nextitem1 = Nothing
        Else
          ' nextref.container is of type Object. We need to convert explicitly
            nextitem1 = CType(nextref.container, Customer)
        End If

    End Get
End Property


Public ReadOnly Property NextItem2() As Customer
    Get
        Dim nextref As ILinkList
        nextref = m_MyLinkList2.NextItem
        If nextref Is Nothing Then
            nextitem2 = Nothing
        Else
            nextitem2 = CType(nextref.container, Customer)
        End If
    End Get
End Property



Public ReadOnly Property PreviousItem1(ByVal Root As Customer) As Customer
    Get
        PreviousItem1 = CType(m_MyLinkList1.PreviousItem(Root.LinkList1), _
        Customer)
    End Get
End Property

Public ReadOnly Property PreviousItem2(ByVal Root As Customer) As Customer
    Get
        PreviousItem2 = CType(m_MyLinkList2.PreviousItem(Root.LinkList1), _
        Customer)
    End Get
End Property
```

```
    Sub Remove1(ByRef Root As Customer)
        Dim llroot As ILinkList
        llroot = Root.LinkList1
        ' Why not just use m_MyLinkList.Remove Root.LinkList1?
        ' Because Root.LinkList1 will be placed in a temporary variable
        ' which is then called by reference. Changes to that temporary
       ' variable will not be magically reflected back to the Root.LinkList1 reference
        ' So we need to use our own temporary variable so that we can
        ' detect changes to that variable on this ByRef call.
        m_MyLinkList1.Remove(llroot)
        If llroot Is Nothing Then
            Root = Nothing
        Else
            Root = CType(llroot.Container, Customer)
        End If
    End Sub

    Sub Remove2(ByRef Root As Customer)
        Dim llroot As ILinkList
        llroot = Root.LinkList2
        m_MyLinkList2.Remove(llroot)
        If llroot Is Nothing Then
            Root = Nothing
        Else
            Root = CType(llroot.Container, Customer)
        End If
    End Sub

End Class
```

Listing 5-8 shows the code for the revised TestForm.vb form. This form adds a second listbox that contains only those objects whose customer name starts with letters before N. Note that the two variables that reference the lists, m_List and m_ListAtoM, are now both Customer types. The form is, in fact, completely oblivious to the ILinkList interface, which can't be used to access the Customer object anyway now that it is no longer inherited. The code for the form is otherwise similar to what you've seen before except that it has been extended to work with two lists.

Listing 5-8. The TestForm.vb form supports two linked lists.

```vb
' LinkList .Net example showing dual lists
' Copyright ©2001 by Desaware Inc.  All Rights Reserved

Public Class Form1
    Inherits System.Windows.Forms.Form

' Note the list roots are now Customers, not LinkList objects
    Private m_List As Customer
    Private m_ListAtoM As Customer


    ' Remove from both lists
    Protected Sub cmdRemove_Click(ByVal sender As System.Object, _
    ByVal e As System.EventArgs) Handles cmdRemove.Click
        Dim currentcustomer As Customer

        currentcustomer = m_List
        Do While Not currentcustomer Is Nothing
            If currentcustomer.CustomerName = CStr(lstCustomers().SelectedItem) Then
                currentcustomer.Remove1(m_List)
                Exit Do
            End If
            currentcustomer = currentcustomer.NextItem1
        Loop

        currentcustomer = m_ListAtoM
        Do While Not currentcustomer Is Nothing
            If currentcustomer.CustomerName = CStr(lstCustomers().SelectedItem) Then
                currentcustomer.Remove2(m_ListAtoM)
                Exit Do
            End If
            currentcustomer = currentcustomer.NextItem2
        Loop

        UpdateList()

    End Sub
```

```vbnet
' In this simple example, every customer with a name >"M is excluded
' from the second list
' Not also how there is no need to use separate Customer
' and LinkList variables - we're always using the Customer interface
' only.
Protected Sub cmdAdd_Click(ByVal sender As System.Object, _
ByVal e As System.EventArgs) Handles cmdAdd.Click
    Dim newEntry As New Customer()
    newEntry.CustomerName = txtCustomerName().Text
    newEntry.Append1(m_List)
    If UCase(strings.Left(newEntry.CustomerName, 1)) <= "M" Then
        newEntry.Append2(m_ListAtoM)
    End If

    UpdateList()
End Sub

' Display the contents of both linked lists.
Private Sub UpdateList()
    lstCustomers().Items.Clear()
    lstAtoM().Items.Clear()

    Dim currentcustomer As Customer
    currentcustomer = m_List
    Do While Not currentcustomer Is Nothing
        lstCustomers().Items.Add(currentcustomer.CustomerName)
        currentcustomer = currentcustomer.NextItem1
    Loop

    currentcustomer = m_ListAtoM
    Do While Not currentcustomer Is Nothing
        lstAtoM().Items.Add(currentcustomer.CustomerName)
        currentcustomer = currentcustomer.NextItem2
    Loop

End Sub

Protected Sub cmdGC_Click(ByVal sender As System.Object, _
ByVal e As System.EventArgs) Handles cmdGC.Click
    gc.Collect()
    gc.WaitForPendingFinalizers()
End Sub


End Class
```

The LinkListVB6-2 sample project shows how you can implement a dual link list using VB6 (except that it still suffers from the circular memory reference problem).

Dealing with Naming Conflicts

You've just learned that VB.NET exposes all of the methods and properties of all inherited objects and interfaces to users of the top-level object. What happens if two interfaces have methods of the same name?

You've actually seen the answer already, though not in a form that directly addressed this problem. The secret is in the use of the Implements statement in method declarations. Listing 5-9 shows the Class1.vb file from the TwoInterfaces project. The example defines two interfaces, both of which contain a method named CommonFunction.

Listing 5-9. Illustration of the implementation of interfaces with duplicate names.

```
' Example of resolving interface name conflicts
' Copyright ©2001 by Desaware Inc. All Rights Reserved

Interface MyFirstInterface
    Sub UniqueFunction()
    Sub CommonFunction()
End Interface

Interface MySecondInterface
    Sub SecondUniqueFunction()
    Sub CommonFunction()
End Interface

Public Class Class1
    Implements MyFirstInterface
    Implements MySecondInterface

    Sub UniqueFunction() Implements MyFirstInterface.UniqueFunction

    End Sub

    Sub SecondUniqueFunction() Implements MySecondInterface.SecondUniqueFunction

    End Sub
```

```
' These could be made private to avoid confusion
Sub CommonFunction() Implements MyFirstInterface.CommonFunction
    Console.WriteLine("Common Function on first interface")
End Sub

Sub CommonFunctionSecondInterface() Implements MySecondInterface.CommonFunction
    Console.WriteLine("Common function on second interface")
End Sub
```

```
End Class
```

The solution, as you see next, requires that you rename one of the methods. The Implements syntax allows you to use different names within a class for implemented functions, thus allowing (actually requiring) you to eliminate duplicate names:

```
' Example of resolving interface name conflicts
' Copyright ©2001 by Desaware Inc. All Rights Reserved
Module Module1

    Public Sub Main()
        Dim c As New class1()
        Dim i1 As MySecondInterface
        c.CommonFunction()
        i1 = c
        i1.CommonFunction()
        Console.ReadLine()
    End Sub

End Module
```

That solves the implementation side but what about the calling side?

The public CommonFunction method (called with the c.CommonFunction call) will display Common Function on first interface. But when you call CommonFunction through the il variable (il.CommonFunction) you'll see Common function on second interface, indicating that the CommonFunctionSecondInterface method was called.

This situation should be avoided due to the possibility of confusion. The easiest way to solve the problem is to hide the accessibility of the method on the class by making it Private. You'll still be able to access the method through an Interface variable because the Interface method is Public.

Of course, with this solution, you'll have to assign the object to a variable of the desired interface in order to call the Interface method.

Inheritance in .NET

The .NET Framework make extensive use of inheritance. The Common Language Runtime supports single inheritance only. If this book were written for C++ programmers, I would go into an in-depth discussion at this point regarding the relative benefits of single versus multiple inheritance. Since I am addressing Visual Basic programmers, there's really not much point in describing multiple inheritance. However, lest you feel that you're missing something, I will say this: as skeptical as I am over the use of inheritance, I assure you that I am ten times more skeptical of multiple inheritance. It adds all sorts of complexities with few benefits. The only framework I've seen that uses it effectively is ATL and that approach is one of the reasons why ATL is so hard to learn. I've only used it once in my own software development efforts, and that time was a mistake.[8]

Everything Is an Object

Any discussion of inheritance with .NET must begin with the humble object.[9] Earlier, you read that the CLR eliminates memory leaks by keeping track of objects and freeing them when they are no longer referenced by a root-level variable. But what of data that isn't an object? How can the CLR manage that data and make sure it is released properly?

This is a trick question.

Under the CLR, every piece of data is an object. Every structure is an object. Even the humble integer is an object. Consider the Module1.vb module from the IntegerObject project shown in Listing 5-10.

Listing 5-10. The IntegerObject console application.

```
' Demonstration that everything is an object.
' Copyright ©2001 by Desaware Inc. All Rights Reserved
Module Module1

    Sub Main()
        console.WritcLine("This is a test")
```

---

8. For those who are wondering, C# does not support multiple inheritance, either.

9. Wait! Haven't we been talking about inheritance throughout this entire chapter? Yes, but that was inheritance as a concept and language feature. Now we'll be focusing on the way inheritance is used in the .NET Framework.

```
    Dim i As Integer = 15
    Console.WriteLine(i.ToString())
    console.WriteLine("Hash is: " + i.GetHashCode().ToString())
    Console.WriteLine("Type is: " + i.GetType().ToString)
    console.WriteLine("Type full name is: " + i.GetType().FullName())
    console.WriteLine("Type assembly qualified name is: " + _
    i.GetType().AssemblyQualifiedName)
  console.WriteLine("Type assembly qualified name is: " + i.GetType().Namespace)

    console.Write("Press Enter to continue")
    console.ReadLine()


  End Sub

End Module
```

Yes, this is an actual console application now supported very nicely by VB.NET. It's a great way to test and explain concepts without having to deal with all the overhead of a form.

The interesting thing about this code is the integer variable 'i'. Even though it is an integer, it is possible to invoke methods on the variable. Who ever heard of an integer with methods?

This happens because the Integer type, like every Variable type, inherits from object. An object has a number of methods. The ToString method returns a string representation of the data in the variable. The GetHashCode method retrieves a hash value for the object, which is helpful for searches when dealing with collections of objects. The Equals method (not shown here) is used to perform value comparisons between objects (allowing you to compare objects based on some internal value as opposed to determining whether two object's variables refer to the same object). The GetType method allows you to retrieve type information for an object—the metadata that describes everything about the object: it's methods, properties, and their parameters.

Here is the resulting output from the IntegerObject program:[10]

```
This is a test
15
Hash is: 15
Type is: Int32
Type full name is: System.Int32
Type assembly qualified name is: System.Int32, mscorlib, Version=1.0....., Cul
ture=neutral, PublicKeyToken=b77a5c561934e089Type assembly qualified name is:
System
Press Enter to continue
```

In the case of the Integer property, the ToString method is the most useful. The other properties are most often used in more complex objects in which the object overrides the built-in functionality to provide a solution that is optimized for its purposes. You'll read more about overriding functions shortly.

Making every data type an object provides the consistency needed for the CLR to manage data in an application. But it's only fair to ask what the catch is. Doesn't adding methods to something as simple as an integer variable have a huge performance impact? Integers are, after all, usually simple variables allocated on a stack. Objects have all sorts of overhead.

The good news is that the CLR has a pretty good way to solve this problem. It turns out that there are two types of objects under .NET. Reference objects are the kind you are familiar with—implemented with classes, stored on the heap, and accessed using references. Value objects are a kind of "lightweight" object that can be stored on the stack. As long as you use Value objects as simple variables (for example, mathematical operations on integer variables), the compiler creates the exact same code you would see with current versions of Visual Basic. Numbers are loaded, stored, and operated on directly. When you try to use a Value object as a Reference object, the CLR performs an operation called boxing in which it wraps the value into an object, performs the requested operation, and then unboxes it. You can create Value objects in Visual Basic using the Structure keyword as you'll read in Chapter 6.

A Look at Forms

Up until now, we've ignored the code added to forms by the form designer. Listing 5-11 shows a part of the LinkListNet2 sample applications. The System.Windows.Forms

---

10. The version and Public key token in the assembly-qualified name will almost certainly differ from what you see depending on whether you are using a beta, a release candidate, an intermediate build, or the final release of the .NET runtime.

namespace has implementations for a variety of Windows-based components (for now, think of a namespace as a way to logically group classes). The new form inherits from the System.Windows.Forms.Form object.

In fact, the complete hierarchy for the Form object is as follows:

Object

MarshalByRefObject

Component

Control

ScrollableControl

ContainerControl

Form

Each Object type inherits the functionality of the previous type. I won't go into details of these types here but it should be obvious that quite a bit of functionality is available to your form before you write a single line of code. This also represents a change from VB6 where a form's functionality is just magically there. The same effect is achieved with VB.NET but you can tell exactly where each new piece of functionality comes from. And you can (if you wish) choose to create objects that inherit from any object along the hierarchy.

As you look at Listing 5-11, keep in mind that every method being called is inherited from one of the base classes. Again, the idea here is not to analyze this code in depth but to illustrate how .NET is based on inheritance.

Listing 5-11. The TestForm.vb file from the LinkListNet2 sample project.

```
' LinkList .Net example using aggregation
' Copyright © 2001 by Desaware Inc. All Rights Reserved

Public Class Form1
    Inherits System.Windows.Forms.Form

#Region " Windows Form Designer generated code "

    Public Sub New()
        MyBase.New()

        'This call is required by the Windows Form Designer.
        InitializeComponent()

        'Add any initialization after the InitializeComponent() call
    End Sub
```

```vb
'Form overrides dispose to clean up the component list.
Public Overloads Overrides Sub Dispose()
    MyBase.Dispose()
    If Not (components Is Nothing) Then
        components.Dispose()
    End If
End Sub
Private WithEvents cmdAdd As System.Windows.Forms.Button
Private WithEvents lstCustomers As System.Windows.Forms.ListBox
Private WithEvents cmdGC As System.Windows.Forms.Button
Private WithEvents txtCustomerName As System.Windows.Forms.TextBox
Private WithEvents cmdRemove As System.Windows.Forms.Button
Private WithEvents label1 As System.Windows.Forms.Label


'Required by the Windows Form Designer
Private components As System.ComponentModel.Container

'NOTE: The following procedure is required by the Windows Form Designer
'It can be modified using the Windows Form Designer.
'Do not modify it using the code editor.
<System.Diagnostics.DebuggerStepThrough()> Private Sub InitializeComponent()
    Me.txtCustomerName = New System.Windows.Forms.TextBox()
    Me.cmdGC = New System.Windows.Forms.Button()
    Me.label1 = New System.Windows.Forms.Label()
    Me.cmdAdd = New System.Windows.Forms.Button()
    Me.cmdRemove = New System.Windows.Forms.Button()
    Me.lstCustomers = New System.Windows.Forms.ListBox()
    Me.SuspendLayout()
    '
    'txtCustomerName
    '
    Me.txtCustomerName.Location = New System.Drawing.Point(88, 24)
    Me.txtCustomerName.Name = "txtCustomerName"
    Me.txtCustomerName.Size = New System.Drawing.Size(136, 20)
    Me.txtCustomerName.TabIndex = 4
    Me.txtCustomerName.Text = ""
    '
    'cmdGC
    '
    Me.cmdGC.Location = New System.Drawing.Point(200, 152)
    Me.cmdGC.Name = "cmdGC"
    Me.cmdGC.Size = New System.Drawing.Size(64, 32)
    Me.cmdGC.TabIndex = 2
    Me.cmdGC.Text = "GC"
    '
```

```
'label1
'
Me.label1.Location = New System.Drawing.Point(16, 24)
Me.label1.Name = "label1"
Me.label1.Size = New System.Drawing.Size(64, 16)
Me.label1.TabIndex = 5
Me.label1.Text = "Customer:"
Me.label1.TextAlign = System.Drawing.ContentAlignment.MiddleRight
'
'cmdAdd
'
Me.cmdAdd.Location = New System.Drawing.Point(200, 72)
Me.cmdAdd.Name = "cmdAdd"
Me.cmdAdd.Size = New System.Drawing.Size(64, 32)
Me.cmdAdd.TabIndex = 0
Me.cmdAdd.Text = "Add"
'
'cmdRemove
'
Me.cmdRemove.Location = New System.Drawing.Point(200, 112)
Me.cmdRemove.Name = "cmdRemove"
Me.cmdRemove.Size = New System.Drawing.Size(64, 32)
Me.cmdRemove.TabIndex = 1
Me.cmdRemove.Text = "Remove"
'
'lstCustomers
'
Me.lstCustomers.Location = New System.Drawing.Point(24, 72)
Me.lstCustomers.Name = "lstCustomers"
Me.lstCustomers.Size = New System.Drawing.Size(160, 108)
Me.lstCustomers.TabIndex = 3
'
'Form1
'
Me.AutoScaleBaseSize = New System.Drawing.Size(5, 13)
Me.ClientSize = New System.Drawing.Size(292, 216)
Me.Controls.AddRange(New System.Windows.Forms.Control() _
{Me.label1, Me.txtCustomerName, Me.lstCustomers, Me.cmdGC, _
Me.cmdRemove, Me.cmdAdd})
Me.Name = "Form1"
Me.Text = "Link List Test 2"
Me.ResumeLayout(False)

End Sub
```

A Closer Look at Inheritance in VB.NET

It's clear that you will be using inheritance a great deal, at least when it comes to inheriting from objects provided by the .NET Framework. It's time to take a closer look at the language features that support object inheritance.

The Customer1 sample project shown next illustrates a classic inheritance example. In this scenario, a business has several types of customers. All of them derive from a base Customer class. This class has the MustInherit attribute, which indicates that you can't actually create an object of type Customer. You can only create objects that inherit from Customer. It is also possible to define a class as NotInheritable—in which case the class is sealed and no further classes may inherit from it:

```
' Customers sample application
' Copyright ©2001 by Desaware Inc. All Rights Reserved
Public MustInherit Class Customer
    Public Name As String
    Public MustOverride Function DefaultNet() As Integer
    Public Overridable Function DisplayTerms() As String
        DisplayName()
        Console.WriteLine("... is net " + CStr(DefaultNet()))
    End Function
    Sub DisplayName()
        Console.WriteLine("Customer is " + Name)
    End Sub

End Class
```

Methods and properties in a class can be marked as Overridable or MustOverride.

If a method is marked as Overridable, the inheriting object can, if it chooses, override the function—providing its own implementation. If a method is not marked as Overridable, an attempt by the inheriting object to create a method with the same name will result in a compile-time error. A method marked as MustOverride indicates that the inheriting class must implement the method. Since it will always be implemented in the inheriting class, there is naturally no need to implement it in the base class.

A property or method not marked is, by default, not overridable. If you inherit from a class, any methods marked as Overridable will also be overridable by any classes that derive from your new class. You can change an Overridable method to no longer be overridable by further derived classes by overriding it in your class and adding the NotOverridable keyword.

In Chapter 10, you'll also learn how to use the Overloads keyword to declare methods that have the same name as a method in a base class but different parameters. I'll leave that out for now to help keep things simple.

Let's take a look at three classes that derive from the Customer class. The Commercial class overrides the DefaultNet function to set the default payment terms for the commercial customer. All of the other methods and properties of this class inherit from the base class:

```
Public Class Commerical
    Inherits Customer
    Public Overrides Function DefaultNet() As Integer
        Return (30)
    End Function
End Class
```

The Individual class also overrides the DisplayTerms string so instead of showing payment terms, it just prints a message that the user must pay immediately:

```
Public Class Individual
    Inherits Customer
    Public Overrides Function DefaultNet() As Integer
        Return (0)
    End Function
    Public Overrides Function DisplayTerms() As String
        DisplayName()
        Console.WriteLine("... must pay immediately")
    End Function
End Class
```

The Government class, in addition to overriding the DisplayTerms method, also defines a new method called BranchInfo that specifies the branch of government for this government entity. In other words, the object extends the functionality of the base class by adding new functionality:

```
Public Class Government
    Inherits Customer
    Public Overrides Function DefaultNet() As Integer
        Return (120)
    End Function
    Public Overrides Function DisplayTerms() As String
        DisplayName()
        Console.WriteLine("... will pay someday we hope")
    End Function
```

```
        Sub BranchInfo()
            Console.WriteLine("Legislative")
        End Sub
    End Class
End Namespace
```

The Module1.vb module shown in Listing 5-12 contains a simple console application that demonstrates the use of these classes.

Listing 5-12. Module1.vb from the Customer1 sample project.

```
' Customers sample application
' Copyright ©2001 by Desaware Inc. All Rights Reserved
Module Module1

    Sub Main()
        Dim store As New Commerical()
        store.Name = "Worst buys"
        store.DisplayName()
        store.DisplayTerms()
        console.Write("Press enter to continue:")
        console.ReadLine()
        Dim Person As New Individual()
        Person.Name = "Jim Smith"
        Person.DisplayName()
        Person.DisplayTerms()
        console.Write("Press enter to continue:")
        console.ReadLine()
        Dim USA As New Government()
        USA.Name = "U.S.A."
        USA.DisplayName()
        USA.DisplayTerms()
        USA.BranchInfo()
        console.Write("Press enter to continue:")
        console.ReadLine()
        Dim BascObject As Customer
        BaseObject = USA
        BaseObject.DisplayName()
        BaseObject.DisplayTerms()
        ' BaseObject.BranchInfo()
        console.ReadLine()

    End Sub


End Module
```

The results are as follows:

```
Customer is Worst buys
Customer is Worst buys
... is net 30
Press enter to continue:
Customer is Jim Smith
Customer is Jim Smith
... must pay immediately
Press enter to continue:
Customer is U.S.A.
Customer is U.S.A.
... will pay someday we hope
Legislative
Press enter to continue:
Customer is U.S.A.
Customer is U.S.A.
... will pay someday we hope
Press enter to continue:
```

Some of the results are obvious. If you call a method on an object that over-rides that of the base class, you get the new method—not that of the base class.

But the final example—in which we create a variable of type Customer, assign it from one of the derived objects, and use it directly—is interesting. The first thing you might notice is that it confirms something I wrote earlier—you do not need to perform an explicit type conversion when converting a derived object to a base object (or base interface). The compiler knows that the object supports the base object or interface and performs an implicit conversion.

The next interesting point is in the DisplayTerms function. We're using a reference to the base object Customer. That base object has its own implementation of DisplayTerms yet when we call DisplayTerms using that base object, we none-theless obtain the method of the Government object. How is this possible?

The Common Language Runtime knows what type of object you are dealing with even though you are accessing it through the base object type. It can determine at runtime that you have overridden the method and can thus call the correct method. This is called polymorphism and is one of the key features of any true object-oriented language. You can change this behavior as well using the Shadows keyword instead of the Overrides keyword. The Shadows keyword indicates that even though a method in the derived class has the same name, it is nevertheless a completely different function and calls through the base object type should not be redirected to the new method.

In this example, it is not possible to call the BranchInfo method using the BaseObject variable. While a derived object can use the methods and properties of a base object, the base object cannot use methods and properties that are added by a derived object.

Chapter 10 goes into more detail on the various attributes and keywords that effect inheritance in .NET.

Solving the Fragile Base Class Problem

Now I'm going to show you one of the coolest features of the CLR and how it solves a problem that, although uncommon, is very serious when it does occur.

The ClassLibrary2 sample project in Listing 5-13 contains a definition and implementation for the same Customer class we used in the previous example. It is, however, defined in a unique namespace because we're going to share this object.

Listing 5-13. Customer class from the ClassLibrary2 project.

```
' ClassLibrary2 example (chapter 5)
' Copyright ©2001 by Desaware Inc. All Rights Reserved
Namespace MigratingBook.Chapter5.ClassLibrary2
    Public MustInherit Class Customer
        Public Name As String
        Public MustOverride Function DefaultNet() As Integer
        Public Overridable Function DisplayTerms() As String
            DisplayName()
            Console.WriteLine("... is net " + CStr(DefaultNet()))
        End Function
        Sub DisplayName()
            Console.WriteLine("Customer is " + Name)
        End Sub
    End Class
End Namespace
```

This project is a class library. When you compile it, you obtain a DLL that can be referenced by other assemblies. This is roughly the same as creating an ActiveX DLL that can be shared by applications except that it lacks many of the advanced features of components you'll learn about later. It does provide a simple and effective way to share code.

The Customer2 sample project is identical to the Customer1 sample project except that it references the Customer class defined in the ClassLibrary instead of containing the class definition internally.

Consider this: the Government object has its own implementation of the BranchInfo. What if, one day, the developer of the Customer object adds his or her own overridable BranchInfo function—without realizing that some derived object may have a method by that name?

The principals of polymorphism suggest that if you call BranchInfo from code in the base class, it will call the function in the derived class. This is, however, fatal because there is no way that the designer of the base class can possibly anticipate what the derived method would do. We can be certain that it will not perform the task that the base class implementation was designed to do.

This problem is called the "fragile base class" problem and can be quite serious. Both C++ and Java suffer from this to one degree or another.

The ClassLibrary3 and Customer3 projects illustrate how this problem is handled under .NET. You'll need to walk through a process to see how the problem occurs and how it is resolved. The sample code for this project shows a "snapshot" during that process.

Begin by modifying the Class1.vb module in the ClassLibrary3 project shown in Listing 5-14.

Listing 5-14. The Customer object from the ClassLibrary3 project.

```
' ClassLibrary3 example (chapter 5)
' Copyright ©2001 by Desaware Inc. All Rights Reserved
Namespace MigratingBook.Chapter5.ClassLibrary3
    Public MustInherit Class Customer
        Public Name As String
        Public MustOverride Function DefaultNet() As Integer
        Public Overridable Function DisplayTerms() As String
            DisplayName()
            Console.WriteLine("... is net " + CStr(DefaultNet()))
            'Console.Write(" Branch is: ")
            'BranchInfo()
        End Function
        Sub DisplayName()
            Console.WriteLine("Customer is " + Name)
        End Sub
        'Public Overridable Sub BranchInfo()
        '    Console.WriteLine("New Branchinfo Function")
        'End Sub
    End Class
End Namespace
```

This initial state corresponds to the previous example. Compile this class library and reference it from the Customer3 project (which is identical to the Customer 2 project you saw earlier). Now, compile the Customer3 project and verify that the executable displays the same results you saw earlier.

Next, uncomment the lines in the previously shown Customer object (Listing 5-14). Compile the DLL and copy it into the same directory as the Customer3 executable you just created.

The BranchInfo method is called from two places: within the base class and in the derived object. Polymorphism says that all calls on the method (even when referenced from the base class) should go to the derived class. However, the actual results are shown here:

```
Customer is Worst buys
Customer is Worst buys
... is net 30
 Branch is: New Branchinfo Function
Press enter to continue:
Customer is Jim Smith
Customer is Jim Smith
... must pay immediately
Press enter to continue:
Customer is U.S.A.
Customer is U.S.A.
... will pay someday we hope
Legislative
Press enter to continue:
```

The sample code provided is a snapshot of the project in this state.

Even in the final object, calls to the BranchInfo function that take place within the base class go to the base class implementation! However, calls to the BranchInfo function that are made to or by the derived function call the derived implementation.

In other words, if you add a method or property to a class or component that is inherited by some other object that has a method or property of the same name and then you compile that component and redistribute it, both the component and the derived executable will continue to work correctly.

Try opening the Customer3 project. You will find that you now have an error in the code! VB.NET detects that you have a method that matches the name of an Inherited method but does not have the Overrides attribute. You can now decide whether to override the base class method (something you should do with caution only after you understand what you are overriding) or use the Shadows[11] keyword to hide the base class implementation from the derived class or change the name of your method.

---

11. The Shadows keyword was not implemented in Beta 1.

Method Visibility

This leaves us with one last subject related to inheritance: visibility and scoping rules. Most of the methods and properties in the samples you've seen have had Public scope (as indicated by the Public attribute for the class members). When a Public member is inherited, it becomes a fully visible member of the derived function.

You can also declare members as Private, Friend, and Protected.

Private functions can only be accessed by the class. They are not accessible or inherited by derived classes. If, in our previous example, the Customer object's BranchInfo function were Private, there would be no problem of possible interference with the BranchInfo method in the Government object.

You are probably already familiar with Friend members from VB6. They are inherited by derived classes but are only visible within an assembly.

Protected members are new to VB.NET. A protected member can be accessed from a derived class and it can be inherited by a class that is further derived from that one. However, it cannot be accessed from outside of a directly derived object.

If you have Class A with protected member MyFunc as follows:

```
Class A
    Protected Sub MyFunc()
    End Sub
End Class
```

…and you derive class B as follows:

```
Class B
    Inherits A
    Public Sub MyPublicFunc()
    End Sub
End Class
```

…then within Class B, you can call the MyFunc method directly—it has been inherited from Class A. However, if you declare a variable of type B in another routine, calls to B.MyFunc will fail. The MyFunc method is only available within the derived Class B; it is not visible to outside functions. You can also define a method to be a Protected Friend member, combining the characteristics of both attributes.

Recap

In this chapter, you learned some critical concepts:

- The .NET Framework relies heavily on inheritance and every variable or class you declare does, in fact, inherit from some object in the framework (even if it is the Object type itself).

- While your classes will always inherit from other classes, they will rarely be inherited by others. In fact, you should, as a matter of routine, mark your classes as NotOverridable in order to prevent others from using them in a manner for which they were not designed.

- For most VB programmers, code reuse is best accomplished through containment; and VB.NET, by solving the circular reference and object navigation problems, has eliminated most of the problems with containment under VB6.

- If you do decide you need to create an inheritable object, use great care in designing it. Even though VB.NET has addressed the fragile base class problem, the solution only deals with being able to deploy updated components without breaking existing code. It does not eliminate the need to recode derived classes when the problem is detected on later builds.

The final verdict: Inheritance is probably the most overhyped feature in VB.NET, one that you should almost never use even while you are always using it.

Memory Management in VB.NET

IN CHAPTER 4, YOU LEARNED that the .NET Framework solves the circular reference problem by keeping track of all the objects used by your application and using garbage collection to free any objects no longer referenced.

In Chapter 5, you learned that every piece of data down to the simplest integer variable is an object.

This means that every item of data you use in your application is subject to the memory management rules of .NET.

Almost....

Value Objects and Reference Objects

The designers of the .NET Framework knew that it would be terribly wasteful to store every item of data down to numeric variables on the heap. Even though the .NET heap is remarkably efficient, it still demands an allocation step that is slower than a simple stack allocation. And there is also the cost of tracking the object and collecting it after it is freed.

Nevertheless, they wanted the ease of use and consistency that comes from deriving every variable from a base Object type.

To resolve this conflict, they ended up defining two types of objects: Reference objects and Value objects.[1]

A Reference object is similar to the COM objects you are familiar with from VB6. When you assign one Reference object to another, you do not make a copy of the data—instead, you simply obtain a new reference to the existing data. Reference objects are always allocated on the heap. Reference objects can inherit from other objects and other objects can, in turn, inherit from them.

---

1. Just to be clear, the terms Reference type and Reference object mean the same thing, as does Value type and Value object in this context.

Value Objects

Value objects are allocated in the application's data segment or on the stack—not on the heap. Value types in VB.NET are created in much the same way as you created user-defined types in VB6 except that you use the new Structure keyword.

Here's an example of a simple structure defined in the ValueType sample program:

```
Public Structure mystruct
    Public AString As String
    Public Sub SetString(ByVal newstring As String)
        AString = newstring
    End Sub
    Public Sub New(ByVal InitialString As String)
        AString = InitialString
    End Sub
End Structure
```

There are some interesting points to consider about this declaration.

First, the structure contains a string. Under VB6, you could define fixed-length strings that would be stored within the structure. Under VB.NET, the String data type is a Reference type.[2] So, here you have a Value type that contains a single variable, which is a Reference type. What then, is the benefit of using a Value type in this case?

There is none. It's the wrong approach.

Value types are best used to create small objects that are mostly based on numeric data types, for example, complex numbers or location coordinates.

Unlike VB6 user-defined types, VB.NET structures can have methods and properties. They can also have constructors: methods used to initialize the structure. There's just one catch, however, constructors you define must have at least one parameter. The default constructor is used by the CLR to initialize the structure to all zeros.

The Button1_Click method in the ValueType sample project appears as follows:

---

2. You'll read a lot more about strings in Chapters 8 and 9—they work very differently from VB6. For now, you just need to know that a string inside a structure is stored as a pointer to a location on the heap. The string data is not stored in the structure itself.

```
Private Sub Button1_Click(ByVal sender As Object, _
ByVal e As System.EventArgs) Handles button1.Click
    Dim a As mystruct
    a.SetString("Hello")
    Dim b As mystruct = a
    Debug.WriteLine("B's String: " + b.AString)
    Dim c As New mystruct("Another string")
    Debug.WriteLine("C's String: " + c.AString)
    Debug.WriteLine("C's ToString: " + c.ToString())

    Dim obj As Object
    obj = c
    ' Boxed into an object
    Debug.WriteLine(obj.ToString())

End Sub
```

This method shows three different ways to initialize the mystruct structure.

The `Dim a As mystruct` statement creates variable 'a' that contains the structure. All of the fields of the structure are initialized to zero using the default constructor (strings are initialized to Nothing). If mystruct were a Reference type in this statement, variable 'a' would be equal to Nothing—Reference objects must be created before they are used. There is no such thing as an invalid or empty Structure variable. Thus, there is no difference between `Dim a As mystruct` and `Dim a As New mystruct` except for the ability to use other constructors with the latter syntax.

VB.NET allows you to initialize variables using the syntax:

```
Dim myvaluetype = initialvalue
```

Thus, the statement:

```
Dim I As Integer = 5
```

…is a valid way to declare an integer and set its initial value to 5.

Structures of the same type can be assigned to each other as well. VB.NET performs a member-by-member copy of the elements of the structure on assignment. Thus, the following is allowed:

```
Dim a As mystruct
Dim b As mystruct
b = a
```

In this example, the previous code is shortened to:

```
Dim a As mystruct
Dim b As mystruct = a
```

The final object, 'c,' uses the overloaded[3] New method to create and initialize the string in one operation, thus:

```
Dim c As New mystruct("Another string")
```

As you can see, you can assign a Value type to a Reference object type with the following code:

```
Dim obj As Object
obj = c
```

When the CLR needs to access a Value type as a reference, it performs an operation called Boxing in which an object is allocated on the heap and members of the Value type are copied onto the newly allocated heap object. The reversal of this process is called Unboxing.

When the button1.Click event executes, the following is sent to the output window:

```
B's String: Hello
C's String: Another string
C's ToString: ValueType.mystruct
ValueType.mystruct
```

This example demonstrates copying structures, structure initialization, and the fact that a boxed Value object still maintains its type information.

The button2.Click event shown in Listing 6-1 provides an even clearer demonstration of the differences between Value and Reference types.

---

3. Overloaded is a term used to describe the existence of more than one method of a given name within a class or structure. The methods only differ by their parameters. Overloading is covered in depth in Chapter 10.

Listing 6-1. Copying Reference and Value type objects.

```
    Private Class myclass1
        Public AString As String
        Public Sub SetString(ByVal newstring As String)
            AString = newstring
        End Sub
        Public Sub New(ByVal InitialString As String)
            AString = InitialString
        End Sub
    End Class


    Private Sub Button2_Click(ByVal sender As Object, ByVal e As System.EventArgs) _
    Handles button2.Click
        Dim S1 As New mystruct("Hello")
        Dim S2 As mystruct
        Dim c1 As New myclass1("Hello")
        Dim c2 As myclass1
        S2 = S1
        c2 = c1
        S2.SetString("Modified")
        c2.SetString("Modified")
        Debug.WriteLine("Struct: " + S1.AString)
        Debug.WriteLine("Class: " + c1.AString)
    End Sub
```

The myclass1 class is virtually identical to the structure and they seem to be initialized in the same way. What happens when you create a copy of the structure and object, then modify the copy? When you click on the button, the AString property values of the original structure and object are displayed in the output window as follows:

```
Struct: Hello
Class: Modified
```

When you modify the copy of a structure, you modify only the copy. When you assign an object reference, you obtain a new reference to the original object—it doesn't matter which Object variable you use to modify or access the object.

Here are some issues to consider when choosing the type of object to create:

- Structures cannot inherit from classes or other structures.

- You cannot inherit from a structure.

- Structure variables always refer to valid data—they cannot be set to Nothing.

- Assigning structures performs a member by member copy—a potentially time-consuming process.

- Structures are compared by comparing the values of each member of the structure.

- Structures never have destructors (finalizers).

- Data members of a structure cannot be initialized to values unless those members are constants. Nor can array members have their initial size specified.

- Microsoft guidelines suggest that the overhead of copying data in Value types exceeds the overhead of garbage collection once the size of the Value type exceeds 16 bytes.

Reference Objects

You may have gotten the idea that I'm not terribly excited by structures. This may seem odd because under VB6, user-defined types had some major advantages over Object types. Because they could hold fixed-length arrays and fixed string data, they offered an efficient way to transfer data in large blocks. They also had less overhead than objects. These advantages are not nearly as compelling under VB.NET.

Arrays and strings inside of structures remain objects created on the heap and managed by the CLR.[4] And the design of the heap makes allocation and deallocation of objects incredibly fast. Allocation of a Reference variable is fast because it is allocated from the free space at the top of the heap.[5] Deallocating a Reference variable consists of assigning it to Nothing or to a reference to some other object—the heap isn't even touched. Of course, this amazing allocation and deallocation performance does come with a price: as you learned in Chapter 4, it is necessary to periodically perform a garbage collection to free up the memory used by unused objects and reclaim them for the free portion of the heap.

Value objects are best when you need large numbers of small objects that are based on other Value types and do not contain members that are Reference types.

---

4. There are ways to more tightly control the layout of members inside of structures and to define fixed-length strings and arrays inside of structures—primarily for use in making API calls or COM interoperability. This will be covered in Part Three of this book.

5. This is a slight simplification in that the CLR maintains separate, free spaces for small and larger objects to improve efficiency.

Otherwise, you'll usually be better off with Reference types. In other words, if you're accustomed to creating and using user-defined types extensively instead of classes, it's time to kick the habit.

Revisiting Garbage Collection

The Common Language Runtime is optimized to handle the rapid creation, release, and collection of small objects. One way that this is accomplished is by keeping track of the age of the objects. Each time an object survives a garbage collection step, it is considered to be in an older generation. It turns out that in typical programs, the longer an object exists, the more likely it is to continue to exist until the program terminates. Newer objects are often either temporary objects or objects that exist during a single function call. When a garbage collection is necessary, the .NET Framework first attempts a Generation Zero collection—an attempt to collect only the newest objects. According to Microsoft, in many cases, small temporary objects will be collected so quickly and efficiently they will never even leave the CPU cache to be written in main memory.

Let's take a closer look at what really happens when an object is collected during the garbage collection process.

Figure 6-1A shows a heap that contains five objects. Two of the objects (marked with the letter 'F') have finalizers attached. This means that the code for these objects contains a Finalizer method. The CLR, in conjunction with the JIT compiler, can identify those objects that have finalizers and keep track of them.

When the garbage collector sees that an object with a finalizer is no longer referenced, it does not delete the object immediately. Instead, it places the object in a separate list of objects that still need to be finalized.

The objects remain in the finalizer heap until a separate background thread runs the finalizers. After the finalizer is run, the object is removed from the finalizer list and will be finally freed during the next garbage collection cycle.[6]

How long does it take from the time you stop referencing an object until the time the finalizer runs?

You don't know.

In fact, the current .NET documentation does not guarantee that finalizers will always be run when an application terminates, though this does seem to be the case.

---

6. That's right, objects with finalizers have to be collected twice: first when it is added to the finalizer list and second when the memory is actually reclaimed.

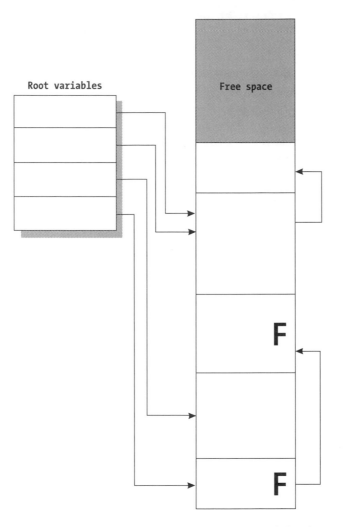

Figure 6-1A. A heap containing two objects with finalizers.

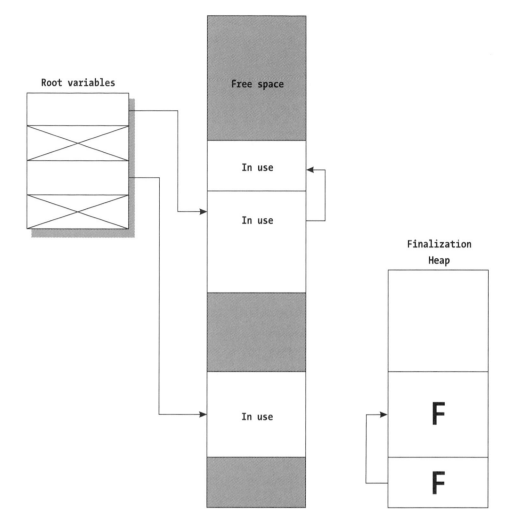

Figure 6-1B. Objects with finalizers are not destroyed when garbage collection occurs.

Finalizers

Few areas better illustrate how different VB.NET is from VB6 than the finalization issue.

VB6 programmers who have studied good object-oriented programming techniques know the "right" way to initialize and terminate components. During the class Initialize event, you initialize members and often allocate any necessary system resources. During a class Terminate event, you perform any necessary cleanup operation. The Terminate event occurs immediately when the last reference to an object is released so you can generally assume that any Object variables are valid during the Terminate event.[7] You can certainly count on the Terminate event taking place, assuring that you can clean up after your application (free system resources, close files, etc.) when your application terminates.

These lessons do not apply to VB.NET.[8]

To see why, take a look at the Undead1 sample application. It contains a class named Undying that is defined as follows:

```
Public Class Undying
    Protected Overrides Sub Finalize()
        Debug.WriteLine("I have been finalized")
    End Sub
End Class
```

The form contains a button named cmdCreate. The cmdCreate button creates and deletes an object using the following code:

```
Private Sub button1_Click(ByVal sender As System.Object, _
    ByVal e As System.EventArgs) Handles button1.Click
    ' Note: unlike VB6, this does create the object
    Dim obj As New Undying()

End Sub
```

Unlike VB6, in VB.NET, the New statement immediately creates an object. In VB6, the New statement simply signals VB to create the object automatically the first time any of the object's methods or properties are accessed.

---

7. When a VB6 application terminates, objects are released in an arbitrary order. Thus, it is possible for object references to be invalid during a class Terminate event. This can even cause memory exceptions.

8. Don't let anyone trick you into thinking you can escape this by switching to C#. The C# language has destructors that look like those of C++ but they work just like the finalizers in VB.NET.

This change also has an impact on clearing object variables. In VB6, if you declare a variable with the New statement as follows:

```
Dim myObject As New SomeObjectType
```

…the myObject object will be created any time it is referenced. If you set the myObject variable to Nothing, then reference it again, it will access a new instance of the SomeObjectType object.

In VB.NET, a SomeObjectType object will be created as soon as the Dim statement is executed. If you then set myObject to Nothing, and try to reference it, you will get a runtime error.

Now try running the application. Click the button. After some indeterminate number of clicks, a garbage collection may occur and the finalizers will be called (note, it might take thousands of clicks or more). Then try terminating the application. All of the finalizers will run when the final garbage collection occurs.

The delay between release and finalization may seem unimportant but it is actually quite significant. If your objects hold resources such as database connections or sockets, the resources held by these released but uncollected objects can have a serious impact on performance and scalability.

The Great Non-Deterministic Finalizer Controversy

Visual Basic 6 (and COM objects in general) provides deterministic finalization— you always know that finalizers will be called and you know when they will be called. As you can see, the CLR does *not* support deterministic finalization. There is no way to know when a finalizer will be called or, in some situations, even if it will be called.

Some VB programmers object strongly to this change and have criticized Microsoft for leaving deterministic finalization out of VB.NET.

Frankly, I'm hard pressed to see how Microsoft could put this feature back in. Remember, the whole reason for using a garbage collection was to eliminate the need for reference counting with its potential for both memory leaks and circular references. The only way I know of to provide deterministic finalization in such an environment is to either perform a garbage collection after each Object variable is modified or to add reference counting back into the environment. The performance impact of doing a garbage collection on each variable change would be prohibitive. Adding reference counting brings back memory leaks and circular reference issues.

Personally, I think the benefits of garbage collection are worth the loss of deterministic finalization.

But there is no doubt that this change does alter the way you should write objects in VB.NET.

Initialization remains largely unchanged. If anything, it is improved because it is now possible to pass parameters when an object is constructed. But the lack of deterministic finalization still has an impact because you may want to minimize resource allocation at that time—waiting instead to allocate resources until they are actually needed.

Instead of waiting until finalization to free resources and perform cleanup, it is advisable under .NET for the client using the object to explicitly tell the object to perform cleanup when the object is no longer needed. The convention is to implement a method named Dispose for this purpose. Performing cleanup during the Dispose method allows you to eliminate the finalization step (which eliminates an extra step during garbage collection and thus improves performance). It is also common for objects to implement both approaches: a Dispose method to allow the client to clean up resources, and a finalizer that performs a "last chance" cleanup if the method is not called.

The InitAndDestruct sample application shows how this can be done. In this example, the Component1 class inherits from System.ComponentModel.Component. A "Component" can use the component designer that allows it to contain other components. The System.ComponentModel.Component class also inherits from the IDisposable interface that defines the Dispose method. Its default implementation of this method calls the Dispose method of these contained components, thus helping to automate the cleanup process.

The Component1 example demonstrates the following features:

- Shared (class) constructor —called the first time any object of a class is created.

- Object constructor —called when an object is created.

- Object finalizer—usually called at some time after an object is released.

- Dispose method—called (by convention) by a client using an object.

The component is defined as shown in Listing 6-2 (some of the designer code has been left out).

Listing 6-2. InitAndDestruct sample program.

```vb
' Initialization and Destruction example
' Copyright © 2001 by Desaware Inc.
Public Class Component1
    Inherits System.ComponentModel.Component


    Shared Sub New()
        MsgBox("Shared component initializer called")
    End Sub

    Public Sub New()
        MyBase.New()

        'This call is required by the Component Designer.
        InitializeComponent()

        'Add any initialization after the InitializeComponent() call
        MsgBox("My component instance created")

    End Sub

    Protected Overrides Sub Finalize()
        MsgBox("My component finalizer called")
    End Sub

    Public Overloads Overrides Sub Dispose()
        MyBase.Dispose()
        MsgBox("I've been disposed")
    End Sub

End Class
```

The component can be tested by a button click function that creates and deletes the object as follows:

```vb
Private Sub button1_Click(ByVal sender As System.Object, _
ByVal e As System.EventArgs) Handles button1.Click
    Dim obj As New Component1()
    ' Dispose of the object when you are done with it - See text
    obj.Dispose()
End Sub
```

The first time you click on the button, you will see that the shared constructor is called, then the object constructor, then the Dispose method (which is called explicitly by the client). The next time you click on the button, only the object constructor and Dispose method are called. The finalizer is called if and when the object is released.

It is important to remember that the Dispose method must be called by the client. The good news is that in many cases, the .NET Framework performs this task for you. For example, when you host a control on a form, that control is added to the form's Controls collection. When a form performs its own cleanup operation (which occurs when the framework calls its Dispose method), the form in turn calls the Dispose method on all of the controls in the Controls collection. However, it has no way of knowing about components you create in your code, such as the Component1 component in this example. You must call Dispose on those objects yourself.

Having the container explicitly call its objects' Dispose method is not an ideal solution. But given the architecture of .NET, it's probably the best that can be done. I still think the benefits of having the CLR perform object cleanup is worth the cost—but I do miss deterministic finalization.

Meanwhile, here are some guidelines to follow with regards to object termination.

- Avoid designs that require object cleanup if you can. Don't implement a finalizer unless you really need it for cleanup.

- If your object does require cleanup, implement the Dispose method.

- Consider creating a Container object (one that inherits from System.ComponentModel.Container) and add any components you use to the object. When you call the Dispose on the Container object, it will automatically call the Dispose method of all of the objects it contains. Remember that the wizard will often do this for you on components that it manages.

- Even if you implement a Dispose method, consider implementing a Finalizer method as a backup to perform necessary cleanup if the Dispose method is not called. With some types of components (like Controls), you can be fairly sure their Dispose method will be called because they must be placed in the Controls collection in order to work and will thus be cleaned up by the framework.[9] But if you are creating a component for use by others, it's quite possible the developers will forget to call Dispose even if you make it clear that you expect it to be called.

---

9. It is possible for you to create controls in code and never use them, in which case, their Dispose method won't be called unless you do it explicitly.

- On Windows NT/2000/XP, most system resources are automatically freed when an application ends. On Windows 95/98/ME, application cleanup is not as reliable.

Off the Deep End—Resurrection Exists

The scenario I'm about to show you is so wild it's almost incomprehensible. It is certainly alien to the experience of virtually every VB programmer.

Follow this chain of reasoning:

- When no root-level variable is referencing an object, it is eligible to be "collected" by the garbage collector.

- If an unreferenced object has a finalizer, it is not collected immediately but is instead added into a list of objects to be finalized. Until it is finalized, the object does still exist.

- Let's say that while the object's finalizer is executed, a root-level variable is set to point to the object such that it is no longer subject to collection.

Surprise! The object, which supposedly has been freed and has had its finalizer execute, is now a valid object and will not be subject to garbage collection! In other words, the "dead" object has brought itself back to life.

Consider the Resurrected class from the Resurrection sample project:

```
Public Class Resurrected

    Public mycontainer As Form1

    Public Sub AreYouThere()
        MsgBox("I am here")
    End Sub

    Protected Overrides Sub Finalize()
        MsgBox("I'm being finalized")
        mycontainer.PriorObject = Me
    End Sub

End Class
```

The class has a public property that will be set to reference the container form. It has a method called AreYouThere that exists simply to give evidence that the object exits. The form has a public property named PriorObject that will reference the Resurrected object. This circular reference, in which the form references the object and the object references the form, is not a problem under VB.NET. Once the form stops referencing the object, it will be collected by the garbage collector.

The form, in addition to the PriorObject property, has four events for four different buttons:

- The Create & Delete button raises the cmdCreate.Click event. This button creates an object and sets its mycontainer property to reference the form. This allows the object to access the form's PriorObject property.

- The Force GC button raises the cmdGC.Click event, which forces an immediate garbage collection and waits for all finalizers to run.

- The Check Prior Object button raises the cmdPrior.Click event that checks to see if the form's PriorObject property is valid. If so, it calls the AreYouThere method of the object.

- The Turn Finalizer Back On button raises the cmdRefinalize.Click event, which reenables the object's finalizer—this will be explained shortly.

The form module is shown in Listing 6-3.

Listing 6-3. Resurrection sample form module.

```
Public PriorObject As Resurrected

Private Sub cmdRefinalize_Click(ByVal sender As Object, _
ByVal e As System.EventArgs) Handles cmdRefinalize.Click
    If Not PriorObject Is Nothing Then
        GC.ReRegisterForFinalize(PriorObject)
    End If
    PriorObject = Nothing
End Sub

Private Sub cmdPrior_Click(ByVal sender As Object, _
ByVal e As System.EventArgs) Handles cmdPrior.Click
    If Not PriorObject Is Nothing Then
        ' Proof that the finalized object still exists!
        PriorObject.AreYouThere()
    End If
End Sub
```

```
Private Sub cmdCreate_Click(ByVal sender As Object, _
ByVal e As System.EventArgs) Handles cmdCreate.Click
    Dim obj As New Resurrected()

    ' The object has a way to reference back to the form
    obj.mycontainer = Me
End Sub

Private Sub cmdGC_Click(ByVal sender As Object, _
ByVal e As System.EventArgs) Handles cmdGC.Click
    ' Force a garbage collection here.
    GC.Collect()
    GC.WaitForPendingFinalizers()
End Sub
```

You can use the Resurrection sample project in Listing 6-3 to demonstrate object resurrection. Try the following:

1. Click on the Create & Destroy button—this creates an object, sets its mycontainer property to reference the form, then releases the object (when the function exits, the form no longer has a variable that references the object).

2. Click on the Force GC button—this forces a garbage collection and object finalization. During finalization, the object uses its mycontainer property to set the form's PriorObject property to reference the object. In other words, the object is now again referenced by a Form (root-level) variable.

3. Click on the Check Prior Object button to show that the object, though finalized, still exists.

4. Now try closing the application. Even though finalizers are called when an application terminates, you will see that the finalizer for the object is not run on shutdown.

How can this be? Once an object's finalizer has been run, it will not be run again, even if the object is brought back to life!

Now run the Resurrection sample program again, repeat the previous steps 1 through 3, then click on the Turn Finalizer Back On button. This button also sets the PriorObject variable to Nothing. Now click on the Force GC button again. You will see that the finalizer runs a second time. The GC.ReRegisterForFinalize method tells the garbage collector that you have brought the object back to life and want its finalizer to run again when the object is collected a second time.[10]

At first glance, you might think I'm spending a lot of time writing about a subtle problem that no developer in their right mind would ever use. And in a sense, that is correct—you are far more likely to see this scenario as a result of a bug than a design choice.

But understanding this process is key to understanding an important technique that you can and should use.

Just as the garbage collector has a ReRegisterForFinalize method, it also has a SupressFinalize method, which allows you to notify the garbage collector that an object does not need to be finalized even though it has a finalizer. This allows you to implement an important optimization. Earlier, I recommended performing cleanup operations in your object's Dispose method using the Finalize method as a backup to perform cleanup if the client neglects to call Dispose. You can call the SupressFinalize method during the object's Dispose method to eliminate this now unnecessary finalization.

Recap

The use of managed memory in the .NET Framework has far-reaching implications on not only the VB.NET language, but on the way you should design your applications.

You learned the difference between Value types and Reference types and that while using user-defined types in VB6 often has significant benefits, those benefits do not translate to the VB.NET Structure type. In other words, in VB.NET, you should prefer classes over structures for all but the smallest structures that contain primarily other Value type data.

You learned that the benefits in reliability and scalability brought about by managed memory (eliminating memory leaks and the circular reference problem) come at a cost—the inability of the CLR to provide deterministic finalization.

This means that VB.NET developers should avoid performing resource cleanup operations during the object's Finalize method. Instead, you should implement a Dispose method after inheriting the IDisposable interface.[11] The Finalize method should be used as a "last chance" backup to perform cleanup in cases where Dispose is not called. If Dispose is called, the GC.SupressFinalize method can be used to eliminate the finalization step, thus improving performance.

---

10. You won't see the message box if you terminate the application because VB.NET is smart enough to know that you are terminating the application and will not raise message boxes at that time.

11. Or, after deriving from a class that that inherits the IDisposable interface.

Finally, you learned that it is possible for dead objects to be brought back to life if you are careless with your object model and you re-reference an object during its finalization step.

Inheritance and memory management, the subjects of Chapters 5 and 6, represent the first two of what I consider to be the three major conceptual challenges that face programmers transitioning from VB6 to VB.NET. These are the two most likely to get VB6 developers into trouble if they either follow previous programming habits or blindly adopt over-hyped language features. In Chapter 7, we will deal with the third of these challenges: multithreading.

VB.NET Multithreading

IN HIS CLASSIC SCIENCE FICTION NOVEL *The Stars My Destination* (Vintage Books, 1996 reprint), Alfred Bester describes a psychokinetic explosive called PyrE—so powerful that a single grain of it can blow up a house. And all that is needed for it to blow up is for anyone to just think at it and want it to explode. The hero of the story has to decide whether to keep it locked up and secret or to spread it around the planet leaving the fate of the world in the hands and thoughts of every single person on earth.

Which brings us to multithreading.

It's a useful technology—one that has the potential to improve your application's real (or perceived) performance. But it is the software equivalent of a nuclear device because if it is used incorrectly, it can blow up in your face. No—worse than that—used incorrectly, it can destroy your reputation and your business because it has nearly infinite potential to increase your testing and debugging costs.

Multithreading in VB.NET scares me more than any other new feature. And as is the case with a number of new .NET technologies, the reason for this has to do with human factors as much as with technology.

Several months before the .NET PDC preview,[1] I was doing a session with Bill Storage at a VBits conference. I asked the audience, which consisted of fairly experienced Visual Basic programmers, whether they wanted free threading in the next version of Visual Basic. Almost without exception, their hands quickly went up. I then asked how many of them actually understood what they were asking for. Only a few hands were raised and there were knowing smiles on the faces of those individuals.

I'm afraid of multithreading in VB.NET because Visual Basic programmers have little in their experience to prepare them for designing and debugging free-threaded applications.[2] VB6 provides enormous protection (along with severe limits) in its implementation of multithreading. The only way to use free threading safely is to understand it and to design your applications correctly.

---

1. The first public preview of Microsoft.NET at the Microsoft Professional Developer's Conference.

2. And before you decide that I'm being hopelessly condescending, let me be clear—I've done free threading for years and I still run into subtle threading bugs. Desaware's NT Service toolkit uses free threading internally and I spent as much time designing, testing, and debugging the thread management as I did developing all of the other features in the package.

Again, I stress, *design your applications correctly.* If your design is incorrect, it will be virtually impossible to patch up the problems later. And again, the potential cost to fix threading problems has no upper limit.

I've always felt that it's my responsibility as an author to not only teach technology but to put it into context and help readers choose the right technology to solve their problems. Because multithreading is such a serious issue, I've decided to take a somewhat unusual approach in teaching it. Instead of focusing on the benefits of multithreading and why you would want to use it, I'm going to start by doing my best to help you gain a healthy respect for the technology and the kinds of problems you will run into.[3] Only towards the end of this chapter, once you understand how to use multithreading, will I discuss scenarios where it is advisable to use it.[4]

A Quick Introduction to Multithreading

As an intermediate-level or experienced Visual Basic programmer, you hopefully have at least a rough idea of what multithreading is. Simply put, Windows is able to run more than one piece of code at a time by rapidly switching between them. But what does that actually mean?

A processor has a number of registers that it uses in order to execute code. An instruction pointer contains the address of the instruction that is executing. A stack pointer contains the address of the program stack that is used for local variables and to keep track of function return addresses. Other registers are used as temporary variable holders. When the OS decides it is time to switch from one piece of code to another, it interrupts the normal instruction flow, saves the contents of the registers, loads the current register values for another piece of code, and starts running it.[5]

So, if code is running on a system, it is running on a thread.

What then is a process?

A process consists of one or more threads that run in their own memory space. When you launch an application in Windows, the process acts as if it has the entire system memory all to itself. It cannot write into another process's memory nor can other processes write into its memory. This provides a high degree of

---

3. In other words, I'm going to try to scare you to death.

4. And before you decide to skip this chapter because you don't ever want to use multithreading, allow me to remind you that, by default, all of your object finalizers run in a separate finalization thread! So, you have the potential of seeing threading problems even if you don't explicitly create any threads!

5. Purists will note that this is a vast oversimplification in these days of pipelined processors and multiprocessor systems but conceptually it's accurate and adequate for our purposes here.

protection and is a key reason why 32-bit Windows operating systems don't crash as much as earlier 16-bit versions.[6]

From the preceding paragraph comes a corollary that is the most important factor to consider when doing multithreaded programming:

All of the threads in a multithreaded application share the same memory space.

So what?

Consider the following scenario.

The Shopping Fiasco

Mr. and Mrs. Consumer are a typical and happy suburban couple. One morning, Mr. Consumer decided to buy Mrs. Consumer the latest wireless Internet appliance. Being a cautious consumer and a bit stretched financially (since he invested his life savings on a one bedroom luxury shack in Palo Alto), he went online and checked to make sure that he had enough available credit to purchase the device. He then drove off to the store to make the purchase.

Meanwhile, Mrs. Consumer was browsing the Web and discovered a sale on the 125GB hard drive that Mr. Consumer coveted (so he would have space to install Office 2005 with its new, optical lip-reading technology). Quickly checking the credit card account, she saw that she had just enough money to purchase the hard drive and promptly placed the order.

Meanwhile, Mr. Consumer had arrived at the Electronics store and after a short forty-five minute wait, had reached the register. Imagine his shock when the cashier called for the person in charge who gently informed Mr. Consumer that his credit card was over the limit and that he had been instructed to demolish the card with a small flamethrower.

Mr. Consumer slunk out of the store in shame wondering what could have possibly gone wrong. Distracted in his despair, he didn't notice where he was walking and was trampled by five thousand rampaging teenagers running to buy the newly arrived Playstation 4 X-Box (the latest innovation of MS-Sony).

What does this have to do with multithreading, you ask?

Everything.

Mr. and Mrs. Consumer were each acting independently and both had full access to the credit card at any time. Mr. Consumer retrieved information about the card but between the time he retrieved the information and the time he used it, that information was changed without his knowledge—with disastrous results.

Mr. and Mrs. Consumer were separate threads of execution that had access to shared memory.

What if the two threads were accessing a single COM object?

---

6. Again, there is some simplification going on here. Windows NT, 2000, and XP have better process isolation than Windows 95/98/ME. Processes have other features besides memory isolation.

COM objects, as you recall, use reference counting to determine how many references to the object exist. If two threads try to change the reference count at the same time, this exact problem can occur. Objects might fail to be decremented on release, resulting in objects that are never destroyed. Or an object may not be incremented correctly resulting in an object that is destroyed while references to it still exist.

The potential for this type of problem exists anytime you have a shared resource or variable.

Why doesn't this problem exist in Visual Basic 6? Because VB6 makes separate copies of all global variables for each thread in a multithreaded application or DLL.[7] This separation is part of Visual Basic 6—not the OS. In VB.NET, global and shared variables are shared among all of the threads in an application. So, dealing with multithreading issues is entirely your responsibility.

Multithreading: A Closer Look

Since my goal is not just to teach you about multithreading but to help you gain a healthy respect for the technology, it seems appropriate now to take a close look at an example. But just to keep things interesting, I'll put you on notice that there are flaws in this program and I won't point them out until later. See if you can spot potential problem areas in the code.

The sample program simulates a client/server scenario. The model is that of a family. The server is a parent who receives a paycheck. The clients are the children who are continuously asking for money that is promptly spent. Simplistic, yes, but the pattern is applicable to many business scenarios.

This sample application is longer than most in this book but I encourage you to take the time to read through and understand it. It is not complex and in order for you to understand the flaws in the application's design, it is important that you be familiar with the code.

The Data Structures

It's my habit, when approaching any application, to think first about the objects implemented by the application. I'm sure, as an experienced, object-oriented programmer, you do much the same.

In this application, the parent and children both have bank accounts. The parent receives deposits in the form of paychecks, the kids in the form of allowances. The basic mechanics of depositing and withdrawing money from an account and maintaining a balance would be similar, if not identical, with both. In fact, since

---

7. To be specific, VB6 global variables are placed in thread local storage.

logically a child's account and parent's account are both bank accounts, it seems clear that an "is a" relationship could exist between them and a generic bank account object:

A child account *is a* bank account.

A parent account *is a* bank account.

In other words, the object hierarchy in this situation lends itself nicely to using inheritance.

Here's the Account class as it appears in the Threading1 sample program. The object maintains an account balance in the m_Account variable. It also keeps a running total of the amount spent and the amount deposited over the life of the account. The object has a Random object, which is an object in the CLR that serves up random numbers and replaces the VB6 Rnd function. The GetRandomAmount function creates a value between zero and one dollar, providing simulated amounts to be spent:

```
Public Class Account
    Protected m_Account As Double
    Protected m_Spent As Double
    Protected m_Deposited As Double
    Private Shared m_Random As New Random()

    ' Returns a random amount from 0 to $1.00
    Protected Shared Function GetRandomAmount() As Double
        Dim amount As Double
        amount = int(m_Random.NextDouble * 100)
        GetRandomAmount = amount / 100
    End Function
```

Listing 7-1 shows that a series of properties exist to allow access to the member variables.

Listing 7-1. Account class properties.

```
    Property Withdrawn() As Double
        Get
            Withdrawn = m_Spent
        End Get
        Set
            m_Spent = Value
        End (ByVal Value As Double)
    End Property
```

```
Property Balance() As Double
    Get
        Balance = m_Account
    End Get
    Set(ByVal Value As Double)
        m_Account = Value
    End Set
End Property

Property Deposited() As Double
    Get
        Deposited = m_Deposited
    End Get
    Set(ByVal Value As Double)
        m_Deposited = Value
    End Set
End Property
```

The Member variables could have been made public or protected but it's always a good practice to expose them through properties so that you can preserve the flexibility to add additional functionality to the properties later.

The Withdraw method takes as a parameter the amount you are trying to withdraw and returns the amount actually withdrawn (which may be less than what was requested if the balance is insufficient). It also adds the amount withdrawn to the total spent. The Deposit method adds the specified amount to the account and to the total deposited. The Clear method allows you to clear the Member variables of the account as shown in Listing 7-2.

Listing 7-2. The Account class Withdraw and Deposit methods.

```
' Attempt to spend a requested amount of money, return
' the amount spent
Protected Function Withdraw(ByVal amount As Double) As Double
    If amount > m_Account Then
        amount = m_Account
    End If
    m_Account = m_Account - amount
    m_Spent = m_Spent + amount
    Return amount
End Function
```

```
    Protected Sub Deposit(ByVal amount As Double)
        m_Account = m_Account + amount
        m_Deposited = m_Deposited + amount
    End Sub

    Public Overridable Sub Clear()
        m_Account = 0
        m_Deposited = 0
        m_Spent = 0
    End Sub

End Class
```

The children's account object is called KidsAccount and inherits from the Account class. This object adds a Member variable named m_FailedRequests. This variable keeps count of the number of times the child wanted to spend money but did not have enough in their account to spend. As you can imagine, this variable will tend to increase quickly.

The GetAllowance method is called to deposit money into the account. Could we have used the Deposit method? Not directly. Since the Deposit method in the base class is protected, it can't be exposed directly from this class. We could have created a new Deposit method and used the Shadows keyword to hide the inherited base class method (and could have still called the base class method using the MyBase object—but you'll read all about this in Chapter 10).

```
Public Class KidAccount
    Inherits Account
    Private m_FailedRequests As Double
    ReadOnly Property FailedRequests() As Double
        Get
            FailedRequests = m_FailedRequests
        End Get
    End Property

    ' Gets an allowance from the parent
    Public Sub GetAllowance(ByVal amount As Double)
        Deposit(amount)
    End Sub
```

The Spend method is called to spend money. It chooses a random amount up to a dollar and tries to spend it. If the balance is zero, the attempt fails and the m_FailedRequests variable is incremented. The Clear method clears both the m_FailedRequests member and the base class members as shown in Listing 7-3.

Listing 7-3. The KidAccount class Spend and Clear methods.

```vbnet
' Tries to spend a random amount of money
Public Sub Spend()
    Dim amount As Double
    amount = GetRandomAmount()
    If amount > m_Account Then amount = m_Account
    If amount = 0 Then
        m_FailedRequests = m_FailedRequests + 1
    Else
        Withdraw(amount)
    End If
End Sub


' Clear the object and base class
Overrides Sub Clear()
    m_FailedRequests = 0
    MyBase.Clear()
End Sub
End Class
```

A class named ParentAccount, which also inherits from Account, represents the parent's account. The GiveAllowance method picks a random amount that is withdrawn from the parent's balance. The amount actually returned should be deposited in the child's account using its GetAllowance method. The DepositPayroll method simply deposits a paycheck in the parent's account as shown in Listing 7-4.

Listing 7-4. The ParentAccount class.

```vbnet
Public Class ParentAccount
    Inherits Account

    ' When called, the Parent Account picks a random allowance
    ' and gives it.
    Public Function GiveAllowance() As Double
        Dim amount As Double
        amount = GetRandomAmount()
        amount = Withdraw(amount)
        ' Return amount actually withdrawn (may be 0)
        Return (amount)
    End Function
```

```
    Public Sub DepositPayroll(ByVal amount As Double)
        deposit(amount)
    End Sub
End Class
```

The Simulator

The FamilyOperation class simulates the operation of a family. It has a member array, Kids(), which contains an array of KidAccount objects, one for each child in the family. The Parent variable is a ParentAccount object representing the parent.

The simulator is designed to run on one or more background threads. This corresponds to the use of a thread pool for managing client requests or (with slight modification) to having each child managed on their own independent thread.

The threads are managed by a variable named Thread that references an array of System.Threading.Thread objects—the thread management object provided by the CLR.

The m_NumberOfKids variable contains the number of child accounts. The m_Stopping variable is set to True to tell the background threads that they need to terminate. The m_Random variable is an object of type Random that is used by the simulator to determine the amount of allowance transferred to the kids:

```
Public Class FamilyOperation
    Private Kids() As KidAccount
    Private Parent As ParentAccount

    Private Threads() As System.Threading.Thread

    Private m_NumberOfKids As Integer
    Private m_Stopping As Boolean

    Private m_Random As New Random()
```

The FamilyOperation object is designed so that you must set the NumberOfKids property before you attempt to run the simulator, but that once set, you may not change the value. The Get functionality is trivial—it simply returns the value of the internal m_NumberOfKids variable. The Set functionality first checks to see if the value is legal—only values between 1 and 50 are allowed. It also checks to see if the value is already set, raising an error if the m_NumberOfKids variable is already set.

The Throw method is the new and recommended way of raising errors in VB.NET. There are a number of different types of exceptions documented in the CLR. The two used here are the ArgumentOutOfRangeException used when a parameter or property value is invalid, and the InvalidOperationException, which indicates that you have attempted an invalid operation. You'll read more about exceptions shortly and learn about the new way of handling errors in Chapter 9.

If the error conditions do not apply, the method goes on to dimension and initialize the child accounts and the parent account as shown in Listing 7-5.

Listing 7-5. The FamilyOperation NumberOfKids property.

```
Property NumberOfKids() As Integer
    Get
        NumberOfKids = m_NumberOfKids
    End Get
    Set(ByVal Value As Integer)
        If Value < 1 Or Value > 50
            Throw New ArgumentOutOfRangeException(_
            "Property must be between 1 and 50")
        End If
        If m_NumberOfKids <> 0 Then
            Throw New InvalidOperationException(_
            "NumberOfKids may only be set once")
        End If
        Dim Kid As Integer
        m_NumberOfKids = Value
        ReDim Kids(m_NumberOfKids - 1)
        For Kid = 0 To m_NumberOfKids - 1
            Kids(Kid) = New KidAccount()
        Next
        Parent = New ParentAccount()
    End Set
End Property
```

The KillFamily method simply sets the m_Stopping variable to True, indicating to the threads that they should exit.[8] You'll see later in this chapter where this comes into play. The ParentPayday method is called to deposit money into the parent's account:

```
Private Sub KillFamily()
    m_stopping = True
End Sub

Public Sub ParentPayday(ByVal Amount As Double)
    Parent.DepositPayroll(Amount)
End Sub
```

8. Rest assured that no actual families were ever killed by this function.

The TotalDepositedToParent, TotalAllocatedByParent, and ParentBalance properties are used to obtain statistics about the parent account.

Logically, the following expression should always be true:

TotalDepositedToParent - TotalAllocatedByParent = ParentBalance

The code for these properties is shown in Listing 7-6.

Listing 7-6. The TotalDepositedToParent, TotalAllocatedByParent, and ParentBalance properties.

```
Public ReadOnly Property TotalDepositedToParent() As Double
    Get
        If m_NumberOfKids = 0 Then Return 0
        Return Parent.Deposited
    End Get
End Property


Public ReadOnly Property TotalAllocatedByParent() As Double
    Get
        If m_NumberOfKids = 0 Then Return 0
        Return Parent.Withdrawn
    End Get
End Property


Public ReadOnly Property ParentBalance() As Double
    Get
        If m_NumberOfKids = 0 Then Return 0
        Return Parent.Balance
    End Get
End Property
```

The TotalGivenToKids, TotalSpentByKids, TotalKidsBalances, and TotalFailedRequests properties are used to obtain aggregate statistics from all of the child accounts. Logically, the following expression should always be true:

TotalGivenToKids - TotalSpentByKids = TotalKidsBalances

The code for these properties is shown in Listing 7-7.

Listing 7-7. The KidsAccount aggregate properties.

```
Public ReadOnly Property TotalGivenToKids() As Double
    Get
        If m_NumberOfKids = 0 Then Return 0
        Dim idx As Integer
        Dim Total As Double
        For idx = 0 To m_NumberOfKids - 1
            Total = Total + Kids(idx).Deposited
        Next
        Return Total
    End Get
End Property


Public ReadOnly Property TotalSpentByKids() As Double
    Get
        If m_NumberOfKids = 0 Then Return 0
        Dim idx As Integer
        Dim Total As Double
        For idx = 0 To m_NumberOfKids - 1
            Total = Total + Kids(idx).Withdrawn
        Next
        Return Total
    End Get
End Property


Public ReadOnly Property TotalKidsBalances() As Double
    Get
        If m_NumberOfKids = 0 Then Return 0
        Dim idx As Integer
        Dim Total As Double
        For idx = 0 To m_NumberOfKids - 1
            Total = Total + Kids(idx).Balance
        Next
        Return Total
    End Get
End Property
```

```
Public ReadOnly Property TotalFailedRequests() As Double
    Get
        If m_NumberOfKids = 0 Then Return 0
        Dim idx As Integer
        Dim Total As Double
        For idx = 0 To m_NumberOfKids - 1
            Total = Total + Kids(idx).FailedRequests
        Next
        Return Total
    End Get
End Property
```

The KidsSpending method forms the heart of the simulator. It consists of a loop that runs continuously until the m_Stopping variable is set to True as shown in Listing 7-8. The simulator performs the following steps:

- It chooses a random child.

- It requests an "allowance" from the parent account. This will be a random value up to one dollar.

- It gives the amount retrieved to the selected child.

- The child is then given the opportunity to spend a random amount of money.

Listing 7-8. The KidsSpending function forms the heart of the simulator.

```
Public Sub KidsSpending()
    Dim ChildIndex As Integer
    Dim Allowance As Double
    Dim thiskid As KidAccount
    Do
        ' Random kid spends some money
        ChildIndex = CInt(Int(m_Random.NextDouble() _
        * CDbl(m_NumberOfKids)))
        thiskid = Kids(ChildIndex)

        Allowance = Parent.GiveAllowance()
        thiskid.GetAllowance(Allowance)

        thiskid.Spend()
    Loop Until m_Stopping

End Sub
```

Obviously, if you were to call that method from your main program, you would run into a serious problem. The function only returns when the m_Stopping variable is set to True, and there is nothing in the function itself that sets that variable. This method is designed to be called from an independent thread. When the method returns, the thread terminates.

The StartThreads method creates a specified number of new threads and starts them. It redimensions the Threads array and creates new Thread objects, each of which receives a delegate to the KidsSpending method.

Delegate?

You may be familiar with the AddressOf operator in VB6 as returning the address (a pointer) to a function in a module. In VB.NET, the AddressOf operator returns a delegate—best thought of as a pointer to a method in a particular object. In this case, it retrieves a pointer to the object's own KidsSpending method.[9]

Each thread invokes the KidsSpending method.

For the purposes of this example, the priority of each thread is set lower than the main user-interface thread. The reason for this is that if you leave the priority equal to the main thread, and launch more than a few threads that do a lot (and the KidsSpending method makes continuous use of the CPU), the performance of the main user-interface thread will be severely impacted since the user interface has equal priority to the CPU-intensive threads.

The IsBackground property is set to True to notify the CLR that the thread you created is intended to be a background thread and should be destroyed automatically if all nonbackground threads are terminated:[10]

```
Public Sub StartThreads(ByVal ThreadCount As Integer)
    If ThreadCount < 1 Then ThreadCount = 1
    ReDim Threads(ThreadCount - 1)
    Dim Idx As Integer
    For idx = 0 To ThreadCount - 1
        Threads(idx) = New Threading.Thread(AddressOf Me.KidsSpending)
        Threads(idx).Priority = _
        System.Threading.ThreadPriority.BelowNormal
        Threads(idx).IsBackground = True
        Threads(idx).Start()
    Next
End Sub
```

---

9. You might be wondering: is it possible to retrieve a delegate to a method in a different object and call it? The answer is yes. In fact, as you'll learn later, this is exactly how events work in VB.NET.

10. Of course, you should never rely on this. As shown in this example, you should always terminate your own background threads. This property just adds some insurance.

The StopThreads method introduces the new VB.NET mechanism for handling errors. The basic idea of killing threads is simple: you first call the KillFamily method, which sets the m_Stopping variable to True. All of the threads should then terminate when they reach the end of their Do loop. The Join() method of the Thread object forces the current thread to wait until the specified thread actually terminates.

In this particular example, the Join method should always work since the threads are started when they are created. But if you call the method before the Threads array is initialized, the GetUpperBound method will raise an exception. This will cause the method to jump directly to the block of code immediately following the Catch statement. In Listing 7-9, the error is simply ignored.

Listing 7-9. The StopThreads method.

```
Public Sub StopThreads()
    Dim Idx As Integer
    Try
        KillFamily() ' Should stop all threads
        For idx = 0 To Threads.GetUpperBound(0)
            ' Wait for thread to terminate
            Threads(idx).Join()
        Next
    Catch
        ' Ignore all errors
    End Try

End Sub

End Class
```

The simulator is not particularly robust in its design. Once stopped, it is assumed that you will create a new FamilyOperation object rather than try to restart the current one. And the error handling is minimal but it is sufficient to demonstrate the use of multithreading to perform background operations.

The simulator form has two text boxes that allow you to specify the number of child accounts and the number of threads. It has three buttons: one to deposit money, one to start the simulator, and one to stop it. It also has a listbox to display the results. The form has a single myFamily variable that references a FamilyOperation object. The StopThreads method is called before the form exits so that the background threads will be stopped even if the Stop button is not clicked:

```
Public Class Form1

    Dim myFamily As FamilyOperation

      'Form overrides dispose to clean up the component list.
       Public Overloads Overrides Sub Dispose()
        MyBase.Dispose()
        If Not (components Is Nothing) Then
            components.Dispose()
        End If
        ' Clean up threads here
        If Not myFamily Is Nothing Then
            myFamily.StopThreads()
        End I
   End Subf
```

The UpdateResults method shown in Listing 7-10 loads the listbox with statistics about the various accounts. Its primary purpose is to make sure that the total deposited less the total withdrawn is equal to the current balance (for both kids and adults).

Listing 7-10. The form's UpdateResults method.

```
Private Sub UpdateResults()
    lstResults.Items.Clear()
    lstResults.Items.Add("Parent:")
    lstResults.Items.Add("- Total Deposited: " + _
    Format(myFamily.TotalDepositedToParent, "0.00"))
    lstResults.Items.Add("- Total Withdrawn: " + _
    Format(myFamily.TotalAllocatedByParent, "0.00"))
    lstResults.Items.Add("- Expected Balance: " + _
    Format(myFamily.TotalDepositedToParent - _
    myFamily.TotalAllocatedByParent, "0.00"))
    lstResults.Items.Add("- Actual Balance: " + _
    Format(myFamily.ParentBalance, "0.00"))
    lstResults.Items.Add("Kids:")
    lstResults.Items.Add("- Total Deposited: " + _
    Format(myFamily.TotalGivenToKids, "0.00"))
    lstResults.Items.Add("- Total Withdrawn: " + _
    Format(myFamily.TotalSpentByKids, "0.00"))
    lstResults.Items.Add("- Expected Balance: " + _
    Format(myFamily.TotalGivenToKids - _
    myFamily.TotalSpentByKids, "0.00"))
    lstResults.Items.Add("- Actual Balance: " + _
    Format(myFamily.TotalKidsBalances, "0.00"))
End Sub
```

A timer displays the updated results in the listbox once every second or two. The Deposit button deposits the specified amount in the parent's account by calling the FamilyOperation.ParentPayday method. The Start button creates a new FamilyOperation object, sets its NumberOfKids property, and then calls the StartThreads method with the requested number of threads. The StopThreads method first stops the threads, then displays the final updated result in the listbox. Listing 7-11 contains the code that performs these operations.

Listing 7-11. The Threading1 form code.

```
Protected Sub Timer1_Tick(ByVal sender As Object, _
ByVal e As System.EventArgs) Handles timer1.Tick
    UpdateResults()
End Sub


Protected Sub cmdDeposit_Click(ByVal sender As Object, _
ByVal e As System.EventArgs) Handles cmdDeposit.Click
    Dim Amount As Double
    Amount = Val(txtDeposit.Text)
    myFamily.ParentPayday(Amount)
End Sub


Protected Sub cmdStart_Click(ByVal sender As Object, _
ByVal e As System.EventArgs) Handles cmdStart.Click
    myFamily = New FamilyOperation()
    Dim Kids As Integer
    Dim Threads As Integer

    Kids = CInt(Val(txtKids.Text))
    Threads = CInt(Val(txtThreads.Text))
    myFamily.NumberOfKids = Kids
    myFamily.StartThreads(Threads)
    lstresults.Items.Clear()
    Timer1.Enabled = True
    cmdStart.Enabled = False
    cmdStop.Enabled = True
    cmdDeposit.Enabled = True
End Sub
```

```
Protected Sub cmdStop_Click(ByVal sender As Object, _
ByVal e As System.EventArgs) Handles cmdStop.Click
    myFamily.StopThreads()
    cmdStop.Enabled = False
    cmdStart.Enabled = True
    cmdDeposit.Enabled = False
    UpdateResults()
End Sub

End Class
```

Testing the Simulator

To become familiar with the operation of the simulator, try an example with the default of ten kids and one thread. Click the Deposit button twenty or thirty times just to get a feel for how the money flows from the parent to the children and is then spent by the children. Figure 7-1 shows a typical simulator display.

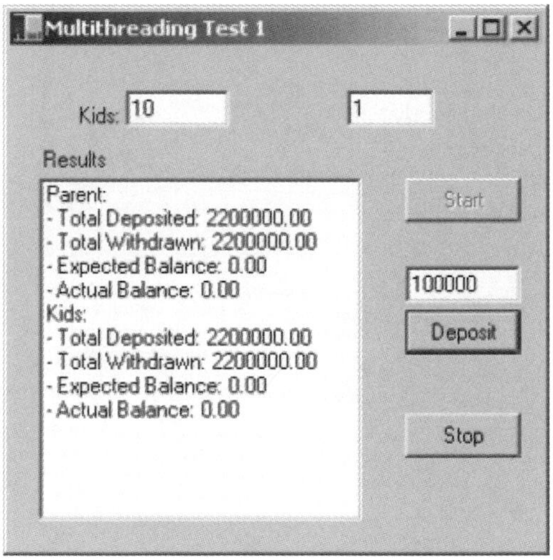

Figure 7-1. Simulator display with a single thread.

Now we've reached the moment of truth. Look over the sample program. Make sure you understand how it works.

Do you see what's wrong with it?

Try running the sample program with ten kids specified using ten background threads. Click on the Deposit button several times—depending on your system you may have to click it a few hundred times to see results similar to those shown in Figure 7-2.

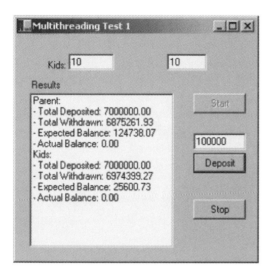

Figure 7-2. Example simulator display with multiple threads.

What went wrong?

Remember, what we are testing here is extremely simple. In the Account object you have two methods:

```
Protected Function Withdraw(ByVal amount As Double) As Double
    If amount > m_Account Then
        amount = m_Account
    End If
    m_Account = m_Account - amount
    m_Spent = m_Spent + amount
    Return amount
End Function

Protected Sub Deposit(ByVal amount As Double)
    m_Account = m_Account + amount
    m_Deposited = m_Deposited + amount
End Sub
```

And it is simple arithmetic to realize that the current account must always equal the amount deposited less the amount spent.

Yet in this example it doesn't.

The only way for it to fail would be if these extremely simple arithmetic operations were to fail. In other words, one or more of these lines must fail:

```
m_Account = m_Account - amount
m_Spent = m_Spent + amount
m_Account = m_Account + amount
m_Deposited = m_Deposited + amount
```

How is this possible?

Let's take a look at the Deposit method again but this time look at the intermediate language (IL) generated for the method as shown in Listing 7-12.[11]

Listing 7-12. Intermediate code for the Account Deposit method.

```
.method family instance void  Deposit(float64 amount) il managed
{
  // Code size       31 (0x1f)
  .maxstack  8
  IL_0000:  nop
  IL_0001:  ldarg.0
  IL_0002:  ldarg.0
  IL_0003:  ldfld      float64 Threading1.Account::m_Account
  IL_0008:  ldarg.1
  IL_0009:  add
  IL_000a:  stfld      float64 Threading1.Account::m_Account
  IL_000f:  ldarg.0
  IL_0010:  ldarg.0
  IL_0011:  ldfld      float64 Threading1.Account::m_Deposited
  IL_0016:  ldarg.1
  IL_0017:  add
  IL_0018:  stfld      float64 Threading1.Account::m_Deposited
  IL_001d:  nop
  IL_001e:  ret
} // end of method Account::Deposit
```

Now, I'm not going to try to teach you the IL language. For one thing, I don't know it. For another, you don't need it. But a bit of guesswork can go a long way towards understanding what is going on. The line:

```
m_Account = m_Account + amount
```

---

11. Obtained using the .NET disassembler. The controversies surrounding the relative ease of disassembling .NET applications (VB or C#) will be covered in Chapter 16.

…looks like it translates into something like:

```
IL_0001:  ldarg.0
IL_0002:  ldarg.0
IL_0003:  ldfld        float64 Threading1.Account::m_Account
IL_0008:  ldarg.1
IL_0009:  add
IL_000a:  stfld        float64 Threading1.Account::m_Account
```

This appears to be loading a pointer to the m_Account parameter into a stack twice. It then loads a register with the value of the top pointer. Next, it loads a pointer to the amount argument. It then adds the two. Finally, it stores the result into the m_Account variable, whose pointer remains on the stack (because it was loaded twice). This will probably make sense to those of you who have ever used RPN (Reverse Polish Notation) with an HP calculator.[12] For the rest of you, don't worry. You don't really need to know exactly what is happening here. All you need to know is that the following sequence is taking place:

- The m_Account variable is loaded into a register.

- The amount parameter is added to the register.

- The result is stored back into the m_Account variable

Here's the question: what happens if two threads just happen to attempt the same operation at the same time? You could have, for example, the following sequence:

1. Thread 1 loads m_Account into a register.

2. The operating system interrupts Thread 1.

3. Thread 2 loads m_Account into a register.

4. Thread 2 adds the amount parameter to the value in the register.

5. Thread 2 stores the result into the m_Account variable.

6. Thread 2 is interrupted.

---

12. Information on RPN can be found at http://www.hpmuseum.org/rpn.htm.

7. Thread 1 adds the amount parameter to the value in the register (which is restored to the value it contained before it was interrupted in step 2)— but note that the current contents of the register do not include the changes made by Thread 2!

8. Thread 1 stores the result of its addition into the m_Account variable, effectively wiping out the value stored by Thread 2.

Result: Two amounts were added to the m_Account variable but the variable only reflects the results of one of those operations!

In other words, because the operating system can perform a task switch at the assembly language-level (even lower than the IL level), you must assume that task switches may take place within individual lines of VB.NET code.

As currently implemented, the members of the Account object are shared among all of the threads of the application.

This is bad enough, but I'd like you to consider one more fact.

In order for the problem to occur here, a very precise combination of sequences of operations and thread switches must occur. What is the chance that this will occur considering that there are only a few places where a thread switch can cause this problem out of thousands of IL instructions?

Well, as you may recall, the allowance used in this example was between zero and one dollar. Assuming an average allowance of fifty cents, and that the error only occurred once to cause the erroneous results in this example, with seven million dollars shown as the transaction total, we're looking at one error in fourteen million executions.

How do you go about debugging code that is going to fail only once every fourteen million times it runs? Especially considering that the error can range from a few pennies vanishing in a banking program to someone dying if the code is running in a medical instrument (or extracting dosage information from a medical database).

I hope you now understand that my initial claim was not extreme at all. There is no upper limit to the potential costs of testing and debugging a multithreaded application.

Does this mean you should never use multithreading?

No.

It does mean that you should understand multithreading before you decide to use it. And it means that you must take the time to properly design your multithreaded application before you write any code. You must ruthlessly seek out any place where variables might be shared and decide how to handle it.

By the way, if you aren't nervous enough, here's one more item to chew on:

Most of the classes in the CLR are *not* thread safe. In other words, calling a CLR object from multiple threads can be just as deadly as accessing a shared variable from multiple threads. You'll read more about this later in the chapter.

Design: Your First Line of Defense

The Threading2 example does not provide a complete solution to the problems of the Threading1 application but it illustrates an approach that is important to understand. Multithreading problems result from access to shared variables by multiple threads. There are several approaches you can take to eliminate these problems:

- Eliminate global variables. If data is not shared among threads, there can be no conflict.

- Allow global variables but allow any given variable to be accessed by only one thread.

- Use synchronization to allow only one thread at a time to access shared data.

The Threading2 example focuses on the first two of these approaches. Instead of allowing each thread to access any of the child accounts, each thread is assigned to a single child account. Even though the child accounts remain shared, each one is accessed only by its assigned thread so no possibility of conflict arises.

In order to accomplish this, there must be a way for each thread to be able to identify itself. Unfortunately, there is no obvious way to pass a parameter to a new thread when it is launched. So, it is necessary to use a shared variable. In this case, the shared variable is the ThreadCounter variable, which is incremented as each thread is created.

Each thread must remember its thread number. This could be stored in a stack variable (for example, one of the KidsSpending method variables) but the Threading2 example shows another way to do this. The ThisThreadIndex variable is defined as shared, making it equivalent to a global variable (shared among all instances of the class, which is irrelevant considering that the application only uses a single instance of the class). But more important is the fact that the variable has an attribute attached. The ThreadStatic() attribute indicates that a separate copy of the variable is created for each thread in the application.[13] Sounds familiar? It should—that's what VB6 does with all global variables. This ability to maintain separate copies of variables for each thread is supported by the operating system using a feature called thread local storage, which is used when you specify the ThreadStatic attribute as well as by VB6 to store global variables.

As each thread is created and executes its KidsSpending method, its copy of the ThisThreadIndex variable is loaded with the current value of the ThreadCounter, which is then incremented.

---

13. Attributes are a *big* subject in .NET as you'll find out in Chapter 11. For now, think of it as a way to provide information to the CLR—in this case, information on how to compile this variable.

Well, actually, the ThreadCounter is first incremented and the ThisThreadIndex is set to one less the new value. As unlikely as it is, there is a possibility that the ThreadCounter variable itself could have a multithreading problem as the threads start up because ThreadCounter is itself shared among all of the threads. To eliminate the possibility of threads interfering with each other (say, two threads obtaining the same thread index), the ThreadCounter variable is incremented using the Threading.Interlocked.Increment method. This is a shared method[14] of the Threading.Interlocked class that performs an atomic increment operation—in other words, the OS cannot interrupt the process of incrementing the variable.[15]

The ThisThreadIndex variable will contain a unique thread number, which is used as an index into the Kids array as shown in Listing 7-13 and ensures that each child account will be accessed by one and only one thread.

Listing 7-13. The Threading2 KidsSpending method.

```
Private Shared ThreadCounter As Integer
<ThreadStatic ()> Private Shared  ThisThreadIndex As Integer

Public Sub KidsSpending()
    Dim Allowance As Double
    Dim thiskid As KidAccount
    ThisThreadIndex = Threading.Interlocked.Increment(ThreadCounter) - 1
    Do
        ' Each kid is managed by a single thread
        'ChildIndex = CInt(Int(m_Random.NextDouble() * _
        CDbl(m_NumberOfKids)))
        thiskid = Kids(ThisThreadIndex)

        Allowance = Parent.GiveAllowance()
        thiskid.GetAllowance(Allowance)

        thiskid.Spend()
    Loop Until m_Stopping

End Sub
```

---

14. Reminder: Shared methods belong to a class but not to a specific object of the class. They can be called without an object.

15. You might be wondering if the Interlocked.Increment method could have been used to correctly increment the m_Account variable in the Account class. The answer is no—this method only increments by one—but you're thinking in the right direction and I'll soon show you a way to apply that technique.

The end result of this change can be seen in Figure 7-3. After numerous clicks of the Deposit button, you'll see that the Parent object is still subject to multi-threading errors because it is still shared. However the Kids objects work correctly. Through this design change, they are effectively no longer shared variables.

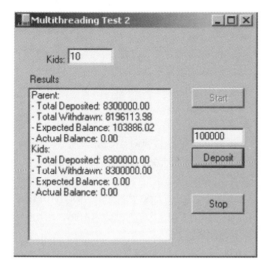

Figure 7-3. Threading2 simulation in action.

Why did I present you with an example that only solves part of the problem?

Because it explains a concept that is fundamental to COM and may be of significance when you start performing advanced operations with VB.NET including those relating to working with COM objects.

COM objects, due to their use of reference counting, are subject to multi-threading problems—the internal reference-count variables are common to all threads using an object. COM defines three different threading models: single threaded, apartment model threading (also known as STA or Single Threaded Apartment), and free threaded (also known as MTA or Multi-Threaded Apartment). The single threaded and apartment model threading approaches are based on the same solution shown here. By limiting all access to an object to the same thread that created the object, these models effectively eliminate threading problems because only one thread can access a given object (and all of its methods and properties).

So you see, VB6 really does a lot of work behind the scenes to make threading safe. It places all global variables into thread local storage (Thread Relative or Thread Static in .NET terms). And it enforces the apartment model for all objects, thus eliminating the need to worry about access by multiple threads on methods and properties.

VB.NET does not provide this safety by default. Thus, it is essential before you start creating threads that you understand how to add this safety to your own applications. The Threading2 example is a start. Let's look at the other tools available to you.

Multithreaded Design: Your Next Best Hope

If your first hope for avoiding multithreading problems is proper design, your second best hope is the proper use of synchronization tools to prevent multiple threads from accessing shared data simultaneously.

The Threading3 sample project shows a brute force approach in which an entire class is synchronized. This means that the methods and properties can only be accessed by one thread at a time. If you have any thread running any method or property in the class, no other thread can access any of the methods or properties of the class. The CLR will block that thread until the first thread exits from the method or property. This example is based on the Threading1 example (in other words, the threads choose random child accounts).

The sample code fragments shown in Listing 7-14 depict the changes to the Account and KidAccount classes.

Listing 7-14. Changes in the Threading3 sample to the Account and KidAccount classes.

```
Imports System.Runtime.Remoting
' Inherits ContextBoundObject
' And KidAccount is synchronized
Public Class Account
    Inherits ContextBoundObject

            .
            .
            .
            .

End Class


' Make the KidAccount synchronized to solve the access problem
<contexts.Synchronization ()> Public Class  KidAccount
    Inherits Account

            .
            .
            .
            .

End Class
```

The first change you'll see is that the Account class now inherits from ContextBoundObject. Originally, the class only inherited from Object (because every type in .NET inherits from object). By inheriting from ContextBoundObject (which, in turn, inherits from MarshalByRefObject and Object), this object inherits additional functionality that allows the CLR to associate a context with the object. A context, among other things, makes it possible to control access from outside of the context. Inheriting from ContextBoundObject has no impact on the Account object itself. But when the CLR runs the KidAccount class, it sees the Synchronization attribute, which tells it that access to the class is restricted to one thread at a time.

Figure 7-4 shows the results of running the Threading3 example after multiple Deposit operations.

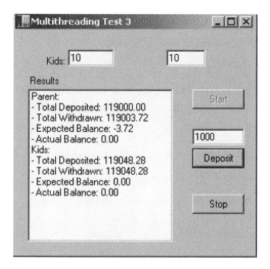

Figure 7-4. Threading3 simulation in action.

As with the Threading2 example, the child accounts work correctly because access to the KidAccount object is synchronized. Like before, the Parent account is not synchronized so it is still subject to multithreading errors as you can see. As you play with the example, you will notice one other fact: the program runs much more slowly than the other examples. I'll discuss general performance issues relating to multithreading later. In this example, the reason for the performance degradation is obvious—every time two threads try to access the same class, one of the threads is blocked. And blocking and restarting a thread is a time-consuming operation.

You already know that synchronization is only critical for two of the methods: Deposit and Withdraw. So, synchronizing all of the methods and properties is overkill and makes performance worse than it would be otherwise.

The brute force approach shown here should be avoided but does have the advantage of being easy to implement. You can simply synchronize all of your classes and be confident that you won't see any synchronization problems. That you may lose some of the benefits of multithreading is another issue.

In addition to the Synchronization attribute, you can give a class the ThreadAffinity attribute. Synchronization tells the CLR that an object can be accessed by any one thread at a time. The ThreadAffinity attribute tells the CLR that an object can only be accessed by the thread that created it—and the CLR will, if necessary, marshal information from one thread to another in order to allow one thread to access the methods and properties of an object that exists in the context of another thread. It's the same concept used in COM to implement the STA (Apartment model) of threading. You should also be aware that these attributes do not synchronize shared methods or properties that are common to all instances of a class.

Roll Your Own Synchronization

The Synchronization and ThreadAffinity attributes provide a simple technique to synchronize all of the methods and properties of a class. One way to measure the advisability of this approach could be found hidden in the beta documentation under the heading "Synchronization Concepts" where the following bullet appears:

- Great for naïve users.

I'm sure this leaves you with as much enthusiasm for this approach as it does me.

Sure, it's easy, but you will almost inevitably end up synchronizing members and properties that do *not* share any data and thus are safe to access without synchronization. The solution is to handle synchronization manually.

The Threading4 sample program illustrates one way to accomplish this using the new VB.NET SyncLock keyword. Behind the scenes, this keyword uses a type of object called a Monitor to synchronize blocks of code. Listing 7-15 shows the changes from the original Threading1 sample program.

Listing 7-15. Threading4 example changes from the Threading1 example.

```
Imports System.Runtime.Remoting
Public Class Account
    Protected m_Account As Double
    Protected m_Spent As Double
    Protected m_Deposited As Double
    Private Shared m_Random As New Random()

    Protected LockingObject As String = "HoldTheLock"
```

```
' Attempt to spend a requested amount of money, return
' the amount spent
Protected Function Withdraw(ByVal amount As Double) As Double
    SyncLock LockingObject
        If amount > m_Account Then
            amount = m_Account
        End If
        m_Account = m_Account - amount
        m_Spent = m_Spent + amount
    End SyncLock
    Return amount
End Function


Protected Sub Deposit(ByVal amount As Double)
    SyncLock LockingObject
        m_Account = m_Account + amount
        m_Deposited = m_Deposited + amount
    End SyncLock
End Sub
        .
        .
        .
        .

End Class
```

The SyncLock keyword takes as its parameter any Reference type object (so you can't use integers unless you box them onto the heap). You could just create an empty class and use it but I chose to use a string here to help identify the object.

When the SyncLock block is opened, the CLR checks to see if any other thread has a lock on the LockingObject variable. If not, the LockingObject variable is locked and the code is permitted to execute. When the SyncLock block ends, the LockingObject variable is unlocked. If, when the SyncLock statement is reached, the LockingObject variable is locked, the current thread is suspended and does not continue to execute until the thread that holds the lock on the object releases the lock.

The nice thing about this approach is that it's easy to implement, it is efficient, and it only synchronizes the code that accesses the shared variables in the Account class.

By synchronizing the base Account class (instead of the derived KidAccount and ParentAccount classes), both the child and parent accounts are correctly synchronized as shown in Figure 7-5.

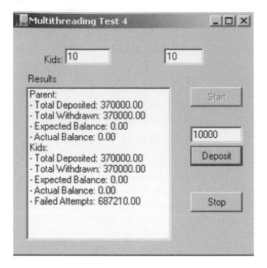

Figure 7-5. Threading4 simulation in action.

This example is very simple but it's worth exploring some of the situations that can arise in more complex scenarios:

What if you have two threads, Thread A and Thread B?

Thread A enters a SyncLock block and locks the LockingObject variable.

Thread B tries to enter a SyncLock block and fails because the LockingObject variable is set.

Meanwhile, Thread A, still in the SyncLock block, starts waiting for an operation that must be performed by Thread B.[16]

Thread A is waiting for Thread B but Thread B is suspended until Thread A ends it's SyncLock on the LockingObject. The result: neither thread can run.

This is called a deadlock. It occurs anytime two threads are suspended waiting for each other or (in more complex scenarios) when a series of threads are waiting in a chain for each other.[17]

Another issue to consider is whether the LockingObject variable should be shared or not. If it were shared, all instances of objects derived from the Account class would be synchronized to each other. This is overkill in this case, because the problems with this application are due to simultaneous access of Object variables of a specific object instance from different threads. However, if the object had any shared variables or Static methods, synchronizing to a shared Object variable would be necessary.

---

16. There are any number of situations where one thread performs services for another. Perhaps Thread B is responsible for a background operation. Or, it contains a class with ThreadAffinity set that must be accessed from that thread.

17. One computer science maxim says, "If deadlock can occur, it will."

Synchronization and Waiting

If you look closely at Figure 7-5, you'll see a new entry at the bottom of the listbox that shows the number of failed attempts. This displays the sum of the m_FailedRequcsts variables for each child object. In other words, this value is incremented every time a child wants to spend money but finds that they don't have any in their account.[18]

If you look again at the KidsSpending method that is performing the simulation as shown in Listing 7-16, you'll see an infinite loop that continues to try to spend money even if the account is empty.

Listing 7-16. The Threading4 KidsSpending method.

```
Public Sub KidsSpending()
      Dim ChildIndex As Integer
      Dim Allowance As Double
      Dim thiskid As KidAccount
      Do
          ' Random kid spends some money
          ChildIndex = CInt(Int(m_Random.NextDouble() _
          * CDbl(m_NumberOfKids)))
          thiskid = Kids(ChildIndex)

          Allowance = Parent.GiveAllowance()
          thiskid.GetAllowance(Allowance)

          thiskid.Spend()
      Loop Until m_Stopping

   End Sub
```

You can see one of the side effects of this approach by looking at the task manager while the program is running.

Anytime you see a process that has a CPU load of 99%, as you do in Figure 7-6, you know you have problems. And indeed, this sample program eats up every spare CPU cycle and slows down system performance considerably. In short, it's a terrible design.

---

18. The large number is an artifact of the huge number of operations performed by this simulator in order to illustrate synchronization problems—unless you're a parent, in which case the number will look perfectly reasonable.

```
Windows Task Manager                              _ |□| x|
File  Options  View  Help

Applications  Processes  Performance

  Image Name          PID   CPU   CPU Time   Mem Usage ▲
  explorer.exe        520    00    0:00:09     3,072 K
  msdtc.exe           532    00    0:00:00     4,624 K
  lissrv.exe          664    00    0:00:00     2,028 K
  tcpsvcs.exe         692    00    0:00:00     2,584 K
  sfmprint.exe        708    00    0:00:00     2,476 K
  photopnt.exe        772    00    0:00:08     1,712 K
  mdm.exe             792    00    0:00:00     2,936 K
  sqlservr.exe        832    00    0:00:00     6,604 K
  regsvc.exe          860    00    0:00:00       756 K
  mstask.exe          876    00    0:00:00     2,888 K
  WinMgmt.exe         900    00    0:00:15       152 K
  dfssvc.exe          960    00    0:00:00     1,264 K
  inetinfo.exe        976    00    0:00:01     9,252 K
  sfmsvc.exe         1044    00    0:00:00     1,324 K
  tp4mon.exe         1232    00    0:00:00     1,040 K
  svchost.exe        1376    00    0:00:00     2,764 K
  devenv.exe         1404    00    0:00:21    39,204 K
  Threading4.exe     1408    99    0:02:29    13,680 K
  taskmgr.exe        1412    01    0:00:00     2,160 K  ▼

                                          End Process

Processes: 30    CPU Usage: 100%    Mem Usage: 133376K / 471244K
```

Figure 7-6. Impact of the threading simulator on system performance.

What you really want is for the simulator to be smart enough to wait for money to appear in a child's account before it tries to spend money. One of the nice things about a multithreaded application is that it is possible to suspend individual threads without stopping the entire program. For example, you can suspend a background thread and not impact the user interface. In fact, a suspended thread that is in a wait mode (such as one waiting for an object locked by a SyncLock call) has virtually no impact on system performance.

The Threading5 sample program addresses this issue. But before looking at that, take a quick look at the following listing that modifies the Account class to use a Mutex object instead of a SyncLock block to synchronize the code.

Listing 7-17. The Threading5 example Account class.

```
Public Class Account
    Protected m_Account As Double
    Protected m_Spent As Double
    Protected m_Deposited As Double
    Private Shared m_Random As New Random()
```

```
Protected myMutex As New Threading.Mutex()
Protected Shared MoneyAvailable As New Threading.ManualResetEvent(False)
    .
    .
    .

Property Deposited() As Double
    Get
        Deposited = m_Deposited
    End Get
    Set
        m_Deposited = Value
    End Set
End Property


' Attempt to spend a requested amount of money, return
' the amount spent
Protected Function Withdraw(ByVal amount As Double) As Double
    Try
        myMutex.WaitOne()
    Catch e As Threading.ThreadInterruptedException
        Return 0
    End Try        If amount > m_Account Then
        amount = m_Account
    End If
    m_Account = m_Account - amount
    m_Spent = m_Spent + amount
    myMutex.ReleaseMutex()
    Return amount
End Function


Protected Sub Deposit(ByVal amount As Double)
    Try
        myMutex.WaitOne()
    Catch e As Threading.ThreadInterruptedException
        Return 0
    End Try        m_Account = m_Account + amount
    m_Deposited = m_Deposited + amount
    myMutex.ReleaseMutex()
End Sub


End Class
```

What is the difference between using the SyncLock approach and a Mutex? In this case, none whatsoever. A Mutex object provides more flexibility in some situations because it is possible to perform wait operations on more than one Mutex at a time. The code was changed in this example only to illustrate that there are other synchronization objects available. An error handler prevents a runtime error from occurring if the thread is interrupted (which will be important as you will see shortly). You should take the time to read the reference material for the System.Threading namespace and familiarize yourself with the various synchronization objects and how they work before you begin to work extensively with multithreading.[19]

The Account class also defines a shared ManualResetEvent object. This object uses Win32 synchronization events (which have nothing to do with the normal term "event" in Visual Basic). This object is shared because the presence of money in this simulation is common to all of the child objects:[20]

```
Protected Shared MoneyAvailable As New Threading.ManualResetEvent(False)
```

The Spend method of the KidAccount class looks to see if the amount available is zero. If so, it calls the MoneyAvailable.WaitOne() method. This method causes the thread to suspend and wait for the ManualResetEvent object to be set by a different thread.

The Wait operation is in a Try block. This is because there are scenarios where the wait can be aborted by the simulator; specifically, when the application is about to terminate, it must interrupt any waiting threads so that the application can exit cleanly.[21] Listing 7-17 depicts how the KidAccount class uses the MoneyAvailable mutex.

---

19. Why don't I cover them all here? Because my purpose is to teach you the concepts behind multithreading and to help you learn to design multithreaded applications in VB.NET with reasonable safety. Rehashing the specifics of synchronization objects that are already well documented has little benefit. One hint: don't limit yourself to the documentation on the object. Look also at the Win32 platform SDK documentation for the underlying synchronization APIs, which goes into more depth on how the various objects work.

20. A cleaner design would associate the ManualResetEvent object with a Parent object, and associate KidAccount objects with a specific ParentAccount object. While it doesn't matter for this simple simulator, it is the kind of issue you would consider when designing class hierarchies for reuse.

21. The threads in this simulator have their IsBackground property set to True so they won't hold the application open once the main application thread terminates. But it's practice to exit all threads before your application terminates rather than counting on the whims of the CLR to do it for you.

Listing 7-17. The Threading5 KidAccount class.

```vbnet
' Make the KidAccount synchronized to solve the access problem
Public Class KidAccount
    Inherits Account

    .

    .

    .


    ' Tries to spend a random amount of money
    Public Sub Spend()
        Dim amount As Double
        ' Always wait until money is available
        ' What would happen if we held the mutex here?
        Try
            If m_Account = 0 Then MoneyAvailable.WaitOne()
        Catch
            ' Interrupt on termination
            Exit Sub
        End Try

        amount = GetRandomAmount()
        If amount > m_Account Then amount = m_Account
        If amount = 0 Then
            m_FailedRequests = m_FailedRequests + 1
        Else
            Withdraw(amount)
        End If
    End Sub
End Sub

End Class
```

The MoneyAvailable ManualResetEvent object is controlled by the parent account. When it attempts to give an allowance and finds that the balance is zero, the MoneyAvailable object is reset, meaning that it is not signaled. When a ManualResetEvent object is signaled, all threads waiting on that object are permitted to run (for example, the wait condition is satisfied). When it is reset to the unsignaled state as done in Listing 7-18, any thread attempting to wait on the ManualResetEvent object will be suspended until it is signaled. The DepositPayroll method sets the ManualResetEvent object to the signaled state, notifying any waiting threads that money is available to spend.

Listing 7-18. The Threading5 ParentAccount class.

```
Public Class ParentAccount
    Inherits Account

    ' When called, the Parent Account picks a random allowance
    ' and gives it.
    Public Function GiveAllowance() As Double
        Dim amount As Double
        amount = GetRandomAmount()
        amount = Withdraw(amount)
        ' Return amount actually withdrawn (may be 0)
        ' If no money is left, stop the process
        ' Note there is still a subtle synchronization bug -
        ' do you see it?
        If m_Account = 0 Then MoneyAvailable.Reset()
        Return (amount)
    End Function


    Public Sub DepositPayroll(ByVal amount As Double)
        deposit(amount)
        ' Set event - let kids know money is available
        MoneyAvailable.Set()
    End Sub
End Class
```

In order to allow the application to shut down cleanly, the StopThreads method has also been modified. If the thread is detected as currently waiting (see Listing 7-19), it is interrupted using the Threads.Interrupt method. This causes an exception to be raised at the point of the wait operation, which (in this example) is caught and ignored.

Listing 7-19. The Threading5 StopThreads method.

```
Public Sub StopThreads()
    Dim Idx As Integer
    Try
        KillFamily() ' Should stop all threads
        For idx = 0 To Threads.GetUpperBound(0)
            ' Wait for thread to terminate
            ' Still potential for rare termination synchronization
            ' problem -
            ' what if it enters wait state after this comparison?
```

```
            If (Threads(idx).ThreadState And _
                System.Threading.ThreadState.WaitSleepJoin) <> 0 Then
                    Threads(idx).Interrupt()
                End If
            Threads(idx).Join()
        Next
    Catch
        ' Ignore all errors
    End Try


End Sub
```

The results of these changes can be seen in Figure 7-7.

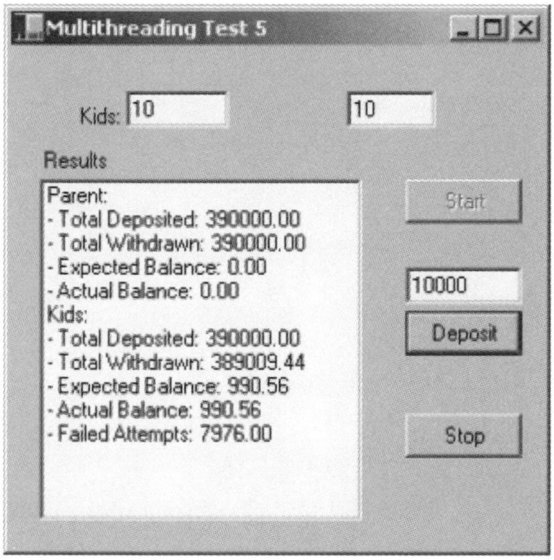

Figure 7-7. The Threading5 simulator in action.

As you can see, the number of failed attempts is much lower. Failed requests do occur during the natural operation of the simulator but once the parent's money is gone and all of the child threads enter the wait state, the attempts stop. If you look at the task manager while this program running, you'll see that during idle times the CPU load is zero.

More Synchronization Subtleties

Earlier in this chapter, I told you that I would be taking the somewhat unusual approach of showing you bad code examples—the intent being to help you understand the kinds of problems that can occur. So far, we've focused entirely on the shared variables in the Account class and on the use of synchronization for waiting. However, the Threading5 sample program is a great illustration of the subtle problems that can potentially occur in the process of adding synchronization to an application.

Which Thread Is Stopped?

The Threading5 example is built on the Threading1 example in which the simulator code is shown in Listing 7-20.

Listing 7-20. The Threading5 KidsSpending method.

```
Public Sub KidsSpending()
    Dim ChildIndex As Integer
    Dim Allowance As Double
    Dim thiskid As KidAccount
    Do
        ' Random kid spends some money
        ChildIndex = CInt(Int(m_Random.NextDouble() * _
        CDbl(m_NumberOfKids)))
        thiskid = Kids(ChildIndex)

        Allowance = Parent.GiveAllowance()
        If (Not m_Stopping) Then thiskid.GetAllowance(Allowance)

        thiskid.Spend()
    Loop Until m_Stopping

End Sub
```

One change is that the m_Stopping flag is tested before calling the GetAllowance method. This is necessary because there is a chance that the GiveAllowance function returned because its thread was interrupted. In that case, calling GetAllowance would cause the thread to be blocked again on a mutex. However, this time it would not be interrupted—thus leading to a potential deadlock state as the main thread waited forever for the thread to terminate.

Onto another subject. As you recall, each thread chooses a random child account each time through the loop. The way the code is structured here, when a child has a zero balance, the thread that is calling that object will be suspended. But since the child accounts are chosen randomly, it is very possible for two or more threads to be blocked while accessing the same child object, while other child objects are not accessed at all. In fact, once the parent account is empty, the chances that free threads will happen to call those children that still have money become increasingly slim as the child accounts run out of money. So, it is virtually certain that many of the child accounts will not have all their money spent when all of the threads become suspended. This is evident from Figure 7-7 that shows money still being held in the child accounts even after the threads are suspended waiting for a parent deposit.

How to fix this?

You could, in the KidsSpending routine, never try to spend money if a child's account balance is zero.

The Surprise Shared Variable

It should already be clear that synchronization problems are caused by access to shared data from multiple threads. Take a close look at the code in Listing 7-21 from the ParentAccount class (which contains a nonsubtle hint to the problem).

Listing 7-21. The Threading5 GiveAllowance and DepositPayroll methods revisited.

```
Public Function GiveAllowance() As Double
    Dim amount As Double
    amount = GetRandomAmount()
    amount = Withdraw(amount)
    ' Return amount actually withdrawn (may be 0)
    ' If no money is left, stop the process
    ' Note there is still a subtle synchronization bug -
    ' do you see it?
    If m_Account = 0 Then MoneyAvailable.Reset()
    Return (amount)
End Function



Public Sub DepositPayroll(ByVal amount As Double)
    deposit(amount)
    ' Set event - let kids know money is available
    MoneyAvailable.Set()
End Sub
```

Do you see it?

Consider this sequence:

- A thread calls the DepositPayroll method.

- A second thread is still running (even though the parent is out of money, there is a finite time where the other threads continue to run because the children are not out of money). That thread simultaneously calls the GiveAllowance method.

- The second thread is interrupted right after doing the test for m_Account = 0.

- The first thread continues running the DepositPayroll method and executes the Deposit method and sets the MoneyAvailable ManualResetEvent object.

- The second thread then proceeds to reset the MoneyAvailable ManualResetEvent object.

If this occurs, child accounts may be suspended unnecessarily.

The chances of this happening are very small—so small that the chances of seeing this problem with this simulator are virtually nil (assuming you'd even be able to detect it from the simulator). But it is possible.

Why does this problem occur?

Because the ManualResetEvent object, MoneyAvailable, is itself a shared variable that can be accessed by multiple threads at once!

That's right. Just because you are using a variable for synchronization purposes doesn't protect it from having its own synchronization problems! If it's a shared variable (as synchronization objects usually are), you may need to use another synchronization method (such as a SyncLock block) to restrict access to that object and the code it is controlling in order to prevent it from creating its own synchronization problems.

In this case, if you placed the comparison line in the GiveAllowance method and both lines of the DepositPayroll method in a SyncLock block (using the same variable), you would avoid this potential problem.

The Termination Problem

Let's take another look at the modified StopThreads routine shown in Listing 7-22.

Listing 7-22. The Threading5 StopThreads routine revisted.

```
Public Sub StopThreads()
    Dim Idx As Integer
    Try
        KillFamily() ' Should stop all threads
        For idx = 0 To Threads.GetUpperBound(0)
            ' Wait for thread to terminate
            ' Still potential for rare termination synchronization
            ' problem -
            ' what if it enters wait state after this comparison?
```

```
            If (Threads(idx).ThreadState And _
                System.Threading.ThreadState.WaitSleepJoin) <> 0 Then
                    Threads(idx).Interrupt()
                End If
            Threads(idx).Join()
        Next
    Catch
        ' Ignore all errors
    End Try


End Sub
```

and the Spent function...

```
Public Sub Spend()
    Dim amount As Double
    ' Always wait until money is available
    ' What would happen if we held the mutex here?
    Try
        If m_Account = 0 Then MoneyAvailable.WaitOne()
    Catch
        ' Interrupt on termination
        Exit Sub
    End Try
    .
    .
    .
```

Consider the following scenario:

- The StopThreads method is called as one thread is in the Spend method and the m_Account member is zero (the child is out of money). The parent is out of money as well so the MoneyAvailable ManualResetEvent object is reset.

- The system switches from the thread in the Spend method to the one running StopThreads.

- The StopThreads method performs its comparison and finds that the thread is not waiting so it skips down to the Join method and waits for the thread to terminate.

- The system switches back to the thread in the Spend method, which detects that the account is empty and calls the WaitOne method to suspend the thread.

- The StopThreads thread is suspended with the Join method waiting for the thread in the Spend method to terminate. But that thread is suspended waiting for money to be available. The result is a deadlock—the application will never terminate.

Again, this is a very subtle problem that is extremely unlikely to happen. Again, it results from the fact that the synchronization objects (both the MoneyAvailable and the Thread object itself) are shared.

The solution here is trickier.

You might try this: SyncLock the Spend method call in the KidsSpending routine. Then put a test for the m_Stopping variable before calling the Spend method as shown here:

```
Public Sub KidsSpending()
        .
        .
        .
        SyncLock someobject
            If Not m_Stopping Then thiskid.Spend()
        End SyncLock
    Loop Until m_Stopping
```

Also place a SyncLock block inside the KillFamily function call.

This prevents the m_Stopping variable from being set to True if the Spend method is being run. Once KillFamily is called successfully, the thiskid.Spend method won't be able to be called because the test against m_Stopping and the Spend call are in the same SyncLock block.

Unfortunately, this solution will lead to a deadlock as threads waiting on the MoneyAvailable ManualResetEvent object hold the lock and prevent not only KillFamily from running but every other thread from running as it tries to call Spend.

Frankly, I don't see a particularly clean solution to this one using the Account classes as written.[22] One approach would be to put a timeout on the Join call. When an exception is raised, find the suspended thread, interrupt it, and reenter the Join. It's messy but it will work.

A better solution is to redesign the Account classes so that they have their own Interrupt methods. When called on a thread, the object would not only exit the current wait in progress but would set a flag (properly synchronized of course) so that the instance could not reenter a wait under any circumstances.

In other words, multithreading does not lend itself to hacked code that evolves. If you see yourself facing these subtle synchronization problems and having a

---

22. Your suggestions are welcome.

hard time seeing how to solve them, it's a good bet that you should go back and take a hard look at your design.

Multithreading also does not lend itself well to normal testing. All but the first of the problems described in this section are only potential problems that are extremely unlikely to happen. The only reason I know about them is because I looked closely at the code and asked myself, "What if…" If you are going to be doing free threading, get used to the idea that you will have to look carefully at your code and at every line (as well as within every line) where threads may interact through shared variables or methods. You'll need to use the best debugger ever created to detect, anticipate and solve these problems—the debugger that exists in your mind.

Remember the Finalizers

It's not an issue in this example because none of the classes here use finalizers but remember, if you are using a finalizer, finalizers run in their own thread. It's safest to assume that your finalizer code can be called as if it were a free-threaded method. The good news being, of course, that you can assume no other methods of that particular object instance will be called at the same time—if they were callable, your object's finalizer would not be running. So, you really only need concern yourself with global or shared variables and not Member variables of the object.

Random Is as Random Does

I leave this section with one last potential problem that you probably never thought of. There is one more shared variable in this application. In the Account class, you'll find the following line:

```
Private Shared m_Random As New Random()
```

Yep, we used a single, random-number generator object to generate all of our random numbers. This object can be shared by all instances of the class on any thread.

Now, who said that this object is thread safe?

I didn't.

Nothing in the documentation suggests that it is thread safe.

That's right folks—burn this thought into your mind right now:

Many of the CLR classes are *not* thread safe.

The documentation of which are thread safe and which are not is unclear at this time. Hopefully, Microsoft will document this for each class. I know that the Console class is thread safe.

I'm virtually certain that the Random class is not. Why? Because the following line2 of code:

```
Dim amount As Double
amount = int(m_Random.NextDouble * 100)
```

...results, once in a very rare while, in an overflow error.

How is it possible for this to cause an overflow error if the m_Random.NextDouble property always returns a value between zero and one? Answer: it can't—unless the m_Random.NextDouble returns a number outside that range. This can be caused by either a bug in the random number generated (possible) or by data corruption caused by it not being thread safe (likely). I've only seen this happen twice in many hours of testing—so, again, you see evidence that it is essential to design multithreading bugs out of your application. You can't test them out.

Forms and controls are not thread safe either. You'll learn in Chapter 13 how to safely access the members of a form from another thread in an application.

The Benefits of Multithreading

Having spent this entire chapter explaining the difficulties and risks of multi-threading, it would not surprise me if most readers are ready to throw up their hands in surrender and swear never to attempt multithreaded programming regardless of any presumed benefits. While that was not exactly my intent, I believe it is preferable to risk having you feel that way as compared to the blind enthusiasm that often results from the more common approach of discussing multithreading in glowing terms—as a feature that ensures huge performance benefits.

However, now that you are familiar with the risks of multithreading, especially free threading, it is essential to understand exactly why multithreading has value. That way, you will be able to evaluate whether multithreading can bring about performance benefits for your specific applications and whether those benefits justify the increased development and testing costs incurred when multithreading is used.

It is very difficult to gauge the benefits of multithreading without understanding the environment in which software will be running. Applications have different issues than components. Components have different issues depending on the host application. Even a component that does not itself create and use threads may need to be thread safe to be used effectively from a free-threaded client.

It is beyond the scope of this book to go into the specific issues related to even common environments under Windows. Fortunately, the issues that come up when evaluating a specific environment invariably relate to a few fundamental benefits of multithreading, which we can discuss here.

Efficient Wait States

The Threading5 sample application illustrates one of the simplest and most useful features of multithreading: the ability of a background thread to enter a highly efficient wait state. Windows supports built-in background operations for many operations such as data transfers over files or sockets (network) and allows a thread to wait for these operations to complete. It provides the capability for a thread to wait for other operations such as the end of a timer interval or the termination of a thread or process. Single threaded applications and components cannot make the best use of these features because if the main thread of an application is allowed to be suspended, the operation of the application or component can be severely impaired. For example, the user interface of such an application would freeze. So, these applications must use a timer and poll the object for completion—an approach that works but is potentially very inefficient.

Visual Basic 6 handles this situation poorly. While ActiveX EXE-based applications can create new threads, method calls to these objects are generally synchronous. This means that if an ActiveX EXE object thread is suspended, it can't return to the calling method, thus blocking the client as well (and often resulting in an OLE Automation timeout). ActiveX DLL components in Visual Basic 6 cannot safely create their own background threads so performing a wait operation ends up suspending the client application thread.[23]

Under VB.NET, you can simply spawn a new thread object, have it perform a wait operation (thus entering a highly efficient wait state), and have it raise an event when the wait is complete.

The nice thing about this approach is that the threads created for this purpose are generally simple and pose few synchronization problems. The main thread sets up the requested operation and launches the new thread. The slave thread performs the requested operation, and then waits for the result. When done, the slave thread can raise an event or set a flag indicating that the operation is complete. It can then terminate, leaving the main thread to pick up the information at its convenience. Generally speaking, the main thread sets up any shared data before even starting the slave thread—so synchronization problems are unlikely. The main thread shouldn't access the shared data until the background thread signals that the data is ready. As long as you use reasonable care, you should not see any synchronization problems with this type of operation. The only trick is to remember to interrupt any waiting threads and allow them to terminate when your component is being disposed.

---

23. I must note at this point that users of Desaware's SpyWorks have long had access to a background-threading component that makes it easy to perform this type of wait operation and generic background operations using Visual Basic 6.

Background Operations

From a conceptual point of view, the idea of background operations is simple. Certainly the threading simulator programmers in this chapter are clear demonstrations of generic background operations using multithreading. The Threading5 example illustrates how Wait operations can benefit from multithreading. Background operations are just an extension of this idea. If your application or component needs to perform a long operation such as a file transfer or an upload, it would be disastrous, in most cases, to perceived performance to have the application wait for that operation to complete. Consider a word processor—it is acceptable to have the user wait while performing a requested file save operation. But an automatically triggered backup operation that freezes the user interface periodically is very annoying. From background printing to spreadsheet recalculations to complex drawings to network transfers—the ability to perform tasks in the background are essential to a modern application. As you will soon read, it is also essential to applications and services that provide features to clients.

The difficulty of implementing this type of multithreading safely depends on the complexity of the application or component and the background operation.

Efficient Client Access

Consider an Internet Web server: it may receive requests from hundreds of different clients. If it could only service one request at a time, performance could be severely impacted. These applications rely on the ability to maintain a pool of threads, and handle a request on an available thread, preventing a single client from blocking the entire service. Note that I wrote "could be" and not "would be." As you'll soon see, the question of multithreading, even in server scenarios, is not obvious or trivial.

One of the major reasons that Visual Basic programmers have long wanted free threading is because services like Internet Information Server (IIS) work best with free-threaded components. Here's why.

Every Web request that comes in to IIS is separate from every other. In order for a Web site to perform anything other than the simplest page view, it needs a way to preserve information (maintain state) between requests from the same user. There are a number of ways to accomplish this, which I won't go into here, but suffice to say that IIS makes it possible for Web-based applications to store information between Web requests. This means, for example, that you can create a Web application that reads information from a database, generates a form, and sends it out to the user. When a request comes back from the same user, the application can continue to run, receiving and processing the request. IIS can help preserve state so that the Web application you write can store information between the time the form is sent out and the time the filled-out form is returned from the user.

In order to work in the most efficient possible manner, IIS likes to assign each request to any available thread.

What happens if your Web application uses a Visual Basic 6 object and requests IIS to store it?

That object is an Apartment Threaded object—meaning that all method and property calls to that thread must occur on the same thread that created the object. If IIS is holding such an object, it must make sure that all requests for that session (the particular user running that particular application) must go to the same thread. What if that thread is busy handling someone else's long operation? The incoming request must then wait until that thread is available.

Now, this is not a terribly fatal situation by any means. It's just usually not as good as if the object had been free threaded. IIS has to put in extra work to keep track of the thread for each object and perform the necessary thread switches.

This scenario can potentially apply to any application or service that handles multiple clients, including business services or components that you have implemented on a server.

The difficulty of implementing this type of multithreading depends on whether you are implementing the server or a component used by the server.

If you are implementing a server that supports multiple clients on a thread pool, you have several concerns:

- You must correctly implement the thread pool with special attention to synchronizing allocation and deal location of threads to clients.

- You must take special care of common functionality or data that is shared among the threads in the thread pool.

- You must take care to isolate the threads or synchronize those areas where threads are allowed to interact with each other.

With regard to components used by these servers, you should become familiar with the requirements and restrictions imposed by the server. If you know that the server is multithreaded and expects components to be free threaded, you must be sure that any Public method and property of your component can be safely called at any time on any thread. If your component can raise events to the server, you should know whether it is safe to raise that event on any thread or if there are any restrictions.

Unfortunately, there is a tendency among many programmers to assume that multithreading is necessary for all client-server type applications (which is another term that describes this scenario). This deserves a closer look.

Evaluating Multithreaded Performance

One of my favorite misquotes goes as follows:

"There are lies, damn lies, and benchmarks."[24]

I believe this is true. Benchmarking is very hard to do correctly and easy to manipulate. If the results of the 2000 presidential election were based on benchmarking instead of the relatively accurate punch card ballots used in Palm Beach, we'd still be waiting for the courts to figure out the results.

In a conference session I used to present on relating to multithreading and scalability, I used a theoretical argument to show that multithreading is not always the best approach for a server application that must support multiple clients. In fact, it can lead to reduced performance in many situations.

This time, since VB.NET does support multithreading, I decided instead to show a practical demonstration of this fact. The numbers you will see later in this chapter are all real results. They are also lies in the sense that you will never be able to reproduce them—there are far too many factors involved. Your machine system is different, your OS is configured differently and you may have other applications running at the same time that will impact these numbers. Still, they are good enough to illustrate the points.

The ThreadPerformance Sample Program

To begin with, the ThreadPerformance sample defines a class named WorkerThread that performs various tasks on request of a client. This class also has the ability to measure the duration of the operation. A System.TimeSpan object is defined by the CLR as an object that contains a measure of time and is great for measuring time differences. The ElapsedTimeForCall property returns a reference to the current TimeSpan object.

A variable called LongDuration is set to True to increase the length of the requested operation. The program uses this to experiment with a mix of different length operations:

---

24. My editor wanted an attribution to this quote. Mark Twain once said, "There are lies, damn lies, and statistics"—but I'm sure Twain would have used benchmarks if computers had existed when he was around.

```
Imports System.Threading

Public Class WorkerThread
    Private myTimeSpan As TimeSpan
    Public ReadOnly Property ElapsedTimeForCall() As TimeSpan
        Get
            Return myTimeSpan
        End Get
    End Property


    Public LongDuration As Boolean
```

The WorkingOperation method simulates a CPU-intensive operation by performing a very long loop. It sets the TimeSpan object initially to the current time, then subtracts the time at the end of the operation. It is intended to be called on each object in an independent thread, allowing us to measure the performance achieved by handling multiple clients on independent threads:

```
Public Sub WorkingOperation()
    Dim counter As Long
    Dim upperlimit As Long
    Dim temp As Long
    myTimespan = TimeSpan.FromTicks(DateTime.Now.Ticks)
    upperlimit = 50000000
    If LongDuration Then upperlimit = 5 * upperlimit
    For counter = 1 To upperlimit
        temp = 5
    Next
    myTimespan = _
    TimeSpan.FromTicks(DateTime.Now.Ticks).Subtract(myTimespan)
End Sub
```

The SynchronousRequest method separates the setting of the myTimespan variable from the operation itself. This is necessary because the SynchronousOperation method for each object will be called in sequence, allowing us to measure the performance of a single thread handling a series of client requests in turn. We're therefore interested in the elapsed time from the start of the first operation, not the time for each one. Otherwise, the SynchronousOperation method is identical to the WorkingOperation method:

```
Public Sub SynchronousRequest()
    myTimespan = TimeSpan.FromTicks(DateTime.Now.Ticks)
End Sub

Public Sub SynchronousOperation()
    Dim counter As Long
    Dim upperlimit As Long
    Dim temp As Long
    upperlimit = 50000000
    If LongDuration Then upperlimit = 5 * upperlimit
    For counter = 1 To upperlimit
        temp = 5
    Next
    myTimespan = _
    TimeSpan.FromTicks(DateTime.Now.Ticks).Subtract(myTimespan)
End Sub
```

The SleepingOperation and SleepingSynchronous methods are similar to
the previous operations except that the client request is not CPU intensive (see
Listing 7-23). These methods measure the performance of a client request that
performs a file, database, or network operation that is perhaps I/O intensive but
does not tie up the CPU.

*Listing 7-23. The WorkerThread module's SleepingOperation and
SleepingSynchronous methods.*

```
Public Sub SleepingOperation()
    Dim sleepspan As Integer
    sleepspan = 1000
    If longduration Then sleepspan = sleepspan * 5
    myTimespan = TimeSpan.FromTicks(DateTime.Now.Ticks)
    Thread.CurrentThread.Sleep(sleepspan)
    myTimespan = _
    TimeSpan.FromTicks(DateTime.Now.Ticks).Subtract(myTimespan)
End Sub

Public Sub SleepingSynchronous()
    Dim sleepspan As Integer
    sleepspan = 1000
    If longduration Then sleepspan = sleepspan * 5
    Thread.CurrentThread.Sleep(sleepspan)
    myTimespan = _
    TimeSpan.FromTicks(DateTime.Now.Ticks).Subtract(myTimespan)
End Sub

End Class
```

The ThreadingPerformance sample program runs as a console application and creates five worker objects and five threads. Several tests are defined. The RunTest function creates five threads, one for each WorkerObject. Note that the thread creation is in a separate loop from the actual thread start operation. This helps improve the accuracy of the measurement by starting the five threads as close to simultaneously as possible.

The RunTest2 method shown in Listing 7-24 uses the SleepingOperation method to test the non-CPU-intensive case. It is otherwise identical to RunTest.

Listing 7-24. Module1 in the ThreadingPerformance sample.

```
Module Module1

    Dim WorkerObjects(4) As WorkerThread
    Dim Threads(4) As Threading.Thread

    Sub RunTest()
        Dim x As Integer

        ' Create the threads
        For x = 0 To 4
            Threads(x) = New Threading.Thread(AddressOf _
            WorkerObjects(x).WorkingOperation)
        Next x

        ' Start the 5 threads
        For x = 0 To 4
            Threads(x).Start()
        Next

        ' Wait for them to finish
        For x = 0 To 4
            Threads(x).Join()
        Next

    End Sub
```

```
Sub RunTest2()
    Dim x As Integer

    ' Create the threads
    For x = 0 To 4
        Threads(x) = New Threading.Thread(AddressOf _
        WorkerObjects(x).SleepingOperation)
    Next x

    ' Start the 5 threads
    For x = 0 To 4
        Threads(x).Start()
    Next

    ' Wait for them to finish
    For x = 0 To 4
        Threads(x).Join()
    Next

End Sub
```

The RunSynchronous and RunSynchronous2 methods first call the SynchronousRequest method to initialize the start time for each object. They then call the SynchronousOperation or SleepingSynchronous methods in sequence, simulating sequential handling of client requests as shown in Listing 7-25.

Listing 7-25. Module1 in the ThreadingPerformance example—continued.

```
Public Sub RunSynchronous()
    Dim x As Integer
    For x = 0 To 4
        WorkerObjects(x).SynchronousRequest()
    Next
    For x = 0 To 4
        WorkerObjects(x).SynchronousOperation()
    Next

End Sub
```

```
Public Sub RunSynchronous2()
    Dim x As Integer
    For x = 0 To 4
        WorkerObjects(x).SynchronousRequest()
    Next
    For x = 0 To 4
        WorkerObjects(x).SleepingSynchronous()
    Next

End Sub
```

As Listing 7-26 shows, the ReportResults method displays the elapsed time for each of the worker objects and the average time for all of the worker objects. The main program calls the various tests twice, once where each client request is of equal length and once where the first client request is significantly longer than the others (accomplished by setting the WorkerObject's LongDuration property to True).

Listing 7-26. Module1 in the ThreadingPerformance example—continued.

```
Sub ReportResults()
    Dim x As Integer
    Dim tot As Double
    Dim ms As Double
    For x = 0 To 4
        ms = WorkerObjects(x).ElapsedTimeForCall.TotalMilliseconds
        tot = tot + ms
        Console.Write(Int(ms).ToString + " ,")
    Next
    Console.Write(" Average: " + Int(tot / 5).ToString())
    Console.WriteLine()
End Sub



Sub Main()
    Dim x As Integer
    For x = 0 To 4
        WorkerObjects(x) = New WorkerThread()
    Next

    Console.WriteLine("Running tests...")
```

```
            Console.WriteLine("CPU-Intensive operations")

            Console.WriteLine("Synchronous Equal length operations")
            WorkerObjects(0).LongDuration = False
            RunSynchronous()
            ReportResults()

            Console.WriteLine("Synchronous one long operation")
            WorkerObjects(0).LongDuration = True
            RunSynchronous()
            ReportResults()

            Console.WriteLine("Multithreaded Equal length operations")
            WorkerObjects(0).LongDuration = False
            RunTest()
            ReportResults()

            Console.WriteLine("Multithreaded One long operations")
            WorkerObjects(0).LongDuration = True
            RunTest()
            ReportResults()


            Console.WriteLine("Non CPU-Intensive operations")


            Console.WriteLine("Synchronous Equal length operation")
            WorkerObjects(0).LongDuration = False
            RunSynchronous2()
            ReportResults()

            Console.WriteLine("Synchronous one long operation")
            WorkerObjects(0).LongDuration = True
            RunSynchronous2()
            ReportResults()

            Console.WriteLine("Multithreaded Equal length operations")
            WorkerObjects(0).LongDuration = False
            RunTest2()
            ReportResults()
```

```
        Console.WriteLine("Multithreaded One long operations")
        WorkerObjects(0).LongDuration = True
        RunTest2()
        ReportResults()

        Console.ReadLine()

    End Sub

End Module
```

ThreadPerformance Program Results

First, let's start with the synchronous results. The actual results you see will differ based on your machine speed and configuration as well as the version of .NET you are using. The synchronous results simulate the behavior of client requests that are received simultaneously but are handled on a single thread, each one in turn:

```
Running tests...
CPU-Intensive operations
Synchronous Equal length operations
2093 ,4186 ,6238 ,8271 ,10284 , Average: 6214
Synchronous one long operation
10184 ,12217 ,14250 ,16303 ,18346 , Average: 14260
```

As you can see, the duration of each CPU -intensive operation is about 2 seconds. So, when handled in sequence, the first takes 2 seconds and the second a total of 4 seconds, 2 spent waiting for the first one to complete and so on.

The average is 6.2 seconds, close to the theoretical average of 6 seconds.

If, however, the first operation is long (in this case about 10 seconds), the impact on the overall performance is huge because each of the shorter requests must wait until the long one is complete.

Let's take a look at what happens when CPU-intensive requests received simultaneously are handled on multiple threads:

```
Multithreaded Equal length operations
8442 ,8331 ,8221 ,8111 ,7991 , Average: 8219
Multithreaded One long operations
15241 ,7921 ,8301 ,8181 ,7921 , Average: 9513
```

When the requests are of equal length, the time for each request is much longer. That's because threading does not magically create more CPU power—the CPU resources is divided among the threads, thus slowing down each operation.

The duration of a bit over 8 seconds is lower than the theoretical time of 10 seconds. This is probably because the algorithm used by the OS to allocate CPU time is not a simple case of dividing 100% of available CPU time to the threads of one particular application. With more threads demanding CPU time, the OS allocates more total OS time to the threads than in the single-thread scenario. In a large system, these values would tend to increase not only because the application would demand more from the system but also due to the overhead that occurs when switching between threads.

When the test is repeated with a long duration in the first worker object, the slow request has no measurable impact on the other objects and thus has a smaller impact on the average performance.

Now compare the single versus multithreaded case. The results lead to an important conclusion.

If client requests are all of similar length and are competing for a scarce resource (like CPU time), overall performance is better handling them in sequence than handling them on separate threads!

It is only when you have mixed-length requests or when threads aren't competing for resources that multithreading becomes advantageous. You should consider carefully the types of requests that you expect your application to handle when determining whether to use multithreading. In some cases, your software can determine at runtime the expected duration of a request and choose to handle short ones sequentially and longer ones on separate threads.

The rules change for scenarios that are not competing for scarce resources (in this case, non-CPU-intensive operations). While the synchronous operations match the theoretical results almost exactly, the multithreaded results achieve the ideal. Since the threads are not doing anything, there is no need to divide the CPU among threads. The fact that CPU cycles are a limited resource has no impact in this case:

```
Non CPU-Intensive operations
Synchronous Equal length operation
1001 ,2002 ,3004 ,4005 ,5007 , Average: 3004
Synchronous one long operation
5007 ,6008 ,7010 ,8011 ,9012 , Average: 7010
Multithreaded Equal length operations
1001 ,1001 ,1001 ,1001 ,1001 , Average: 1001
Multithreaded One long operations
5007 ,1001 ,1001 ,1001 ,1001 , Average: 1802
```

When considering the differences between competing and noncompeting scenarios (in this case, CPU-intensive and non-CPU-intensive operations), it's important to keep in mind that these represent two extremes. Few client requests demand the full attention of any resource. But even if the client request requires waiting on a file I/O, database, or network operation, the operation itself (once the wait expires) demands CPU and other resources.

Recap

Though multithreading is familiar to most VB6 programmers, the complexities and dangers of multithreading are actually well hidden in VB6. Those complexities and dangers become a significant issue in VB.NET.

You learned that the risks of multithreading come about due to the ability of threads to share data, and that because the OS can interrupt operations at the assembly language level, you must assume that such interruptions can occur within individual lines of VB code. Even an operation as simple as $A = A + 1$ can fail if multiple threads attempt to execute it simultaneously and A is shared among the threads.

Worse, the chances of an error occurring can be incredibly small. The examples shown in this chapter exhibited an error rate of one in millions of operations and those errors can involve anything from a program freezing due to a deadlock to subtle inaccuracies in calculations. It is, therefore, not enough to rely on testing to detect multithreading problems. One must carefully design multithreaded applications to control access to shared objects and variables ruthlessly.

You learned several techniques for synchronizing threads and protecting blocks of code. You also learned that the CLR has many resources for synchronization beyond those shown here.

Finally, assuming you did not give up in terror over the risks involved in multithreaded software design, you learned that when used properly, multithreading can be a powerful tool to improve both the real and perceived performance of an application. Multithreading can actually reduce the load that an application places on a system by eliminating the polling necessary to handle certain wait operations in VB6.

Part III

Code

"God is in the details."

—Ludwig Mies van der Rohe

CHAPTER 8

Data Types and Operators

IN PART ONE OF THIS BOOK, we covered strategic issues relating to the .NET Framework—what it is and where it fits into both Microsoft's world and yours. In Part Two, we covered key concepts—those language-related ideas that must be understood lest old habits lead one to seriously flawed architectural decisions.

This part of the book is devoted to code—specifically, the ways the language has been changed. My focus here will not be on the specifics of the changes themselves but on the consequences of those changes and the impact they will have on the way you code.

It is perhaps a measure of the magnitude of the changes facing Visual Basic developers that we must begin by looking at the fundamental data types of the language.

The Numeric Types

Table 8-1 lists the numeric data types supported by VB6 and VB.NET. The number in parentheses is the size of the type in bytes. The CLR column shows the name of the variable type within the CLR—the runtime system used by VB.NET and all .NET languages.

Table 8-1. Numeric Data Types Supported by VB6 and VB.NET

VB6 TYPE	VB.NET TYPE	CLR TYPE
Byte (1)	Byte (1)	System.Byte
String * 1(1)	Char (2)	System.Char
Boolean (2)	Boolean (4)	System.Boolean
N/A	Decimal (12)	System.Decimal
Currency (8)	N/A	N/A
Double (8)	Double (8)	System.Double

Table 8-1. Numeric Data Types Supported by VB6 and VB.NET (Continued)

VB6 TYPE	VB.NET TYPE	CLR TYPE
Integer (2)	Short (2)	System.Int16
Long (4)	Integer (4)	System.Int32
N/A	Long (8)	System.Int64
Single (4)	Single (4)	System.Single

Take a close look. If you have had any doubts that VB.NET is really a new language, this table alone should put the subject to rest. Changing the fundamental numeric data types of a language is already a huge change. Sure, a conversion program can handle most data type porting for you—but that doesn't change the fact that a VB.NET program looks very different from a VB6 program.

String * 1 versus Char

Okay, this is a cheat. There is no Char data type in VB6. So why do you need a Char data type in VB.NET? Because there are no fixed-length strings in VB.NET (a subject I'll discuss later in this chapter). Sure, you could handle characters by using the first character of a dynamic string but that's a very expensive operation in terms of performance because all VB.NET strings are allocated on the heap. True, heap allocation on VB.NET is fast but it is still not as efficient as the stack allocation used with the Char data type. The Char type is a 16-bit value—large enough for a Unicode character. That's why I've included it here as a numeric type even though it really falls into a gray area.

Boolean

Booleans are now 4 bytes instead of 2, a fact that should have no impact on most programs.

I remember, in the early days of Visual Basic, getting into huge arguments over the nature of the Visual Basic Boolean variable. The problem, in a nutshell, is that while a Boolean variable supports only two values (True and False, represented by the values –1 and zero), Visual Basic 6 performs what looks like Boolean operations on Integer variables.

For example, the VB6 code:

```
If 4 And 8 Then
    Debug.Print "Should be true"
Else
```

…evaluates to False and the line is not printed. The VB6 "And" and "Or" operators are actually bitwise operators. When applied to a number, they work correctly only if True is always represented by –1 and False is always represented by zero. When applied to two numbers, you can obtain logically inconsistent results. In this case, the numbers 4 and 8 (being nonzero) are logically True, thus the expression 4 And 8 should intuitively return True. However the bitwise And of 4 and 8 results in zero, which is False.

This could lead to incorrect results, especially when using API functions that tend to return 1 for True. For example, The IsWindow API function returns 1 if a window handle is valid. In other words:

- If IsWindow(*validwindow)* works correctly because 1 is evaluated as True.

- If Not IsWindow(*validwindow*) fails because Not 1 evaluates to –1, which is also True!

So, VB programmers (especially those using API functions) must be exceedingly careful to always compare results to zero and never depend on the actual value being compared if an expression is involved.

VB.NET uses the System.Boolean object that can only be True or False. Microsoft made a valiant effort in Beta 1 to bring some sanity to Visual Basic's traditional handling of Boolean variables by attempting to redefine the And and Or operators to always represent logical Boolean operators. Microsoft also defined new BitAnd and BitOr operators to handle bitwise operators. Under such a scenario, logical operators such as Not, And, and Or would only work with Boolean types (or variables converted to Boolean types), thus there would be no possibility of ambiguity. If you wanted to perform bitwise operations, you had to use the BitNot, BitAnd, and BitOr operators.

Unfortunately, a number of shortsighted VB6 programmers managed to convince Microsoft that this change somehow violated the principals that made Visual Basic great and Microsoft, for some equally incomprehensible reason, caved.

As a result, VB.NET continues to define True as –1 and to combine logical and Boolean operators into the same command.

You can see this in the BooleanExample project in Listing 8-1.

Listing 8-1. The Boolean sample project.

```
' Demonstration of boolean variables
' Copyright ©2001 by Desaware Inc.
' All Rights Reserved.
Module Module1

    Sub Main()
        Dim A As Boolean
        Dim I As Integer
        A = True
        I = CInt(A)
        Console.WriteLine("Value of Boolean in Integer is: " + I.ToString())
        Console.WriteLine("Value of  a System Boolean in Integer is: " +
I.ToString())

        I = 5
        A = CBool(I)
        Console.WriteLine("Value of Boolean assigned from 5 is : " + A.ToString())
        I = CInt(A)
        Console.WriteLine("And converted back to Integer: " + I.ToString())
        Console.WriteLine("5 And 8: " + (CBool(5) And CBool(8)).ToString)
        Console.WriteLine("5 And 8: " + (5 And 8).ToString())
        Console.ReadLine()
    End Sub

End Module
```

The results are as follows:

```
Value of Boolean in Integer is: -1
Value of  a System Boolean in Integer is: -1
Value of Boolean assigned from 5 is : True
And converted back to Integer: -1
5 And 8: True
5 And 8: 0
```

Boolean variables can only be True or False. As long as you perform logical operations with Boolean variables, you won't have a problem. But remember that if VB.NET sees a numeric variable instead of a Boolean variable, it will perform a bitwise operation, which can result in unforeseen bugs.

Currency and Decimal

The Decimal type replaces the Currency type. It provides greater resolution (12 bytes versus 8) and the decimal position is not fixed. This change is unlikely to have any significant impact on your code. The biggest advantage of the change is that it is a true .NET native type and should be well supported by any .NET components across all .NET languages.

Integers, Longs, and Shorts

The change of VB Integers from 16 to 32 bits and Longs from 32 to 64 bits is one of the most controversial changes to VB.NET. Integers have always been 16 bits in Visual Basic, which was fine as long as you stuck with VB. But VB programmers who used the Win32 API had to adapt to the fact that in the 32-bit C++ world (and thus in all of Microsoft's documentation), Integers are 32 bits. So VB programmers had to constantly remember that an API "short" is a VB Integer and an API "Integer" is a VB Long.

When it came to VB.NET, Microsoft had a choice. They could change the size of Integer to 32 bits and thus make the term Integer consistent across all .NET languages and documentation. Or they could keep the VB Integer at 16 bits and perhaps come up with a new Int64 type.

Changing the definition of Integer has the advantage of making the VB documentation consistent with the rest of the .NET documentation. But it will make things more difficult for VB programmers who continue to code in both languages. One can almost hear the mental gears grinding as you switch from VB6 to VB.NET and back.

Personally, I favor the change. I think, in the long term, the benefits of consistency with the rest of the .NET Framework will be worth the change. However, I admit to being biased—as someone who works extensively with both the Win32 API and the Microsoft namespaces, consistency across .NET is more important to me than consistency with old code. But I admit this is a tough one and those who disagree have a strong case.

As long as you are programming with VB.NET, keep in mind that Integers are the most efficient data type on 32-bit operating systems. You should avoid Longs unless you really need the 64-bit range.

Also, be prepared for the possibility that Integer may be redefined to 64 bits on some future 64-bit version of the CLR, at which time I assume Microsoft will define an explicit 32-bit data type for those who must use 32-bit variables.

Unsigned Types

Visual Basic .NET does not support unsigned variables. But before you get too upset about this lack, be aware that the unsigned variable types defined in the CLR are not CLS compliant. In other words, if you use unsigned variables in public methods, properties, or data structures of an assembly, there is no guarantee that other CLS-compliant languages can use the assembly.

This means that for most programmers, unsigned variables (if they existed in VB.NET) would only be usable within individual assemblies.

The only other area in VB6 in which there is a desire for unsigned variable types is when accessing the Win32 API—which makes extensive use of unsigned variables. This need, as you will see later, has also largely vanished as VB.NET programmers are much more likely to use the .NET Framework classes than direct API calls. When you do use API calls, the PInvoke namespace handles conversions for you automatically to and from signed variables (as you'll see in Chapter 15).

So, while some may miss unsigned data types and even use their lack when advocating that VB programmers learn C# instead of VB.NET, it's a minor loss and a weak argument.

About the CLR

The third column in Table 8-1 shows the name of the data types as they are known by the CLR. I've listed them to make an important point: one of the key features that Microsoft claims for .NET is the ability of languages to work together.

Unfortunately, Microsoft has portrayed this feature in a rather silly way, focusing on the fact that you can build applications easily out of multiple .NET languages. Given the fact that the features supported by the three biggest .NET languages (C++, C#, and VB.NET) are very similar,[1] it's likely that the vast majority of programmers will pick the one they are most familiar with and stick to it.

A better way to look at this feature is this: the ability of components built out of different languages to work together is fundamental to .NET—and a vast improvement over the type-library-based translation provided by COM or the completely manual translation provided by the Declare statement when making API calls.

As you can see Table 8-1, every data type in VB.NET is actually a data type in the .NET CLR and is usable from any other .NET language that adheres to the Common Language Specification.

Non-Numeric Data Types

Microsoft did not limit their changes to just the numeric data types.

---

1.   Virtually identical if you are writing managed code.

Goodbye Variants (and Good Riddance)

I never liked variants. I won't go into all the reasons why here—I actually discuss it at length in my earlier book on developing COM/ActiveX components.[2] But here's a quick rundown:

- Variants are slow.

- Variants require runtime type checking if you want your software to be robust for various types of input.

- Variants promote hidden conversions that aren't always what you want (evil type coercion).

- Variants lead to bugs that are more likely to appear at runtime, such as "empty" variables and conversion errors or overflows.

- Variants are slow (in case you missed it the first time around).

The only place variants had a real use in Visual Basic 6 were in situations where you had no choice because you were using a database or object model that required them; or in cases where you needed to do limited parameter overloading (a single function that could accept more than one type of data).[3]

I say, good riddance.

Variants Are Not Objects

There is a tendency among some to look at the Object type as a kind of variant since it can reference every data type. Even Microsoft's documentation suggests that the Object type is the replacement for the Variant type. This is inaccurate.

A variant is a variable that references a block of memory, which can contain different types of data. The block of memory itself contains a field that indicates the type of data contained in the variant. The OLE subsystem exposes a number of functions for clearing and setting variants and for converting the contents of variants from one type to another.

Figure 8-1 shows what happens when you declare a variant and assign it to a number and then a string.

---

2. *Developing COM/ActiveX Components with Visual Basic 6: A Guide to the Perplexed* (Que, 1998).

3. A feature that is supported directly in the VB.NET language.

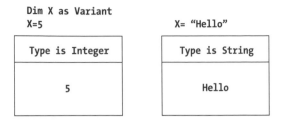

```
Dim X as Variant
X=5                                    X= "Hello"
```

Type is Integer
5

Type is String
Hello

Figure 8-1. The contents of a variant change on assignment.

As you can see, the contents of the Variant variable change when the Variant variable is assigned a value and the internal type information is modified according to the assigned data type.

Figure 8-2 illustrates that a completely different process occurs when you assign an object under VB.NET.

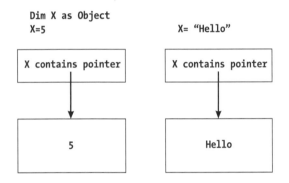

```
Dim X as Object
X=5                                    X= "Hello"
```

X contains pointer

X contains pointer

5

Hello

Figure 8-2. Object assignment changes the reference.

During the initial assignment x = 5, an integer value is boxed into an object and given the value 5. Variable *x* contains a reference (pointer) to this boxed integer value. When you then assign variable *x* to a string, *x* contains a reference to a String object that is allocated on the heap. What happens to the Integer object? It is now unreferenced and will be destroyed during the next garbage collection.

The ability of the Object type to reference any type of variable is a consequence of the fact that all data types in the .NET Framework inherit from the Object type. It has no relation at all to variants.

Determining Object Types

While the Object type is not a variant, it can serve the purpose of a generic variable able to reference many types of objects. Just as the VarType operator existed to determine the type of a variable, it is possible to determine the type of object that is being referenced by an Object variable (or any other variable for that matter). This is done through a process called reflection, presumably because it makes it possible to reflect back to the code information about the objects, method, properties (and other metadata) associated with an assembly. Reflection will be covered in depth in Chapter 11.

You can retrieve the type of any object because the GetType method is part of the System.Object class (which is the base class for every .NET object). The DataTypes sample program illustrates this, as shown here:

```
Module Module1
    Sub Main()
        Dim o As Object
        o = 5
        console.WriteLine(o)
        console.WriteLine(o.GetType.FullName)
        o = "Hello"
        console.WriteLine(o)
        console.WriteLine(o.GetType.FullName)
        console.ReadLine()
    End Sub
End Module
```

When run, the following results are displayed:

```
5
System.Int32
Hello
System.String
```

The Type object returned by the GetType method has many properties that allow you to find out information about an object or class. The FullName property allows you to obtain the complete object name. The GetTypeCode method allows you to obtain a numeric type code value, which is more efficient to use in your code.

Miscellaneous

If you multiply two Integer objects (32 bits) and an overflow occurs, the result will be a Long (64 bits).

Strings

There are two big changes in VB.NET with regards to strings. The first change, and the one most likely to impact existing programs, is that fixed-length strings are no longer supported in VB.NET. Fixed-length strings in VB6 come in handy when working with fixed record sizes and have the advantage of being allocated on the stack. All strings in VB.NET are dynamic and are allocated on the heap.

The second change, which is more subtle and less likely to impact your code, is that strings in VB.NET are immutable—they never change. This means that any function or operator that seems to modify a string is actually returning a new string. This makes life easy for the CLR, which doesn't need to worry about overflowing string buffers or moving strings on the heap when they change. It is also efficient in that string literals can be shared. The most important consequence of immutability is that strings are relatively safe to use in a multithreaded environment. True, you can still run into problems when sharing String variables among threads but you don't need to worry about different threads modifying the contents of strings at the same time.

The most important reason for immutability is one that you'll probably never notice and relates to the way objects are passed as parameters. You'll read more about this in the next chapter.

The System.Text.StringBuilder class can be used to efficiently construct strings that are easily modifiable. However, Visual Basic programmers will probably stick with the very flexible Mid statement, which is even easier to use.

The Strings sample program in Listing 8-2 illustrates how VB.NET can share string literals.

Listing 8-2. The Strings sample program.

```
Module Module1

    Sub Main()
        Dim A As String
        Dim B As String
        A = "Hello"
        B = "Hel" + "lo"
        console.WriteLine(A = B)
        console.WriteLine(A Is B)
```

```
        Mid(A, 1, 1) = "X"
        Mid(B, 1, 1) = "X"
        console.WriteLine(A = B)
        console.WriteLine(A Is B)
        console.WriteLine(a)
        Console.ReadLine()
    End Sub

End Module
```

...which results in the following output:

```
True
True
True
False
Xello
```

A and B are both set to the string Hello at compile time (the compiler is smart enough to determine that B is, in fact, set to Hello and to reference the same string literal). Not only are A and B equal but they reference the same object (as you can see from the Is statement). If strings could be modified, VB.NET would not be able to combine literals in this fashion because changes to one variable could change the other.

Once the first character in both strings is modified, the strings remain equal but they no longer refer to the same object.

The String$ function has been removed from VB.NET. That's because the String object itself has a number of powerful constructors. For example, you can create a string of length N that contains all nulls using the line:

```
s = New String(Chr(0), N)
```

Arrays

There are two major changes to arrays in VB.NET, one of great significance and the other is relatively unimportant to most programmers.

The big change is that all arrays are zero based. This means that the line:

```
Dim X(10) As Integer
```

...always creates an array with eleven entries indexed zero to 10. It is the equivalent of the VB6 declaration:

```
Dim X(0 To 10) As Integer
```

Many VB programmers will miss the flexibility of being able to set the base for arrays. C++ and C# programmers are, of course, accustomed to this. From a programmer's viewpoint, this change has one advantage: it enforces consistency on array usage. Programmers who use multiple array bases in an application are more likely to create bugs due to the natural confusion that results from mentally shifting gears between bases. Having a consistent array base tends to improve the readability of code as well as developer's ability of to understand code they did not write. As things stand, VB.NET programmers will probably continue with their previous VB6 habits using either zero-based arrays or using '1'-based arrays and simply ignoring entry zero.

Normally, I'm a huge fan of having the language protect the developer but, frankly, I think Microsoft blew it on this one. My first thought was that their reasoning had something to do with the .NET Framework—but then I took a closer look at the Array class and found that it supports array bounds as shown in Listing 8-3.

Listing 8-3. The ArrayExample sample program.

```
Module Module1

    Sub Main()
        Dim X As Array
        Dim I As Integer
        Dim Lengths(0) As Integer
        Dim LowerBounds(0) As Integer

        Lengths(0) = 10
        LowerBounds(0) = 1

        X = Array.CreateInstance(GetType(System.Int32), Lengths, LowerBounds)

        Try
            X.SetValue(5, 0)
        Catch e As Exception
            Console.WriteLine(e.Message)
        End Try

        X.SetValue(6, 1)
        Console.WriteLine(X.GetValue(1))

        Console.ReadLine()


    End Sub

End Module
```

The Array type is the generic array type on which all arrays (including VB arrays) are based. How do you know this? Because you can invoke all the Array object methods on an array declared using Visual Basic. The sample program in Listing 8-3 creates a generic array variable named X and creates an instance of the array containing integers with the length set to 10 and the lower bound set to 1. It then attempts to set two indexes in the array, index zero (which shouldn't exist) and index 1. The resulting output is as follows:

```
An exception of type System.IndexOutOfRangeException was thrown.
6
```

The IndexOutOfRangeException exception is raised when you try to access index zero. Index 1 works fine.

The code shown here is too awkward for most practical use by VB programmers. It does, however, illustrate that the .NET Framework supports array bounds.

So, why did they remove this capability from VB.NET?

While the .NET Framework Array object supports different lower bounds, the Common Language Specification requires that all arrays have a zero base. The CLS represents the common denominator, which, if a language complies with it, that language will be able to interoperate seamlessly with assemblies written in every other CLS language.

Microsoft had a choice: they could allow user-defined bases in the CLS and add that feature to C++ and C#; they could take user-defined bases out of VB.NET; or they could leave the CLS as is and allow VB.NET to create non-CLS-compliant assemblies.

Their choice is obvious but you don't have to like it. Personally, I would rather have seen them add the feature to C++ and C# than pull it from VB. I do agree with their decision (painful as it is) to enforce CLS compliance on VB.NET programmers—since VB programmers (more than any others) make extensive use of component-based development.

No Fixed Arrays

All VB.NET arrays can be redimensioned. This is unlikely to matter to most VB programmers but has consequences with regards to handling API calls (as you will see in Chapter 15).

Dates

VB.NET uses the .NET Framework System.DateTime object type. The biggest change for VB programmers is that there is no longer an easy conversion to and from double. The DateTime class does, however, have methods to convert to and from OLE automation date format (double). The good news is that the DateTime object is very rich and includes the ability to easily compare dates and times and add or subtract a period from a DateTime variable.

Enums

Enums are almost unchanged from VB6 days, at least in terms of syntax. The biggest change is that Enums are treated like any other declared type. In other words, the Enum statement can be preceded by the Public, Private, Protected, and Friend access specifiers, as well as the Shadows keyword to control the visibility of the Enum to derived classes or other assemblies.

The biggest change to Enums for VB.NET is that the Enum base class provides a variety of methods to convert to and from the string (named) representation of an enumerated value and the value itself.

From a programming perspective, the only real change for Enums is their support for the Flags attribute as shown Listing 8-4, the EnumExample program.

Listing 8-4. The EnumExample program.

```
' Enumeration example
' Copyright ©2001 by Desaware Inc.
' All Rights Reserved

Module Module1

    Enum E
        A = 5
        B
        C = 6    ' B and C will both be 6
    End Enum

    <Flags()> Enum B
        A = &H1
        B = &H2
        C = &H4
    End Enum

    Enum C
        A = &H1
        B = &H2
        C = &H4
    End Enum
```

```
    Sub F(ByVal X As E)
    End Sub


    Sub FB(ByVal X As B)
    End Sub


    Sub Main()
        Dim I1, I2, I3 As Integer
        I1 = E.A : I2 = E.B : I3 = E.C
        ' We can't use ToString directly on the enumeration value because
        ' that returns the enumeration name, not the value
        Console.WriteLine(I1.ToString() + I2.ToString() + I3.ToString())
        F(E.C)
        FB(B.A Or B.C Or B.B)
        Console.WriteLine(E.Format(GetType(E), 5, "G"))
        Console.WriteLine(C.Format(GetType(C), (C.A Or C.C), "G"))
        Console.WriteLine(B.Format(GetType(B), (B.A Or B.C), "G"))
        Console.ReadLine()
    End Sub


End Module
```

The first two results illustrate the fact that more than one entry in an Enum can have the same value—in this case, e.b and e.c are both 6. The Format method of an enumeration retrieves the Enum name for a given value—a handy feature for debugging or report generation:

```
566
A
```

Enums are typically used in two ways: to provide a list of more or less sequential numeric constants or to provide a list of flags—constants where each has a single bit set, which are designed to be combined using the Or operator. The F and FB functions illustrate the way these two types of Enums are typically used.

The Flags attribute on an Enum tells the runtime that the Enum parameters are intended to be combined using bitwise logical operators. The implementation of the Format method uses reflection to read the attribute before it returns the member name.[4] Thus, the C Enum returns the value of the Enum but the B Enum, which has the Flags attribute specified, returns A|C: the C++/C# syntax for two members combined using a bitwise Or operator. The output, then, is as follows:

---

4. The Format operator takes as parameters the enumeration type, the value to format, and a
    formatting code where "G" indicates to return the enumeration value name if possible.

5
A, C[5]

It is also possible that the Flags attribute will be used to provide improved feedback to the developer in the IntelliSense pop-up.[6]

Declarations

The story with VB.NET declarations is short and sweet. The language allows you to declare multiple variables on one line with variables A and B as shown in the Declarations sample project. This is relatively unimportant.

VB.NET allows you to initialize both variables and arrays at declaration time as shown with variables C and D. This is nothing short of wonderful:

```
Module Module1

    Sub Main()
        Dim A, B As Integer
        Dim C As Integer = 6
        Dim D() As String = {"A", "B", "C", "D", "E"}
        Dim E As Integer, F As String
    End Sub

End Module
```

Array initializers use the { } characters—the first time these characters have been part of Visual Basic's syntax.

By the way, the DefType (DefInt, DefLong, etc.) declarations are gone. This is no great loss as they only served to reduce both code readability and consistency among VB applications.

Conversions and Type Checking

With all the hype around VB.NET, it's easy to miss one of the most important and exciting new features in the language. The fact that it is also one of the most annoying features does not…well, let's start from the beginning.

---

5. According to the documentation, "A|C" should be returned. In Beta 2, "A, C" is returned. Which is correct? Only time will tell.

6. I've seen no evidence of this in the current beta but it's still a good idea to use the Flags attribute in preparation for later versions or third-party debug tools or utilities.

Visual Basic 6 and earlier versions have a feature called evil type coercion. A classic example of this is shown here:

```
Sub Evil()
    Debug.Print 15 + "15" + "15"
End Sub
```

```
Sub Main()
    Evil
End Sub
```

This results in 45 being displayed in the Debug window.

VB6 essentially tries to be intelligent about what types of conversions you wish to perform. It's also very cooperative with regards to even simple and obvious conversions, such as that from Long to Integer.

The problem with this approach is twofold: sometimes VB6 guesses wrong and fails to warn you when a variable conversion has a chance of raising a runtime error.

One might argue that this is not really a problem. VB6 guesses right most of the time, especially with programmers experienced enough to avoid the obvious problems. And automatic conversions prevent a developer from seeing warnings, most of which can safely be ignored because the developer really does know what he or she is doing.

The flaw in this argument is that it does not take into account the actual distribution of costs during the software life cycle. As annoying as warning messages are and as annoying as it is to perform explicit conversions, these annoyances are inexpensive to fix. The original software developer eliminates them during the process of getting the code to compile for the first time. They might cost a few extra minutes in the development process but that's it.

Once a bug passes the initial developer, costs rise dramatically. There are bug-tracking costs within the organization; communications increase between developers attempting to identify bugs and assign them to the correct developer; and there are testing costs both to test each fix and to regression test the program to ensure new flaws weren't introduced.

And if the bug survives into the released product, the costs can become astronomical.

VB.NET adds a new option called Strict Type Checking, which is, unfortunately, not the default setting for new VB.NET projects.

The very first thing you should do is enable this option for all new projects.[7]

You'll quickly get used to using conversion functions when needed and you'll find that the reminders by the compiler will help you to write better code. They'll remind you to consider using different variable types. They'll remind you which object or interface you are really accessing. They'll help you eliminate bugs before anyone else has a chance to see them.

I feel so strongly about this that not only do all the examples in this book have Option Strict on, but I won't even acknowledge the possibility of leaving it off when discussing the migration to VB.NET. The only case where you might even consider leaving Option Strict off is for a direct porting scenario using the Upgrade Wizard. All new code and most migrated code should leave it on.

The rules for Strict Type Checking are quite simple. Anytime you convert a variable from one type to another, the compiler checks to see if there is any chance of information loss such that a conversion runtime error might occur. Listing 8-5 illustrates this.

Listing 8-5. The Conversions sample program.

```
Module Module1

    Sub Main()
        Dim I As Integer, L As Long
        I = 50
        L = I
        Console.WriteLine(L)
        L = 50
        I = CInt(L) ' Explicit cast needed here
        Console.WriteLine(I)
        L = &H100000000
        Try
            I = CType(L, Integer)
        Catch E as Exception
            Console.WriteLine(E.Message)
        End Try

        Console.WriteLine(I)
        Console.ReadLine()

    End Sub

End Module
```

---

7. In Beta 1, Option Strict was enabled by default. Unfortunately, Microsoft decided to change the default to disabled with Beta 2. Normally, I would criticize them roundly for this decision but I'm so grateful that Option Strict exists at all that I will at least try to avoid being insulting, even though it really is a terrible mistake.

An Integer can be converted implicitly to a Long because a Long variable can hold every possible Integer variable. The reverse is not true. When you run this program, you'll see the following results:

```
50
50
An exception of type System.OverflowException was thrown.
50
```

Listing 8-5 shows two ways to convert an Integer to a Long, the CInt and the CType functions. These conversion functions are needed to tell the compiler that yes, you actually do know what you are doing in assigning a Long to an Integer variable. Without them, you would see a compile-time error. Both CInt and CType perform the same operation—CType is the generic function that can be used to convert from any type to any other (at least where a conversion is supported).

Conversions and Classes

In Chapter 5, you saw the CType operator used to convert objects from one type to another. The rules for implicit and explicit conversions for objects are similar to the rules used with Value type variables.

You can implicitly convert from a derived class to a base class. This makes sense because a derived class effectively "contains" the base class and has all the methods and properties of the base class.

You can also implicitly convert from a class to an interface that is implemented by the class.

You must explicitly convert from a base class to a derived class. Since the object referenced in this case may or may not actually be the derived class, there is the risk of a runtime error if the conversion fails.

You must explicitly convert from an interface to a class. Since the object referenced in this case may or may not actually be the correct class, there is the risk of a runtime error if the conversion fails.

The ObjectConversions sample program in Listing 8-6 illustrates this. It defines interface I, class A (which implements interface I), and class B, which inherits from class A. The comments in the program point out the rule that applies for each conversion.

Listing 8-6. The ObjectConversions sample program.

```
Module Module1
    Interface I
        Sub MyInterfaceFunc()
    End Interface

    Class A
        Implements I
        Protected Overridable Sub MyFunc()

        End Sub
        Public Sub MyPublicFunc()

        End Sub
        Public Sub MyInterfaceFunc() Implements I.MyInterfaceFunc

        End Sub
    End Class

    Class B
        Inherits A

    End Class

    Sub Main()
        Dim myA As New A()
        Dim myB As New B()
        Dim myAReference As A
        Dim myBReference As B
        Dim myIReference As I

        myAReference = myA  ' Same type - ok
        myAReference = myB  ' Base type - implicit
        myIReference = myA  ' Implemented interface - implicit

        myA = CType(myIReference, A)    ' I pointer may be any object - _
        ' explicit Can't tell until runtime if it will work

        Try
            myB = CType(myIReference, B)    ' Here it doesn't work
        Catch e As Exception
            Console.WriteLine(e.Message)
        End Try
```

```
        myIReference = myB  ' Implemented Interface - implicit
        ' B inherits from A, inherits I as well

        Console.ReadLine()

    End Sub

End Module
```

Conversions and Structures

At this time, VB.NET does not support custom conversions of structures that you create. For example, if you created a complex data type and wanted the ability to directly assign it from an Integer or Long value (either implicitly or explicitly), you would not be able to do so. Instead, you should follow the convention of implementing a Shared function by the name FromXxx(source type).

For example, you might define:

```
Shared Function FromLong(ByVal l As Long) As YourStructureType
```

Operators

Most of the operator changes are straightforward and covered adequately in the "Language Changes" section of the Visual Studio.NET documentation.

The AndAlso and OrElse Operators

As discussed earlier in this chapter, the And and Or operators in VB.NET continue to work as they did in VB6. However, Microsoft added two new operators that only work on Boolean types: the AndAlso and OrElse operators. Listing 8-7 illustrates how these operators work.

Listing 8-7. Demonstration of the AndAlso and OrElse operators.

```vb
' Illustration of shortcutting operators
' Copyright ©2001 by Desaware Inc. All Rights Reserved
Module Module1

    Class A
        Public ReadOnly Property IsTrue() As Boolean
            Get
                Console.WriteLine("IsTrue was called")
                Return True
            End Get
        End Property

        Public ReadOnly Property IsFalse() As Boolean
            Get
                Console.WriteLine("IsFalse was called")
                Return False
            End Get
        End Property

    End Class


    Sub Main()
        Dim testvar As New A()
        If testvar.IsFalse And testvar.IsFalse Then
            Console.WriteLine("After IsFalse And IsFalse")
        End If
        If testvar.IsFalse AndAlso testvar.IsFalse Then
            Console.WriteLine("After IsFalse AndAlso IsFalse")
        End If

        If testvar.IsTrue Or testvar.IsTrue Then
            Console.WriteLine("After IsTrue Or IsTrue")
        End If
        If testvar.IsTrue OrElse testvar.IsTrue Then
            Console.WriteLine("After IsTrue OrElse IsTrue")
        End If
        Console.ReadLine()
    End Sub

End Module
```

This program results in the following output:

```
Before IsFalse And IsFalse
IsFalse was called
IsFalse was called
Before IsFalse AndAlso IsFalse
IsFalse was called
Before IsTrue Or IsTrue
IsTrue was called
IsTrue was called
Before IsTrue OrElse IsTrue
IsTrue was called
```

As you can see, the AndAlso and OrElse operators will not evaluate conditional terms unnecessarily. Once one term in an And expression is False, evaluating others is pointless since any False term guarantees a False result. These operators can result in a substantial performance improvement, especially when the conditional terms are properties that take time to evaluate.

String Operators

Earlier in the chapter, you saw that VB6 can occasionally perform conversions that lead to unexpected results, for example, 15 + "15" could result in 30. Strict Type Checking prevents such automatic conversions and also eliminates the need for a separate Concatenation operator for strings. Basic programmers can thus return to the more intuitive "+" operator to concatenate strings as shown in the following code from the Operators sample program:

```
' Console.WriteLine(15 + "15" + "15") ' Compile error
Console.WriteLine("Evil Typing")
Console.WriteLine(15.toString + "15" + "15")
```

This results in 151515.

You can, of course, stick with the '&' Concatenation operator as well. One thing to watch out with strings (which doesn't directly relate to operators but could lead to some confusion) has to do with character numbers.

The VB.NET intrinsic commands count string characters in the way you are accustomed, from 1 through the length of the string. However, the String .NET class (on which String variables are based) counts characters from a base of zero. Thus, the following code from the Operators example:

```
Dim A As String = "ABCD"
Console.WriteLine("String Characters")
Console.WriteLine(instr(A, "C"))
Console.WriteLine(A.IndexOf("C"))
```

...will result in:

```
String Characters
3
2
```

Concatenation Operators

VB.NET incorporates a set of new Concatenation operators that will be familiar to C++ programmers. These operators perform an operation on a variable and assign the result back to the variable. For example:

A = A + B can be replaced with A += B

This is illustrated in the Concatenators function in Listing 8-8 from the Operators example.

Listing 8-8. Concatenation operations.

```
Sub Concatonators()
    Dim S As String
    Dim A As Integer
    S = "Hello"
    S += " Everybody"
    A = 5
    A += 10
    Console.WriteLine("Concatonators")
    Console.WriteLine(S)
    Console.WriteLine(A)
End Sub
```

Which results in:

```
Concatonators
Hello Everybody
15
```

Table 8-2 lists these new operators.

Table 8-2. VB.NET Concatenation Operator

A &= B	A = A & B (string concatenation)
A *= B	A = A * B
A += B	A = A + B
A /= B	A = A / B
A -= B	A = A–B
A \= B	A = A \ B
A ^= B	A = A ^ B

These operators can make code more concise and readable so I encourage you to make use of them.

Eqv and Imp

The Eqv VB6 operator is replaced by the "=" operator (which does the same thing).

The Imp VB6 operator can be replaced by:

(Not A) Or B ' For logical operations

Recap

In this chapter, you learned how the .NET architecture demanded significant changes in the fundamental data types of VB.NET and how they work. In order for VB.NET to be CLS compliant, its data types must be based on .NET data types.

The most important change for most VB developers is the appearance of Strict Type Checking. This chapter did not discuss the behavior of VB.NET when Strict Type Checking is disabled under the assumption that anyone foolish enough to turn off Strict Type Checking isn't smart enough to read this book in the first place.[8] It goes without saying that you should leave Option Explicit[9] on as well.

---

8. Yes, I realize that this is a very strong way of putting it (and insulting, a behavior I try to avoid)—but darn it, Strict Type Checking is *important!* From the perspective of the total cost to develop software, it may be the single most important new feature in VB.NET. So, if you turned it off or forgot to turn it on, I promise not to tell anyone if you promise to turn it on and fix your code (bet you find some bugs you didn't know you had).

9. Requires variable declarations. Same issues as Strict Type Checking—'nuff said.

While making these fundamental changes, Microsoft's developers took the opportunity to perform some language cleanup as well. They added declaration initialization—a huge improvement, especially with regards to array initialization (always awkward in VB6). And they tossed in a handful of Concatenation operators that those of us who also program in C++ and C# will welcome to Visual Basic.

CHAPTER 9

Language Syntax

NOW THAT YOU'VE SEEN the changes to Visual Basic's underlying Data types and operators, let's look at the changes to the language itself. In this chapter, I'll cover those language changes *not* related to objects and object-oriented programming—those deserve a chapter of their own.

Keep in mind that this chapter is not intended to be a comprehensive reference of all of the changes to the language. That you will find in the Visual Studio.NET online documentation. In fact, I strongly encourage you to review the section of online documentation entitled "What's New in Visual Basic" before you read any further. As always, my goal is to place those changes in context and to explore how they are likely to impact your code.

Function Calls and Parameters

Visual Basic.NET incorporates a number of changes to functions, some significant and some subtle but nonetheless important.

Rational Calling Mechanism

VB6 distinguishes between subroutines and functions. Functions always return values and return zero if no return value is specified. Subroutines never return values. You can call functions and subroutines using the following syntax:

VB6 function call syntax

```
x = F(Y)              ' If you wish to use the result
F Y                   ' If you do not need to use the result
Call F(Y)             ' If you do not need to use the result
F (Y)                 ' Forces Y to be passed by value
```

VB6 subroutine call syntax

```
F Y
Call F(Y)
F (Y)    ' Forces Y to be passed by value
```

It's bad enough having two ways to call methods (with and without parenthesis) but it gets worse. Given function F, what is the difference between the following calls?

```
x = F(Y)
F (Y)
```

Yes, in one case you are using the result and in the other you are not. But there's more. If parameter Y to function F is declared to be ByRef, the first call will pass Y by reference and the second will pass Y by value. This can be a source of subtle and unexpected bugs.

Under VB.NET, the following syntax is used to call functions and subroutines:

```
x = F(Y)        ' If you wish to use the result (not allowed for subroutines)
Call F(Y)       ' if you do not need to use the result
F (Y)           ' if you do not need to use the result
F()             ' Calling a function with no parameters
```

Function calls always use parentheses, even if the function has no parameters. Subroutines and functions are called the same way except that subroutines can't return a result.

You can still use parentheses to force a call by value, in which case the syntax appears as follows:

```
F ((Y))         ' Force a call by value
```

Microsoft's documentation notes that some of the changes from VB6 to VB.NET are to clean up the language. The function-calling syntax is an excellent example of a cleanup that was long overdue.

Returning Values

Visual Basic.NET offers several options for returning values—one of the few cases where the language increases the number of ways to perform a basic operation:

```
Function F(ByRef x As Integer) As Integer
   Return (6)
   Return 6
   F = 6
End Function
```

The Return statement appears in C++ and C# and was probably added to provide a consistent approach for those writing in multiple languages. Personally, I like the Return statement a great deal more than the assignment-to-the-function-name approach. It results in more readable code and reduces the chance that you'll overlook returning a result—especially if your function has multiple exit points.

Unfortunately, the Visual Basic.NET compiler, unlike the C# compiler, does not warn you if you neglect to return a value from a function. I hope Microsoft will reconsider this decision and at least add a warning option.

ByVal Is Now Default

Parameters are now passed ByVal by default. Frankly, I never understood why Visual Basic used ByRef parameters by default. True, ByRef calls are more efficient in VB6, but from a developer's perspective, you run an increased risk of bugs if you accidentally modify parameters within a function. It turns out that the performance advantage of ByRef calls is much smaller in VB.NET. The reason for this will become apparent in the next section.

The ByVal Calling Convention—It's Not What You Think

In VB6, the ByVal and ByRef operators are fairly easy to understand. When you pass a parameter by value, a copy of the variable is placed on the stack and passed as a parameter to the function. If the function modifies the parameter, it does not modify the calling variable, only the copy. When you pass a parameter by reference, a pointer to the variable is passed so changes made to the parameter within the function modify the value of the calling variable as well.

The only exceptions to these rules under VB6 are strings in Declare statements (which pass a null terminated ANSI string to the API function) and objects.

Let's consider for a moment what happens when you pass an object as a parameter to a function. The following applies to both VB6 and VB.NET.[1]

---

1. There are, of course, differences in the actual implementation of the calls primarily due to the fact that VB6 uses COM to obtain a second reference to an object (specifically, a QueryInterface call), whereas .NET uses a simple assignment along with its usual memory management to keep track of root-level variables.

Figure 9-1 shows what happens when you pass an object parameter by reference. The function receives a pointer to the calling Object variable.

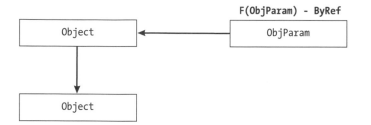

Figure 9-1. An object parameter passed by reference.

Figure 9-2 illustrates what happens when a parameter is passed by value. The function receives an Object variable that contains an additional reference to the object.

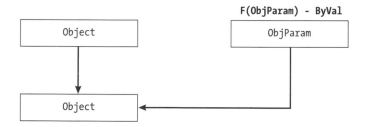

Figure 9-2. An object parameter passed by value.

It's important to realize that even though the variable is passed by value, what is passed is a copy of the Object variable—not a copy of the object itself. In other words, the ByVal and ByRef attribute refers to the variable that references the object and not to the object itself. Objects are not copied when passed by value. ByVal just assures that the calling variable will continue to reference the same object after the call.

The ObjectParams sample program in Listing 9-1 illustrates this with a simple object that has a single Public property. There are two functions that use a ByRef call and two that use a ByVal call: one simply modifies the X property; the other assigns the parameter to a new instance of the MyObject object.

Listing 9-1. Passing objects as parameters.

```
Class MyObject
    Public X As Integer
End Class

Public Sub FObjByRef1(ByRef Y As MyObject)
    Y.X = 5
End Sub

Public Sub FObjByRef2(ByRef Y As MyObject)
    Y = New MyObject()
    Y.X = 5
End Sub

Public Sub FObjByVal1(ByVal Y As MyObject)
    Y.X = 5
End Sub

Public Sub FObjByVal2(ByVal Y As MyObject)
    Y = New MyObject()
    Y.X = 5
End Sub

Public Sub ObjectTests()
    Dim A As New MyObject()
    Dim B As MyObject = A
    A.X = 1
    Console.WriteLine("Initial state")
    Console.WriteLine("Are A and B the same? " + (A Is B).ToString())
    Console.WriteLine("A.x: " + A.X.ToString() + " B.x " + _
                    B.X.ToString())
    FobjByRef1(B)
    Console.WriteLine("After FobjByRef1")
    Console.WriteLine("Are A and B the same? " + (A Is B).ToString())
    Console.WriteLine("A.x: " + A.X.ToString() + " B.x " + _
                    B.X.ToString())
```

```
            A.X = 1
            B = A
            FobjByRef2(B)
            Console.WriteLine("After FobjByRef2")
            Console.WriteLine("Are A and B the same? " + (A Is B).ToString())
            Console.WriteLine("A.x: " + A.X.ToString() + " B.x " + _
                            B.X.ToString())
            A.X = 1
            B = A
            FobjByVal1(B)
            Console.WriteLine("After FobjByVal1")
            Console.WriteLine("Are A and B the same? " + (A Is B).ToString())
            Console.WriteLine("A.x: " + A.X.ToString() + " B.x " + _
                            B.X.ToString())
            A.X = 1
            B = A
            FobjByVal2(B)
            Console.WriteLine("After FobjByVal2")
            Console.WriteLine("Are A and B the same? " + (A Is B).ToString())
            Console.WriteLine("A.x: " + A.X.ToString() + " B.x " + _
                            B.X.ToString())
        End Sub
```

The ObjectTests function produces the following results:

```
Initial state
Are A and B the same? True
A.x: 1 B.x 1
After FobjByRef1
Are A and B the same? True
A.x: 5 B.x 5
After FobjByRef2
Are A and B the same? False
A.x: 1 B.x 5
After FobjByVal1
Are A and B the same? True
A.x: 5 B.x 5
After FobjByVal2
Are A and B the same? True
A.x: 1 B.x 1
```

The object setup initializes the X property to 1 and assigns B and A to reference the same object.

After the FobjByRef1 call, the property value is set to 5 as you would expect. B and A still refer to the same object because the function parameter Y is not modified.

The FobjByRef2 call assigns the Y parameter to a new object. Because the call was made by reference, the calling variable B is set to reference the newly created object. The X property is modified only for the new object, thus A remains at its initial value of 1.

The FobjByVal1 call illustrates an important point. Even though the object is passed by value, the property value of the object is modified.

The FobjByVal2 call is subtle. The Y parameter is set to a new object and the X property of that object is modified. However, that new object is assigned to Y, which is a temporary variable—not a reference to the calling variable. The X property of that new object is modified. When FobjByVal2 returns, B is unmodified. B continues to refer to the original object (which is also referenced by variable A) whose X property was never modified. What happens to the object that was created in the function? When the FobjByVal2 function returns, the temporary Y Object variable goes out of scope and no longer references the newly created object. That object being unreferenced will be deleted during the next garbage collection.

This behavior has always been present in Visual Basic 6 but was relatively unimportant to most programmers, who tended to use the ByRef default and simply avoided setting the Object variable unless they had reason to do so.

However, this behavior is much more important to understand under Visual Basic.NET. Why? Because in VB.NET, every variable is an object.

Before you get too worried, let me elaborate on one point:

Value type objects (such as numeric variables, structures, and those other objects that inherit from the System.ValueType class) work as you would expect. When you pass them as parameters using ByVal, a copy of the Value type object is passed.

Passing Value Type Parameters

The ObjectParams sample program in Listing 9-1 also includes a demonstration of passing Value type objects as parameters. The code in Listing 9-2 is virtually identical to that of the Object type but the results are very different.

Listing 9-2. Passing structures as parameters.

```
Structure MyStruct
    Public X As Integer
End Structure

Public Sub FStructByRef1(ByRef Y As MyStruct)
    Y.X = 5
End Sub
```

```
Public Sub FStructByRef2(ByRef Y As MyStruct)
    Y = New MyStruct()
    Y.X = 5
End Sub

Public Sub FStructByVal1(ByVal Y As MyStruct)
    Y.X = 5
End Sub

Public Sub FStructByVal2(ByVal Y As MyStruct)
    Y = New MyStruct()
    Y.X = 5
End Sub

Public Sub StructTests()
    Dim A As MyStruct
    Dim B As MyStruct
    A.X = 1
    B = A
    Console.WriteLine("Initial state StructTests")
    Console.WriteLine("Are A and B the same? " + _
    (A.Equals(B)).ToString())
    Console.WriteLine("A.x: " + A.X.ToString() + " B.x " + _
    B.X.ToString())
    FStructByRef1(B)
    Console.WriteLine("After FStructByRef1")
    Console.WriteLine("Are A and B the same? " + _
    (A.Equals(B)).ToString())
    Console.WriteLine("A.x: " + A.X.ToString() + " B.x " + _
    B.X.ToString())
    A.X = 1
    B = A
    FStructByRef2(B)
    Console.WriteLine("After FStructByRef2")
    Console.WriteLine("Are A and B the same? " + _
    (A.Equals(B)).ToString())
    Console.WriteLine("A.x: " + A.X.ToString() + " B.x " + _
    B.X.ToString())
    A.X = 1
    B = A
    FStructByVal1(B)
    Console.WriteLine("After FStructByVal1")
    Console.WriteLine("Are A and B the same? " + _
    (A.Equals(B)).ToString())
```

```
      Console.WriteLine("A.x: " + A.X.ToString() + " B.x " + _
      B.X.ToString())
      A.X = 1
      B = A
      FStructByVal2(B)
      Console.WriteLine("After FStructByVal2")
      Console.WriteLine("Are A and B the same? " + _
      (A.Equals(B)).ToString())
      Console.WriteLine("A.x: " + A.X.ToString() + " B.x " + _
      B.X.ToString())

   End Sub
```

There are several important changes to the code that result from the use of Value types. For one thing, there is no need to use the New operator to create an instance of the structure. Value type variables always refer to an object—there is no concept of "Nothing" for Value type objects.

The Equals method is used to compare the structures. This is necessary because VB does not allow you to override the = operator for user-defined structures. The Equals method can, however, be overridden if you wish. In this case, we're using the default Equals method implementation, which performs a shallow compare— a simple, member-by-member comparison of the structure members.

Here are the results:

```
Initial state StructTests
Are A and B the same? True
A.x: 1 B.x 1
After FStructByRef1
Are A and B the same? False
A.x: 1 B.x 5
After FStructByRef2
Are A and B the same? False
A.x: 1 B.x 5
After FStructByVal1
Are A and B the same? True
A.x: 1 B.x 1
After FStructByVal2
Are A and B the same? True
A.x: 1 B.x 1
```

The first thing you may notice is that the meaning of the question "Are A and B the same?" has changed. It will only be True (in this case) when the X property of both objects is equal.

The FStructByRef1 causes the X property of the B object to be set to 5, thus A and B are no longer equal when the function returns. The FStructByRef2 call has the same result but for a different reason. The Y parameter is set to a new structure (thus modifying the B calling variable) and sets its X property to 5.

Both of the ByVal cases result in no change to the B calling value. This proves that the Y parameter did, in fact, receive a copy of the entire structure.

All of the Value type parameters work this way. This includes Boolean, Byte, Char, Decimal, Double, Enum, Single, Integer, Short, Structures, and Long. Their behavior as ByVal and ByRef parameters will be what you intuitively expect.

This list does, however, leave us with two notable exceptions: String variables and Arrays.

Passing Strings as Parameters

String variables deserve special consideration because they are among both the most frequently used objects and because their behavior is a bit nonintuitive. The ObjectParams sample program in Listing 9-3 has been modified to use strings. The only major change is the new FStringByRef3 function, which does not change the contents of the string, it just assigns the first character to its existing value. The intent of this unusual operation will become clear shortly.

Listing 9-3. Passing strings as parameters.

```
Public Sub FStringByRef1(ByRef Y As String)
    Mid$(Y, 1, 1) = "A"
End Sub

Public Sub FStringByRef2(ByRef Y As String)
    Y = "Hello"
End Sub

Public Sub FStringByRef3(ByRef Y As String)
    Mid$(Y, 1, 1) = Mid$(Y,1,1)
End Sub

Public Sub FStringByVal1(ByVal Y As String)
    Mid$(Y, 1, 1) = "A"
End Sub

Public Sub FStringByVal2(ByVal Y As String)
    Y = "Hello"
End Sub
```

```
Public Sub StringTests()
    Dim A As String = "Hello"
    Dim B As String
    B = A
    Console.WriteLine(chr(10) + "Initial state StringTests")
    Console.WriteLine("Are A and B the same? " + (A Is B).ToString())
    Console.WriteLine("A: " + A + " B: " + B)
    FStringByRef1(B)
    Console.WriteLine("After FStringByRef1")
    Console.WriteLine("Are A and B the same? " + (A Is B).ToString())
    Console.WriteLine("A: " + A + " B: " + B)
    A = "Hello"
    B = A
    FStringByRef2(B)
    Console.WriteLine("After FStringByRef2")
    Console.WriteLine("Are A and B the same? " + (A Is B).ToString())
    Console.WriteLine("A: " + A + " B: " + B)
    A = "Hello"
    B = A
    FStringByRef3(B)
    Console.WriteLine("After FStringByRef3")
    Console.WriteLine("Are A and B the same? " + (A Is B).ToString())
    Console.WriteLine("Are A and B equal? " + (A = B).ToString())
    Console.WriteLine("A: " + A + " B: " + B)
    A = "Hello"
    B = A
    FStringByVal1(B)
    Console.WriteLine("After FStringByVal1")
    Console.WriteLine("Are A and B the same? " + (A Is B).ToString())
    Console.WriteLine("A: " + A + " B: " + B)
    A = "Hello"
    B = A
    FStringByVal2(B)
    Console.WriteLine("After FStringByVal2")
    Console.WriteLine("Are A and B the same? " + (A Is B).ToString())
    Console.WriteLine("A: " + A + " B: " + B)


End Sub
```

Keeping in mind that strings are objects, let's go through the results line by line:

```
Initial state StringTests
Are A and B the same? True
A: Hello B: Hello
```

The initial state for each test has both A and B referencing the same object. In other words, there exists a single String object that contains the text "Hello." Variables A and B are the same object (as evidenced by the True result to the Is operator). The contents of A and B are also equal (obviously, since they reference the same object):

```
After FStringByRef1
Are A and B the same? False
A: Hello B: Aello
```

The FStringByRef1 method assigns a character in the string using the Mid$ statement:

```
Mid$(Y, 1, 1) = "A"
```

Think about it. The Y parameter being passed by reference refers to the same object as A. Thus, you would think that modifying a character in that string would modify string A as well. Remember that in the Object Parameters example earlier, modifying the X property of the object through the Y variable also modified the X property of the A variable that referenced the same object.

In fact, the Mid$ function did not modify the String object that was referenced by Y. It actually created a new string with a different first character and assigned it to the Y parameter, which (being passed by reference) also modified the B variable.

Why did this happen? Because strings are immutable (as discussed in Chapter 8). Any operation that seems to modify a string actually creates a new string. So, while B was modified to reference the new string, variable A continued to reference the original Hello string:

```
After FStringByRef2
Are A and B the same? True
A: Hello B: Hello
```

The FStringByRef2 function assigns the Y parameter to a new string that is equal to the original string value:

```
Y = "Hello"
```

Intuitively, you might expect B to reference a new String object that contains the value Hello. Yet, it turns out on return that B and A still reference the same object! This occurs because the VB.NET compiler is smart about string literals. It sees that you are assigning Y with the string Hello and that it already has this string in the internal string table. So, it simply sets Y to reference the same string literal object. This is a process called Interning and is possible because of the immutability of strings—the CLR knows that the literal can't be changed so it can safely assign String variables to the same literals when possible.

This process is made even clearer by the FStringByRef3 example, which, on the surface, does not modify the string at all:

```
Mid$(Y, 1, 1) = Mid$(Y,1,1)
```

Yet, the result indicates that A and B are no longer the same, even though they are equal!

```
After FStringByRef3
Are A and B the same? False
Are A and B equal? True
A: Hello B: Hello
```

In other words, A and B now reference different variables that happen to have the same contents. Why did this happen? Even though the string is unchanged, the CLR can't tell that the string is being assigned to a literal. In order to maintain the immutability of the string, it must assign Y to a new string even if it happens to have the same contents as before.

The ByVal functions produce the following results:

```
After FStringByVal1
Are A and B the same? True
A: Hello B: Hello
After FStringByVal2
Are A and B the same? True
A: Hello B: Hello
```

These results are exactly what you would expect if the String object were a Value type—the changes do not impact the calling function (unlike the Object parameters example where changing the X property of a ByVal object was reflected in the X property of the calling variables as well). This works due to the immutability of strings. Changes to the contents of the string cannot be reflected in the calling variable because the contents of a string never change. Instead, a new string is created and assigned to the Y parameter. Since the Y parameter was passed by value, changes to that parameter do not modify the B calling variable.

Note that because assigning a string by value does not actually make a copy of the string, there is no performance benefit to passing strings ByRef! So, go ahead and pass strings ByVal unless you have good reason to do otherwise.

Passing Arrays as Parameters

Arrays are objects. Unlike strings, they are not immutable. This means that you would expect the same results you saw earlier with the Object parameters example. Changes to an element of the array should always impact the object even if the array is passed ByVal (just like to the X property of MyObject). Assignment to the Y parameter should only impact the calling variable if the call is made by reference.

I've omitted the source code due to space considerations (you can find it in the ObjectParams sample program). The results, as shown in Listing 9-4, are exactly as you would expect.

Listing 9-4. Passing arrays as parameters.

```
Initial state ArrayTests
Are A and B the same? True
Array A:
1, 2, 3, 4, 5
Array B
1, 2, 3, 4, 5
After FArrayByRef1
Are A and B the same? True
Array A:
5, 2, 3, 4, 5
Array B
5, 2, 3, 4, 5
After FArrayByRef2
Are A and B the same? False
Array A:
1, 2, 3, 4, 5
Array B
2, 3, 4, 5, 6
After FArrayByVal1
Are A and B the same? True
Array A:
5, 2, 3, 4, 5
Array B
5, 2, 3, 4, 5
After FArrayByVal2
Are A and B the same? True
```

```
Array A:
1, 2, 3, 4, 5
Array B
1, 2, 3, 4, 5
```

Let's take a moment and summarize what you've learned here:

1. Value type objects behave in a way that is intuitive. When passed by value, a copy of the variable is passed to the function and changes to the variable cannot impact the calling variable. When passed by reference, a pointer to the variable is passed to the function and changes to the parameter can impact the calling variable.

2. Objects are less intuitive. The ByVal and ByRef attributes refer to the variable that references the object and not the object itself. Objects are not copied when passed by value. ByVal just assures that the calling variable will continue to reference the same object after the call. Method and property calls to the object can modify the object.

3. Arrays are objects and follow the rules just mentioned in item 2.

4. Strings are objects but their perceived behavior is modified by the fact that strings are immutable. Because no method or property call can actually modify a string, when passed by value, it may seem as if a copy were made but that is not the case. One consequence of this is that passing a String object ByVal has the same performance as passing it ByRef (unlike the case in VB6 where passing a string by value has severe performance implications due to the need to copy the string).

The nice thing about parameter passing in .NET is that it *does* follow consistent rules—even if they do take some getting used to.

Optional Parameters Require Default—No Is Missing

Visual Basic.NET requires that you specify default values for optional parameters (with VB6, you can leave off the default value and the missing parameters will be set to zero or to the empty string depending on variable type).

Because Visual Basic.NET does not support variants, it naturally does not support variant optional parameters and thus no longer requires or supports the IsMissing statement used to determine whether a variant parameter was missing.

ParamArrays

ParamArrays allow you to pass a variable number of parameters to a function. In VB6, ParamArrays are implemented as follows:

```
Public Function A(ParamArray V() As Variant)
   Dim x As Integer
   If IsMissing(V) Then
      Debug.Print "V is missing"
   Else
      For x = 0 To UBound(V())
         Debug.Print V(x)
      Next x
   End If
End Function
```

The variants (if present) are passed by reference. You must use the IsMissing function to determine if parameters are present before enumerating the entries in the array.

In Visual Basic.NET, the parameter array can be defined as any type (including Object, should you need to support different types of objects as parameters). The array is passed ByVal (with all that implies as discussed previously in this chapter).

If no parameters are specified when the function is called, the array is a zero-length array which can be enumerated directly as shown:

```
Public Sub ParamArrayTest1(ParamArray ByVal A() As Integer)
    Dim x As Integer
    For x = 0 To uBound(A)
        Console.WriteLine(A(x))
    Next
End Sub
```

The UBound function returns –1 for zero-length arrays, thus simplifying the code needed to enumerate the array entries.

Scoping Rules

When programmers discuss the scope of a variable, they are really talking about two things: the visibility of a variable and the lifetime of a variable. Visibility determines where in the code you are able to access a variable. Lifetime determines when the variable is created and destroyed.

The scoping rules for modules, objects, and assemblies will be discussed in Chapter 10 because they relate more closely to the object-oriented features of the language than to the language syntax. Here, we'll explore changes to variable scope within a function.

Consider the following VB6 example from the ScopingVB6 sample project:

```
Sub Main()
    Dim Counter As Integer
    ' X = 3  ' Variable not defined at this point
    For Counter = 1 To 3
        If True Then    ' Always enter this block
            Dim X As Integer
            Debug.Print X
            X = Counter
        End If
    Next Counter
    Debug.Print "Outside of block: " & X
End Sub
```

This code displays the following results in the Immediate window:

```
0
1
2
Outside of block 3
```

The code illustrates several key points about scoping in VB6:

- You can't access a variable until it is declared.

- VB6 initializes variables to zero.

- The visibility of X is the entire block once it is declared (for instance, you can access the variable outside of the block in which it is defined).

- The lifetime of X is the duration of the function call (in other words, you can exit and reenter the block and the value will remain unchanged). Initialization occurs when the function is entered—not when the block is entered.

- You can't declare two local variables of the same name in a function.

Now, consider the equivalent code in VB.NET from the Scoping sample project:

```
Module ScopingMod

    Sub Main()
        Dim Counter As Short
        ' X = 3  ' Variable not defined at this point
        For Counter = 1 To 3
            If True Then '  Always enter this block
                Dim X As Short
                Console.WriteLine(X)
                X = Counter
            End If
        Next Counter
        'Console.WriteLine("Outside of block: " & X)
        Console.ReadLine()
    End Sub
End Module
```

This code results in the output:

```
0
1
2
```

The big change here is that it is no longer possible to access the variable outside of the block in which it is defined. The VB.NET Upgrade Wizard will move local variable declarations out of a block if necessary in order to make the variables visible wherever they are called.

Just to place this subject in context, consider how the new C# language handles this situation as shown in Listing 9-5, the ScopingCSharp example.

Listing 9-5. The ScopingCSharp example.

```
static void Main(string[] args)
{
                short counter;
                //short x;
                //x = 50;  // Variable not defined at this point
                for(counter = 1;counter<=3;counter++)
                {
```

```
                    if (true)
                    {
                              short x=0;        // C# requires initialization
                              Console.WriteLine(x);
                              x= counter;
                    }
              }
              //Console.WriteLine("Outside of block: " + x.ToString());
              Console.ReadLine();
}
```

This code results in the output:

```
0
0
0
```

The lifetime of *x* is still the life of the function; however, the C# language forces you to initialize variables before you use them and performs the initialization at the point of declaration. This had a slight performance impact but does give you improved predictability (though it's unlikely you'll miss this kind of bug during development).

The really interesting code is in C++ as shown in Listing 9-6, the ScopingC++ example.

Listing 9-6. The Scoping C++ example.

```
int main(void)
{
    short counter;

    short x;
    x = 50;  // Variable not defined at this point
    for(counter = 1;counter<=3;counter++) {
        if (true) {
                          short x; // C# requires initialization
                          Console::WriteLine(x);
                          x= counter;
                  }
              }
    Console::WriteLine(x.ToString());
    Console::ReadLine();
    return 0;
}
```

This results in the output:

```
0
1
2
50
```

To be fair, the C++ compiler does warn about the uninitialized variable. However, the really interesting aspect of this code is that a block can define a nested local variable of the same name. When x is defined in the inner block, it temporarily shadows the x declared in the outer block.

The disadvantage of this approach is that you can have multiple variables by the same name in a single function, which can lead to confusion.

The advantage is that you can keep variable declarations in close proximity to where they are used in individual blocks, reusing variable names at will.

I'll be honest—this is one feature in C++ I miss, even though the C#/VB.NET approach results in code that is marginally easier to read.[2]

Static Variables

A Static variable is one whose lifetime is the duration of the entire program but whose visibility is limited to the function in which it is declared. Static variables are initialized the first time a function is called and remain unchanged for subsequent calls of the same function.

In VB6, it is possible to declare a Static function in which all variables in the function would be static by default. In all my years as a Visual Basic programmer, I have never declared a Static function—so, I can't say I was too troubled when I heard about this change.

Static variables are specific to object instances. This is shown in Listing 9-7, the Statics sample project.

Listing 9-7. The Statics sample project.

```
Class C
    Public Shared Sub SharedTest()
        Static x As Integer
        x = x + 1
        console.WriteLine(x)
    End Sub
```

---

2. I'm also conflicted about spending this much space on a relatively unimportant issue. I can only excuse this in saying that sometimes language features are interesting for their own sake and I tend to feel that a good understanding of scoping—even the subtle issues—is important.

```
    Public Sub Test()
        Static x As Integer
        x = x + 1
        console.WriteLine(x)
    End Sub
End Class

Module Module1

    Sub Main()
        Dim c1 As New C()
        Dim c2 As New C()
        c1.Test()
        c1.Test()
        c2.Test()
        c2.Test()
        c.SharedTest()
        c.SharedTest()
        console.ReadLine()
    End Sub

End Module
```

This code results in the following output:

```
1
2
1
2
1
2
```

Variables c1 and c2 point to different instances of class C objects. The results indicate that the Test method for each object has its own copy of the Static variables, as does the SharedTest method.[3]

Note: There will inevitably be a certain amount of confusion between static and shared variables as you learn more about Microsoft.NET. The reason for this is that the keyword Static in C++ and C# is used to define both shared and static variables. As you read documentation, white papers, and articles on .NET, there will be times when the author forgets to include both C# and VB.NET terminology.

---

3. You'll read more about shared methods and variables in Chapter 10.

However, if you follow these simple rules, you should be able to avoid confusion:

- VB.NET Shared variables are variables shared among all instances of a class.

- VB.NET Shared class methods are not associated with a particular object (you'll read about this in Chapter 10).

- Static local variables have visibility only within the method or function in which they are defined but their lifetime is the duration of the program.

- If you ever hear the term "static" applied to a class method or class variable, it means shared.

Error Handling

Let's begin our discussion of error handling by agreeing on one fundamental fact:
Error handling in Visual Basic 6 sucks.[4]
Of course, to be completely fair, error handling in C++ does as well.
There are probably a few of you VB6 programmers who are aghast wondering what could possibly be wrong with the good ol' On Error Goto statement, not to mention numerous C++ programmers who think I've completely lost my senses because C++ already has the Structured Exception Handling capabilities I'm about to tell you about.
Bear with me. I have good reasons for both statements.

The Old Way

Before looking at the way VB6 handles errors, I'd like to take you to a lower level and examine the source of those errors. Runtime errors can occur under the following circumstances:

- While accessing a method or property of a COM object.

- During an API call.

- During a VB6 language operation (for example, a numeric overflow).

Let's look at these one at a time.

---

4. Pardon my language but sometimes one must reach out to borderline colloquialisms to properly express a sentiment without descending into obscenity.

One of the requirements of an object model (like COM) is that it have a standard and consistent error-reporting mechanism. Without such a mechanism, it is impossible for components to notify calling clients that errors have occurred. Without a standard, it would be impossible for components written by one user using a particular language to work correctly with components written by another user in that or any other language.

The error mechanism under COM is based on a 32-bit value called an HRESULT. I won't go into detail on HRESULTs here (they are covered in-depth in MSDN and in my book *Developing COM/ActiveX Components with Visual Basic 6*, [Que, 1998]). Suffice to say that they divide errors into possible sources[5] (such as ActiveX controls, Automation, or system errors) and error numbers. COM method and property calls and virtually every OLE subsystem API return HRESULT values that can be interpreted in a standard manner. In addition, an object can implement an interface called ISupportErrorInfo, which allows a component to provide additional information about an error to a client, such as a text message, source information, and even a help-file location for information about the error.

Errors that occur in API functions are indicated by the result of the function. Every function defines its own error values. Some functions indicate an error by returning –1, some by returning zero, some by returning any nonzero value. Additional information about an error is usually available by calling the GetLastError API function, which returns an error value based on a list of standard errors defined in the winerror.h header file that comes with the Windows Platform SDK (and Visual C++). The inconsistent form of API function return values is indicative of the haphazard evolution of the Windows API. The GetLastError return values were defined as part of the evolution from 16 to 32-bit Windows. The standard API error values are also mapped into one of the categories of HRESULT codes.

Errors that occur during language operations such as overflows or array boundary errors raise runtime errors that can only be handled in VB6 using the On Error Goto statement. Because VB6 handles COM method and property access for you behind the scenes, it is also able to raise runtime errors when an error occurs in a COM component by mapping the HRESULT values it returns into a VB runtime error.

VB6 Error Handling

In Visual Basic, you can use the On Error Goto statement to trap errors. What's wrong with this approach?

---

5.   The term "Facility" is used to define an error category. A Facility Code is the value indicating the source category of the error.

- You can only have one error handler active in a particular function or sub-routine. It is possible to trap some errors and pass others to calling functions but this ability to "nest" error handlers is at the function level and cannot be done within a function.

- When an error occurs, your error-handling code must evaluate the Error type based on a line number or Error type.

- A routine with complex error handling results in Spaghetti code in which it is difficult to determine the flow of control for a function.

- The On Error Resume Next statement, while eliminating Spaghetti code, clutters your code if you include inline error checking everywhere an error can occur.

- The inconsistency of error sources (especially for VB programmers who use API functions) tends to encourage error management inconsistencies in VB programs. It's not unusual to see VB programs where some functions return error values and others raise errors.

VC++ Error Handling

Visual C++ programmers have long pointed to error handling as one of the areas that proves the superiority of C++ over Visual Basic. You see, Visual C++ supports something called Structured Exception Handling that is far superior to the On Error Goto syntax of Visual Basic. I'll tell you about Structured Exception Handling shortly but before I do, let me tell you why the C++ crowd is wrong.

You see, while it is true that VC++ supports Structured Exception Handling, and it is true that it is better than On Error Goto, it is also very poorly supported in the Windows environment on VC++ 6.0.

Why? Consider these problems:

- API calls, which are much more common in VC++, still return error code results instead of raising errors that can be detected using Structured Exception Handling.

- COM method and property calls, which VB6 has the courtesy of mapping into runtime errors, simply return HRESULT values for C++ programmers. Thus, they, too, are not automatically supported using Structured Exception Handling.

- Most C++ runtime and library errors are not handled by Structured Exception Handling. In fact, they generally aren't handled at all, resulting in Memory exceptions, which, at best, can invoke a just-in-time debugger and, at worst, will crash your application (except on Windows 95/98/ME where they can crash your system as well).

In other words, having Structured Exception Handling built into he language has very little benefit if it's not supported by the software libraries and objects that comprise the environment for which you are programming!

Which brings us to .NET

Structured Exception Handling

What is Structured Exception Handling? The key word here is structure. Visual Basic, C#, and C++ all belong to a language category called a block-structured language. These languages allow you to define blocks of code that are handled as a unit. In other words, you can code structures in the form:

If *something,* then execute *a block of code.* Otherwise, execute *another block of code* where each block of code can be of any size and can contain additional nested blocks of code.

C# and C++ delineate blocks using the { and } characters. Visual Basic delineates blocks using the syntax of the language itself. The exact syntax doesn't matter. The idea is that you can group code into blocks that can be executed based on a decision without having to apply the decision to each line of code within the block.

Structured Exception Handling simply applies this principle to error handling. The syntax for Structured Exception Handling looks something like this:

```
Try
    some block of code
Catch a type of error [When condition]
    some block of code to execute if that error occurs
Catch another type of error [When condition]
    some block of code to execute if that error occurs
Finally
    A block of code to execute before leaving the Try block
End Try
```

Each block of code can contain additional blocks of code, including additional Try…End Try blocks!

Exception objects represent types of errors. All exceptions should inherit from a class called System.Exception. You can use multiple Catch statements to catch different types of errors. You can optionally add a When term to a Catch statement to specify an additional condition to apply to the Catch block. A Catch block will be executed only if the specified Error type occurs and the condition specified by the When term is True.

That's all there is to it.

The important change for VB.NET isn't so much the language syntax—as important as that is—and it's not that every VB language runtime error raises an exception that can be caught using Structured Exception Handling, which is something you would expect. The really important change is that *every error that can occur in every method or property of every .NET Framework class or object raises an exception that can be caught using Structured Exception Handling!*

Having the Try…End Try syntax is nice. Having it built into the environment from the ground up is fantastic. What's more, .NET interop will map errors for any COM objects you use into exceptions as well![6]

So, the only place you won't have errors compatible with Structured Exception Handling are with API calls and those are much less common under VB.NET than VB6 anyway (as you will see in Chapter 15).

Overview of the ErrorHandling Sample Project

The ErrorHandling sample project illustrates Structured Exception Handling. A close examination of the code will help you understand not just how it works but how you should use it.

The ErrorHandling sample is a console application that does some simple file processing. It reads numbers from a file and writes to the console the results of 100 divided by each number. Before going into the details of the code, Listing 9-8 depicts a quick pseudocode[7] description of the program.

Listing 9-8. A pseudocode description of the Error-Handling sample project.

```
Sub Main
Try
        Try
                Open the file
        Catch—file not found
                Create the file and write sample data
```

6. Interop is the term used to describe .NET's ability to work with COM. You'll learn more about interop in Chapter 15.
7. Pseudocode is a way to describe a program. It has the structure of actual code but a syntax that is intended to be understood by a reader, not a computer.

```
        Catch—any other error
                Exit the program
        End Try


        Try
                Read a line of the file
                Try
                        Display 100/the numeric value of the line
                Catch—Line can't be converted into a number
                        Do some error handling
                Catch—Division by zero
                        Do some error handling
                Catch—any other error
                        Throw it to the next level with some extra information
                End Try
        Catch—Any error
                Do some error handling
        Finally
                Close the file and delete it
End Try
Finally
        Console.ReadLine
End Try
End Sub
```

The first thing that happens in Sub Main is the declaration of a Try block. You might think this occurs in order to catch and handle any error that takes place in this program. And *that*…is a good reason to place your entire program in a Try block. At the very least, it allows you to display your own runtime error message instead of the one provided by the .NET Framework. For example, you could display the .NET error message along with information such as a contact Email address or phone number. You could even have your error-handling code log detailed error information including a complete stack trace and send it to your tech support team via the Internet! Just be sure your error handler has its own error trapping if you do anything sophisticated.

However, in this case, I have a completely different reason for placing the entire program in a Try block. You've probably noticed that most of the sample programs in this book that are based on Console applications end with a Console.ReadLine statement. The reason for this is obvious: it keeps the Output window open until the user presses the Enter key, which makes it possible to see the results. The problem in this ErrorHandling sample project is that some of the caught errors require the program to exit immediately; the best way to do that is by using the Exit Sub command. But how can you see the results if you use Exit Sub, which, upon exiting the Main routine, immediately closes the Output window (since the Console.ReadLine command never executes)?

The answer is to put all of the code inside a Try block and put the final Console.ReadLine statement in the Finally block.

The code inside a Finally block is guaranteed to run before the Try Block exits. It "trumps" the Exit Sub and Exit Function statements. In other words, if I call the Exit Sub or Exit Function statement inside a block of code in a Try…End Try block, all of the pending Finally blocks will execute before the subroutine actually exits.

This represents a dramatic change in the meaning of the Exit Sub and Exit Function statement but also represents an improvement—since the great failing of the Exit Sub and Exit Function statements was the difficulty they presented in performing any necessary cleanup. In VB6, you end up either performing cleanup each time you call Exit Sub or performing a Goto to a block of common exit code that ends with an Exit Sub or Exit Function call.[8]

The program uses nested Try blocks. This demonstrates one of the biggest advantages of Structured Exception Handling over the old On Error Goto statement. It helps you partition your error handling, even within a function. Sure, you could accomplish this with On Error Goto by having several error-handling blocks and using multiple On Error Goto statements to redirect errors to those blocks, but the result is code that is hard to read and follow as the program flow jumps out and then back.

Nested Try blocks also eliminate the need for a Resume statement. Any place you want to be able to handle an error and then continue running, simply add another nested Try block!

The ErrorHandling Sample Project In-Depth

Now, let's take a close look at the program code.

The example uses two constants intended to illustrate the results of different design choices. When the ShowErrors constant is True, an error message is displayed to the console when an invalid number is found in the file—either a line that can't be converted into an integer, or a number (such as zero) that results in a division error. When the ThrowOnBadFormat constant is True, if a line is found that can't be converted into an integer, the sample throws an error to be processed by the next block up (in this example, a higher Try block; but in a component, it might represent passing the error up to the client after some error processing):

---

8. The Goto statement is, of course, evil. However, using it to perform centralized cleanup before exiting a function is one of the few places in VB6 where it is less evil than the alternative of placing the cleanup code at each exit point. Another place where Goto is acceptable in VB6 is, of course, the On Error Goto statement—simply because you have no choice. In VB.NET, neither of these exceptions is applicable so Goto is even more evil than it is in VB6.

```
' Error Handling example
' Copyright ©2001 by Desaware Inc. All Rights Reserved
Imports System.IO
Module Module1

    Const ShowErrors As Boolean = False
    Const ThrowOnBadFormat As Boolean = True
```

The first step is to open a Try block whose primary purpose in this example is to force the Console.ReadLine statement to always execute by placing it in a Finally block:

```
Sub Main()
    Dim FileToRead As String
    Try
        ' Putting everything in a Try Block allows catching
        ' Exit Sub easily
        FileToRead = CurDir + "\TestFile.txt"
        Dim TestFile As FileStream
```

The next Try block prepares the file for reading. If the file exists, it is opened. If not, it is created. If any error occurs that would prevent the file from being read, the program exits.

File I/O is another area that has changed significantly and one that I will go into further in Chapter 12.

The FileStream object inherits from Stream, an object designed to manipulate streams of data. A FileStream object allows you to read and write data in a file. If the file exits, the FileStream will be successfully created. If not, the FileNotFoundException exception will be raised. But what about other types of errors? This block has a second Catch statement that catches the generic Exception object.[9]

Here's a question: if the FileNotFoundException type inherits from System.Exception; and System.Exception matches any error, but the FileNotFoundException matches only "file not found" errors; how do you know that the FileNotFoundException handler (and not the more generic System.Exception handler) will catch the "file not found" error?

Simple: the FileNotFoundException comes first.

When a runtime error occurs, the program checks the list of Catch statements and goes down the list one by one until it finds one that matches the error that occurred. This means you should always place the most specific error handler first in the list:

---

9. See the block starting with the line `Catch E2 As Exception` farther down in the listing.

```
Try
    TestFile = New FileStream(FileToRead, FileMode.Open, _
    FileAccess.Read)
Catch E As FileNotFoundException
    ' If the file isn't found (typically the case),
    ' create a new one
```

If the file is not found, we create a file and attempt to write some sample data to the file. This is accomplished by first creating a new FileStream object (this time with the Create flag set), then creating a StreamWriter object that is associated with that FileStream. A StreamWriter object has methods to read and write various types of data to and from a stream.

After the data is written, it must be flushed out. Why? Because a FileStream object uses buffering to improve performance and we want to make sure that the data is written before we reset the file position to the start of the file in preparation for reading the data back.

If the file cannot be created or any error occurs in writing the file, an exception occurs. In this case, we simply catch the generic System.Exception object and leave the program as it doesn't really matter why the problem occurs—the program cannot continue from that point.

```
Try
    TestFile = New FileStream(FileToRead, FileMode.Create, _
    FileAccess.ReadWrite)
    Dim Writer As New StreamWriter(TestFile)
    Writer.WriteLine("8")
    Writer.WriteLine("7")
    Writer.WriteLine("0")
    Writer.WriteLine("ABC")
    Writer.WriteLine("5")
    ' Don't forget to Flush!!!!
    Writer.Flush()
    TestFile.Seek(0, SeekOrigin.Begin)
Catch CantCreate As Exception
    ' Unlikely to happen with this example
    Console.WriteLine("Can't create or write the file")
    Exit Sub
End Try
Catch E2 As Exception
    Console.WriteLine("Some other error occurred")
    ' Note: Exit Sub does not avoid Finally blocks!
    Exit Sub
End Try
```

At this point, the file is open and ready to read. If it weren't, the program would have already exited. The next step is to read the file. Another Try block is opened here, not just to catch errors but mostly to define a Finally block in which the file can be closed and deleted (the file is deleted just for illustrative purposes in this example). A Do loop is going to loop through the file reading one line each time:

```
' If we got this far, the TestFile is open

Try
    Dim Reader As New StreamReader(TestFile)
    Do
        Dim I As Integer, S As String
        Dim Result As Integer
```

We enter another Try block for each line. Why? Because most of the errors that occur in this block are going to be recoverable—meaning that they are intended to be handled and not to prevent the rest of the entries in the file from being read:

```
Try
    S = Reader.ReadLine()
    I = CInt(S)
    Result = 100 \ I
    Console.WriteLine(Result)
```

The DivideByZeroException is fairly self-explanatory. The interesting thing about this block is the use of the Exit Try statement to exit a Try block. The Exit Try statement transfers control to the line after the End Try block. However, any code in a Finally block will execute even if you use an Exit Try statement. The ShowErrors constant allows you to experiment with this statement:[10]

```
Catch DivByZero As System.DivideByZeroException
    If Not ShowErrors Then Exit Try
    Console.WriteLine("** Divide by zero **")
```

The System.InvalidCastException exception occurs when the line read from the file can't be converted into an integer.[11] In this case, if the ThrowOnBadFormat constant is True, an exception will be thrown—but what exception?

---

10. Yes, I know—in this particular example, it would have been better to make the Console.WriteLine statement conditional on ShowErrors rather than use the slightly convoluted logic and Exit Try statement. But then I wouldn't have been able to show you the Exit Try statement. Truth is, you probably won't use Exit Try unless your error-handling code is quite complex.

11. The term "Cast" can be thought of as the C++/C# term for conversion.

You can throw any exception you wish using the Throw statement. Simply create a new Exception object and pass it as a parameter to the Throw statement. You can use any of the standard exception types or create your own—simply create a new class that inherits from System.Exception or any of the other unsealed exception classes. In this case, we're throwing another System.InvalidCastException object but putting in our own error message. Not only that, but the original Bad-Conversion exception object is passed as a parameter called the InnerException. An inner exception is used to indicate that an exception you are throwing was triggered as a result of another exception, thus providing additional information to the higher-level block:

```
Catch BadConversion As System.InvalidCastException
    If ShowErrors Then Console.WriteLine("** " + S + _
    " is not a number **")
    If ThrowOnBadFormat Then Throw New _
    System.InvalidCastException( _
    "My own exception happened here", BadConversion)
```

If any other errors occur (which is unlikely but possible), the error is simply rethrown:

```
Catch OtherErrors As Exception
    ' This catch block is meaningless!
    Throw OtherErrors
End Try
```

What would happen if another error occurred and was not caught by this code? That's right—it's a trick question. Errors that aren't matched to a Catch block automatically go to the next Try block! The end result is exactly as if we had caught the error and then threw it again. So, this Catch block does nothing and should not be here.

In the context of the current Try Block—in cases where a Throw statement is used (either the Catch OtherErrors block or when a System.InvalidCastException error occurred while the ThrowOnBadFormat constant is True)—the error will be propagated out of the Try block and further parsing of the file will stop. But if a conversion error occurs while the ThrowOnBadFormat constant is False or a division by zero error occurs, no error is thrown; thus the file continues to be read and the function continues with the Loop statement:

```
Loop While Reader.Peek <> -1
```

Why use the Reader.Peek method (which returns –1 when the end of a file is reached)? Why not just catch the exception that occurs when the end of file is reached and stop reading at that point?

Then answer is a bit philosophical. The two exceptions we do catch, division by zero and a format error, represent (in the context of this example) real errors. The presumption is that this file is created by a user or other source and, if formatted correctly, will never have the number zero and will never have a non-numeric text. In other words, both of these conditions represent error conditions—format errors in the file.

But the end of a file is not an error (in this example). The program is designed to read to the end of a file, which means it is expected that, at some point, the end of a file will be reached.

An expected behavior is not an exception.

Exceptions should be reserved for exceptional conditions—for errors or unexpected behavior. So, yes, you could catch the end of a file using an exception—but it's poor design and will make your application harder to read and ultimately support.

When would an end of file be a legitimate exception?

What if the first line in the file represented the number of lines in the file and you then entered a loop to read that exact number of lines? In that case, an end of file would represent an unexpected error and handling it with an exception would be appropriate.

The Catch block shown next illustrates how a container might handle a thrown exception. It writes a custom error message to the console along with the exception message and that of any inner exception. It then writes out a stack trace (take that, VB6!):

```
Catch E As Exception
    ' How you might catch an error coming from another assembly
    Console.WriteLine(ControlChars.CrLf + _
    "An internal error occurred")
    Console.WriteLine("Message: " + E.Message)
    Console.WriteLine("Source Message: " + _
    E.InnerException.Message)
    Dim F As Integer, S As New StackTrace(E)
    Console.WriteLine("StackFrame: ")
    For f = 0 To S.FrameCount - 1
        Console.WriteLine(S.GetFrame(f).ToString())
    Next F
```

We're now almost finished unwinding from the various Try blocks. These ensure that the file is closed and deleted. In this example, since the file was created here in this application, there's no real possibility of being unable to delete the file. However, if you were concerned about this, you could always place another Try block inside of a Finally block. In this example, even if one of these were to fail, the outer-level, Unhandled exception Catch block that follows would catch it. Finally, the Console.ReadLine statement is called:

```
    Finally
        ' We're virtually certain to close ok
        TestFile.Close()
        ' Delete could fail though due to security
        File.Delete(FileToRead)
    End Try


Catch Unhandled As Exception
    ' Just in case we overlooked something here.
    ' YOU should control which errors are propogated outward!
    Console.WriteLine("An unhandled exception occurred " + _
    Unhandled.Message)
Finally
    Console.ReadLine()
    End Try
End Sub

End Module
```

I encourage you to experiment with this program. I won't show you the results here since there are many different possibilities. Among the options to try include:

- Experiment with the values of the ShowErrors and ThrowOnBadFormat methods.

- Add Throw statements to try forcing different errors at different places.

- Add Exit Sub statements in Catch blocks to verify that the Finalize statement runs regardless.

- Add Exit Try statements in Catch blocks to verify that the Finalize statement runs regardless.

- Add When terms to Catch statements to apply additional conditions to exception handling blocks.

What about On Error Goto?

Visual Basic.NET still supports the good ol' On Error Goto statement and the Err object. Perhaps Microsoft's developers figured they would get enough grief over the language changes and couldn't take the heat on this one. Or, maybe it was an act of mercy for those who do plan on porting existing VB6 code because Structured Exception Handling uses a radically different code organization than the On Error Goto statement. Most likely, it was an act of expedience—designing the Upgrade Wizard to correctly convert existing code based on the On Error Goto statement to Structured Exception Handling would be quite a challenge.

If you do find yourself porting code and you know your error handling works, it probably makes sense to stick with On Error Goto—the benefits of Structured Exception Handling are greatest when it is incorporated into the original design.

But for all new development, bite the bullet and use Structured Exception Handling. It will help you create code that is more reliable and stable and ultimately has a lower total cost of ownership.

Other Language Changes

In this section, I'll quickly review the other major changes to the language, again avoiding those that relate to object-oriented programming (the subject of the next chapter).

Control Flow Changes

When was the last time you used Gosub, On...Gosub, or On...Goto?

I have never used any of these terms with Visual Basic—they are holdovers from the old days of BASIC when the language was not a block-structured language.

If you are using Gosub because it allows you to define a reusable block of code in a function without the trouble of passing variables, consider using a class or structure to hold the variables and pass a reference to the class as the parameter to a function. The resulting code will be much more readable and easier to support.

The While...WEnd block is now a While...End While block. This represents a minor syntax change that is easy to adjust to and makes the language more consistent internally.

Elimination of Differentiated String Functions

A number of VB6 functions exist in two forms, one that returns a variant, the other that returns a string. These are shown in Table 9-1.

Table 9-1. VB6 Functions That Exist in Both Variant and String Form

VB6 DIFFERENTIATED STRING FUNCTIONS	
Chr	Chr$
CurDir	CurDir$
Dir	Dir$
Format	Format$
Hex	Hex$
LCase	LCase$
Left	Left$
LTrim	LTrim$
Mid	Mid$
Oct	Oct$
Right	Right$
RTrim	RTrim$
Space	Space$
Trim	Trim$
UCase	UCase$

The idea (one assumes) in VB6 is to use the form of the function that is most efficient. In other words, if you are using variants, use the form that returns a variant; when using strings, use the form that returns a string. Unfortunately, in practice, most smart programmers tend to avoid variants but forget to use the string form of the function. This results in a performance penalty as VB6 converts the string result into a variant within the function and then converts it back into a string during the assignment.

Visual Basic.NET uses a single form for each of these functions and always returns a string (which makes sense since variants no longer exist).

This is yet another example of a worthwhile language cleanup brought to us by the good folks at Microsoft.[12]

Other Minor Changes

In VB.NET, UBound returns –1 when applied to a zero-length array. Read the descriptions of arrays in Chapter 8 for further information on VB.NET array changes.

Commands That Have Vanished

Visual Basic's original success came about to a large degree from its innovative philosophy towards Windows programming. VB's great power came from encapsulating the power of the Win32 API into the language itself. That's what made Visual Basic an easy language for creating Windows applications. Part of this ease of use came from simplification—instead of learning dozens of tricky API commands you only needed to learn a handful of VB commands to obtain a great deal of functionality. Fortunately, you could also selectively access the Win32 API in cases where you needed the richer functionality supported by the underlying system.

Over the years, Visual Basic has evolved to add new capabilities and commands. VB6 may still be the easiest way to write Windows applications but you'd be hard-pressed to really call it "easy"—the learning curve has grown considerably.

With Visual Basic.NET, the language undergoes somewhat of a philosophical shift. Yes, the language still encapsulates features of the operating system. However, it's really no longer the language that is doing the encapsulation but rather the .NET Framework itself. Most language commands and Data types map directly into .NET methods and objects.

In some cases, Microsoft chose to simply remove the commands in the language that implemented certain functionality, requiring that you use framework objects directly instead.

All of this means more power to VB.NET programmers than has been available in the past but at the price of increased complexity and a higher learning curve.[13]

Vanishing Graphics Commands

The following Visual Basic 6 methods and properties are *not* supported in VB.NET:
    PSet, Scale, Circle, and Line

---

12. One must give credit where credit is due and if, occasionally, it sounds like a soap opera commercial, attribute this to my valiant effort to keep things entertaining as well as informative.

13. Not that I'm complaining, mind you—I respect the choice and my own software will benefit greatly from it. Nevertheless, the tradeoff is an important one to understand.

Similar functionality (or the equivalent) is provided in the System.Drawing or System.Graphics namespaces. You'll read more about how to migrate code that uses these commands and methods in Chapter 12.

Before you cry bitter tears about the loss of these functions, allow me, for the moment, to remind you of the notation for the VB6 Line method:

```
object.Line [Step] (x1, y1) [Step] - (x2, y2), [color], [B][F]
```

Can you honestly say that this is anything less than an embarrassing hack? It's totally inconsistent with the format of methods in general. Whoever thought of this thing in the first place?

When Microsoft's developers decided to do a "language cleanup," they may have eliminated much that is familiar and certainly imposed on us the need to learn a great deal. But the term cleanup implies that much of what was thrown away was "dirty"—and the truth is, in most cases, that implication is correct. It certainly applies here.

Good riddance to bad code.

Vanishing Variant Commands

With the disappearance of variants, many of the functions that existed to work with variants have vanished as well.

IsNull and IsEmpty are meaningless. You can determine if a Reference type object references Nothing by using the Is operator:

```
If obj Is Nothing Then…
```

Value type objects may be set to zero (and have all their members set to zero) but the variables themselves always exist and are always valid.

IsObject is meaningless—every variable in VB.NET is an object so this would always return True. You can use reflection to determine if a variable is a Reference or Value type object. You'll read more about this in Chapter 11.

The VarType and TypeName functions are also handled using reflection as you'll see in Chapter 11.

Vanishing Math Commands

The .NET Framework includes classes to perform a variety of math operations. The Abs, Atn, Cos, Exp, Log, Sgn, Sin, Sqr, Tan, Rnd, and Round functions have been eliminated from VB.NET, requiring you to use the math libraries directly. In addition, some of the names of the System.Math functions do not correspond exactly to the VB6 versions, specifically, Atn becomes Atan, Sgn becomes Sign, and Sqr becomes Sqrt.

The MathVB6 sample project shown here illustrates the use of some these functions in VB6:

```
Option Explicit

Sub Main()
    Randomize
    Debug.Print Rnd()
    Debug.Print Sqr(4)
    Debug.Print Round(1.4), Round(1.6)
    Debug.Print Sgn(-1), Sgn(0), Sgn(1)
    Debug.Print Atn(0)
End Sub
```

After running this code through the Upgrade Wizard (and converting it into a console application for the sake of clarity), the following VB.NET code results:

```
Option Strict Off
Option Explicit On
Module modMath

        'UPGRADE_WARNING: Application will terminate when Sub Main() finishes. _
         Click for more: ms-help://MS.MSDNVS/vbcon/html/vbup1047.htm
    Public Sub Main()
        Randomize()
        Console.WriteLine(Rnd())
        Console.WriteLine(System.Math.Sqrt(4))
        Console.WriteLine(VB6.TabLayout(System.Math.Round(1.4), _
        System.Math.Round(1.6)))
       Console.WriteLine(VB6.TabLayout(System.Math.Sign(-1), System.Math.Sign(0),
_
        System.Math.Sign(1)))
        Console.WriteLine(System.Math.Atan(0))
        Console.ReadLine()
    End Sub
End Module
```

Let's first consider the Sqr, Round, Sgn, and Atn functions. These map directly into the System.Math.Sqrt, System.Math.Round, System.Math.Sign, and System.Math.Atan functions.

This leads one to wonder, why bother removing the original functions from the language when they could have easily mapped those functions to the equivalent System.Math methods. Why force VB.NET programmers to use the System.Math library?

My guess is that they did this to encourage VB programmers to make use of the richer set of functions provided by the System.Math library directly. Many elements, such as the Log10 function or the built-in value for Pi (which, in VB6, must be derived—often based on formulas provided in the Help file) are built into the System.Math namespace. There's a certain logic to having all of your math functions available in the same place, whether it is in the language itself or in a namespace. Microsoft chose to place them in the namespace and it's hard to fault them for the choice.

The Rnd function is trickier. It is mapped to the VBMath object that is part of the Microsoft.VisualBasic namespace. But you also have the option of using the System.Random class that offers more flexibility than the Rnd function. There are a number of cases where the Upgrade Wizard will choose a built-in function, whereas you may be able to obtain better results with one of the general system classes. You'll see more of these throughout the rest of the book.

Other Commands That Have Vanished

The LSet and RSet functions only work with strings. Structure assignment is member-by-member under .NET.

The System.Diagostics.Debug class replaces the Debug object. Debug.Print is replaced by the System.Diagnostic.Debug.Write and WriteLine methods.

The String$ function has been replaced by the String object constructor as illustrated in Chapter 8.

The Microsoft.VisualBasic and Compatibility Namespaces

If you explore Microsoft's marketing material about the .NET Framework and Visual Basic.NET, one statement you'll see repeated often is that Visual Basic.NET is a "first class" .NET language. It's easy to miss the significance of this statement. More than anything else, it means to Visual Basic programmers that VB.NET is not an afterthought, not a sideline, not a "crippled" or "toy" language in the .NET environment. Visual Basic.NET is, in Microsoft's eyes, a full-featured .NET language capable of taking complete advantage of .NET's features for the creation of CLS-compliant code (which is, in their eyes, the only kind of code you should be creating with .NET anyway).[14]

---

14. A view that I share.

It's one thing to see this in a marketing brochure or on the PowerPoint slides of a keynote session. It's another thing to see it from a technology perspective—and nothing illustrates this better than the Microsoft.VisualBasic namespace.

Consider a language such as C++ or C. The syntax of both of these languages is very simple with remarkably few keywords. For much of their functionality, they historically rely on vast runtime libraries like the C runtime library, MFC, or ATL class libraries. In the .NET world, the syntax of these two languages as well as that of the new C# language remains simple and the functionality is provided by the .NET class library.

Just for fun, bring up the Object Browser and take a look at the Microsoft.VisualBasic namespace. You won't see certain VB keywords such as If, Then, or For. But you will see virtually every other VB command, function, or enumeration value.

In other words, most of Visual Basic's commands are provided by a namespace in the .NET Framework, which is the case for every other .NET language.

To truly illustrate this, consider the CSharpOrVB example program in Listing 9-9 written in C# that has a reference to the Microsoft.VisualBasic namespace:[15]

Listing 9-9. The CSharpOrVB example program.

```csharp
using Microsoft.VisualBasic;
namespace CSharpOrVB
{
        using System;

        /// <summary>
        ///            Summary description for Class1.
        /// </summary>
        class Class1
        {
            static void Main(string[] args)
            {
                    String s = "This is a test";
                    Console.WriteLine(Strings.Mid(s, 6, 4));
                    Console.ReadLine();
            }
        }
}
```

15. You'll need to explicitly add a reference to the Microsoft.VisualBasic.NET runtime using the Add References command in the Project window.

That's right. Visual Basic.NET and C# are so tied into the .NET Framework that not only can VB.NET use all the framework classes that C# can, but C# can actually reference and use Visual Basic.NET commands!

I don't know about you but this blows me away.

The Microsoft.VisualBasic namespace contains the functions and methods for Visual Basic. Net and also includes elements designed to make it easier for you to use VB6-style code in Visual Basic.NET.

We're Off to See the Wizard

Many people will tend to try to learn VB.NET by writing VB6 code and seeing what the Upgrade Wizard produces as a result. Unfortunately, because it turns off Option Strict, this approach will tend to teach the wrong lessons.

Consider the XOrVB6 example project, which contains the following code:

```
Option Explicit

Sub Main()
    Dim Var1 As Integer
    Dim Result As Integer

    Result = Var1 XOr 5

End Sub
```

When you run this program through the Upgrade Wizard, you'll get the following result:

```
Option Strict Off
Option Explicit On
Module XOrMod

        'UPGRADE_WARNING: Application will terminate when Sub Main() finishes. _
          Click for more: ms-help://MS.MSDNVS/vbcon/html/vbup1047.htm
        Public Sub Main()
                Dim Var1 As Short
                Dim Result As Short

                Result = Var1 Xor 5

        End Sub
End Module
```

Now try turning Option Strict back on. You'll see an error due to an implicit type conversion from Integer to Short. There are many other cases where the Upgrade Wizard will create code that performs implicit type conversions or late bound method calls that require Option Strict to be off. Each of those conversions and method calls represents a potential runtime error—a potential error that could be designed out of your application using Strict Type Checking.

If you must port code, using the Upgrade Wizard as a first step is probably a necessity. However, as I stated in Part One of this book, I believe it will not make economic sense to port code in most cases. VB.NET is best used for new code development.

The Compatibility Choice

One choice faced by every VB.NET programmer is whether you should use the Microsoft.VisualBasic namespace or the .NET Framework. After all, there are many VB.NET-native functions that can be accomplished using .NET methods.

If you expect that you may one day want to port your application to another language like C#, it might make sense to avoid the native VB.NET functions (even though, as you saw, those are callable from C# and there is no rational reason to port your VB.NET code to C# anyway).

I therefore recommend that you feel free to stay with the native VB.NET functions (from the Microsoft.VisualBasic namespace), avoiding only those in the Microsoft.VisualBasic.Compatibility.VB6 namespace.

Why? Because the functions in the Microsoft.VisualBasic namespace (excluding the Compatibility.VB6 namespace) are those that have survived Microsoft's cleanup of the language. Those in the Compatibility.VB6 namespace are holdovers maintained for the sake of the Migration Wizard.

You should, however, invest the time needed to become familiar with the .NET equivalents for VB functions. In some areas, such as File I/O, the .NET Framework provides vastly more capability and flexibility than the traditional Visual Basic File I/O commands.

Here are a selection of examples of places where the built-in functions overlap the .NET Framework and recommendations on how to handle them.

Rnd (Revisited)

The VB.NET Rnd function takes an optional parameter that controls the return value. The typical usage is to call the function without a parameter (which retrieves the next value in the random number sequence). However, depending on whether the value is smaller, greater, or equal to zero, the result will be a constant based on the seed value, the next number in the sequence, or on a repeat of the last random number generated.

The Rnd function returns a floating-point value between zero and 1 (excluding 1).

There is no direct equivalent to the Rnd function in the .NET Framework. Instead, .NET provides the System.Random class. After you create an instance of this class, you can use the following methods to obtain random numbers:

Next—Returns a random integer value (32 bits).

NextDouble—Returns a random value between zero and 1 (excluding 1).

NextBytes—Loads a Byte array with random data.

You can specify a seed value by passing a value to the System.Random constructor; however, the default uses a seed based on the date and time (meaning there is no need to use a Randomize statement).

This is an excellent example of why the wizard uses the VB.NET runtime library to implement a function. Because the System.Random object does not have a method with similar functionality, it takes several lines of code to mimic the behavior of the Rnd function. It is much easier (and, in fact, clearer) to use the built-in function in this case when translating code from VB6 to VB.NET.

However, for new code, it may be better to use the System.Random class directly and avoid the additional overhead required to process the Rnd function.

Constants

The .NET Framework, like the Win32 API and VB6, makes extensive use of constant values. These values might be mathematical constants like Pi; color values like Red, Green, or Blue; or flags for use in operations such as opening a file.

The difference between the .NET approach and prior approaches has to do with the scope of those constants.

Constants in .NET tend to be exposed either as Enumeration objects or as Shared properties of a class. For example, let's say you wanted to append a CRLF character to a string.

The following are equivalent:

```
a = a + ControlChars.CrLf
a = a + Constants.vbCrLf
```

The Microsoft.VisualBasic.Constants namespace includes many (but not all) constants with a vb prefix—from characters to message box options. The Microsoft.VisualBasic.ControlChars namespace only contains control characters.

In the same way, you can use the System.Drawing.Color object to obtain color constants instead of using the old VB colors such as vbRed and vbBlue.

Sure, it's a bit of extra effort to use the actual .NET constants but once you know where they are, not only will your code be easier to read, it will be easier to support. Why? Because enumerations are typed variables and a function that takes an enumeration as a parameter will accept only its own constants without error. For example, MsgBox functions will only accept values from the MsgBoxStyle enumeration. Not only that but the IntelliSense window will only show values from that enumeration, making coding easier.

Visual Basic 6 is forced to use the vb prefix on constant names because every time you add a reference to a new library, its constants are merged into the global namespace for your application. If one application defines a constant named FAILED as –1 and another defines it as zero, the actual value of FAILED in your application depends on which type library is first on the reference list. Thus, the potential for confusion and error is huge. Visual Basic (and other COM library developers) addressed this by adding a prefix to their constant values—one that was hopefully unique. In .NET, the hierarchical nature of namespaces minimizes the possibility of confusion because when you import a namespace that uses an enumeration, the enumeration values in your code will always include the enumeration name. The only time they don't is when you explicitly import the enumeration itself—and then presumably you know what you're doing.

Strings and Compatibility

One historic strength of the BASIC language (in all its variations) is string handling. The .NET Framework also includes classes and objects to manipulate strings.

My recommendation is that you stick with the familiar Visual Basic methods for most situations. They are easy to use and generally map directly to their equivalent .NET methods (or even provide functionality not built into .NET). The only exception is performance-critical areas where you should perform a comparison to see if there is a faster .NET object solution. For example, if you are building a string by concatenating values, the StringBuilder class (which is designed specifically for that purpose) is dramatically faster than appending strings.

You should familiarize yourself with the .NET Framework classes listed in Table 9-2 as well.

Table 9-2. String-related Classes in .NET

NAMESPACE	CONTENTS
System.String	Base class for all VB.NET strings. Includes general-purpose string manipulation methods.
System.Text.Encoding	Useful for converting to and from ASCII, Unicode, and other text formats.
System.Text.StringBuilder	Useful for building and modifying strings. Unlike strings, the contents of String-Builder objects are not immutable
System.Text.RegularExpressions	A powerful class for parsing and manipulating strings using Regular Expressions.[16]

As mentioned earlier, the String$ function has been replaced by the String object constructor.

File I/O and Compatibility

The Microsoft.VisualBasic namespace continues to support traditional File I/O in the form of the Open, Close, Get, Put, Input, Print, and related statements.

The .NET Framework includes powerful, stream-based File I/O in the System.IO namespace. An in-depth description of these classes can be found in the .NET online reference. A more tutorial-style description of these classes can be found in the Visual Studio.NET documentation in the section "Visual Studio.NET/Visual Basic, and Visual C#/ Visual Basic Programming/Processing Drives Folders and Files/File, Drive and Folder Access with Visual Basic.NET."

Meanwhile, the FileIO example provides an illustration of how you might read the contents of a text file into a Text control in VB.NET. Listing 9-10 shows how you can use the OpenFileDialog class to access the File Open common control. Once you obtain a file name, you can use the OpenFileDialog class to obtain a Stream object for the file. A separate StreamReader object is used to actually read the contents of the stream. Confusing? It certainly takes getting used to. My own

---

16. The concept of Regular Expressions is beyond the scope of this book. If you are not familiar with it, I encourage you to examine the namespace documentation and seek out additional information on the subject. You'll be amazed at the things you can do with Regular Expressions.

attempt to shed some light on the occasionally confusing set of classes available for File I/O with VB.NET can be found in Chapter 12.

Listing 9-10. Code from the FileIO sample application shows how to read the contents of a file.

```
Protected Sub MenuItem2_Click(ByVal sender As Object, _
ByVal e As System.EventArgs) Handles menuItem2.Click
    OpenFileDialog1 = New OpenFileDialog()

    openFileDialog1.InitialDirectory = "c:\"
    openFileDialog1.Filter = "txt files (*.txt)|*.txt"
    openFileDialog1.FilterIndex = 1
    openFileDialog1.RestoreDirectory = True
    If OpenFileDialog1.ShowDialog() = dialogresult.OK Then
        Dim fs As Stream
        fs = openfiledialog1.OpenFile()
        Dim sr As New StreamReader(fs)
        TextBox1.Text = sr.ReadToEnd()
        TextBox1.SelectionLength = 0
    End If
End Sub
```

Recap

This chapter focused on the language syntax differences between VB6 and VB.NET. You learned how architectural changes such as the elimination of variants and COM result in surprisingly minor changes in syntax yet have far-reaching consequences. An in-depth discussion of subtle changes in scoping and parameter passing will (hopefully) help you to avoid equally subtle bugs in the code you write. Above all, you gained an understanding of the reasoning behind many of the language changes and how they should result in code that is more stable, readable, and supportable.

This chapter also covered the new, exception-based error-handling syntax, which is dramatically more powerful than the old VB6 On Error Goto statement—now and henceforth to be considered evil.[17]

---

17. It has long been known that the Goto statement is evil. It is about time the On Error loophole be closed. For those interested in reading further, I refer you to Edsger W. Dijkstra's classic work, "Goto Statement Considered Harmful," currently available at the Association for Computing Machinery's Web site at http://www.acm.org/classics/oct95.

There are many cases in which you can perform a task using either the VB.NET language libraries or the .NET class library. There are no hard and fast rules as to which to use in any given case. However, if you use the VB.NET Upgrade Wizard as a learning tool, upgrading VB6 code to see what results and you see code generated by the wizard that uses the Microsoft.Visualbasic.Compatibility.VB6 library, **ignore that code!** Instead, take the time to learn to perform that task using the native VB functions or the .NET Framework classes.

Objects In-Depth

CHAPTER 5 ALREADY WENT into a great deal of depth on inheritance and object-oriented programming in Visual Basic.NET. The focus in that chapter was primarily on the concepts behind object-oriented programming and inheritance, as well as the syntax necessary to explain those concepts. In this chapter, we'll cover additional issues relating to classes and objects. Those issues covered in Chapter 5 will be given rather short shrift here for obvious reasons.

The Parts of a .NET Application

In Chapter 9, you learned about scoping within a function. Scoping at the class, module, assembly, and application domain-levels is considerably more complicated. Before you can understand scoping in .NET, it is necessary to look much more closely at the way .NET applications are put together.

You've read a little bit about assemblies in previous chapters. And you've probably read about assemblies and application domains in the .NET documentation. Chances are pretty good that you're still confused. My goal in the next few pages is not only to bring together all of the bits of information on the subject scattered throughout the documentation but to do so in a reasonable facsimile of plain English.

Application Domains

In the VB6 world (and programming before .NET in general), you dealt with two types of executables: EXE files and DLL files. They had the following characteristics:
An EXE file…

- runs in a separate process.

- is isolated from all other processes (no shared memory).

- is allowed to execute based on system security settings (NT/2000/XP only).

- has one main thread and may create others.

- may (optionally) expose objects via OLE (ActiveX EXE).

- represents a loading boundary (you can't load part of an EXE into memory).

- is debugged independently of any other process.

When we use the term "application" or "program," we are usually referring to EXE files.

A DLL file...

- is loaded at runtime by a client process.

- shares memory space with other DLLs loaded by the process and the process itself.

- is allowed to load based on system security settings (NT/2000/XP only).

- shares the main thread of the process and may create new threads.[1]

- may (optionally) expose objects via OLE (ActiveX DLL).

- represents a loading boundary (you can't load part of a DLL into memory).

- cannot be debugged independently of the calling process.

While .NET does represent a major change to developers, it is still based on Windows and uses EXE and DLL files, which work exactly as they always have. Why, then, introduce the confusion of assemblies and application domains? In other words, if EXE and DLL files continue to work as they always have and .NET applications continue to be made up of EXE and DLL files, why confuse the issue?

Like many of the changes in .NET, this is a consequence of a feature that at first glance, may seem completely unrelated and one you already know.

You know that the CLR manages memory very tightly. You know that pointers are not allowed with managed memory. The existence of pointers would make it impossible to accurately determine if an object or variable is in use (which is necessary for garbage collection to work). Pointers also allow errors to occur whcre code may corrupt application memory or even that of the .NET runtime. In fact, one of the key goals behind managed memory is to prevent memory leaks and memory corruption.

Curiously enough, this was the same reason that 32-bit Windows instituted the idea of separate process spaces in the first place.[2] The isolation of memory

---

1. VB6 DLLs cannot create their own threads without using a third-party component.

2. In 16-bit Windows, memory was shared, so memory access errors in one application could bring down other applications or the entire system.

spaces is, in fact, the most significant difference between EXEs and DLLs. Every EXE loads into its own memory space, whereas every DLL loads into the same memory space as the EXE that loads it.

But now under .NET, because the CLR tightly controls access to all objects, it is possible to apply the same level of isolation within parts of a process. In other words, you could theoretically create a software component that is implemented by a DLL but specify that the objects and variables of that component are completely isolated from the application that uses it and every other component in the process. The only way to do this outside of .NET would be to create the component in a single-use ActiveX EXE—every time an instance of the component was created, a new process would be launched. Obviously, it is much more efficient to take the .NET approach—launching processes has a great deal of overhead. Not only that but in the ActiveX EXE approach, each component must have its own thread.[3] Because .NET components are implemented in DLLs, they are perfectly capable of sharing threads. Figures 10-1A and 10-1B show how one might implement an application that uses three components, which perform standalone tasks such as implementing a business rule or running a Web application.

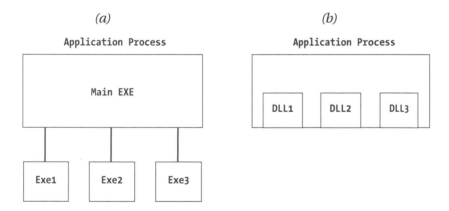

Figure 10-1. (a) Process isolation guarantees that the components cannot interfere with each other. (b) Application domains are implemented by DLLs loaded into the main process and share memory from the perspective of the operating system yet are completely isolated from each other by the CLR.

The .NET Framework has a name for a set of objects designed to work together and be deployed together but are isolated from each other in managed memory. They are called an application domain.

---

3. Remember, we're talking about single-use ActiveX EXE components. Multiple-use components can share threads but you don't get the process memory isolation.

An application domain can be deployed as an EXE file with additional optional DLL files.[4]

An application domain can also be deployed as one or more DLL files. When the application domain's DLLs are loaded into memory, they are isolated from other application domains in the process.

An application domain…

- consists of one or more executable files (EXE or DLL) that are intended to be deployed together.

- is isolated from other application domains in memory.

- is allowed to execute based on .NET security considerations (see Chapter 16).

- may run in its own thread (EXE launched) or share threads (depending on the host process).

- represents an unloading boundary (you can load parts of an application domain but must unload the entire application domain at once).

- may be debugged independently of other application domains.

- may expose objects for use by other application domains (or OLE through COM interop). Access to objects of one application domain by another must be accomplished via proxies—not shared memory.

How you deploy an application domain depends upon the type of application. Stand-alone programs typically deploy an application domain in an executable file. In this case, the term "application domain" corresponds closely to the traditional EXE-based application.

Web services typically deploy application domains as DLLs. This allows each service to run safely within the Web server process while preventing them from interfering with each other. It is even possible to debug individual application domains from among those running under the host.

When you deploy an application domain, you deploy all of the EXE and DLL files that it uses. However, .NET has its own way of looking at these files and the way code is organized within them.

---

4. An application domain may include other types of files as well, such as resources and configuration files. However, in this chapter, we are only concerning ourselves with code and executable files.

Assemblies

You've just read that an application domain is comprised of one or more executable files. Does this mean that all of the executable files must be loaded at once?

No.

Just as a traditional Windows program can load individual DLLs on demand or launch ActiveX EXE servers as needed, so can an application domain load individual assemblies on demand. In fact, the term "assembly" describes the smallest entity that can be separately loaded by an application domain.

An assembly…

- is the smallest granularity for loading code (assemblies are unloaded when the application domain unloads).

- is made up of a single executable or DLL file in VB.NET (other languages allow an assembly to be made up of multiple executable files).

- is the smallest versionable component in .NET.

- is only loaded if allowed to run under the current security settings.

- can determine if all of its dependent assemblies are present and allowed to run before it runs.

Figure 10-2 illustrates the general structure of a .NET application. This figure is applicable to an ASP-like scenario where each application domain represents a different Web application or Web service. All of the application domains run under the same process (the one that handles ASP), sharing threads as determined by the process. Each application domain is made up of one or more assemblies, each of which is implemented by one or more executable files.[5] A standalone VB.NET application would have a single process containing a single application domain made up of one or more assemblies.[6]

You'll read more about application domains and assemblies in Chapter 16 when I discuss deployment and versioning.

---

5. VB.NET allows only one executable file per assembly.

6. You can write VB.NET applications that host other application domains but that will not be a common scenario.

Process

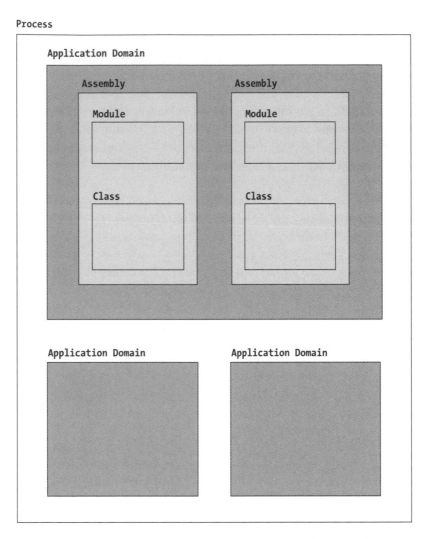

Figure 10-2. The relationship between processes, application domains, and assemblies.

Scoping in VB.NET

As you may recall, scoping actually consists of two separate issues: object lifetime and object visibility (also sometimes referred to as accessibility).[7] Lifetime has to do with how long an object exists. Visibility and accessibility have to do with whether you can access that object from any given line of code.

In order to understand VB.NET scoping, it is first essential to understand the concept of namespaces.

---

7. If, within an application, your code can see a method or variable, it can also access it.

Namespaces

Application domains and assemblies determine the structure of a VB.NET program from the perspective of versioning, loading, and deployment. Namespaces determine the structure of a VB.NET program from the perspective of scoping.

Every type of object in VB.NET has a name and is part of a namespace.

The idea of a namespace is actually quite simple: every type name within a namespace must be unique. As a simple example, two different applications might each have a class named Class1. However, if you try to create two Class1 classes in the same namespace, you'll get an error. Under .NET, you can create two different Class1 classes as long as they are in different namespaces.

To illustrate this, try the following:

1. Create a new VB.NET console application.

2. Go to the Project Properties dialog box (right-click on the project in the Solution Explorer Window and select Properties).

3. Clear the Root Namespace text box.

4. Add a Namespace block to the program as follows:

```
Namespace MovingToVB.CH10.Class1Example
    Module Module1

        Sub Main()

        End Sub

    End Module
End Namespace
```

Under VB.NET, the project properties dialog sets the default namespace for an assembly. If you wish to override your assembly's namespace, you will typically clear this entry because anything in the Root Namespace text box will become the prefix to any name you define in the Namespace command. In other words, if I left the Class1Example entry in the text box, the namespace would be defined as Class1Example.MovingToVB.CH10.Class1Example instead of MovingToVB.CH10.Class1Example.

Add two Class1 classes into the Namespace as follows:

```
Namespace MovingToVB.CH10.Class1Example
    Class Class1

    End Class

    Class Class1

    End Class
```

Obviously this does not work. You'll see an error along the lines of "Class1Example\Module1.vb(2): class 'Class1' and class 'Class1' conflict in namespace Class1Example." [8]

Well, duh, of course you can't have two classes with the same name.

Now change the program as follows:

```
Namespace MovingToVB.CH10.Class1Example
    Class Class1

    End Class

    Module Module1
        Dim c1 As New Class1()
        Dim c1b As New Class1ExampleNS2.Class1()
        Sub Main()

        End Sub

    End Module
End Namespace

Namespace MovingToVB.CH10.Class1ExampleNS2
    Class Class1

    End Class

End Namespace
```

---

8. If you try to compile at this point, you'll also see an error that Sub Main is not defined in the Namespace. Go back to the Project Properties dialog and set the startup object to the correct Namespace.

You now have two Class1 classes defined in the same assembly! But there is no conflict because each one is in a separate namespace. As you can see, it is easy for code in one namespace to access a type in another—you just need to identify the namespace when you specify the type.

You've just seen that an assembly can define code for more than one namespace.[9] While I would not generally recommend that you define multiple namespaces in one file, it is not unreasonable to use different namespaces in *different* files within a project. In fact, the hierarchical nature of namespaces lends itself to this approach. If you look at the Microsoft System namespace, you can see that it has many second-level namespaces below System. Most of them reside in a single DLL (assembly). Namespaces are often used to group-related classes in this way.

You should not, however, use multiple namespaces within an assembly without good reason. Giving each assembly its own namespace is intuitive and will reduce the potential for confusion by those using the assembly.

Architecture and Deployment

If you look in the Chapter 10 Namespaces directory, you will see a project group called ConsoleApplication1 with two projects: ConsoleApplication1 and GroupSupport. The root namespace for both projects has been cleared. Listing 10-1 shows the Module class for the ConsoleApplication1 project module.

Listing 10-1. File module1.vb in project ConsoleApplication1.

```
Imports MovingToVB.CH10.Organization.Members
Namespace MovingToVB.CH10.Organization
    Class Organization

    End Class

    Module Module1

        Sub Main()
            Dim org As New Organization()
            ' The following two lines are identical - because of imports
            Dim grp As New CH10.Organization.Members.MemberCollection()
            Dim grp2 As New MemberCollection()
```

9. Remember, in VB.NET, a project translates into a single assembly.

```
                  ' Note, this one is in another assembly!
                  ' But is in the same namespace!
                  Dim sorter As New CH10.Organization.Members.MemberSorter()
                  Dim sorter2 As New MemberSorter()
            End Sub

      End Module
End Namespace


Namespace MovingToVB.CH10.Organization.Members
      Class GroupMember

      End Class
      Class MemberCollection

      End Class
End Namespace
```

Listing 10-2 shows the class1.vb module for the GroupSupport project module.

Listing 10-2. File class1.vb in project GroupSupport.

```
Namespace MovingToVB.CH10.Organization.Members
      Public Class MemberSorter


      End Class
End Namespace
```

The ConsoleApplication1 project contains two namespaces: the MovingToVB.CH10.Organization namespace defines the main program and classes to manage a hypothetical organization; the objects used to manage members of the organization are in a second namespace named MovingToVB.CH10.Organization.Members.

The interesting thing about the ConsoleApplication1 project is the Member-Sorter class—it isn't part of the project! The MemberSorter class is defined in the GroupSupport project referenced by the ConsoleApplication1 project.[10] Yet, it is still part of the MovingToVB.CH10.Organization.Members namespace.

That's right—a namespace can cross multiple assemblies!

---

10. To add this reference: In the Solution Explorer window, right click on the References item for the project and select Add-Reference. Then select the Projects tab and choose the GroupSupport project.

Why would you want to do that?

Let's say that the MemberSorter class is a rather large and complex class that is rarely used. Logically, it belongs in the MovingToVB.CH10.Organization.Members namespace because it is closely related. However, it's silly to always load the code for a class that is rarely used. By placing the MemberSorter class in a separate assembly, it can be loaded only when needed.

In fact, in a sophisticated deployment scheme (say, one that is deployed through the Internet), you can even create a scenario where the GroupSupport assembly is not even installed until it is needed!

In other words, the use of namespaces makes it possible for developers to completely separate the logical organization of classes from the deployment and security strategy for the classes. You can organize your classes in a manner that is easy to understand, maintain, and document, yet distribute them into assemblies based on other considerations such as efficiency of loading, security, or deployment. The architecture of your application need not match the deployment scenario.

Of course, from a developer's perspective, this flexibility imposes an additional responsibility. Now you need to design not only the objects and their relationships but also determine which assemblies hold which objects. I think the flexibility gained by this approach justifies the added effort.

The Imports Statement

The Imports statement is used to provide a shortcut when referring to elements in a namespace. When you import a namespace, you can access the objects in that namespace directly without the full namespace name. This can be seen in the Sub Main function of the ConsoleApplication1 project, in which the MemberCollection and MemberSorter classes are referenced both through the full name and directly.

What happens if a namespace you import has a class with the same name as one in the current namespace? In that case, the class within the current namespace takes precedence. You can still access the class in the other namespace but you must use its full name. If you import two different namespaces that contain classes with the same name (and a class with that name is not defined in the current namespace), you will also get an error because the compiler cannot determine which of the two imported namespaces take precedence.

What happens if two assemblies are defining classes in the same namespace and try to define a class with the same name? In that case, you'll get an error—the fact that you can't have two classes with the same name in a namespace applies even if the classes are in two different assemblies.

What happens if you extend another namespace like the System namespace? Then your assembly and any other assembly that references yours will see that extension. And it will work until Microsoft adds a class to the System namespace that conflicts with yours, at which point your code will break. The lesson being, don't extend other people's namespaces!

The Imports statement can also be used to import an Enumeration object, which allows you to access fields of the enumeration without qualifying them with the enumeration name.

For example, normally, in order to access the CrLf constant, you must use the form:

```
Dim S As String = ControlChars.CrLf
```

However, if you add the line:

```
Imports Microsoft.VisualBasic.ControlChars
```

…you can access CrLf:

```
Dim S As String = CrLf
```

It is easy to get confused between referencing and importing a namespace.

You reference a namespace by adding a reference to the namespace (or rather, an assembly that implements the namespace) using the Solution window or project settings dialog box. Once you reference a namespace, you can access all of its objects and methods by specifying the fully qualified name of the object.

The Imports statement allows you to define a shortcut to currently referenced namespaces and objects so that you need not type the fully qualified name each time you use an object from the namespace.

Names and Namespaces

In VB6 and COM, Microsoft solved the problem of object naming conflicts by using GUIDs—globally unique identifiers—to identify objects. In .NET, namespaces are in the hierarchical, humanly readable form that you've seen here. You should try to choose a root namespace that is certain to be unique—for example, the name of your company.

But what if two conflicting namespaces are installed on a system?

In most cases, you still won't have a problem because unless you install your assembly in the global assembly cache, your assembly will only see a namespace in assemblies that it has referenced.

But what if a referenced assembly changes its namespace in a way that is somehow incompatible with your assembly?

The answer is that unless you allow it or do so explicitly, nobody can change the assembly that yours references. Assemblies can use "strong" names—in which the name of the assembly is a composite of the assembly name, version, signature, and other information that uniquely identifies that specific assembly from any other version. As long as your application is bound to a specific assembly by its strong name, you need never worry about someone making changes that can break compatibility.

You'll read more about assembly names and versioning in Chapter 16.

Scoping 1: The Namespace Level

There are four types of objects you can define at the Namespace level: Class, Module, Structure, and Enum.

Each of these can be given a scope of Friend, or Public.[11]

	ASSEMBLY/PROJECT	EVERYWHERE
Public	Visible	Visible
Friend	Visible	Hidden

Sample code illustrating the visibility of these types can be found in the AssemblyScoping sample program.[12]

The scope of the object at this level represents the maximum overall visibility for all of the elements within the object. For example, a Public variable within a Public class will be visible and accessible to everyone with access to the namespace.

Classes, Structures, and Enums should be familiar to you from both your VB6 experience and previous chapters in this book. But it's worth taking a moment to review the Module type.

As you may have noticed, there is no difference between files in VB.NET—they all have the extension .VB and all have the same internal structure. Modules in VB.NET are similar to classes in the way they work except for two critical differences:

1. You can't create an instance of a module.

2. The elements of a module are visible even if you do not include the module name, throughout all code where the module is visible. In other words, Public functions and variables of a module can be used like global variables and functions in a VB6 standard module.

---

11. The Private, Protected, and Protected Friend attributes apply to elements inside classes and will be discussed shortly. Beta 1 supported private elements at the Namespace level, which were given visibility only within the current file.

12. The AssemblyScoping sample has a variety of declarations at different scopes but does not actually do anything. It's fairly clear and there seems little need to include a listing in this book.

Curiously enough, C# does not allow you to create modules. It can, however, use modules defined in VB.NET applications, as you can see in the ModuleScoping sample application (which is included with the sample code but not presented here in print).[13]

Inheritance Rules

Visual Basic.NET does not allow you to increase the scope of a base class using a derived class. In other words, a Friend class can inherit from a Public class (because the visibility of all inherited members would be less than Public). However, a Public class *cannot* inherit from a Friend class. Doing so would make it possible for public members of the Friend class to be visible outside the legal scope of the Friend class.

In order to inherit from a class, the derived class must (obviously) be able to access the base class.

Inheritance Control

Use the MustInherit keyword to indicate that it is not possible to create an instance of a class. You can only create instances of classes that derive from the class.

Use the NotInheritable keyword to indicate that no other class can derive from your class. You can't define protected members in a NotInheritable class (there isn't much point in doing so anyway since the protected keyword only has meaning in the context of inheritance as you'll see in the next section).

Use the Shadows keyword when defining a class within a class to indicate that the included class overrides the definition of a member class in the base class. In other words,[14] say you have the following code in Listing 10-3 from the Inheritance1 sample project.

Listing 10-3. Code from the Inheritance1 sample project.

```
Class A
    Class B
        Sub Test()
            Console.WriteLine("A.B.Test")
        End Sub
    End Class
```

---

13. This project is also easy to follow and is thus not included as a listing in the book.

14. And if ever a sentence needed other words, that last one does.

```
        Class D
            Sub Test()
                Console.WriteLine("A.D.Test")
            End Sub
        End Class

    End Class

    Class C
        Inherits A
        Shadows Class B
            Sub Test()
                Console.WriteLine("C.B.Test")
            End Sub
        End Class

    End Class

    Module Module1

        Sub Main()
            Dim abref As New A.B()
            Dim cdref As New C.D()
            Dim cbref As New C.B()
            abref.Test()
            cdref.Test()
            cbref.Test()
            Console.ReadLine()
        End Sub

    End Module
```

When run, the program displays:

```
A.B.Test
A.D.Test
C.B.Test
```

The definition of class B inside of class C overrides the definition of class B inside of class A because of the Shadows keyword.

Shadowing is the default behavior in this case, so if you leave the Shadows keyword off, the program will produce the same output but the compiler will indicate a warning to remind you that shadowing is taking place and that you should add the Shadows keyword.

Scoping 2: The Class Level

Within classes or modules, scoping attributes determine the visibility of individual members—the methods, properties, and fields of the class.[15]

Here is a quick review of the accessibility terms:

- Public—Element is visible outside of the class in which it is defined.

- Private—Element is not visible outside of the class in which it is defined.

- Friend—Element is visible outside of the class in which it is defined but only within the assembly in which the class is defined.

- Protected—Element is not visible outside of the class in which it is defined except that it is visible to derived classes.

- Protected Friend—Element is visible outside of the class in which it is defined but only within the assembly in which the class is defined, and within derived classes.

This subject was discussed at some length in Chapter 5, so what follows in Tables 10-2 and 10-3 is not so much a tutorial as a comprehensive summary of the scoping of class members. The ClassScoping sample project contains the code on which the following information was verified. The sample is included with the source code for the book but is not shown in print.

Table 10-2. Public Classes (X Indicates Visibility)

	PRIVATE	FRIEND	PROTECTED	PROTECTED FRIEND	PUBLIC
In the class	X	X	X	X	X
Reference to a base class from inside a derived class		X	X	X	X
Reference to a derived class from within the derived class		X		X	X
Reference to a class from inside the assembly		X		X	X
Reference to a class from outside the assembly					X

---

15. I'll be referring to classes but the scoping attributes work the same way with modules and structures except for issues relating to inheritance, which only apply to classes. Remember that the scoping attributes also refer to classes and structures that are members of other classes.

Table 10-3. Friend Classes (X Indicates Visibility)

	PRIVATE	FRIEND	PROTECTED	PROTECTED FRIEND	PUBLIC
In the class	X	X	X	X	X
Reference to a base class from inside a derived class		X	X	X	X
Reference to a derived class from within the derived class		X		X	X
Reference to a class from inside the assembly		X		X	X
Reference to a class from outside the assembly					

An Inherited method can be hidden outside of a derived class (even if it's a Friend or Public method) using the Shadows keyword.

You should always set the scoping of your classes and methods within the class to the least visibility necessary for the application. This serves to reduce the complexity of the application and to minimize the chances that those using your assemblies might call a method in error.

Threading and Scope

Don't forget the big difference between the treatment of global variables in VB6 and VB.NET. Global variables in VB6 are specific to a single thread. This means that if you create a multithreaded DLL or EXE in VB6, each thread has its own copy of the global variables. In VB.NET, global variables are shared among all threads unless you specifically mark them as local to a thread using the ThreadStatic attribute (as shown in Chapter 7).

Note that the Upgrade Wizard does not convert VB6 global variables to thread local VB.NET variables nor does it warn you about this difference.

More about Classes

Determining the scope of your classes and their members is perhaps the most important aspect of object-oriented design next to the definition of the object model itself. Now let's take a look at a few additional features that you must know related to classes.

Shared Members

You can add the Shared attribute to any class variable. The syntax is:

```
Private Shared SharedVariable As Integer
```

Shared variables are shared among all instances of a class. There are a number of common uses for this feature:

- To keep track of the instances of a class. For instance, you could use a collection to maintain a reference to all instances of a class or a counter to keep a running total of instances that exist.

- To precalculate data used by all items of a class. For example, a Mutual Fund class might have shared variables that contain the average performance of different classes of mutual funds to make it easy to compare a given instance of the class with those averages.

- To define variables needed for shared procedures.

Shared variables can, of course, also have Friend, Protected, Friend Protected, and Public scope as well.

A Shared procedure can be called without an instance of the class. It cannot access nonshared members of the class.

Programmers sometimes create classes that contain nothing but shared procedures and members as a way to group general-purpose functions that don't require instances of the objects to be created. However in VB.NET, you can use modules to accomplish this.

The AssemblyScoping project contains this code, which demonstrates the use of shared members and procedures:

```
Public Class SharingDemo
    Public Shared SharedVariable As Integer
    Public NotSharedVariable As Integer
    Shared Sub ShowShared()
        Console.WriteLine("Access using Shared Procedure: " _
        & SharedVariable.ToString)
    End Sub
End Class
```

The following code shows how you can access the Shared class:

```
Dim sh As New Scoping.SharingDemo()
Dim sh2 As New Scoping.SharingDemo()
sh.SharedVariable = 5
Console.WriteLine("5 indicates value was shared: " _
& sh2.SharedVariable.ToString)
Console.WriteLine("Access without instance: " _
& Scoping.SharingDemo.SharedVariable.ToString)
Scoping.SharingDemo.ShowShared()
```

Shared members can be accessed through an Instance variable or by directly using the class name.

When we talk about the scope of shared members of a class, we are talking about more than just the accessibility of the member—we are also talking about the scope in which the value is shared. In other words, if you have a Public shared member in a Public class, that member will have the same value for every instance of the class throughout the entire application domain. What's more, it will have the same value in any classes that derive the member as well. This means that shared members should not be thought of as a place to stash data whose meaning can be defined by the derived class.

The class in which they are defined must control the meaning and use of shared members. As with any member, you should use the most restrictive scope you can with shared members.

MyBase and MyClass

Two special keywords exist to help you qualify methods called in an inheritance situation.

The MyBase keyword is used in a derived class to call a method on the base class. This is useful when you have a method in the derived class that overrides or shadows a method in the base class and you need to access the original base class method.

The MyClass keyword works in the opposite direction. If you have a function in the base class that you wish to make sure calls a function in the base class (and not a possibly overridden version of that function), use MyClass to ensure that the base class version is called.

The MyBaseMyClass sample application in Listing 10-4 illustrates this.

Listing 10-4. The MyBaseMyClass sample program.

```
Module Module1

    Class A
        Overridable Sub Test()
            Console.WriteLine("A.Test called")
        End Sub
        Sub ACallsTest()
            Console.Write("A Calls Test directly: ")
            Test()
            Console.Write("A Calls MyClass.Test: ")
            MyClass.Test()
        End Sub

    End Class

    Class B
        Inherits A
        ' What happens if you use Shadows on the Test function instead of Overrides?
        Overrides Sub Test()
            Console.WriteLine("B.Test called")
        End Sub
        Sub BCallsTest()
            Console.Write("B Calls Test directly: ")
            Test()
            Console.Write("B Calls MyBase.Test: ")
            MyBase.Test()
        End Sub
    End Class


    Sub Main()
        Dim aref As New A()
        Dim bref As New B()
        Console.WriteLine("Object A")
        aref.ACallsTest()
        Console.WriteLine("Object B")
        bref.ACallsTest()
        Console.WriteLine("Object B")
        bref.BCallsTest()
        console.ReadLine()
    End Sub


End Module
```

The output from this program is as follows:

```
Object A
A Calls Test directly: A.Test called
A Calls MyClass.Test: A.Test called
Object B
A Calls Test directly: B.Test called
A Calls MyClass.Test: A.Test called
Object B
B Calls Test directly: B.Test called
B Calls MyBase.Test: A.Test called
```

The first three lines are obvious—a class A object can only reference its own methods regardless of whether the method is called directly or through the MyClass qualifier.

The fourth and fifth lines are more subtle—the object is an instance of class B but the code that is running is a method in class A inherited by class B. The first call to Test will call the overridden version. In order for the class A code to call the class A version of the Test function, it must use the MyClass qualifier.

The final two lines are also obvious. When the Test function is called from class B, the class B method is called unless MyBase is specified.

As an experiment, change the attribute for the Test function in class B from Overrides to Shadows. The results are as follows:

```
Object A
A Calls Test directly: A.Test called
A Calls MyClass.Test: A.Test called
Object B
A Calls Test directly: A.Test called
A Calls MyClass.Test: A.Test called
Object B
B Calls Test directly: B.Test called
B Calls MyBase.Test: A.Test called
```

The difference occurs when you call the ACallsTest method from an object of type B. When the ACallsTest method calls Test, it will call an overridden Test function in a derived class. But it will not call a derived function that Shadows a base class method.

Overrides means that a derived method is intended to replace a base class method anytime it is called, whether through a reference to the base class or a reference to the derived class. Shadows means that a derived method should only replace a base class method when called through the derived class.

The MyClass and MyBase qualifiers are not actually class references—you can't pass them as parameters. They also don't break scoping rules; for example, you can't use MyBase to access a private member of the base class. You can use them on shared members as well as instance members.

In the case of the MyBase qualifier, the member does not need to be in the immediate base class—VB.NET will search down the inheritance chain to find the first method of the name that matches the call.

Nested Classes

One of the nice new features of VB.NET is the ability to nest classes or structures within other classes. Nested classes and structures are ideal for organizing data within a class—especially if you have a large and complex class.

At the same time, most developers prefer to keep their objects relatively small and simple so you'll probably end up using nested classes less than you might expect.

Scoping of nested classes is just like that of other members. Thus, a Private class is inaccessible outside of its container class. Visual Basic.NET does not allow you to increase the visibility of a contained class by exposing them through properties or the return values of methods. In other words, you can't have a Public class method that returns an instance of a Private or Friend class.

Methods and Properties

So far, in this chapter, you've learned about scoping of classes and class members along with the underlying .NET concepts needed to understand the scoping rules. Now let's take a look at the methods and properties that make those objects actually do something.

Function Overloading

One of the coolest new features of VB.NET is support for function overloads. Consider what would happen if you placed the following three declarations in a VB6 class or module:

```
Sub Print(ByVal X As Integer)
Sub Print(ByVal X As String)
Sub Print(ByVal X As SomeObject)
```

In VB6, you'll get an error because you can't have multiple functions or sub-routines with the same name. In VB.NET, these declarations are legal. The optional Overloads keyword can be used to explicitly indicate overloading as shown here:[16]

```
Overloads Sub Print(ByVal X As Integer)
Overloads Sub Print(ByVal X As String)
Overloads Sub Print(ByVal X As SomeObject)
```

In fact, you can have as many versions of a function or subroutine as you wish. The only rules are that: first, any functions must return the same result type; and second, VB.NET must be able to unambiguously resolve which function to call based on the parameters. Different overloaded functions can contain not only different type parameters but also different numbers of parameters.

Overloaded functions are used frequently in the .NET Framework. For example, the Console.WriteLine function that has been used so often in the sample programs you've seen so far is actually declared thus:

```
Public Overloads Shared Sub WriteLine()
Public Overloads Shared Sub WriteLine(Boolean)
Public Overloads Shared Sub WriteLine(Char)
Public Overloads Shared Sub WriteLine(Char())
Public Overloads Shared Sub WriteLine(Decimal)
Public Overloads Shared Sub WriteLine(Double)
Public Overloads Shared Sub WriteLine(Integer)
Public Overloads Shared Sub WriteLine(Long)
Public Overloads Shared Sub WriteLine(Object)
Public Overloads Shared Sub WriteLine(Single)
Public Overloads Shared Sub WriteLine(String)
Public Overloads Shared Sub WriteLine(UInt32)
Public Overloads Shared Sub WriteLine(UInt64)
Public Overloads Shared Sub WriteLine(String, Object)
Public Overloads Shared Sub WriteLine(String, Object())
Public Overloads Shared Sub WriteLine(Char(), Integer, Integer)
Public Overloads Shared Sub WriteLine(String, Object, Object)
Public Overloads Shared Sub WriteLine(String, Object, Object, Object)
```

VB.NET looks at the parameters you've passed to the WriteLine function and calls the version that is appropriate for the functions specified.

The nice thing about function overloading is that it actually simplifies applications. To see why, ask yourself what is easier to remember: a single function,

---

16. If you define methods with different signatures in a class, overloading is the default behavior and you do not need to use the Overloads keyword.

WriteLine (which takes different parameters), or fifteen different function names (such as WriteStringLine, WriteIntLine, etc.)?

While the use of the Overloads keyword is optional when overloading methods within a class, it is important when working with derived classes. There are three possible scenarios when defining a method in a class that has the same name as one in a base class.

1. Derived and base class methods have the same signature (parameters and return type).

    • Use Overrides to provide polymorphism (the derived method will be called even if the object is referenced through the base class). If there exist other methods with the same name but different parameters in the base class, use Overrides and Overloads.

    • Use Overrides and NotOverridable to provide polymorphism but prevent the method from being inherited by subsequent derived classes. If there exist other methods with the same name but different parameters in the base class, use NotOverridable, Overrides, and Overloads.

    • Use Shadows (the default) to always access the method based on the type of reference. References to the derived class always reference the method in the derived class and any methods with the same name in the base class are hidden. References to the base class always access the method in the base class.

2. Derived and base class differ by signature (parameters and return type).

    • Use Shadows (the default) to always access the method based on the type of reference. References to the derived class always reference the method in the derived class and any methods with the same name in the base class are hidden. References to the base class always access the method in the base class.

3. Derived and base class differ by parameters only.

    • Use Overloads to allow overloaded access to either the derived method or the base class method depending on the parameters used.

    • Use Shadows (the default) to always access the method based on the type of reference. References to the derived class always access the method in the derived class and any methods with the same name in the base class are hidden. References to the base class always reference the method in the base class.

Here are some (relatively) simple rules that should help you make sense of the use of Overrides, Shadows, and Overloads:

- If you aren't inheriting from another class, don't worry about any of these keywords. If you have two or more methods that differ only by parameters, they will be overloaded automatically.

- Use Shadows anytime you derive from a class and want to hide the base class methods. Method calls through a variable with the base class type will never go to a method in the derived class. Method calls through a variable with the derived class type will never go to a method in the base class.

- Use Overrides anytime you derive from a class and want the method to be called based on the true type of the object, regardless of whether the object is referenced by a variable of the base class type or the derived class type.

- Use Overloads anytime you add a method whose name matches that of a base class method but whose parameters differ from any base class method with that name. Once you use Overloads in your derived class, you'll need to add it to each method with that name.

- Use NotOverridable to indicate that an overridden method may not be over-ridden in turn by another derived class (one that derives from your class).

Still confused? The VB.NET compiler will prompt you as you enter your code. I've found that just following its instructions will invariably lead me to the results I'm looking for.

The use of overloading is fairly intuitive once you become familiar with it but it turns out that there are some less intuitive uses of overloading—especially when you consider that different overloaded methods need not share the same scope.

Constructors

Constructors are functions that are called when an object is created. In VB.NET, constructors have the name New and take the form:

```
Public Sub New()
    MyBase.New()
End Sub
```

A constructor that takes no parameters is called a default constructor. You may not define a default constructor for a structure because structures have an automatic default constructor that sets all of the structure fields to zero.

It is usually necessary to call MyBase.New() in the constructor so that the base class's constructor is called as well. Constructors are not inherited.

Like other methods, you can overload constructors as well. This allows you to not only provide multiple initializations for your objects but also to control the ability to create the objects in the first place.

Scoped Constructors

The Overloads solution contains two projects, the ClassExamples class library and the OverloadsTest console application. The ClassExamples class library defines three classes—the first, InternalClass1, has two constructors: the default constructor is private and the parameterized constructor is public. Because they are in the same class, there is no need to use the Overloads keyword to specify that the two constructors overload each other. The InternalClass1 class is shown in Listing 10-5.

Listing 10-5. The ClassExamples class library.

```
Public Class InternalClass1
    Private m_Name As String
    Shared Sub New()
        Console.WriteLine("Shared constructor called")
    End Sub
    Private Sub New()
        m_Name = "Default"
    End Sub
    Public Sub New(ByVal NewName As String)
        m_Name = NewName
    End Sub

    Public Shared Function GetDefaultObject() As InternalClass1
        Return New InternalClass1()
    End Function

    Public Sub Test()
        Console.WriteLine("Test in InternalClass1, name is: " & m_Name)
    End Sub
End Class
```

What use is a Private constructor? After all, it can only be created within a class.

Private constructors are useful when an object needs to create additional instances of itself or when you want to enforce creation of an object through a Shared method of the class as shown in the GetDefaultObject call in the OverLoads solution example.

What is the difference between using a parameterized constructor and creating the structure using a Shared method?

The only difference is that if you use a parameterized constructor, the object is actually created. If the object is a complex one and derived from other objects, the creation process itself might involve a fair amount of overhead (as may the termination).

If there is any doubt as to whether the object should be created—say, if the creation of the object is allowed only for certain sets of parameters-it is better to use a Shared method. The method can return Nothing or raise an exception in the event of an error and need not actually create the object.

You can even make all of the constructors of the object private, allowing creation of the object only through a Shared method. Because the class itself is Public, there is no problem with visibility of the object and its methods outside of the file or even outside of the assembly. But since there is no Public constructor, it is impossible to create an object of that type using the New operator! You can only create it using the Shared method.

The InternalClass2 example builds on this idea by defining the default constructor as a Friend function as shown here:

```
Public Class InternalClass2
    Friend Sub New()
        MyBase.New()

    End Sub

    Public Overridable Sub Test()
        Console.WriteLine("InternalClass2 Test called")
    End Sub

    Public Sub Test(ByVal x As Integer)
        Console.WriteLine("InternalClass2 Test(ByVal x as integer) called")
    End Sub
End Class
```

A partial listing of the Class1 class shows that it contains a method able to create and return InternalClass2 objects:

```
Public Class Class1
```

```
        Public Function GetInternalClass2() As InternalClass2
            ' You can do additional initializaion here, or
            ' even security checks
            Return New InternalClass2()
        End Function
End Class
```

The InternalClass3 class shows how the Overloads keyword is used to overload methods in an inherited class:

```
Public Class InternalClass3
    Inherits InternalClass2
    Public Overloads Overrides Sub Test()
        Console.WriteLine("InternalClass3() Test called")
    End Sub
    Public Overloads Sub Test(ByVal S As String)
        Console.WriteLine("InternalClass3 Test(ByVal s as String) called")
    End Sub

End Class
```

The OverloadsTest program is in a separate assembly. This means that it is unable to create InternalClass2 objects directly since it has no access to its Friend scoped constructor. The program shown in Listing 10-6 illustrates how it is possible to use the scope of constructors to control the ability to create objects.

Listing 10-6. The OverloadsTest program.

```
Module Module1

    Sub Main()
        ' Can't create with private constructor
        ' Dim c As New ClassExamples.InternalClass1()

        ' Can create with public constructor
        Dim c As New ClassExamples.InternalClass1("MyTestName")
        c.Test()

        ' Can access private constructor via public method
        Dim c2 As ClassExamples.InternalClass1 = _
        ClassExamples.InternalClass1.GetDefaultObject

        ' Can never create InternalClass2 directly
        ' Dim c2 As New ClassExamples.InternalClass2()
```

```
    ' But can using other class and Friend constructor
    Dim cls1 As New ClassExamples.Class1()
    Dim c3 As ClassExamples.InternalClass2 = cls1.GetInternalClass2
    c3.Test()
    Console.WriteLine(ControlChars.CrLf & "InternalClass3")
    Dim cls3 As New ClassExamples.InternalClass3()
    cls3.Test("hello")
    cls3.Test(5)
    cls3.Test()
    Console.ReadLine()

    Console.ReadLine()
  End Sub


End Module
```

You can create InternalClass3 objects even though they inherit from the InternalClass2 class (which cannot be created due to the lack of a Public constructor). This is because constructors are never inherited so the limited scope of the base constructor won't impact the derived class.

Shared Constructors

Classes can define Shared constructors in addition to instance constructors. Shared constructors are called the first time any object of a specified type is created. The InitAndDestruct sample from Chapter 5 and the Overloads solution example in this chapter both demonstrate how Shared constructors are defined.

Instancing Revisited

VB.NET classes don't have an instancing property. This doesn't mean that the capability is lacking, just that it is implemented differently.

Visibility of an object, whether it is private to an assembly or public, is controlled using the Scope attribute for the class (in other words, is the class Public or Friend?).

Whether an object is creatable or not depends on the scope of the object's constructors. Give a constructor a Private or Friend scope to prevent creation of the object outside of an assembly.

Global access—the ability to access an object without qualifying it—can be accomplished by importing the namespace in which the class is defined using the Imports statement.[17]

Automatic creation of an object when it is accessed is not supported. You must use the New statement to create the object.

Methods versus Properties

Many programmers find it difficult at times to decide whether a given member should be a property or a method. The confusion is perfectly understandable given that a parameterized property can do anything a method can do. In fact, as far as functionality is concerned, there is *no real difference* between a Read Only property that returns a value and a method that returns a value.

But knowing this also lets you take the first step towards deciding in cases where no value is returned.

Rule: If you want to perform an operation that does *not* return a value, use a method.

That's about the only hard and fast rule. The following are just some very strong suggestions.

Use Property Procedures

If you wish to expose a simple data element like an integer or string—one that could be exposed through the syntax:

```
Public Class SomeClass
    Public A As Integer
End Class
```

---

17. Remember the difference between importing a namespace and referencing a namespace? Add a reference to a namespace to allow access to its objects from within an assembly. After referencing a namespace, you can import it or any of its objects to allow your assembly to access them without having to specify the fully qualified name each time.

…you should instead use property procedures:

```
Public Class SomeClass
    Private m_B As Integer
    Public Property B() As Integer
        Get
            Return (m_B)
        End Get
        Set (ByVal Value As Integer)
            m_B = value
        End Set
    End Property

End Class
```

Why? Because even though it is more work in the initial coding, it gives you more flexibility. For example, you can add error checking or validation easily at a later time. With VB6, this choice is extremely important because you cannot switch from public properties to property procedures without breaking compatibility. VB.NET is much better about this since it doesn't actually wire up the calls until JIT time. So, you can switch to property procedures later without breaking code. Nevertheless, it's a good habit to get into.

One thing is clear, however. Anytime you have the option to go with a public field or a property procedure, you should definitely use the "property" syntax and not the "method" syntax.

Keep Properties Simple

While you can define parameterized properties, it is only common to do so with indexers—where a property has a single index parameter that is typically used to provide a property index into an element of an array or data set. If you find you need more than one parameter, chances are you should choose a method instead of a property.

Avoid properties that return arrays, especially if the contents of the array are a snapshot of a current set of data that may not remain valid as the program continues to run.

Avoid Side Effects

If accessing the member has observable side effects—for example, makes changes to more than one member or property—you should use a method instead of a property. Functionality within property procedures should be generally limited to error checking, validation, and signaling a change to the property's value via events or other mechanisms. The one common exception to this is when the property itself changes the behavior of the object in some way. In that case, many programmers still prefer to use a property procedure.

Other Times to Use Methods

You should use methods to implement conversions of one type to another.

You should also use methods when the order of execution matters. Most programmers assume that you can set or read properties in any order whereas there is an understanding that methods must often be called in a specific order.

Property Procedures

VB.NET introduces several changes to property procedures when compared to VB6. You've already seen the major change in many of the code examples in the book so far. The syntax of property procedures has changed. Property Get and Set procedures have been combined. Property Let procedures have been eliminated along with all previous distinction of setting objects versus variables (remember, everything in VB.NET is an object). The ReadOnly and WriteOnly attributes are used with property procedures to specify if a property is read only or write only.

The VB.NET approach has the advantage of a slightly cleaner syntax. The Get and Set procedures are forced to be close to each other. On the other hand, I suspect any halfway competent VB6 programmer kept the Property Get and Property Set methods near each other anyway.

The real gripe that many VB6 programmers have about the new syntax is that the accessibility of the Property Set/Let procedures and Property Get procedures must be the same. In VB6, it is very common to have a Public Property Get procedure and a Private or Friend Property Set procedure to create properties that could only be set from within a component or application but could be read by outside clients.

Frankly, I'm not very happy with this change either. But I think it's important to place the blame where it's deserved, and in this case, the fault is not with the VB.NET design team. The requirement that Property Get and Set procedures have the same scope is part of the common language specification (CLS). It thus applies to C# and managed C++ as well as VB.NET.

So, unless (and until) Microsoft decides to change the CLS, your best bet is to use Public ReadOnly property procedures and use a separate Friend or Private scope method to set the internal property value.

Default Properties

Consider the following VB6 code:

```
myVariable = "Hello"
```

What does this line do? Is it assigning a string to a String variable?

What if myVariable is an object? Will this result in a runtime error? Or, if it has a default property, is the string being assigned to that property? If so, which property is being set?

And what if myVariable is a variant? Is it reassigning the variant to be a string? What if the variant contained an object with a default property?

You don't know.

You can't know unless you find out not only the type of the myVariable variable and whether it's an object, but also the structure of the object and whether it has a default property.

Now consider the same line of code in VB.NET.

Variable myVariable is a String or Object variable that is being assigned to reference a String object containing the value Hello.

That's it. No ambiguity. No confusion.

Default properties in VB6 are a costly shortcut. Though they save developers a few keystrokes, developers pay for the convenience with time spent chasing subtle bugs and with long-term support costs.

Personally, I don't think I've ever created a class with a default property. The few times I've added a default property to a control, I've regretted it. When I reference default properties of common objects like text boxes, I always write out the full notation txtEditControl.Text = "string" instead of relying on the default property. I think I've been pretty consistent about encouraging others to do the same.

VB.NET only allows default properties that are parameterized (since a parameterized property is not subject to the ambiguity of a simple assignment). This is most commonly used with indexers.

The Properties sample project shown in Listing 10-7 illustrates this.

Listing 10-7. The Properties sample project.

```
' Properties sample application
' Copyright ©2001 by Desaware Inc.

Module Module1

    Class DefaultTest
        Implements IDisposable
```

```
            Private Shared MyClasses As New ArrayList()

            Public Name As String

            Public Sub New(ByVal myname As String)
                MyBase.New()
                MyClasses.Add(Me)
                Name = myname
            End Sub

            Default Public ReadOnly Property OtherDefaultTestObjects(ByVal _
            idx As Integer) As DefaultTest
                Get
                    Return CType(MyClasses.Item(idx), DefaultTest)
                End Get
            End Property

            Public Shared ReadOnly Property OtherObjectCount() As Integer
                Get
                    Return myclasses.Count
                End Get
            End Property

            Public ReadOnly Property MyIndex() As Integer
                Get
                    Return myclasses.IndexOf(Me)
                End Get
            End Property

            Public Sub Dispose() Implements IDisposable.Dispose
                MyClasses.Remove(Me)
            End Sub


    End Class
```

```
    Sub ShowOtherObjects(ByVal obj As DefaultTest)
        Dim x As Integer
        Console.WriteLine("This object is: " & obj.Name)
        Console.WriteLine("Other objects are: ")
        For x = 0 To DefaultTest.OtherObjectCount - 1
            If x <> obj.MyIndex Then
                Console.WriteLine(obj(x).Name)
            End If
        Next
        Console.WriteLine()

    End Sub

    Sub Main()
        Dim obj1 As New DefaultTest("Firstobject")
        Dim obj2 As New DefaultTest("Secondobject")
        Dim obj3 As New DefaultTest("Thirdobject")

        ShowOtherObjects(obj2)
        obj2.Dispose()
        obj2 = Nothing
        ShowOtherObjects(obj3)
        Console.ReadLine()
    End Sub

End Module
```

The Properties sample program illustrates a number of the techniques you've
learned in Chapters 4 and 5 and in this chapter.

The DefaultTest class demonstrates how you can have a class keep track of all
instances of the class that have been created with minimal effort on the part of the
code that uses the class. A shared ArrayList named myClasses maintains a list of
the created objects. Each object is added to the list during its constructor call.

The default property OtherDefaultTestObjects is an indexer that returns references to objects in the internal object list making it possible for any object to
retrieve a list of all other DefaultTest objects created.

The OtherObjectCount property is a shared ReadOnly property that retrieves
the total number of objects currently stored in the myClasses collection. It's a
tough call as to whether this should be a property or a method. Since it's shared,
you can call OtherObjectCount either using an instance of the DefaultTest object
or directly using the syntax "DefaultTest.OtherObjectCount" (as shown in the
ShowOtherObjects method). The MyIndex property returns the index of a particular object instance in the myClasses collection.

The Dispose method is very important and must be called by the client when the instance is set to Nothing. Why? Doesn't VB.NET automatically handle object cleanup?

Well, VB.NET *does* automatically free up unreferenced objects—specifically, objects that are not somewhere in the chain from a root-level variable. However, the myClasses collection is itself a root-level variable! So if you reference an object in that array, it will not be freed. The Dispose method removes the object from the myClasses collection, allowing the object to be freed properly.

In other words, VB.NET does a great job of freeing up variables that are no longer referenced by your application. But it is certainly possible for you to create your own memory leaks if your design doesn't free up unneeded objects. The Main method shows how you should dispose of objects like components that implement the IDisposable interface.[18]

The ShowOtherObjects method demonstrates the use of the default property.

Parameterized Properties

When you have parameterized properties, all of the parameters are passed ByVal. This is intended to avoid possible side effects that might occur if the property procedure modifies a parameter. I realize that some people have complained about this change but I think it's fair to say that any case where you need the called function to modify a parameter is probably better handled by a method.

Properties as ByRef parameters

It turns out there is another benefit from the requirement that all property procedure parameters be passed by value.

Consider the PropByRef example shown in Listing 10-8.

Listing 10-8. The PropByRef example.

```
Class PropClass
    Private m_Member As String
    ' Overloads keyword is options in this example
    Overloads Property Member() As String
```

---

18. You may have noticed that the Dispose method in forms is marked as Overloaded and Overrides. That's because the Form object derives from the Control class, which not only implements Dispose (which you can override) but implements a second version of Dispose that takes a Boolean parameter—thus the need to also specify Overloads.

```
        Get
            Return m_Member
        End Get
        Set (ByVal Value As String)
            m_Member = Value
        End Set
    End Property


    Overloads Property Member(ByVal x As Integer) As String
        Get
            Return (m_Member)
        End Get
        Set (ByVal Value As String)
            m_Member = Value & " called with " & x.ToString()
        End Set
    End Property



End Class



Module Module1

    Sub FunctionSetsString(ByRef s As String)
        s = "Hello"
    End Sub


    Sub Main()
        Dim obj As New PropClass()
        FunctionSetsString(obj.Member)
        Console.WriteLine(obj.Member)
        FunctionSetsString(obj.Member(5))
        Console.WriteLine(obj.Member)
        Console.ReadLine()
    End Sub

End Module
```

The PropClass class contains a private string member that can be accessed through two overloaded functions called Member. Both versions of the Member method return the contents of the private string member. But they differ in the way they set the member. The parameterless Member method simply assigns the string; however, the second Member method stores the value of the index parameter as well. This makes it possible to determine which overloaded member actually set the string value.

The FunctionSetsString method takes a single String variable by reference and sets the string to Hello.

The Sub Main function calls the FunctionSetsString function passing the Member property of the PropClass class by reference.

In VB6, this would result in a temporary variable being created and loaded with the value of the Member property. That temporary variable would then be passed as a parameter to the FunctionSetsString function. As a result, even though it was passed by reference, the Member property of the PropClass class would never actually be changed by the FunctionSetsString function—only the temporary variable would be modified.

In this example, however, the following results are displayed:

```
Hello
Hello called with 5
```

This indicates that not only was the property passed correctly by reference but the correct version of the property was passed, including all the parameter values used to access the property.

In other words, the following takes place:

- VB.NET reads the member and loads the value into a temporary variable.

- VB.NET then calls the FunctionSetsString function.

- The resulting value is then used to set the property using the same member and parameters used to read the property.

Clearly, in order to perform this operation with reasonable reliability, two conditions must be followed:

1. The property procedure parameters must remain unchanged. If the parameters could change between the time the value is read and written back, the results might range from confusing to a major corruption of data. For example, if the parameter were an index to an internal array, the wrong entry could be written on return from the FunctionSetsString call.

2. The accessibility of the Get and Set procedure must be identical. If they aren't, a runtime error can occur depending on the location of the calling code and which methods are in scope.

I can't tell you if the ability to pass properties by reference is the feature that dictated the requirement that all property procedure parameters be passed by value. Nor can I tell you whether it influenced the decision to require Get and Set property procedures to have the same scope. If so, I'd say it was probably a high price to pay. On the other hand, there's probably a good chance they made the changes to property procedure parameters and scoping for other reasons already mentioned and then discovered as a side effect that they could now pass properties by reference.

With what I do know of Microsoft, I can make one pretty sound guess though: I'll bet there were some interesting, knock-down drag-out arguments among their developers about these particular decisions.

Events and Delegates

I suspect, by this point, some readers have been wondering when I'd get around to mentioning events. I expect most VB.NET books discuss events much earlier. But I have my reasons for procrastinating on this one.

First of all, in their simplest form, events in VB.NET work almost the same as they do in VB6. Consider this code that demonstrates how a button click-event is detected in VB.NET:

```
Private WithEvents button1 As System.Windows.Forms.Button

Me.button1 = New System.Windows.Forms.Button()

Private Sub button1_Click(ByVal sender As System.Object, _
    ByVal e As System.EventArgs) Handles button1.Click
    MsgBox("Simple Event Clicked", MsgBoxStyle.Information, _
    "Event arrived")
End Sub
```

In VB.NET, forms, buttons, and other controls are all just different types of classes and they raise events, as would any other class. Thus, the variable that references a button is declared using the WithEvents statement and then assigned with the New statement.

The syntax of the event handler itself is changed somewhat. Instead of an event by the name button1_Click being magically defined (as is the case in VB6), you can create a subroutine with any name and use the Handles keyword to indicate which event it handles. In other words, the prior button1_Click subroutine shown could be defined:

```
Private Sub OhNoTheButtonWasClicked(ByVal sender As System.Object, _
    ByVal e As System.EventArgs) Handles button1.Click
    MsgBox("Simple Event Clicked", MsgBoxStyle.Information, _
    "Event arrived")
End Sub
```

The name of the subroutine doesn't matter. The Form Designer Wizard will automatically create a subroutine with the name *control_eventname* but the name of the subroutine does not matter—only the event name after the Handles keyword matters.

So, from one perspective, VB.NET event handling is very much like that of VB6—and there was no great urgency to cover event handling in earlier chapters.

But it turns out that in reality, event handling in .NET is radically different from not only VB6 but also from events under COM in general. Understanding how events work requires a good understanding of how objects work in .NET—which is the other reason I wanted to wait until this point to cover the subject.

Worst of all, the documentation on how events work is (at least from my perspective) excruciatingly convoluted if not bordering incomprehensible. It is my sincere hope that I'll be able to do better in the section that follows.

In order to put VB.NET events into context, I'd like to start with a quick review of how events are dealt with in VB6 and COM. This is not so much to help you understand how events work outside of .NET but rather to help bring together into one place information that you probably already know so you can clearly identify everything you need to forget if you want to have any chance of understanding how .NET does things.

Events, Callbacks, and COM

What is an event?

Well, when an event is raised, a method is called on your object.

What's the difference between a method being called directly and being called by an event?

From a purely conceptual point of view, it's just a matter of perception.

Consider two objects: the Client object is part of your program and creates a Server object to perform some task. This is illustrated in Figure 10-3. The Server object has the ability to notify the client when it needs to. The conceptual difference between a method call and an event has to do with the direction of the call. When you make a method call from your application, you control when the call is made—it is part of the normal program flow of your application. Events can be thought of as method calls that arrive outside of the normal flow of control—method calls that your application needs to respond to.

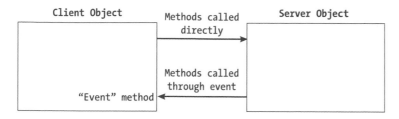

Figure 10-3. A simple event scenario.

In VB6, there are two distinct event mechanisms. The first of these is the regular event mechanism in which you define events using the "Event" syntax and then reference the Server object using the WithEvents keyword. I'll discuss this one further shortly. The other mechanism is the callback, or OLE callback, mechanism. With OLE callbacks, the Client object passes a reference to itself to the server. This allows the server to directly call methods on the Client object.

I won't go into any detail on the advantages and disadvantages of these approaches or how they work—I cover that at length in my book *Developing COM/ActiveX Components with Visual Basic 6* (Que, 1998). The important thing for you to realize is that when you use OLE callbacks, the server holds a reference to the Client object. Since the client also holds a reference to the server, you have a classic case of a circular reference. This means that until one of those references is released, neither object can be destroyed.

While this approach is fine in certain cases, it goes without saying that COM needs an event mechanism that is not subject to the circular reference problem. This mechanism is based on entities called connection points in which an object is able to expose information about the events it can raise. The information consists of the event name and a list of the event parameters. The object expects the client (event sink) to expose methods that accept those event parameters. These connection points are implemented using a set of standard COM interfaces that not only expose the event information but also define how a Server object should maintain a list of all connected clients so that a single event can be raised on multiple clients at once. Most importantly, these interfaces require the Server objects to store a weak reference to the client. This means that even though the server can call a method on the Client object, the client reference it holds does not count as a reference on the client from the perspective of COM reference counting. This allows the Client object to be destroyed even though it is sinking events.

The connection-point event mechanism is quite complex.[19]

Fortunately, NET applications do not suffer from the circular reference problem. This means that most of the complexity of event handling under COM is no longer needed.

---

19. This is one of the many situations where VB6 programmers have been somewhat spoiled by the work going on behind the scenes to make complex operations look simple.

You can, of course, use callbacks in .NET by passing a reference to the Client object to the server. But .NET defines a better and more flexible mechanism that works on a method-by-method basis.

Delegates

One essential part of any event mechanism (whether COM-based or using OLE callbacks or under .NET) is the need for the Server object and Client object to agree on both the parameters and the return value of the Event method. Another part is a mechanism for the server to hold a reference to the object and the method to be called. An object called a Delegate shown in Figure 10-4 performs both tasks.

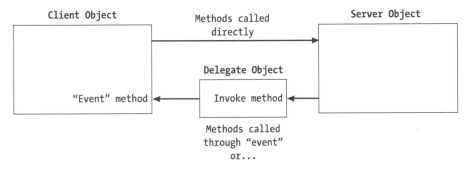

Figure 10-4. Methods called by way of a delegate.

A Delegate object defines a prototype or signature for a method call—that is, an exact set of parameters and return types for the call.[20] When you define a delegate using the Delegate keyword, you're actually creating a new class that derives from the base Delegate class. This new class (which is given the name of the delegate) specifies the parameters and return types for that delegate.

For example, the statement:

```
Delegate Sub DelegateWithStringSignature(ByVal S As String)
```

from the Delegates sample project, actually defines a new class named Delegate-WithStringSignature that will only work for methods that take a single string parameter and return no result.

The AddressOf operator in VB.NET returns a delegate that refers to a specific method.

---

20. To be completely accurate, objects derived from the Delegate base class define the signature.

Say you have a class named CalledClass that is defined as follows:

```
Class CalledClass
    Public Sub WriteMessage(ByVal s As String)
        Console.WriteLine("Called Class Write message of " & s)
    End Sub
End Class
```

Then you create a delegate of type DelagateWithStringSignature:

```
    Dim c As New CalledClass()
    Dim d1 As DelegateWithStringSignature
    d1 = AddressOf c.WriteMessage
```

This creates a delegate that not only has the correct signature (a single string parameter) but also references the WriteMessage method of a specific CalledClass object.

You can call the WriteMessage method of that object using either of the two approaches shown here:

```
d1.Invoke("Test")
c.WriteMessage("Test")
```

Delegates without Objects

You may be wondering what all this has to do with events? After all, the CalledClass class in this example has nothing to do with events, right?

Right. But delegates are what make events work in VB.NET. So bear with me as we study delegates in-depth before looking specifically at how they work with events.

The Delegates sample project in Listing 10-9 shows that a delegate need not be associated with a specific object. It can also be used to call Shared methods and even functions and subroutines in modules.

Listing 10-9. The Delegates sample project.

```
Class CalledClass
    Shared Sub SharedMessage(ByVal s As String)
        Console.WriteLine("Called CalledClass.SharedMessage with parameter: " & s)
    End Sub
```

```
        Public Sub WriteMessage(ByVal s As String)
          Console.WriteLine("Called CalledClass WriteMessage method with parameter: " & s)
        End Sub
End Class


Class OtherCalledClass
    Sub WriteMessage(ByVal s As String)
        Console.WriteLine("Called OtherCalledClass WriteMessage method with __
        parameter: " & s)
    End Sub
End Class


Module StdModule
    Sub ModuleWriteMessage(ByVal s As String)
        Console.WriteLine("AddresssOf works in standard module too")
    End Sub
End Module
```

The following code is in Sub Main for the project:

```
        Dim c As New CalledClass()
        Dim o As New OtherCalledClass()
        Dim BadObject As New ObjectWithNoWriteMessage()
        Dim d1 As DelegateWithStringSignature
        Dim obj As Object
        Dim Params() As Object = {"DynamicParam"}


        ' The two following lines are identical
        d1 = New DelegateWithStringSignature(AddressOf c.WriteMessage)
        'd1 = AddressOf c.WriteMessage

        d1.Invoke("Test")
        d1.DynamicInvoke(Params)
        Dim d2 As DelegateWithStringSignature = AddressOf _
        CalledClass.SharedMessage
        Dim d3 As DelegateWithStringSignature = AddressOf o.WriteMessage
        Dim d4 As DelegateWithStringSignature = AddressOf _
        StdModule.ModuleWriteMessage

        d2.Invoke("Test2")
        d3.Invoke("Test3")
        d4.Invoke("Test4")
```

The three delegates, d1, d2, and d3, illustrate how you can call a method on a specific object, on a Shared method for a class, or on a function in a standard module. The DynamicInvoke method provides a mechanism to specify the parameters at runtime. You'll see shortly why you might need to do this. The results of the code so far are as follows:

```
Called CalledClass WriteMessage method with parameter: Test
Called CalledClass WriteMessage method with parameter: DynamicParam
Called CalledClass.SharedMessage with parameter: Test2
Called OtherCalledClass WriteMessage method with parameter: Test3
AddresssOf works in standard module too
```

Late Binding

The Invoke method relies on the compiler to know two things: the parameter count and types to use in the Invoke call, and that the object actually *does* expose a method that can be called by the delegate.

The .NET Framework also allows for late binding in which the object and method name are not known until runtime. You can even use delegates in cases where the parameter count and types are not specified until runtime. You'll learn more about late binding in Chapter 11 but for now, let's take a look at how you can accomplish this with delegates.

A new object that does not support the WriteMessage method is defined here:

```
Class ObjectWithNoWriteMessage
    Sub BadWriteMessage()

    End Sub
End Class
```

A Delegate type is also defined with a signature that takes no parameters:

```
Delegate Sub DelegateWithNoParam()
```

In this example, the delegate is created using the CreateDelegate method, which allows you to specify the type of delegate, the object, and the name of the method as shown:

```
                Console.WriteLine(ControlChars.CrLf & "Late binding example 1")

                Dim d5 As DelegateWithStringSignature
                Dim c As New CalledClass()
                d5 = CType(System.Delegate.CreateDelegate(GetType(_
                DelegateWithStringSignature), c, "WriteMessage"), _
                DelegateWithStringSignature)
                d5.Invoke("Test")
                Try
                    d5 = CType(System.Delegate.CreateDelegate(GetType( _
                    DelegateWithStringSignature), BadObject, _
                    "WriteMessage"), DelegateWithStringSignature)
                    d5.Invoke("Test")
                Catch e As Exception
                    Console.WriteLine(e.Message)
                End Try
```

The name of the method can be a variable, thus, the binding of the object and method to the delegate does not take place until this code runs. When you try to bind the BadObject object to the delegate, the operation will fail because this object does not have a WriteMessage method. It would also fail if the object had a WriteMessage method that did not match the signature of the DelegateWithStringSignature type (for example, if it did not have a single string parameter). The code produces the following result:

```
Late binding example 1
Called CalledClass WriteMessage method with parameter: Test
Error binding to target method.
```

It is also possible to create a generic method that can call any delegate passed to it even if they have different parameter types. This is shown in the following LateBoundCaller function:

```
    Public Sub LateBoundCaller(ByVal d As [Delegate])
        Dim params() As Object = {"Test"}
        Try
            d.DynamicInvoke(params)
        Catch e As Exception
            Console.WriteLine(e.Message)
        End Try
    End Sub
```

You can pass any type of delegate to this function because every Delegate type inherits from the Delegate base class (and you can always reference a derived object using a base type variable). In this example, we'll pass two completely different delegates to the LateBoundCaller function:

```
Console.WriteLine(ControlChars.CrLf & "Late binding example 2")

Dim d6 As DelegateWithNoParam = AddressOf BadObject.BadWriteMessage
LateBoundCaller(CType(d1, System.Delegate))
LateBoundCaller(CType(d6, System.Delegate))
```

The first call will work because delegate d1 is a DelegateWithStringSignature type. But the second one should fail because the DelegateWithNoParam delegate can't accept any parameters. Sure enough, the results are as follows:

```
Late binding example 2
Called CalledClass WriteMessage method with parameter: Test
Parameter count mismatch
```

Other Applications of Delegates

As you can see, delegates provide a powerful mechanism for calling functions. You can specify the name of a method and its parameters at runtime—a task that is difficult in VB6.[21] You can pass delegates as parameters, which means that a function can be designed to perform an operation on a delegate provided by the caller. A classic example of this is a sort routine where the method to perform the comparison of two items is passed as a delegate parameter to the routine.

We'll use this ability along with the ability to use delegates for API callbacks to demonstrate in VB.NET a classic application of enumerating all of the top-level windows in a system.[22]

The EnumWindows API requires a callback function, which is called with a window handle and a user-defined parameter for each top-level window in the system. The delegate can be defined thusly:

```
Delegate Function EnumWindowsCallback(ByVal hWnd As Integer, _
ByVal lParam As Integer) As Integer
```

---

21. VB6's CallIndirect function allows you to specify the method name and parameters at runtime but the number and types of parameters is fixed. An article at `http://www.desaware.com` entitled "Implementing Indirect Calls on ActiveX/COM Objects" shows how to use SpyWorks to handle the general case of indirect calls—but it's still nowhere near as easy as it is in VB.NET.

22. You'll read a lot more about calling API functions from VB.NET (and why you'll rarely need to do it) in Chapter 15.

Note that the parameters and return value are defined as Integers (32-bit values) and not Longs.[23]

A module contains the declarations for the EnumWindows function and for the GetWindowText function, which will be used to retrieve window names where available. It contains a callback function named ShowWindowNamesCallback that matches the EnumWindowsCallback delegate signature. The ShowWindows-Names method uses the AddressOf operator to obtain a delegate that references the ShowWindowNamesCallback function and passes it to the EnumWindows function. These functions are defined as follows:

```
Module StdModule
    Public Declare Ansi Function EnumWindows Lib "User32" _
    (ByVal proc As EnumWindowsCallback, ByVal pval As Integer) As Integer
    Public Declare Ansi Function GetWindowText Lib "User32" Alias _
    "GetWindowTextA" (ByVal hWnd As Integer, ByVal WindowName As _
    String, ByVal BufferLength As Integer) As Integer

    Public Function ShowWindowNamesCallback(ByVal hWnd As Integer, _
    ByVal lParam As Integer) As Integer
        Dim windowname As New String(Chr(32), 255)
        Dim TrimmedName As String
        GetWindowText(hWnd, windowname, 254)
        TrimmedName = Left$(windowname, InStr(windowname, Chr(0)) - 1)
        If TrimmedName <> "" Then Console.WriteLine(TrimmedName)
        Return (1)
    End Function

    Public Sub ShowWindowNames()
        EnumWindows(AddressOf ShowWindowNamesCallback, 0)
    End Sub

End Module
```

So far, this code looks a lot like the comparable code in VB6. Now things begin to get interesting. Consider the WindowHandles class shown here:

---

23. I expect this to be the most common error programmers will make when attempting to use API functions from VB.NET.

```
Class WindowHandles
    Private col As New Collection()
    Public Sub New()
        MyBase.New()
        EnumWindows(AddressOf GetWindowHandlesCallback, 0)
    End Sub

    Private Function GetWindowHandlesCallback(ByVal hWnd As Integer, _
    ByVal lParam As Integer) As Integer
        col.Add(hWnd)
        Return (1)
    End Function

    Public Sub ShowAllWindows()
        Dim hwnd As Integer
        For Each hwnd In col
            Console.Write(Hex$(hwnd))
            Console.Write(", ")
        Next
        Console.WriteLine()
    End Sub

End Class
```

When this class is created, it calls EnumWindows, passing to it a delegate to the GetWindowHandlesCallback method of the object. Each time the GetWindowHandlesCallback method is called, the window handle it receives is stored in a collection, which can be dumped to the console using the ShowAllWindows method.

As you can see, the EnumWindows method, by taking a delegate as a parameter, can perform different operations depending on the delegate that it receives.

But even more exciting, the EnumWindows callback can call back to a method associated with a specific object. This is much better than in VB6 where the AddressOf operator can only return pointers to functions in standard modules.[24]

Events (at Last)

At last it's time to look at how events work in VB.NET. The first thing you need to know is that delegates have one more capability that is essential for use with events. When you define a Delegate variable in VB.NET, you are actually defining a

---

24. How does .NET do this, given that the EnumWindows function can only work with function pointers and knows nothing about objects or object instances? Well, you're accustomed to VB6 doing magic behind the scenes—consider this VB.NET's brand of magic.

new Delegate type that derives from an object of type System.MulticastDelegate (which itself derives from the base System.Delegate type). Multicast delegates are able to hold references to multiple methods. When the Invoke method of the delegate is called, all of the referenced methods are called. This is illustrated in Figure 10-5.

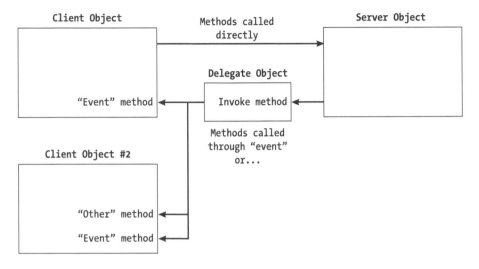

Figure 10-5. Multicast delegates.

Approaches for Handling Events

The EventExample program is a Windows application with one form that has four button controls and three Option button (RadioButton) controls. Each of the controls demonstrates a different aspect of event handling in VB.NET.

The control named SimpleEvent works as described at the start of the "Events and Delegates" section in this chapter. The form designer adds a declaration of the Command button using the WithEvents keyword to indicate that you wish VB.NET to wire up the events for you. The designer creates the button1_Click method: and the Handles keyword tells the language to automatically create a delegate for the button1_Click method and connect it to the button1.Click event:

```
Private WithEvents button1 As System.Windows.Forms.Button

Private Sub button1_Click(ByVal sender As System.Object, _
ByVal e As System.EventArgs) Handles button1.Click
    MsgBox("Simple Event Clicked", MsgBoxStyle.Information, _
    "Event arrived")
End Sub
```

Button2 (labeled "Other Approaches") demonstrates that this is but one possible approach.

The EventClass class defines two events, FirstEvent and SecondEvent. The SecondEvent event follows the convention of having the first parameter be a reference to the object that raised the event. The FirstEvent event ignores this convention.

These two events both define delegates, however, it's not obvious that this is the case.

When you call the RaiseEvent function, what you're really doing is calling the Invoke method of the delegate.

But that's all happening behind the scenes in VB.NET:[25]

```
Public Class EventClass
    Public Event FirstEvent(ByVal myData As Integer)

    Public Event SecondEvent(ByVal Sender As Object, _
    ByVal myData As Integer)

    Public Sub Test1()
        RaiseEvent FirstEvent(5)
    End Sub

    Public Sub Test2()
        RaiseEvent SecondEvent(Me, 5)
    End Sub

End Class
```

We'll be using this class to demonstrate different ways of handling events.

The Button2_Click event simply calls the Test1 and Test2 methods on two different instances of the EventClass object as follows:

```
Private Sub button2_Click(ByVal sender As System.Object, _
ByVal e As System.EventArgs) Handles button2.Click
    ec.Test1()
    ec2.Test2()
End Sub
```

The ec1 and ec2 objects are defined differently:

```
Private ec As New EventClass()
Private WithEvents ec2 As EventClass
```

---

25. Things are a bit trickier in C#—but we won't worry about that here.

As you can see here, the ec2.SecondEvent event is connected to the EventClass_SecondEvent function using the Handles keyword in exactly the same way as button1.Click was connected to the button1_Click method:

```
Private Sub EventClass_SecondEvent(ByVal obj As Object, _
ByVal i As Integer) Handles ec2.SecondEvent
    MsgBox("EventClass_SecondEvent called", _
    MsgBoxStyle.Information, "Event arrived")
End Sub
```

The ec object is not defined using the WithEvents keyword. With VB6, you'd be out of luck. But with VB.NET, you can connect the event dynamically using the AddHandler statement as shown:

```
AddHandler ec.FirstEvent, AddressOf EventClass_FirstEvent

Private Sub EventClass_FirstEvent(ByVal i As Integer)
    MsgBox("EventClass_FirstEvent called", _
    MsgBoxStyle.Information, "Event arrived")
End Sub
```

The simple explanation is that the AddHandler function connects the EventClass_FirstEvent method to the ec.FirstEvent event.

Here's what's really happening.

The ec object defines an event named FirstEvent. But you already know that FirstEvent is actually a delegate that the ec object can use to raise events.

You also know that the AddressOf operator returns a delegate.

So, what the AddHandler command is actually doing is taking the delegate for the EventClass_FirstEvent method and adding it to the ec.FirstEvent delegate. I know the idea of adding a delegate to another delegate sounds strange. Think of it this way:

- A Delegate is an object that can call a specified method.

- A Multicast delegate is an object that can call many methods.

- When you add a delegate to a multicast delegate, you're simply adding another method to the list of methods called by that multicast delegate.

When you add a delegate to an event (which is implemented with a multicast delegate) you're just wiring up another method to call when the event is raised. What happens if you use the AddHandler method to add a delegate to an event that is already being handled? You already know that the ec2 object is connected to the EventClass_SecondEvent method. Now we'll connect it to another method as well:

```
AddHandler ec2.SecondEvent, AddressOf AnotherSecondEventHandler

Private Sub AnotherSecondEventHandler(ByVal obj As Object, _
ByVal i As Integer)
    MsgBox("AnotherSecondEventHandler called", _
    MsgBoxStyle.Information, "Event arrived")
End Sub
```

When you click on button2, you'll see three message boxes indicating that the EventClass_FirstEvent, EventClass_SecondEvent, and AnotherSecondEventHandler methods are called.

The AnotherSecondEventHandler method also illustrates an important point: the name of the method is completely irrelevant. The use of the "classname_eventname" syntax is purely a convention.

Inherited Events

Events are inherited, as are methods and properties.

The DerivedEventClass class shown here illustrates a number of additional issues relating to events, some of which relate to inheritance and others that apply to events in general. The first item of interest is that you can define an event based on a Delegate type (which is not surprising when you recall that an event *is* a delegate).

You can also create shared events just as you can have shared delegates. A shared event can be raised without a specific object instance:

```
Public Delegate Sub EventTemplate(ByVal Obj As Object, ByVal i As Integer)

Public Class DerivedEventClass
    Inherits EventClass
    Shared Event ASharedEvent()

    ' Note alternate form of declaration - These are identical
    'Event DerivedEvent(ByVal obj As Object, ByVal i As Integer)
    Event DerivedEvent As EventTemplate
```

The InternalHandler method handles the SecondEvent event from the base class. Derived classes in general have the ability to sink base class events. It is possible for clients using this class to receive events inherited from the base class as well as those raised by the derived class. If you want to prevent users of a derived class from receiving events of the base class, you can use the Shadows keyword to hide the base class event by defining a Private event of the same name. This Private event will not be accessible outside of the class.

The DerivedEventClass Test2 method hides the base class method of the same name. It calls the base class Test2 method and also raises the shared event:

```
Public Sub InternalHandler(ByVal obj As Object, _
ByVal i As Integer) Handles MyBase.SecondEvent
    RaiseEvent DerivedEvent(Me, i * 2)
End Sub
Private Shadows Event FirstEvent(ByVal Mydata As Integer)

Public Shadows Sub Test2()
    MyBase.Test2()
    RaiseEvent ASharedEvent()
End Sub
```

```
End Class
```

The DerivedEventClass object is defined WithEvents in the form. It is connected to the DerivedEventHandler method using the Handles keyword. It is also connected to the AnotherSecondEventHandler method using the AddHandler command. That's right, the AnotherSecondEventHandler method is handling two events from two different objects. In fact, any method can sink any number of events from any number of objects—as long as the signature of the method matches the signature of the event delegate. You'll see another example of this shortly.

The shared event is referenced by the class name rather than the object name for the sake of clarity. I could have referenced it using an object instance (dec.ASharedEvent) but using the class name emphasizes the fact that it is a shared event. The shared event connects to a method in exactly the same way as an object event. The code that demonstrates the use of the DerivedEventClass is invoked by the button3.Click event as shown:

```
Private WithEvents dec As DerivedEventClass

    AddHandler dec.SecondEvent, AddressOf AnotherSecondEventHandler

    AddHandler DerivedEventClass.ASharedEvent, AddressOf _
    SharedEventHandler
```

```
Private Sub DerivedEventHandler(ByVal obj As Object, _
ByVal i As Integer) Handles dec.DerivedEvent
    MsgBox("DerivedEventHandler called", MsgBoxStyle.Information, _
    "Event arrived")
End Sub

Private Sub SharedEventHandler()
    MsgBox("Shared event handler", MsgBoxStyle.Information, _
    "Event arrived")
End Sub

Private Sub button3_Click(ByVal sender As System.Object, _
ByVal e As System.EventArgs) Handles button3.Click
    dec.Test2()
End Sub
```

Once Again with Delegates

The DerivedEventClass class includes a SpecialEventHandler public delegate and the TestSpecialEvents method to invoke it. Because this delegate is not defined using the Event keyword, it will not appear as an event in the IntelliSense drop-down windows or in the type information. However, this doesn't mean that it can't be used much like an event would be used:

```
Public SpecialEventHandler As EventTemplate

Public Sub TestSpecialEvents()
    SpecialEventHandler.Invoke(Me, 6)
End Sub
```

The SpecialEventHandler delegate is first assigned to a delegate that points to the FirstSpecialEventHandler method of the form. Next, another delegate is created that references the SecondSpecialEventHandler method of the form. Then the SpecialEventHandler delegate is assigned from a combination of the two previous delegates using the Delegate class Combine method.

Now, the FirstSpecialEventHandler and SecondSpecialEventHandler methods are connected to the dec.SpecialEventHandler delegate. When the dec object calls the SpecialEventHandler.Invoke method, both of the form methods will be called.

In other words, this mechanism works exactly the way events do except that with events, VB.NET does some work behind the scenes to make life easier. The following code illustrates this "non-event" approach:

```
dec.SpecialEventHandler = AddressOf FirstSpecialEventHandler
      Dim EventToCombine As EventTemplate = AddressOf _
      SecondSpecialEventHandler
      dec.SpecialEventHandler = _
      CType(dec.SpecialEventHandler.Combine( _
      dec.SpecialEventHandler, EventToCombine), EventTemplate)

   Private Sub FirstSpecialEventHandler(ByVal obj As Object, _
   ByVal i As Integer)
      MsgBox("FirstSpecial event handler", MsgBoxStyle.Information, _
      "Event arrived")
   End Sub

   Private Sub SecondSpecialEventHandler(ByVal obj As Object, _
   ByVal i As Integer)
      MsgBox("SecondSpecial event handler", MsgBoxStyle.Information, _
      "Event arrived")
   End Sub

   Private Sub button4_Click(ByVal sender As System.Object, _
   ByVal e As System.EventArgs) Handles button4.Click
      dec.TestSpecialEvents()
   End Sub
```

Handling Multiple Events

Some VB6 programmers have complained about the lack of support for control arrays in VB.NET. While it's true that VB.NET does not support control arrays, this doesn't mean you can't perform the same tasks in other ways. Here is an example of code that allows three different Option buttons to share the same event:

```
Private Sub Options_CheckedChanged(ByVal sender As System.Object, _
ByVal e As System.EventArgs) Handles radioButton3.CheckedChanged, _
radioButton2.CheckedChanged, radioButton1.CheckedChanged
   Dim params() As Object
   Dim NameValue As Object
   NameValue = sender.GetType.InvokeMember("Text", _
   Reflection.BindingFlags.Public Or _
   Reflection.BindingFlags.Instance Or _
   Reflection.BindingFlags.GetProperty, Nothing, sender, params)
   Debug.WriteLine(CStr(NameValue))
```

```
Dim rb As RadioButton
rb = CType(sender, RadioButton)
Debug.WriteLine(rb.Name & " " & rb.Text)

End Sub
```

The Options_CheckedChange method is linked to the CheckedChanged event of three different Option buttons by specifying multiple events after the Handles statement. By now, I'm sure you realize this could have been accomplished using the AddHandler statement as well. You must add this code yourself—Visual Studio does not have a mechanism to do it automatically.

The sender parameter indicates which radio button raised the event. Since there is no control array, there is no Index property available to distinguish between event sources. Depending on your application, you can use whichever properties are suitable to distinguish between sources—for example, the Name property, Text property, or position. You can read properties from the sender using reflection (which is the subject of the next chapter). Consider the cryptic InvokeMember method shown here as a preview of things to come. For now, suffice to say it will retrieve the specified property of the sender control.

If you are sure all of the controls are of the same type, you can also assign the sender to an object of the control type and access the property directly as shown in the second approach, which uses variable rb declared as a RadioButton.

If you are sure all of the controls are the same type, does that mean…

That's right—if you use this approach for implementing control arrays, you aren't limited to using the same type of control in the array. Why, you can even create form arrays!

Removing Handlers

You'll notice the following statements in the Dispose method of the form:

```
RemoveHandler ec.FirstEvent, AddressOf EventClass_FirstEvent
RemoveHandler ec2.SecondEvent, AddressOf AnotherSecondEventHandler
RemoveHandler DerivedEventClass.ASharedEvent, _
AddressOf SharedEventHandler
RemoveHandler dec.SecondEvent, AddressOf AnotherSecondEventHandler
```

The RemoveHandler statement disconnects a method from an event. Doing so is overkill in this particular example since the application shuts down when the form is closed. But it can be important in other circumstances.

Let's say you create ten Client objects and use the AddHandler statement to connect them to an event in a Server object. Then let's say you no longer need those Client objects and clear the references to them in your program.

Because VB.NET solves the circular reference problem, those Client objects will be freed, right?

Wrong.

The Server object is still holding a reference to those objects in its event delegate. As long as you are holding a reference to the Server object in your application, VB.NET will consider those delegates to be references to the Client objects.

So, it is very important to remember to use the RemoveHandler method to remove event connections that you added in order to allow your objects to be properly freed.

What about events declared using the WithEvents keyword? Those are unlikely to be a problem because the reference to the event source is itself freed when the module sinking the events is freed. For example, if you use WithEvents to connect to a control on a form, deleting a reference to the form is sufficient to cause the form and all of its contained objects to be freed since none of them will trace back to a root-level variable in your application.

Recap

This chapter focused on objects under VB.NET. Since this is not a book for new or inexperienced programmers, we had the luxury of dealing with more advanced concepts instead of introducing basic concepts (such as the importance of classes and how properties and methods work). Instead, you learned how .NET applications fit together and how namespaces represent a way of logically organizing classes that is independent of their physical organization in assemblies.

Next, we covered virtually every aspect of how classes work under VB.NET, emphasizing the scoping changes that are a consequence of both the architecture of .NET applications and the introduction of inheritance to the language. You also learned about changes to the way methods and properties work in .NET and the reasons for those changes.

Finally, you learned about events and the new concept of delegates, which form the foundation of how events work in .NET.

Reflection and Attributes

YOU'VE SEEN CODE like this in Visual Basic 6:

```
Public Class TestClass
    Public X As Integer
    Private Y As Integer
End Class
```

The class and the class members have a characteristic of Public or Private. Think of these as attributes of the class or member. Now look at the following VB.NET code:

```
<Modified("Dan", "1/10/2001")> Public Class TestClass
        <Modified("Dan", "1/13/2001") Public X As Integer
        Private Y As Integer
End Class
```

The information between the <> brackets are also attributes.[1] This represents a major addition to the Visual Basic language—but what does it really mean?

To understand the significance of this change, we'll need to back up a bit.

On Compilers and Interpreters

Let's begin with a look at the fundamental difference between compilers and interpreters.[2]

Compilers and interpreters represent two very different ways of processing code. An interpreter is a program that reads another program and performs the operations that it specifies as illustrated in Figure 11-1.

---

1. Don't try to use the "Modified" attribute shown here in your code until you finish the chapter and understand where it comes from.

2. The explanation that follows refers to "pure" interpreters and compilers. In practice, there are many hybrid approaches where interpreters have compiler like features and vice versa.

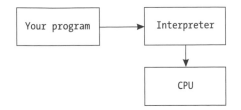

Figure 11-1. Operation of an interpreter.

For example, a BASIC interpreter might see the line:

```
A = 5
```

and internally store 5 in some location in memory that it has labeled "A." Because interpreters are actually reading the source code and performing the operations it describes, they have all of the information about the original source program available at all times. This makes it easy to perform certain tasks such as allowing you to break in the middle of a program, modify code and continue, examine variables and change their values, and even enter lines of code in an Immediate window and process them outside of the normal program sequence.

Interpreters don't always work directly on the original source code. It is common for interpreters to preparse or precompile the original source to an intermediate code (in some cases, called "P-Code"). But it is always possible to go back and rederive the source from this preparsed code, thus maintaining the ability for developers to work at the source-code level.

The main disadvantage of interpreters is that they tend to be slow. The interpreter is constantly translating the source code or P-Code and following its instructions.

A compiler translates source code into the native code of a computer as illustrated in Figure 11-2.

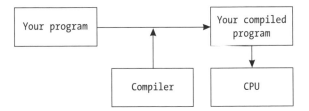

Figure 11-2. Operation of a compiler.

When the compiler sees the line:

```
A = 5
```

it figures out the machine code that performs that operation and outputs it into the resulting executable file. Once the compiler has done its job, it no longer has a role to play in the execution of the program. Because the resulting program is in native code, it can achieve excellent performance (depending on the quality of the compiler).

Once a program is compiled, it no longer needs the original source code to run—thus, compilers have the ability to throw out that information, resulting in smaller and more efficient programs. Unfortunately, throwing out the original source code makes it virtually impossible to debug a program. You need the source information to identify variables and interpret the flow of a program while it is being debugged. For this reason, compilers can produce debug versions of files that hold the original source code along with information on which source lines produce a given block of executable code. Even so, it is difficult for debuggers to let you modify code and continue execution because code modifications typically require existing code to move and that would invalidate existing memory and code pointers. Modern development environments do allow a limited degree of capability to edit and continue[3] but it is not nearly as fast or simple as with an interpreter.

Visual Basic 6 offers the best of both worlds. When you work in the development environment, VB6 provides a true interpreter with all of the development benefits associated with interpreters. But VB6 also has a full native-code compiler. One of the most remarkable features of VB6 is that the interpreter and compiler result in the same functionality for any given program.

Visual Basic.NET is a compiler. For many VB6 programmers, this alone will take getting used to. I've been developing using Visual C++ for some time so I am quite comfortable with the Visual Studio.NET environment but I confess that I do miss the VB6 interpreter-based environment. I understand why Microsoft made the choice to combine the environments and the new IDE *does* have some very cool features. However, I do miss that VB6 interpreter.

One Compiler, Two Compiler…

As you learned in Chapter 4, Visual Basic.NET and C# do not actually compile to native code. They compile source programs into assemblies that contain intermediate language (IL) code and a manifest that contains information on all of the objects in the program as shown in Figure 11-3.

---

3. It is not clear from the current beta how well this feature will work in the final version of VB.NET.

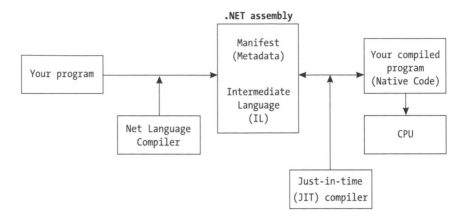

Figure 11-3. Operation of a .NET language.

The program is not compiled into native code until the JIT (just-in-time) compilation phase that takes place either at load time (the first time the assembly is loaded) or at install time. The object information in the manifest is used to build the links to the objects in the assembly and their methods and properties. It is also used to allow the assembly to build links to other assemblies. The manifest information and intermediate code is never discarded, making it possible for the JIT compiler to recompile the assembly if necessary—say, if a new dependent assembly is installed. This ability to resolve method and property calls to updated assemblies helps eliminate component DLL Hell conflicts that are so common with COM components. I'll have more to say on this issue shortly.

Compile Time versus Runtime

The idea of compile-time and runtime is very familiar to C++ and assembly language programmers but not as familiar to VB6 programmers. Consider the following pseudocode program:

```
If ABooleanConstantOrVariable Then
    Code block 1
End If
#If  ABooleanConstant Then
    code block 2
#End If
```

Code block 1 will or will not execute depending on the value of ABooleanConstantOrVariable. Even if the code never runs (because of the value of the conditional term), the code will always be present in the program.

When the program reaches the If statement, it will check the value of ABooleanConstantOrVariable and decide whether to run the code block based on the result. The conditional term is said to be evaluated at runtime because it is evaluated while the program is running.

The #If and #End If statements are evaluated once when the program is compiled. The ABooleanConstant constant is defined as a constant in the project property settings or as a compile line option. If the ABooleanConstant constant is True, code block 2 is included in the program. If it is False, code block 2 is completely eliminated—as if it were a comment. In either case, the conditional itself is not included in the program. This is referred to as conditional compilation—a block of code is included or not based on a conditional statement that is evaluated at compile-time (not runtime). VB.NET supports conditional compilation as well.

Conditional compilation is a powerful tool for managing different software configurations while maintaining a single source file. Each software configuration can have its own compile-time constants that can control inclusion or exclusion of code based on the configuration.

I've used conditional compilation to incorporate special debugging code in debug builds, to create custom configurations with tracing code specific to that configuration, and to support localization efforts where code changes were needed between builds for different languages.

Attributes

The conditional compilation capabilities of VB.NET are comparable to those of VB6. But VB.NET also supports attributes—a feature that plays a role both at compile-time and potentially at runtime. The first thing you need to know about attributes is that they are accessible to the compiler. That means that the compiler can examine the attributes of a class, method, or property and change its compilation based on the attribute. This is obvious for language attributes like Public or Private that control the scope of an object. But it is also true for attributes that are part of the .NET Framework. For example, if you mark a class as synchronized (as shown in Chapter 7), the compiler will create the necessary IL code (which will then JIT compile into native code) to support synchronization of the class.

But the real magic of attributes derives from the fact that the attribute information for objects in .NET is kept in the assembly manifest—which means (as you read a few pages back) that this information is never discarded.

And it can be queried at runtime.

The process of examining the attributes of code and other information kept in an assembly manifest is called reflection. We'll look more closely at attributes later. First let's take a closer look at reflection.

Reflection

To demonstrate reflection, consider the following class and enumeration from the Reflection sample project:

```
' Reflection and attributes example
' Copyright ©2001 by Desaware Inc. All Rights Reserved

Public Class Class1

    Public Class TestClass
        Public X As Integer
        Private Y As Integer
    End Class

    Public Enum TestEnum
        FirstMember = 1
        SecondMember = 2
    End Enum
End Class
```

Our goal is to be able to open the assembly containing this class and not only detect the class and enumeration but also detect the name and types of members of the class and obtain a list of the enumeration values.

Exploring the Manifest

The first thing we do is import the System.Reflection namespace. This provides a shortcut to the objects in the namespace (the System.Reflection namespace is automatically referenced as part of any .NET application). The System.Reflection namespace contains the objects needed to read the manifest:

```
' Reflection and attributes example
' Copyright ©2001 by Desaware Inc. All Rights Reserved

Imports System.Reflection
Module Module1

    Sub Main()
        AssemblyTypes()
        Console.ReadLine()
    End Sub
```

The AssemblyTypes function obtains a list of all of the public types defined by the current executing assembly:

```
Sub AssemblyTypes()
    Dim TypeIndex As Integer
    Dim A As System.Reflection.Assembly
    Dim ATypes() As Type
    ' We're going to explore the current assembly
    A = A.GetExecutingAssembly()
    ' Find all the types exposed by this assembly
    ATypes = A.GetTypes()
```

The GetExecutingAssembly method is a static method. I could have called it without referencing a specific object using the syntax A = System.Reflection.Assembly.GetExecutingAssembly() (or Reflection.Assembly.GetExecutingAssembly, or [Assembly].GetExecutingAssembly) as well. There are other static methods that allow you to open assemblies given an assembly name, DLL name, or namespace. The GetTypes() method returns an array of all the types defined in the assembly. The AssemblyTypes method continues as follows:

```
For TypeIndex = 0 To UBound(ATypes)
        ' Note the full name of each type
        Console.WriteLine("Type: " + ATypes(TypeIndex).FullName)
        ' If it's an enumeration, list the enumeration values
        If ATypes(TypeIndex).IsEnum Then
            Dim EnumStrings() As String
            ' Get the names
            EnumStrings = System.Enum.GetNames(ATypes(TypeIndex))
            Console.WriteLine("   Enumeration names are: ")
            Dim estemp As String
            For Each estemp In EnumStrings
                ' Display the names, and each value
                Console.WriteLine("      " + estemp + " = " + _
                System.Enum.Format(ATypes(TypeIndex), _
                System.Enum.Parse(ATypes(TypeIndex), estemp), "D"))
            Next
        End If
```

The function loops through the array. The IsEnum property of the Type variable is True if the type represents an enumeration. If that is the case, the function uses the static GetNames method of the System.Enum type (the type on which all enumerations are based), which retrieves a string array containing the names of all of the enumeration values. The static Parse method of the System.Enum type returns an enumeration value for a specified enumeration value name. The static Format method converts the enumeration value into a numeric value.

If the type of member is a nested type (a type that is defined within the assembly and is not one of the types that implements the assembly itself), the ShowMembers function is called to show the members of that type. Both the class TestClass and the TestEnum enumeration will be detected as nested types:

```
' For nested types (which represent those defined by
' the programmer within the assembly)
' Show all of the members
If ATypes(TypeIndex).MemberType = _
MemberTypes.NestedType Then
    ' Show the custom attributes - This will be added
    ' in the next example
    ' ShowCustomAttributes( _
    ' ATypes(TypeIndex).GetCustomAttributes())
    ShowMembers(ATypes(TypeIndex))
End If
Console.WriteLine()
    Next

End Sub
```

The ShowMembers function obtains a list of all members for a given data type. Actually, to be completely accurate, it obtains only those members that are fields. You could also enumerate properties, methods, interfaces, and so on.

```
Sub ShowMembers(ByVal ThisType As Type)
    Dim Index As Integer
    Dim idx2 As Integer
    Dim members() As MemberInfo
    ' Find all of the field members for ThisType
    ' You could search for methods, properties, interfaces, etc. as well.
    ' Find both private and public instance members (but not static)
    members = ThisType.FindMembers(MemberTypes.Field, _
    BindingFlags.Public Or BindingFlags.Instance _
    Or BindingFlags.NonPublic, Type.FilterName, "*")
```

The FindMembers method of the Type data type retrieves an array of MemberInfo entries for the members we are searching for. In this case, only fields are being retrieved. The BindingFlags parameter indicates which members should be found based on the .NET runtime's ability to bind to a member. In this case, we're looking for both public and private members and only those members that require an instance of an object (for example, no static members). We're using the default Type object filter and accepting fields with any name.

We then loop through each of the members and display further information about the member:

```
For index = 0 To ubound(Members)
    Dim fi As FieldInfo
    ' Since we know it's a field, it's safe to cast to
    ' FieldInfo here.
    fi = CType(Members(Index), FieldInfo)
```

The FieldInfo data type is derived from the MemberInfo type and allows us to extract in-depth information about field members. The CType operator casts the MemberInfo object into a FieldInfo variable. It works because every one of the MemberInfo objects found is, in fact, a FieldInfo object—we know this because the FindMembers method searched only for fields.

The FieldInfo FieldType property allows us to determine the member type. The Attributes property can be checked to see if the member is private or public:

```
' Pull the name and the type of the field
Console.Write("  Member: " + members(Index).Name + _
" Type:" + fi.FieldType.ToString())
' And read the field attribute to determine if it's public
' or private
If (fi.Attributes And FieldAttributes.Public) <> 0 Then
    Console.WriteLine(" - is Public")
End If
If (fi.Attributes And FieldAttributes.Private) <> 0 Then
    Console.WriteLine(" - is Private")
End If
' This will be added in the next example
' ShowCustomAttributes(fi.GetCustomAttributes())
        Next index
    End Sub
```

The results are as follows:

```
Type: Reflection.Module1

Type: Reflection.Class1
```

```
Type: Reflection.Class1+TestClass
  Member: X Type:System.Int32 - is Public
  Member: Y Type:System.Int32 - is Private

Type: Reflection.Class1+TestEnum
  Enumeration names are:
    FirstMember = 1
    SecondMember = 2
  Member: value__ Type:System.Int32 - is Public
```

As you can see, the System.Reflection namespace makes it easy to obtain information about an assembly at runtime. The rest of this chapter will focus on the ramifications of this capability.

Custom Attributes

Where do attributes come from? Some are built into the language. Others are defined as part of the .NET Framework. But you can also create your own attributes.

The Attributes sample project demonstrates how you can create attributes that store custom information such as revision history in an assembly manifest.

An attribute is defined by creating a class that inherits from the System.Attributes class. The name of the class takes the form *attributename*Attribute. In this example, the Modified attribute is defined by creating a class named ModifiedAttribute. When you use an attribute, you can use the attribute name with or without the "Attribute" suffix. Thus, for the AttributeUsage attribute, you can use either AttributeUsage or AttributeUsageAttribute.

The new attribute class itself uses an attribute to control how the new attribute will work. The AttributeUsage attribute has a constructor that takes an AttributeTargets enumeration as a parameter. The AttributeTargets enumeration is a flag enumeration that defines what types of objects support this enumeration. In this example, the Modified attribute can be applied to methods, properties, classes, and fields as you can see in the following code:

```
' Reflection and Attributes example II
' Copyright ©2001 by Desaware Inc. All Rights Reserved

Public Class Class1
    <AttributeUsage (AttributeTargets.Method Or _
      AttributeTargets.Property Or _
      AttributeTargets.Class Or AttributeTargets.Field, _
      AllowMultiple:=True)> Public Class ModifiedAttribute
        Inherits System.Attribute
```

You can also set two properties in the AttributeUsage attribute: the Inherited property determines whether your new attribute will be inherited by any derived classes on which it applies; and the AllowMultiple property specifies whether you can apply the attribute to an object more than once.

Of course, this raises an interesting question. How can you set properties in a constructor?

Attribute Constructors

Consider a simple class:

```
Class MyClass
    Public Sub New()
    End Sub
    Public X As Integer
End Class
```

You can create this class using:

```
Dim C As New MyClass()
```

But there is no way to set the X field in the constructor unless you create a constructor that takes an integer parameter:

```
Public Sub New(ByVal NewX As Integer)
    X = NewX
End Sub
```

When creating an attribute class, you can (of course) define multiple constructors. But attributes have an additional capability. Here's a simple attribute named MyAttribute that can be applied only to classes:

```
<AttributeUsage(AttributeTargets.Class)>Class MyAttributeAttribute
    Inherits System.Attribute
    Public Sub New()
    End Sub
    Public X As Integer
End Class
```

Naturally, it can be applied using the default constructor as shown here:

```
<MyAttribute()> Public Class B

End Class
```

But as you can see, one of the limitations of attributes is that you can't add additional code to invoke methods at the time the attribute is applied. It is possible to invoke methods on attributes when accessing them through reflection but that doesn't help you at the time they are applied. You can, however, set property and field values using the familiar named-property syntax shown here:

```
<MyAttribute(X:=5)> Public Class B

End Class
```

This means that it is practical to define attributes with many properties or fields and set them when the attribute is applied without creating long and complex constructors.

The := assignment operator is familiar to many VB programmers because it can be used to pass named parameters to functions. This usage, where it allows you to specify the values of properties, is unique to attributes.

Back to the Modified Attribute

We now return to the Modified attribute. Based on the AttributeUsage settings, the attribute can be applied to methods, properties, fields, and classes. It can also be applied more than once to an object. The Modified attribute is designed to keep track of code modifications within the code—and it makes sense to allow it to be applied multiple times because a given code element can be modified multiple times.

In addition to the code shown earlier, this attribute defines three public fields: Author, ModDate, and SomeIntValue. As Listing 11-1 shows, it defines a constructor that sets the author and modification date.

Listing 11-1. Definition and use of a custom attribute.

```
Public Class Class1
    <AttributeUsage (AttributeTargets.Method Or _
      AttributeTargets.Property Or _
      AttributeTargets.Class Or AttributeTargets.Field, _
      AllowMultiple:=True)> Public Class ModifiedAttribute
        Inherits System.Attribute
```

```
    Public Author As String
    Public ModDate As String
    Public Sub New(ByVal SetAuthor As String, ByVal SetModDate As String)
        MyBase.New()
        Author = SetAuthor
        ModDate = SetModDate
    End Sub
    Public Overrides Function ToString() As String
        Return ("Modified by " + Author + " on " + ModDate)
    End Function
    Public SomeIntValue As Integer

End Class
```

The ModifiedAttribute class also overrides the ToString method to display a modification notice. The following code defines a class named TestClass that was modified once by Dan on 1/10/2001. It contains a field X that was modified twice: once by Dan and once by Joe. This attribute also sets the SomeIntValue field to 5 for no reason other than to show you that this actually works:

```
<Modified("Dan", "1/10/2001")> _
Public Class TestClass
    <Modified("Dan", "1/13/2001"), _
     Modified("Joe", "1/25/2001", SomeIntValue:=5)> _
    Public X As Integer
    Private Y As Integer
End Class

Public Enum TestEnum
    FirstMember = 1
    SecondMember = 2
End Enum
End Class
```

Viewing Custom Attributes

The code to show custom attributes is built on the Reflection example shown earlier (in the "Reflection" section of this chapter). The line:

```
ShowCustomAttributes(fi.GetCustomAttributes(True))
```

is added to the ShowMembers function. It uses the GetCustomAttributes method of the FieldInfo class to obtain an array of custom attributes for the field.

The line:

```
ShowCustomAttributes(ATypes(TypeIndex).GetCustomAttributes(True))
```

is added to the AssemblyTypes method. It calls the GetCustomAttributes method to obtain an array of custom attributes for the classes found by the Assembly-Types method.

The ShowCustomAttributes method is defined as follows:

```
Private Sub ShowCustomAttributes(ByVal TheAttributes() As Object)
    Dim ca As System.Attribute
    Dim idx As Integer
    For idx = 0 To UBound(TheAttributes)
        ca = CType(TheAttributes(idx), System.Attribute)
        Console.WriteLine("      Attribute: " + ca.ToString())
    Next
End Sub
```

The ShowCustomAttributes method accepts an array of objects as a parameter because an array of objects is returned from the GetCustomAttributes method. All of the objects in the array will be custom attributes that derive (like all custom attributes) from the System.Attribute class. The routine loops through each entry in the array, references the object using a variable of type System.Attributes, and then calls the ToString method to display the custom attributes.

While there is no mechanism to call methods on an attribute class when the attribute is applied to an object, it is easy to call attribute methods when working with the attribute object itself using reflection.

When you run the sample program, you get the following results:

```
Type: Attributes.Class1

Type: Attributes.Class1+ModifiedAttribute
      Attribute: System.AttributeUsageAttribute
  Member: Author Type:System.String - is Public
  Member: ModDate Type:System.String - is Public
  Member: SomeIntValue Type:System.Int32 - is Public

Type: Attributes.Class1+TestClass
      Attribute: Modified by Dan on 1/10/2001
  Member: X Type:System.Int32 - is Public
      Attribute: Modified by Joe on 1/25/2001
      Attribute: Modified by Dan on 1/13/2001
  Member: Y Type:System.Int32 - is Private
```

```
Type: Attributes.Class1+TestEnum
   Enumeration names are:
      FirstMember = 1
      SecondMember = 2
   Member: value__ Type:System.Int32 - is Public


Type: Attributes.Module1
```

As you can see, you can use reflection to read the Modified attribute. You could create a utility that uses reflection to document an assembly, extracting not only the object names and properties but also the author and modification information or any other information for which you create an attribute. Just as the runtime uses attributes defined by the .NET Framework to control the behavior of objects and applications, you can read attributes while your application is running to modify the behavior of your own applications.

When you start developing components or controls in VB.NET, you'll find yourself using attributes such as Browsable, Category, Description, and Bindable that are defined in the System.ComponentModel class. These attributes control the way the .NET designer works with those properties. For example, if you use the Category component to specify that a property belong to the Appearance category, the property will appear with other Appearance category properties in the property browser when you work with the component at design time. The property browser uses reflection to obtain category information for each property.[4]

In addition to the examples described in this chapter, the DumpLib sample application extends the Reflection and Attributes examples to show how to extract method, property, and parameter information for every object in an assembly. The application builds a simple database of object members and enumerations for an assembly and outputs them in common separated value (CSV) format.[5]

Binding

When an assembly is loaded for the first time, the JIT compiler uses the information in the manifest to compile the intermediate language (IL) code into native code. Member access in the resulting code is very efficient—the compiler can establish the locations of the members and generate direct calls to those addresses.[6] This is called early binding.

---

4. That's right—with VB.NET you are concerned with not only compile time and runtime but also design time. Of course, any VB developer who has ever written an ActiveX control is familiar with this concept.

5. I created the DumpLib program to help compare VB6 methods and constants with those in VB.NET during development of this book. It's included here as an additional example of reflection techniques, with no further description.

Early binding is used any time the object type and member are known to the compiler.

Early Binding and DLL Hell

COM also uses early binding and, like .NET, can use early binding when the object type[7] and member are known to the compiler. Let's say you have a COM program that uses an object in a COM DLL. The application looks at the type library of the DLL and binds the member access based on that information. This means that if the application has a pointer to an object in the DLL, it will access properties or methods based on that pointer.

But what happens if someone rebuilds the DLL after modifying its source code in a way that rearranges the members in one of the DLL's objects?

The COM application doesn't know that the members have moved. So, when it tries to access those members—say, calling a method based on the hard-coded information defined for the previous version—it ends up accessing the wrong method or an illegal method on the new DLL. This is why it is so important under COM to make sure new DLLs are completely compatible with their previous versions. A compatibility error can easily cause a Memory exception. Even changing the order of members in an object can lead to incompatibilities. Changing member names or parameters can lead to even worse problems.

A .NET application also uses early binding except that it bases the native code on the manifest in the .NET DLL that is being called instead of on a type library. But a .NET compiler does one more thing when it creates the application's assembly: it stores in the application's manifest, a digital signature to the .NET DLL assembly that it is using.[8] Any time the application loads, it checks to see that the signature of the DLL matches the one stored when the application was built.

Let's say the author of the .NET DLL builds a newer version of the DLL and, in the process, changes the order of the methods of its objects—perhaps also adding some additional members.

When the application that uses the DLL is loaded, it discovers that the signature of the DLL has been changed. Assuming that the application is configured to allow use of updated components,[9] the CLR will realize that any early bound calls might fail. So, it discards the cached native code version of the application and recompiles it using the JIT compiler and the manifest information from the new DLL.

---

6. I am going to completely duck the specific details of the low-level implementation of early binding—whether the function call is direct, through a vtable (virtual function table), pointer offset, etc. It's enough to know that early binding is fast, and involves hard coding of pointer or offset values.

7. The correct term under COM would actually be Interface type, to be completely accurate.

8. This is a simplification. In fact, the information stored depends on your build settings. You'll learn more about this in Chapter 16.

9. You can configure an assembly to require a specific version of a DLL.

What if the creator of the updated DLL made an error and changed a parameter of a method call?

In that case, the JIT compiler would catch the error during compilation and the application would fail to load.

Now, do you see why .NET assemblies keep both the manifest information and intermediate language around even after they've been compiled to native code?

Because early binding can be used safely in .NET applications, many of the reasons for using late binding in COM applications are avoided.

Late Binding

Late binding occurs when an application calls a method by figuring out the location of the member at runtime. In other words, the program has the name of the member and derives the location using the type information of the object being called. With late binding, the member may not actually exist so it is important to trap for errors to handle that situation.

Late binding under COM is implemented using an interface called IDispatch that is implemented by every VB6 class. This interface has a method called Invoke that takes the name of a method or property and calls it with parameters you specify.[10] Visual Basic 6 uses late binding when you call a method using the generic Object type.

Visual Basic.NET can use late binding in this manner as well, though it does not use COM or IDispatch to do so. You'll learn how .NET implements late binding later in this chapter. For now, let's take a quick look at one way to use late binding in .NET—the wrong way—as shown in Listing 11-2.

Listing 11-2. The wrong way to do late binding in VB.NET.

```
' Late binding example #1
' Copyright ©2001 by Desaware Inc. All Rights Reserved

Option Strict Off

Interface ITestInterface1
    Sub Test()

End Interface

Interface ITestInterface2
    Sub Test()
End Interface
```

---

10. Those of you who are COM experts will recognize this as a slight simplification but there really is no need to go into GetIdsOfNames and dispatch IDs here.

```
Class A
    Implements ITestInterface1
    Implements ITestInterface2
    Sub Test1() Implements ITestInterface1.Test
        Console.WriteLine("Test1 called")
    End Sub
    Sub Test2() Implements ITestInterface2.Test
        Console.WriteLine("Test2 called")
    End Sub
End Class

Module Module1

    Sub Main()
        Dim obj As Object
        Dim Aclass As New A()
        Dim it1 As ITestInterface1
        Dim it2 As ITestInterface2

        Aclass.Test1()
        Aclass.Test2()
        obj = Aclass
        obj.Test1()
        obj.Test2()
        Try
            obj.Test3()
        Catch e As Exception
            console.WriteLine("Late binding error: " & e.Message)
        End Try

        it1 = Aclass
        it1.Test()
        obj = it1
        Try
            obj.Test()
        Catch e As Exception
            Console.WriteLine("Can't late bind to implemented interface")
        End Try
        Console.ReadLine()
    End Sub

End Module
```

Here are the results:

```
Test1 called
Test2 called
Test1 called
Test2 called
Late binding error: Method "LateBinding1.A.Test3" not found.
Test1 called
Can't late bind to implemented interface
Test1 called
```

The Aclass.Test1 and Aclass.Test2 calls are early bound, calling the Test1 and Test2 methods implemented directly by the class.

The obj.Test1 and obj.Test2 methods are late bound. Because they are called on the Object type (which does not itself have a Test or Test2 method), the CLR must find the method at runtime and call it. As you can see, an attempt to call Test3 fails with a "Member not found" exception.

As with VB6, you can also reference an object through one of its implemented interfaces. However, you cannot use late binding on an implemented interface. In VB6, when you assign an interface to the Object type, you have access to whichever interface was last assigned to the object variable and you can access the methods of that interface through the object variable. This does not work with VB.NET.

Why is this the wrong way to do late binding?

Because of the very first line of the program:

```
Option Strict Off
```

As I've mentioned earlier, you should always use strict type checking with your VB.NET applications. This very example proves the point—the invalid call to obj.Test3() would not be found until runtime. It is always better to catch problems such as this at compile-time. That's why Visual Basic.NET does not allow late binding of this type with Option Strict on.

Late Binding—The Right Way

Now that you've turned Option Strict back on, allow me to show you how you can still use late binding with VB.NET.

As mentioned previously, COM uses the IDispatch interface to perform late binding. This requires objects that support late binding to implement IDispatch. The implementation must know about all of the members that the object wishes to expose using late binding and must implement calls to those methods and properties when the IDispatch.Invoke method is called. This can be quite complex, though the process of generating this code is automated when creating COM components using ATL or MFC. VB6, of course, does this for you automatically.

With .NET applications, all of the information needed to access any object method can be found in the manifest. Thus, it is should be no surprise that late binding is tied in with reflection.[11]

The IndirectCall sample application allows you to specify a function to call and parameter. The application form is shown in Figure 11-4.

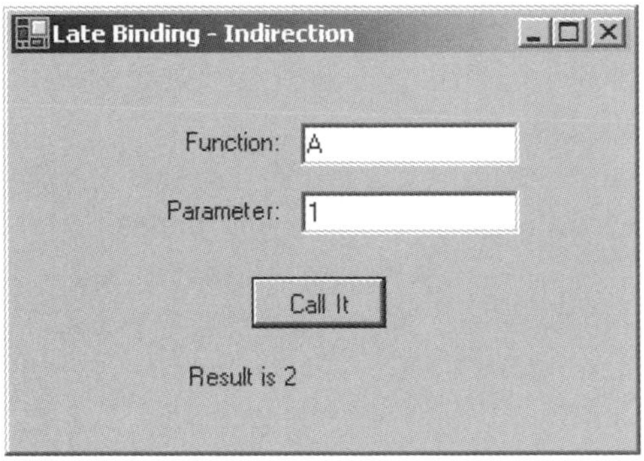

Figure 11-4. The IndirectCall sample application form.

The text boxes are named txtFunction and txtParameter. The button is named cmdCallIt and the Label control below the button that holds the result is named lblResult. The myTestClass class shown here is used to demonstrate late binding to a function (or indirect calls to a function—both terms have the same meaning in this context):

```
Class myTestClass
    Public Function A(ByVal InputValue As Integer) As Integer
        Return InputValue * 2
    End Function
    Public Function B(ByVal InputValue As Integer) As Integer
        Return InputValue * 3
    End Function
    Public Function C(ByVal InputValue As Integer) As Integer
        Return InputValue * 4
    End Function
End Class
```

---

11. In Chapter 10, you learned how late binding can also be accomplished using delegates. Remember, delegates also have the necessary information to perform late binding since they are bound to a specific object and/or method and signature.

The cmdCallIt_Click event shown in Listing 11-3 demonstrates how to use reflection to perform the indirect call.

Listing 11-3. Using InvokeMethod to perform late binding.

```
Private Sub cmdCallIt_Click(ByVal sender As System.Object, _
ByVal e As System.EventArgs) Handles cmdCallIt.Click
    Dim obj As New myTestClass()
    Dim T As Type
    Dim Params(0) As Object
    Dim result As Integer
    ' Note we box the integer here
    Try
        Params(0) = CInt(txtParameter().Text)
    Catch ex As Exception
        MsgBox("Must enter a number")
        Exit Sub
    End Try
    T = obj.GetType()
    Try
        result = CInt(T.InvokeMember(txtFunction().Text, _
        Reflection.BindingFlags.Default Or _
        Reflection.BindingFlags.InvokeMethod, Nothing, obj, Params))
        lblResult().Text = "Result is " + result.ToString()
    Catch ex As Exception
        MsgBox(ex.ToString())
    End Try

End Sub
```

The myTestClass object's GetType method is used to obtain the type information for the object (which is pulled from the manifest). The Type object's InvokeMember function performs the function call.

The first parameter to the InvokeMember function is the name of the member. The BindingFlags parameter gives guidance to the CLR on how to bind to the member. In this case, we choose the default binding search and specify that we wish to invoke a method. The next parameter is the object that does the binding—we specify Nothing to use the default binder (a custom binder can be created if, for some reason, you need additional control on which member is chosen when InvokeMember is called). The next parameter is the object whose method needs to be called. Remember, the InvokeMethod method is not invoked on the myTestClass object—it is invoked on a Type object that contains the type information for the myTestClass object. So, you must provide a reference to the actual object whose method you wish to call. Finally, we come to the parameters—an array of objects. The InvokeMethod member has additional overloads that provide support for named parameters or culture information (which lets you handle cases where the method needs to be called as if it were in a different culture).[12]

Dynamic Loading

Our final example in this chapter takes late binding to its logical extreme—demonstrating the ability to dynamically choose not only the method to call but the object and assembly as well.

The DynamicLoading solution contains two subprojects. The first, the LaterBinding assembly, contains the following class:

```
' Demo of very late binding
' Copyright ©2001 by Desaware Inc. All Rights Reserved
Public Class LoadItDynamically
    Public Sub Test()
        MsgBox("The LoadItDyamically Test method was invoked", _
        MsgBoxStyle.Information, "Important message")
    End Sub
End Class
```

The LaterBinding assembly has its root namespace set to MovingToVB.LaterBinding. It is then compiled into its own DLL. Our goal is to load the DLL at runtime, create an instance of the LoadItDynamically class, then call its Test method. This is accomplished in the second subproject, LaterBindingCaller, using the code in Listing 11-4.

Listing 11-4. The LaterBindingCaller project.

```
' Later Binding example
' Copyright ©2001 by Desaware Inc. All Rights Reserved.
Imports System.Reflection
Module Module1

    Sub Main()
        Dim A As Reflection.Assembly
        Dim LaterBindingDLL As String
        Dim obj As Object
        Dim Params() As Object
```

---

12. Culture is the .NET term for locale—in other words, what country and language do you wish to use for culture-specific operations?

```
' Navigate to the other DLL
LaterBindingDLL = CurDir() & _
"\..\..\laterbinding\bin\laterbinding.dll"
A = A.LoadFrom(LaterBindingDLL)

obj = A.CreateInstance("MovingToVB.LaterBinding.LoadItDynamically")
obj.GetType().InvokeMember("Test", BindingFlags.Default Or _
BindingFlags.InvokeMethod, Nothing, obj, Params)
End Sub

End Module
```

As you can see, the code is quite simple. The assembly is loaded using the Assembly.LoadFrom method, which accepts a DLL name as a parameter and loads the assembly. The assembly's CreateInstance method creates an object given a fully qualified object name.

Once the object is created, the InvokeMember is called as in the IndirectCall sample project.

Recap

In this chapter, we began by reviewing the differences between compilers and interpreters as a lead-in to understanding the difference between compile-time and runtime. You learned how attributes are primarily compile-time entities, potentially much more powerful than traditional conditional compilation. But you also learned that even though attributes exist primarily to control compilation, they can also be used to influence runtime behavior.

Next, you learned how reflection can be used to read the manifest of an assembly and how the information you read can include not only object and member names but their attributes as well. You saw how to create custom attributes and how they can be used to document assemblies or can be accessed at runtime to modify the behavior of an assembly.

Finally, we looked at binding. You saw how early binding is efficient under both COM and .NET architectures but how under COM, early binding is the root of incompatibility problems. You then learned how .NET solves the problem by keeping both the manifest and IL code around so it can recompile assemblies as needed.[13]

To finish, you saw the wrong and right way to do late binding under .NET, even to the extreme of loading an assembly and object at runtime in order to call a late bound method.

---

13. True, this has been described earlier but I think you'll now better understand why things in .NET work the way they do.

Interlude

BEFORE I CONTINUE, I think we need to have a heart to heart talk.

I need you to know what to expect from the remaining chapters and what not to expect.

You see, so far, my job has been fairly easy.

In Part One, I could do a comprehensive job of discussing the key strategy issues that face you in moving to VB.NET.

In Part Two, I could go into great depth in teaching the core concepts you need to know to design good VB.NET applications.

And in the last four chapters, I was able to do what I hope was a good and thorough job of covering the changes to the VB.NET language syntax itself.

But the rest of these chapters are different. They all deal with changes to the language that relate to the .NET Framework classes or runtime. Some of them deal with features from VB6 that have been replaced by entire .NET namespaces. Some of them deal with fundemental architectural changes such as the new forms engine or new Web application and Web service technologies. Some of them deal with .NET Framework concepts that are completely new to VB.NET programmers. In all of these cases, the functionality you'll be dealing with is represented at a minimum by dozens of objects, each of which has many methods and properties. In some cases, the functionality is represented by multiple namespaces, each with dozens of objects and their associated members.

If you expect a comprehensive treatment of each of these areas you will be disappointed. The truth is that many of them are deserving of entire books by themselves![1]

What's an author to do?

The only thing I can do—adhere to what I set out to do at the beginning. This book is not intended to replace or rehash Microsoft's documentation. It is intended to act as a bridge to VB.NET—to teach the core concepts and lend commentary.

And strategy.

And the most important strategy you *must* apply to the chapters that follow is this:

> You *must* learn to read the online documentation. You must feel
> comfortable exploring namespaces, objects, and their methods.
> And you must be willing to experiment with objects and their
> methods and properties.

---

1. This is a comment you will hear often in the chapters that follow. Oh, and by the way, if *you'd* like to write one, please let me know.

Many VB6 programmers fell into a terrible habit of not doing so. They had good reason: the Microsoft documentation was very unfriendly to Visual Basic programmers. C++ declarations are, in some cases, so difficult to port to VB6 that I ended up writing a book whose sole purpose was to teach VB programmers to read MSDN and create declarations for VB6 programs.[2] Many of the functions defined in MSDN's documentation were not compatible with Visual Basic and it was often difficult to decide which ones were and which were not compatible.

All of this has changed.

VB.NET is a fully CLS-compliant language. The .NET Framework classes are fully compatible with VB.NET. All of Microsoft's documentation includes the VB.NET syntax for the method and property calls. Many of the examples are in VB.NET. Even in cases where a VB.NET example is not present, the C# example will translate directly almost line-by-line to VB.NET—and the actual code for accessing a method or property in C# or VB.NET is virtually identical.

For my part, I will attempt to give you a jump start into the concepts you need to know and will point out key classes that you will be dealing with. But I can't possibly cover everything you'll need to know, nor document all of the little details you'll need in order to convert ways of doing things in VB6 to VB.NET. Each control and object will have its own issues to deal with. You must be willing to read the MSDN documentation and do it on your own. As time goes on, there will be other books from Apress and other publishers that will help you with specific areas. I'll probably do additional articles, chapters, Ebooks, and books on various .NET-related subjects as well.

For now, think of what follows as an introduction to the .NET part of VB.NET (as compared to the core language part that has been the focus up until now). My goal will be primarily to help you become familiar with what is available and to lay the proper groundwork for you to build on as you continue to learn VB.NET. In each chapter, I will cover the key strategies and concepts associated with that part of .NET and even include some code examples. Just remember that there's a whole lot more code out there where this came from and be ready to keep exploring on your own.

---

2. *Dan Appleman's Win32 API Puzzle Book and Tutorial for Visual Basic Programmers* (Apress, 1999) for those of you still doing VB6.

Part IV

The Wonderful World
of .NET

"The journey of a thousand miles begins with one step."

—Lao Tsu

.NET Namespaces–
The Grand Tour

GOOD MORNING, LADIES AND GENTLEMEN, and welcome to your grand tour of the Microsoft .NET namespaces. Your tour guide today will be Mr. Daniel Appleman, a veteran tour guide who will not only point out the sights on this journey, but will regale you with tales of the old days going back as far as Visual Basic 1. So, lean your chairs back, buckle in, and keep your eyes on the scenery.

The Most Important Things to Keep in Mind When Dealing with the .NET Namespaces

There are two things that you need to learn and remember from this chapter even if you learn nothing else from what follows.

It's All about the Frameworks

In VB6, Visual Basic does a lot of magic for you. ActiveX EXEs work differently from ActiveX DLLs, standard applications, IIS Applications, UserControls, and so on. The differences between these applications are, to a large degree, determined by the way VB itself works.

But in Visual Basic.NET, the compiler dictates the syntax of the language you are using—*nothing else.*

Let me stress this again.

Visual Basic.NET performs *no* magic. The only thing special about the VB.NET compiler is that it knows how to process a group of text files that contain VB.NET keywords organized according to certain language rules.

Microsoft's new C# language performs no magic. The only way it differs from VB.NET is in its ability to process text files that contain C# language syntax.

All of the magic—all of the cool features—from forms to Web applications, services to class libraries, .NET controls to components, and Web services—all of them are consequences of the .NET class library and the Common Language Runtime. Even the design time behavior of components, controls, and windows derive from behavior specified by classes you create, which derive from classes in the .NET Framework and from attributes you define that also derive from classes in the .NET Framework.

To be very specific, the language doesn't matter.

A VB.NET form and a C# form might as well be the same code. The only way they differ is in the syntax of the language used to derive classes from .NET Framework classes and call methods on those classes.

When you compare this book to the inevitable flood of VB.NET books, I'm sure you'll find that most of them start out by showing how to create Windows form-based applications, Web form-based applications, or Web services. In doing so, they might get you started faster in some ways but they also miss the point. In .NET, you don't start with forms and build from there. Forms are nothing but a result of deriving classes from .NET base classes. So, logically, you first need to learn about inheritance and object-oriented programming, then learn the .NET Framework. Once you've learned those, learning to use forms, Web applications, or any other type of application is accomplished by learning about the methods of the base class upon which your classes are derived as well as the rules for extending those classes through inheritance. That's why most of the code you've seen so far has been in the form of console applications. Console applications allow us to focus on the principals of the code being covered without the distraction of the more complex .NET namespaces.

Remember, now that you know how VB.NET differs as a language from VB6, almost everything else you need to know relates to the .NET Framework classes or the operation of the Common Language Runtime.[1]

Which brings us to the second most important thing to know and remember.

.NET Is Designed for Visual Basic.NET Programmers

Think for a moment about the world of Windows development excluding Microsoft.NET.

How do you think C++ programmers learn to do Windows programming?

Most start out (when possible) with a beginner's book—one that hopefully does a better job explaining the concepts than Microsoft's documentation (which really isn't designed for beginners—it is much more of a reference than a teaching tool).

Intermediate and advanced programmers as well as those who need to use newer technology not yet covered in books, rely on two sources:

1. They read Microsoft's documentation.

2. They read advanced, topic-specific books when available.

---

1. Among the notable exceptions is the VB.NET Declare keyword used to access API functions. I've left coverage of this until later in the book because the importance of API access is drastically reduced as compared to VB6.

They can read Microsoft's documentation because it is, without fail, designed for C++ programmers. API declarations include C++ headers. Many API parameters are difficult to use and manipulate from VB6. Many COM interfaces use data types that are not supported by VB6.[2] All of the architectural assumptions relating to the code are based on software development using C++—assumptions that are often completely incompatible with VB6.

As a result, most Visual Basic programmers are not accustomed to relying on Microsoft's documentation for the information they need. They look to books to provide VB "translations" of the Microsoft documentation.

Let me be honest, I've been a beneficiary of this—my book *Visual Basic Programmer's Guide to the Win32* API (Sams, 1999) succeeded because it filled a real need for VB6 programmers who could not effectively work with the Win32 API without a great deal of advanced knowledge.

But imagine if the Win32 API had been designed for VB programmers—if every function had a VB declaration and the sample programs included versions in VB6 as well as C++.

Would my book have succeeded?

Certainly not as it did.

Oh sure, I probably would have sold some copies—there are some people who just don't like the Microsoft documentation, or want a printed version (and don't want to take the trouble of printing out their own copy from the electronic docs). And I would hope that such a book would have included insights or examples that provided value beyond the documentation.

But it's clear that if Microsoft had designed the Win32 API for VB programmers, the vast majority of VB programmers would have relied on the Microsoft documentation and not bought my book.[3]

Which brings me to my point.

The .NET Framework documentation is written for Visual Basic.NET programmers. Every single class and method is usable from VB.NET.[4] The documentation includes the VB.NET calling syntax along with that of C# and C++.

So, please, resolve now to start a new habit:

READ THE .NET FRAMEWORK DOCUMENTATION FIRST!!

If you are one of those VB6 programmers who, when faced with a problem, start looking for books, articles, tips, or techniques to help you and are afraid to tackle the Microsoft documentation, it is time to grow up. The Microsoft .NET documentation should now be your *first* resource; their examples, the first place you look.

---

2. Although, with the aid of third-party add-ons like Desaware's SpyWorks, VB6 programmers can call or implement these otherwise incompatible interfaces.

3. And my own career would have undoubtedly gone in a completely different and unknowable direction.

4. Except for those few that are not compatible with the Common Language Specification—and you don't want to use those anyway.

Don't get me wrong—there will be a flood of books on the .NET Framework. And many of them will be very useful, teaching advanced techniques, offering better explanations, providing material more targeted to beginners or experts or focusing on examples unique to certain types of applications. Others will serve specific purposes, such as helping VB6 programmers migrate to the new technology.[5]

But you no longer need books or articles to show you how to perform common operations or simple tasks. You no longer need a translation layer from VB to the world of "serious" Window development.

Let the Tour Begin

If you've done any traveling, you've faced the task of familiarizing yourself with a new city. There are two common ways to do this. One is to buy a guidebook. The other is to take one of those day or half-day tours that cover the high points and a bit of the history of the place.

The rest of this chapter will be a cross between these two approaches.

Neither a guidebook nor a tour guide would ever try to tell you every detail about every sight along the way. Neither will I.

During one of my false starts working on this chapter, I thought I might list the objects of the framework and maybe a line or two about each one, listing key methods along the way. It seemed to go rather slowly so I took a break and did a count and discovered over 6700 objects defined in the global assembly cache (classes and enumerations)[6]—my list of objects alone would have taken over one hundred pages even if I had used only a single line for each object.

And that would serve to do little more than rehash material you already have in your hands—something I am loath to do.

That is why this chapter is not a "reference" to the .NET namespaces. My goal is to survey the namespaces and point out how they relate to each other and some of the cool things you can do with them. Hopefully, by the time you've read it, you will have a good understanding of how at least some of the various pieces of the .NET Framework fit together.

I'll also try to cover the key concepts behind many of the namespaces to help you lay a solid foundation on which you can build.

The idea here is based on the principal that 90% of solving any problem lies in knowing that a solution is possible. My job here is to show you some of what is possible so you will know where to look to solve your own problems.

---

5. An example of which you have in your hands right now.

6. There are over 2700 loaded by default in the base framework classes when you create a new Windows application. These numbers are based on object counts from the Deriviations2 sample application you'll read about later in this chapter.

Reading the Map

One of the most useful parts of any guidebook is a map. Now, I could draw one of those cute block diagrams of the major components of the .NET Framework, but I found in my own explorations that I needed more powerful tools. So, I'd like to bring to your attention the three most important tools for navigating through the namespaces.

The MSDN Reference

The .NET Framework SDK documentation will be your primary resource for information. The ".NET Framework Class Library" section within the MSDN documentation will be your primary reference. It is organized by namespace. Within each namespace, objects are sorted alphabetically.

This reference is best suited for finding details of specific objects and methods. It is also useful for browsing, though browsing through the entire reference is not a quick and easy task.

The "Programming with the .NET Framework" section is useful for learning about specific topic areas. Do not limit yourself to only the VB.NET documentation in the Visual Studio portion of the online documentation. Remember, the .NET Framework documentation is designed for VB.NET programmers.

Finally, don't neglect the sample code section. Most of the samples are in VB.NET. Those that aren't are easy for VB.NET programmers to understand because the framework calls are nearly identical in both languages.

The WinCV Tool

WinCV is a tool that comes with the .NET Framework SDK that allows you to view classes. It uses reflection to extract the members of a class that you specify.

Use the WinCV tool if there are any inconsistencies between the documentation and the actual function to identify the members that actually exist for an object.[7]

The Derivation2 Project

As I was making my own way through the namespaces, I realized that the biggest limitation to the existing documentation was the way it was organized. Organizing methods by namespace is good for grouping classes by high levels of functionality

---

7. Microsoft's documentation is more likely to suffer from lack of depth or clarity than inaccuracy—but it has been known to happen, especially with new products or during major product revisions.

but does not help with lower-level grouping. For example, how do you obtain a list of all possible exceptions that can be raised by the runtime or of all of the attributes you can use with component development?

Fortunately, the very architecture of the .NET Framework provides a mechanism to easily answer these kinds of questions. Because .NET is based on inheritance, objects are naturally grouped according to the classes from which they derive.

For example, to answer the query, "show me all of the exceptions that can be raised by the system," I just need to ask, "show me all objects that inherit from the class System.Exceptions.SystemException." These are listed in Table 12-1.

Table 12-1. System Exceptions (Partial List—Core DLLs Only)

System.AppDomainUnloadedException

System.ApplicationException

System.ArgumentException

System.ArgumentNullException

System.ArgumentOutOfRangeException

System.ArithmeticException

System.ArrayTypeMismatchException

System.BadImageFormatException

System.CannotUnloadAppDomainException

System.Configuration.ConfigurationException

System.Configuration.Install.InstallException

System.ContextMarshalException

System.Data.ConstraintException

System.Data.DataException

System.Data.DBConcurrencyException

System.Data.DeletedRowInaccessibleException

System.Data.DuplicateNameException

System.Data.EvaluateException

System.Data.InRowChangingEventException

System.Data.InvalidConstraintException

System.Data.InvalidExpressionException

System.Data.MissingPrimaryKeyException

System.Data.NoNullAllowedException

System.Data.OleDb.OleDbException

Table 12-1. System Exceptions (Partial List—Core DLLs Only) (Continued)

System.Data.ReadOnlyException

System.Data.RowNotInTableException

System.Data.SqlClient._ValueException

System.Data.SqlClient.SqlException

System.Data.SqlTypes.SqlException

System.Data.SqlTypes.SqlNullValueException

System.Data.SqlTypes.SqlTruncateException

System.Data.StrongTypingException

System.Data.SyntaxErrorException

System.Data.TypedDataSetGeneratorException

System.Data.VersionNotFoundException

System.DivideByZeroException

System.DllNotFoundException

System.Drawing.Printing.InvalidPrinterException

System.DuplicateWaitObjectException

System.EntryPointNotFoundException

System.Exception

System.ExecutionEngineException

System.FieldAccessException

System.FormatException

System.IndexOutOfRangeException

System.InvalidCastException

System.InvalidOperationException

System.InvalidProgramException

System.IO.DirectoryNotFoundException

System.IO.EndOfStreamException

System.IO.FileLoadException

System.IO.FileNotFoundException

System.IO.InternalBufferOverflowException

System.IO.IOException

System.IO.IsolatedStorage.IsolatedStorageException

System.IO.PathTooLongException

System.MemberAccessException

Table 12-1. System Exceptions (Partial List—Core DLLs Only) (Continued)

System.MethodAccessException

System.MissingFieldException

System.MissingMemberException

System.MissingMethodException

System.MulticastNotSupportedException

System.Net.CookieException

System.Net.ProtocolViolationException

System.Net.Sockets.SocketException

System.Net.WebException

System.NotFiniteNumberException

System.NotImplementedException

System.NotSupportedException

System.NullReferenceException

System.ObjectDisposedException

System.OutOfMemoryException

System.OverflowException

System.PlatformNotSupportedException

System.RankException

System.Reflection.AmbiguousMatchException

System.Reflection.CustomAttributeFormatException

System.Reflection.InvalidFilterCriteriaException

System.Reflection.ReflectionTypeLoadException

System.Reflection.TargetException

System.Reflection.TargetInvocationException

System.Reflection.TargetParameterCountException

System.Resources.MissingManifestResourceException

System.Runtime.InteropServices.COMException

System.Runtime.InteropServices.ExternalException

System.Runtime.InteropServices.InvalidComObjectException

System.Runtime.InteropServices.InvalidOleVariantTypeException

System.Runtime.InteropServices.MarshalDirectiveException

System.Runtime.InteropServices.SafeArrayRankMismatchException

System.Runtime.InteropServices.SafeArrayTypeMismatchException

Table 12-1. System Exceptions (Partial List—Core DLLs Only) (Continued)

System.Runtime.InteropServices.SEHException

System.Runtime.Remoting.MetadataServices.SUDSGeneratorException

System.Runtime.Remoting.MetadataServices.SUDSParserException

System.Runtime.Remoting.RemotingException

System.Runtime.Remoting.RemotingTimeoutException

System.Runtime.Remoting.ServerException

System.Runtime.Serialization.SerializationException

System.Security.Policy.PolicyException

System.Security.SecurityException

System.Security.VerificationException

System.Security.XmlSyntaxException

System.ServiceProcess.TimeoutException

System.StackOverflowException

System.SystemException

System.Threading.SynchronizationLockException

System.Threading.ThreadAbortException

System.Threading.ThreadInterruptedException

System.Threading.ThreadStateException

System.Threading.ThreadStopException

System.TypeInitializationException

System.TypeLoadException

System.TypeUnloadedException

System.UnauthorizedAccessException

System.UriFormatException

Table 12-1 illustrates yet another aspect of the way the framework is organized by namespace. It is easy to pick out of the list those exceptions that relate to threading—they are all grouped together towards the end of the list with the prefix System.Threading.

In addition to finding all of the objects that inherit from a particular object, the Derivation2 project also displays the inheritance tree for any object and can be used to find all objects that implement a particular interface.

The Derivation2 project takes a rather brute force approach using reflection to load type information for every object referenced by the application domain (the project references all of the major .NET namespaces). It then uses a linear search through all of the derivation trees and interface lists for all of the objects to obtain the list of objects that implement or inherit from the specified object.[8]

The complete project (as always) is in the source code for the book. The source listings are not included in the book because this project is just a different application of techniques you read about in Chapter 11.

As we proceed through the rest of this chapter, I'll point out other places where you can use the Derivation2 tool to provide a map of objects on which you can do further research.

If It's Tuesday, It Must Be System

The System namespace contains certain core classes that are used all the time.

Truly Base Classes

There are three classes on which every other class in the namespace is built.

System.Object

This is the base type on which every object is based (Value or Reference type). The ToString method is among the most important. Even if you don't need it in your program, it's a good idea to override this method in classes you define so that you can obtain some sort of humanly readable rendition of a class for debugging purposes.

System.Type

This class is used extensively for reflection. It represents the type of any object.

- Look for the GetType method on both this class and others to retrieve type information for an object or to retrieve type information from an assembly manifest.

- A large number of properties with the prefix Is... can be used to determine if an object is a particular type, such as a Class or Enumeration, or has a particular attribute, such as Private or Public.

---

8. The brute force approach shown here is not terribly efficient but was easy to code. I was initially concerned about performance issues and was quite sure I'd have to redesign the application to be more efficient. I was pleasantly surprised to find that despite the large number of objects (I estimate over twenty-five thousand), the performance was quite acceptable. Clearly, Microsoft's emphasis on rapid creation and handling of objects has paid off.

- Use the Assembly property to determine the assembly for any object.

- Use the BaseType property to find the base type of a class (see the Derivations2 sample project for this chapter).

- A wide variety of methods can be used to determine the members of the associated object. You can obtain lists of methods, properties, fields, etc.

- Use the InvokeMember method to perform a late bound call on an object.

System.ValueType

This is the base type for all Value type objects. It overrides the Equals method to perform a member-by-member comparison of members of the Value type (structure). This makes sense because while Reference type Object variables are considered equal when they reference the same object, Value type objects are considered equal when they contain the same data.

Core Language Support Classes

These are classes that you may not use directly but which form the foundation on which .NET languages are based. For example, System.Int32 represents the integer primitive for VB.NET and C#. You should be familiar with them for two reasons: first, because knowing your language data types are .NET Framework classes reminds you that they are also objects and can use the System.Object or System.ValueType object methods, and second, because some of these classes contain additional methods you can use that are not built into the language.

System.Array

You'll rarely use this class directly but keep in mind that all VB.NET arrays derive from this base class. One interesting method of this class is the Sort method, which can be used to sort arrays as shown in the following example from the Misc1 project:

```
Sub ArrayDemo()
    Dim A() As Integer = {5, 4, 10, 2, 1}
    Array.Sort(A)
    Dim i As Integer
    Console.WriteLine("Array Tests")
    For Each i In A
        Console.WriteLine(i)
    Next
    Console.WriteLine()
End Sub
```

This displays the sorted array.

System.Random

This class provides greater ability to create random numbers than you have with the Rnd function. This includes the ability to load a buffer with random data. Refer to Chapter 9 for more information on this class.

System.String

Visual Basic.NET keeps VB's traditionally strong set of String functions. In most cases, you will continue to use the native VB String functions. However, the String class (on which VB strings are based) provides some interesting methods to be aware of. These include the ability to pad strings, to remove characters from strings, to easily convert strings to characters and character arrays, and to parse strings based on separator characters. Consider this example from the Misc1 sample application:

```
Public Sub StringSprintDemo()
    Dim S As String = "a,b,c,d,e,f"
    ' This slightly bizzare syntax takes the string "," and extracts the _
    first character
    Dim Separators() As Char = {",".Chars(0)}
    Dim SArray() As String
    SArray = S.Split(Separators)
    For Each S In SArray
        Console.WriteLine(S)
    Next
End Sub
```

This results in:

```
a
b
c
d
e
f
```

Remember that String objects are immutable.

System.Text (Namespace)

The System.Text has a number of additional classes that work closely with the String class to provide additional capability.

Of these, perhaps the most useful is the StringBuilder class. This class provides many of the same capabilities as the String class except that it is not immutable. In other words, changes made to a StringBuilder object—by adding or removing characters or otherwise changing the string—actually modify the contents of the StringBuilder object. This makes the StringBuilder object an efficient tool for building strings from small strings (since it does not require creation of multiple objects during the string assembly process).

The System.Text namespace also includes a variety of objects for encoding and decoding strings into Byte arrays. This is where you'll find objects to convert strings to and from ANSI and Unicode.

Date and Time Classes

There are a number of objects that help you deal with dates, times and durations.

System.DateTime

This object holds a date and a time and is the replacement for the VB6 Date variable type. It has a great many methods that provide the ability to:

- Load an object with the current date and time.

- Compare two DateTime objects.

- Display the date and/or time in a variety of formats.

- Convert to and from an OLE style date (double precision floating point value).

- Load a DateTime object from a string representation of a date and/or time.

- Add or subtract a duration to or from a DateTime object.

- Extract specific year, month, day, etc. information from the object.

- Handle leap years and UTC/local time conversions.

System.TimeSpan

Whereas the DateTime object contains a specific date or time, the TimeSpan object contains a time span—a duration or interval. It contains methods to load the object from various types of durations (hours, minutes, seconds, ticks, etc.). You can add, subtract, and compare TimeSpans.

System.TimeZone

This object is used to manipulate time zone information. It provides the ability to determine the local time zone, the offset from UTC, and to determine if daylight savings time is applicable.

General-Purpose System Classes

System.AppDomain

This class manages application domains.

- The GetCurrentThreadId static method can be used to obtain the identifier of the current running thread.

- The BaseDirectory and RelativeSearchPath methods can be used to determine directory and path information for your application domain.

- Includes methods to load, unload, and enumerate assemblies. Also includes the ability to load objects from assemblies.

System.Console

This class makes it easy to create console applications. In fact, as you've seen already, it is much easier to create console applications than full Windows applications in VB.NET—and they are more efficient.

Console applications use three streams—they read from an input stream, they write to an output stream, and they report errors to an error stream. By default, the input stream is the keyboard, the output stream is the console display of a Command Line window, and the error stream also writes to the console display. You use the Read, ReadLine, Write, and WriteLine methods to access these streams.

The Console class makes it possible to redirect any of these streams to a TextReader or TextWriter object. You'll read more about those later in this chapter.

System.Environment

This class allows you to obtain information about the running process. It replaces a number of API calls and methods handled in VB6 by the VB6 App object. Information you can retrieve includes:

- The command line.

- The current directory.

- The machine name.

- The operating system version.

- The amount of memory in use.

- The assembly version.

- The logical drives mapped to the system.

- A current stack trace.

- The current tick count (time elapsed since the system was started).

- And, of course, the current set of environment variables.

Here's a simple example from the Misc1 project:

```
Sub EnvironmentDemo()
    Console.WriteLine(Environment.CurrentDirectory)
    Console.WriteLine(Environment.OSVersion.ToString)
    Console.WriteLine(Environment.SystemDirectory)
    Console.WriteLine()
End Sub
```

…which results in:

```
D:\CPBknet\Src1\CH12\Misc1\bin
Microsoft Windows NT 5.0.2195.0
J:\WINNT\System32
```

System.GC

This class controls the CLR garbage collection operation. Refer to Chapter 6 for examples that use the GC class.

System.MarshalByRefObject

This class is the base class for any object that needs to be marshaled by reference outside of the application domain. As you learned in Chapter 10, application domains represent the line of memory isolation in .NET (as compared to processes that represent the line of memory isolation for other Windows applications). This means that pointers are not considered valid outside of an application domain.

Any time you wish to reference an object from outside an application domain, a proxy object is created. Method and property calls to the proxy object are translated into method and property calls on the real object—a process called marshaling. Marshaling is generally handled by the CLR with no effort on your part.

When an object derives from System.MarshalByRefObject, it indicates to the CLR that it must create a true proxy where every method or property call on the proxy object is marshaled to the actual object. This is different from the less frequently used **System.ComponentModel.MarshalByValueComponent** object in which the contents of an object are serialized, the data passed outside of the application domain, and a copy of the component created using the serialized data. Serialization is discussed later in this chapter.

Exceptions

Refer to the documentation for each class method to find out what exceptions it can raise. Exceptions are divided into categories, each of which is defined by a class derived ultimately from System.Exception. You should derive your own exception types from System.ApplicationException.

Each Exception class translates into a different HRESULT when .NET components are used with COM.

Exceptions generally fall into two categories: those defined by the user and those defined by the system. There is a philosophical decision you need to make: should you define custom exceptions for cases where you throw an exception? Or, should you throw system exceptions when they are appropriate for the error that occurred?

Personally, I believe it is fine to raise errors defined by the system when they accurately describe the error condition. If anything, I prefer to use system exceptions when available because they are most familiar to clients using components that I develop. However, if a system exception does not meet your needs, I encourage you to derive your new exception from System.ApplicationException and not from one of the exceptions derived from System.SystemException. Use the Derivation2 tool shown earlier in the chapter to obtain a list of all system exceptions.

System.Exception

This is the base class for all exceptions. Class methods allow you to determine the source of the exception, a message describing the exception, a help file that has additional information on the exception, and so on. You can also generate a stack trace based on the exception.

System.ApplicationException

This class derives from Exception and offers the same features. It is intended for all exceptions thrown by an application (as compared to those thrown from the CLR). You should derive any custom exceptions from this class, not System.Exception

System.SystemException

This class derives from Exception and offers the same features. It is intended for all exceptions thrown by the system and most exceptions raised by the CLR derive from this class.

Attributes

You learned about attributes in Chapter 11. Attributes can be queried at runtime using reflection and can modify the behavior of the compiler and designers as well. To obtain a list of available attributes, use the Derivation2 tool to find all objects that derive from System.Attribute. There are several types of attributes you will want to look at more closely:

- Attributes that control the application's runtime behavior. These include attributes like System.ThreadStaticAttribute.

- Attributes that impact the assembly. These are found mostly in the System.Reflection namespace and are set in the Assembly.vb file. Of these, the Assembly version is probably the most important.

- Attributes for component development. These are mostly found in System.ComponentModel and have a huge impact on the way the component designer handles components—especially their properties. For example, you can control exactly how a property appears in the property browser even to the point of creating custom property editors to be used from the designer.

- Look for attributes in the System.Diagnostics namespace to control the behavior of the debugger.

The following are some of the more important attributes you will use.

System.Attribute

This is the base class for all attributes.

The shared GetCustomAttributes member can be used to obtain the custom attributes for a type.

System.AttributeUsageAttribute

This attribute is used when defining new attributes (which inherit from System.Attribute). Use it to specify whether derived objects can inherit your new attribute and if it can be applied more than once.

System.ThreadStaticAttribute

Use with shared class members or global variables to specify that a separate instance of the variable be created for each thread. The variables will be placed in thread local storage.

System.Reflection.AssemblyVersionAttribute

Sets the version of the assembly. See Chapter 16 for more information on versioning.

Interfaces

The System namespace also defines a number of frequently used interfaces.

IAsyncResult

Classes that perform asynchronous operations implement this interface. Code using those classes can use this interface to determine the status of an asynchronous operation or to obtain a handle that can be used on a wait operation to wait for the asynchronous operation to complete. Look for this interface on file I/O classes and network socket classes (use the Derivation2 tool to obtain a list of objects that implement this interface).

ICloneable

You've already learned about the difference between the assignment of a Value type object and a Reference type object. When you use the Equal operator on a Value type object, the default implementation performs a shallow (member-by-member) copy of the fields of the object. This means that if a structure contains objects and you assign it to another structure, both structures will reference the same objects.

The Equals method of a Reference type object simply assigns to the new variable a reference to the original object.

The ICloneable interface provides a standard mechanism to create clones of both Reference and Value type objects. When you implement this interface, you define a Clone method that should create a completely independent copy of the original object. Listing 12-1 from the Misc sample project illustrates how this is done.

Listing 12-1. Demonstration of the ICloneable interface.

```
Class WillClone
    Implements ICloneable
    Public X As Integer
    Public Y As String
    Public Function Clone() As Object Implements ICloneable.Clone
        Dim n As New WillClone()
        n.X = X
        ' When you're cloning, you'll usually want to clone internal objects as well
        n.Y = String.Copy(Y)
        Return n
    End Function
End Class


    Public Sub WillCloneDemo()
        Dim obj1 As New WillClone()
        obj1.Y = "Test"
        Dim obj2 As WillClone = obj1
        If obj1 Is obj2 And obj1.Y Is obj2.Y Then
            Console.WriteLine("Objects are the same")
        End If
        obj2 = CType(obj1.Clone(), WillClone)
        If (Not obj1 Is obj2) And (Not obj1.Y Is obj2.Y) And (obj1.Y = obj2.Y) Then
            Console.WriteLine("Objects are not the same but strings are equal")
        End If
    End Sub
```

Both lines will print when the WillCloneDemo method is called.

IComparable

The IComparable interface works for object comparison the same way ICloneable works for object assignment. It is intended to allow you to define a way to compare two objects for the purpose of sorting and determining content-based identity. Over four hundred framework objects implement this interface.

Implement this interface in cases where you wish to be able to compare objects based on their content.

IDisposable

In Chapter 6, you learned that the CLR does not provide deterministic finalization in object Finalize events. The .NET Framework does provide a consistent method for deterministic finalization that relies on the cooperation of containers. If an object implements the IDisposable interface, it is, in effect, notifying users of the component that before they discard the component, they should call the Dispose method on that interface. Failure to do so can prevent the component from cleaning up properly.

You should implement IDisposable on components that you wish to have participate in this convention. You should also have backup cleanup in your Finalize event just in case the component user does not call the Dispose method.

The Visual Studio component designer will automatically write code to call the Dispose method on components inserted using the designer.

Other Cool System Classes

These are classes in the System namespace that you should know about just because they do cool things.

System.BitConverter

Ever wonder how data is actually stored for various data types? The BitConverter class can convert any primitive data type into an array of bytes and vice versa, for example, the following code from the Misc1 sample project:

```
Sub BitConverterDemo()
    Dim d As Double = 1.5E+64
    Dim BitArray() As Byte = BitConverter.GetBytes(d)
    Console.WriteLine(BitConverter.ToString(BitArray))
    Console.WriteLine(BitConverter.ToDouble(BitArray, 0))
End Sub
```

...displays:

```
78-FB-EF-EE-42-3B-42-4D
1.5E64
```

System.Uri, System.UriBuilder

These objects help you work with universal resource locators. They contain methods to build URLs, convert from relative to absolute URLs, split URLs into their component parts, and otherwise manipulate them in various ways. The following example from the Misc1 sample project illustrates a few of the capabilities of the System.Uri class:

```
Public Sub URIDemo()
    Dim u As New Uri("http://www.desaware.com")
    console.WriteLine(u.Host)
    Console.WriteLine(u.Port)
    Console.WriteLine(u.Scheme)
End Sub
```

This code displays the following result:

```
www.desaware.com
80
http
```

Collections

Visual Basic.NET has a Collection type that looks, feels and works more or less like the Collection object you are used to (the big difference being that it references the Object type instead of the nonexistent Variant type).

As nice and familiar as the VB Collection object is, it is no longer the only game in town. Even those of you who were using the VB Dictionary object will now find that it has a lot of company.

Before examining the new types of collections, let's take a closer look at what makes a collection work.

The Microsoft.VisualBasic.Collection class, like most other collection classes, implements three interfaces:

- System.Collections.ICollection—This interface includes a Count method to obtain the number of objects in a collection and additional methods to determine if a collection is thread safe and to allow synchronized access to the collection.

- System.Collections.IEnumerable—This interface exposes an object that implements the IEnumerator interface, allowing object-by-object access to the collection. The For...Each operator works with any object that implements the IEnumerable interface.

- System.Collections.IList—This interface provides list type access into a collection. It includes methods to add, remove, and find objects in a collection. The Item property of this interface is often the default property for a collection object, allowing direct indexed access to the items of the collection.

Dictionaries implement the System.Collections.IDictionary interface. These are collections that include a key value pair and permit rapid lookup based on a key as well as enforcement of unique keys.

System.CollectionBase and Custom Collections

Those of you who have read my book *Developing COM/ActiveX Components with Visual Basic 6* know that I always recommend using strongly typed collections in cases where the collection is public. This avoids the need to add error checking to your code to watch for cases where someone using your component adds an object to your collection that your code does not know how to handle. In that book, I showed how to use aggregation to create industrial-strength collections.

Visual Basic.NET makes it much easier to create strongly typed collections. All you need to do is inherit from the CollectionBase class, which is designed for this purpose. The CollectionDemo project illustrates this with the code in Listing 12-2.

Listing 12-2. Module1.vb from the CollectionDemo project.

```
' For...Each collection demonstration
' Copyright ©2001 by Desaware Inc. All Rights Reserved

Module Module1
    Enum MyFish
        OneFish
        TwoFish
        RedFish
        BlueFish
    End Enum


    Public Class FishCollection
        Inherits CollectionBase
        Public Function Add(ByVal Value As MyFish) As Integer
            MyBase.List.Add(Value)
        End Function
        Public Sub Insert(ByVal index As Integer, ByVal value As MyFish)
            List.Insert(index, value)
        End Sub
```

```vb
Public Function IndexOf(ByVal value As MyFish) As Integer
    Return List.IndexOf(value)
End Function

Public Function Contains(ByVal value As MyFish) As Boolean
    Return List.Contains(value)
End Function

Public Sub Remove(ByVal value As MyFish)
    List.Remove(value)
End Sub

Public Sub CopyTo(ByVal array() As MyFish, ByVal index As Integer)
    List.CopyTo(array, index)
End Sub

Default Property Item(ByVal index As Integer) As MyFish
    Get
        Return CType(MyBase.List.Item(index), MyFish)
    End Get
    Set(ByVal Value As MyFish)
        MyBase.List.Item(index) = Value
    End Set
End Property

Protected Overrides Sub OnInsert(ByVal index As Integer, ByVal value As Object)
    If Not TypeOf (value) Is MyFish Then
        Throw New ArgumentException("Invalid type")
    End If
End Sub

Protected Overrides Sub OnSet(ByVal index As Integer, ByVal oldValue As Object, _
 ByVal newValue As Object)
    If Not TypeOf (newValue) Is MyFish Then
        Throw New ArgumentException("Invalid type")
    End If
End Sub
```

```vb
        Protected Overrides Sub OnValidate(ByVal value As Object)
            If Not TypeOf (value) Is MyFish Then
                Throw New ArgumentException("Invalid type")
            End If
        End Sub

    End Class


    Sub Main()
        Dim col As New Collection()
        Console.WriteLine("VB Collection  Type is: " & col.GetType.FullName)

        Dim F As New FishCollection()

        Dim il As IList
        F.Add(MyFish.OneFish)
        F.Add(MyFish.TwoFish)
        F.Add(MyFish.RedFish)
        F.Add(MyFish.BlueFish)
        il = F
        Try
            il.Add("Something not a fish")
        Catch e As Exception
            Console.WriteLine(e.Message)
        End Try

        Dim afish As MyFish
        For Each afish In F
            Console.WriteLine(afish.ToString)
        Next

        afish = F(1)
        Console.WriteLine(afish.ToString)

        Console.ReadLine()

    End Sub

End Module
```

The program defines an Enum type named MyFish. The FishCollection
collection only handles this type of object. The Add, Insert, IndexOf, Contains,
Removes, and CopyTo methods accept only MyFish type objects. Each method

need only call the corresponding method on the base object (which accepts any type of object). The Item property is a default property (which is permitted since it has a parameter) that also calls the base class Item property.

In addition to implementing the expected collection methods, we also override OnInsert, OnSet, and OnValidate. These are methods provided by the base class to allow a derived class to perform additional tests or validation before an operation is performed. In this case, we use it to verify that the object is, in fact, of the correct type.

Why is this necessary?

What happens if you reference the class using a variable of type IList instead of using the Variable type itself? The IList will reference the base class implementation of this interface, which allows generic objects to be inserted. Fortunately, the class was designed to allow additional type (or other) verification to be performed by the derived class, thus closing this "back door."

Inside Collections

You can add enumeration capability (the ability to use the For…Each syntax to enumerate contents) to any object by implementing the IEnumerable interface. The code to do this is shown in the ForEach sample project in Listing 12-3.

Listing 12-3. Implementing the IEnumerable interface.

```
Public Class PseudoCollection
    Implements IEnumerable
    Private DummyData() As String = {"One Fish", "Two Fish", "Red Fish", _
    "Blue Fish"}

    Function GetEnumerator() As IEnumerator Implements _
    IEnumerable.GetEnumerator
        Dim myEnumerator As New EnumeratorClass()
        ReDim myEnumerator.Snapshot(UBound(DummyData))
        DummyData.CopyTo(myEnumerator.Snapshot, 0)
        Return myEnumerator
    End Function

    Public Class EnumeratorClass
        Implements IEnumerator

        Dim CurrentIndex As Integer = -1
        Public Snapshot() As String
```

```
    ' Set current state before first entry
    Sub Reset() Implements IEnumerator.Reset
        CurrentIndex = -1
    End Sub


    ReadOnly Property Current() As Object Implements IEnumerator.Current
        Get
            Return (Snapshot(CurrentIndex))
        End Get
    End Property


    Function MoveNext() As Boolean Implements IEnumerator.MoveNext
        CurrentIndex += 1
        Return (CurrentIndex <= UBound(Snapshot))
    End Function


End Class
```

The PseudoCollection class contains a String array that can be enumerated. The first step is to implement the IEnumerable interface. This interface exposes a single method, GetEnumerator, which returns a reference to a separate Enumerator object that implements the IEnumerator interface.

When GetEnumerator is called, the current state of the data is stored in the SnapShot array, which is a copy of the data at the time the GetEnumerator function is called. The IEnumerator interface's Reset, Current, and MoveNext methods are used to iterate through the stored data.

You can, of course, create full-featured custom collections on your own by implementing IList, IComparable, and ICollection if you wish. But you'll probably find that the two approaches shown here will suffice for most purposes.

Other Collections

When I started discussing collections, I mentioned that you had many options beyond using the native Visual Basic collection class (Microsoft.VisualBasic.Collection). In fact, the System.Collections namespace and System.Collections.Specialized namespace have numerous collections. For example, the ForEach sample program demonstrates the use of a SortedList collection in Listing 12-4.

Listing 12-4. Using the SortedList collection.

```
Dim I() As Integer = {3, 8, 4, 6, 10, 7, 9}
Dim C As New Collections.SortedList()

Dim x As Integer
For x = 0 To UBound(I)
    C.Add(I(x), I(x))
Next

Dim IntegerIterator As Object

Console.WriteLine("Array iteration")
For Each IntegerIterator In I
    Console.Write(IntegerIterator.ToString & ", ")
Next
Console.WriteLine(ControlChars.CrLf & "Collection iteration")

Dim DictIterator As DictionaryEntry
For Each DictIterator In C
    Console.Write(DictIterator.Value.ToString & ", ")
Next

Console.ReadLine()
```

A self-sorting collection is a nice idea. The rest of this section will list some others.

This is not a complete list. I encourage you to explore the System.Collections and System.Collections.Specialized namespaces on your own. Note that most of these collections are not thread safe.

System.Collections.ArrayList

This is a nice, general-purpose collection object.

System.Collections.BitArray

This collection defines an array of bits, each of which can be set to True or False. This provides the most compact possible storage for large numbers of flag bits.

But perhaps the most intriguing use for this object is that it can be initialized from a Byte array. This allows you to take other data types (converted, perhaps, using the System.BitConverter object) and test or set individual bits in the data.

System.Collections.DictionaryBase

Use this to implement your own strongly typed dictionaries.

System.Collections.HashTable

This class implements a hash table. This is a high-performance, dictionary-style collection designed for rapid access to any object.

System.Collections.Queue

Implements a first-in, first-out queue.

System.Collections.SortedList

This is a dictionary in which the items are sorted by key value.

System.Collections.Stack

Implements a last-in, first-out stack

System.Collections.Specialized.BitVector

This object lets you divide a 32-bit number into multiple fields, each of which can be accessed directly. For those of you familiar with C++, it is similar to the BitField construct in C++.

System.Collections.Specialized.String

This is a collection that is type safe for use with strings.

Drawing

I have no doubt someone will write an entire book just on the subject of drawing and graphical output. Fortunately, the important concepts you need to understand can be covered even in the short space available here. However the way to approach those concepts depends on how you are accustomed to using graphic operations in your VB6 applications.

If You Are Accustomed to Using the VB6 Graphic Methods...

Forget everything you know about graphic output, including most of what you know about working with bitmaps. The Visual Basic graphic primitives such as Line, Circle, and PSET are gone, never to return. Even simple assignments such as copying images by using code like this:

```
Picture1.Picture = Picture2.Image⁹
```

...are now gone.

Forget all that nonsense about working with twips (with all the fuzzy round-off errors in control locations and font sizes that resulted). Pretty much everything you do from now on will be in pixels. Properties such as ScaleMode, ScaleWidth, and ScaleHeight are gone. Oh, you can still do complex scaling but you'll be doing it using the features provided by the .NET Framework.

The good news is that you will now have more vastly powerful graphics capabilities available to you.

The bad news is that you're going to have to do some serious studying before you'll know enough to use them.

In the next few pages, I'll try to get you started off on the right foot.

If You Are Accustomed to Using Win32 API Calls for Graphic Operations...

Forget everything you know about graphic output.

No, just kidding.

You're actually in luck. You'll be able to get up to speed very quickly with the new graphic environment. Those of you who have read the chapters on graphics in my book, *Visual Basic Programmer's Guide to the Win32 API*, will be able to read through the following pages quickly, focusing on changes from the Win32 API.

---

9. The PictureBox Image property is similar to the Picture property in VB6 but will only retrieve a reference to a previously assigned image, not the current contents of the window.

Goodbye GDI, Hello GDI+

GDI refers to the Graphical Device Interface. In ancient days,[10] a program that wanted to display or print information needed intimate knowledge of the output device. It needed to know the size of the output device and the specialized instructions for that device. This meant that every program would need to implement separate drawing code for each device, window, or screen resolution.

The Windows GDI library provides a device-independent approach to graphical output. Applications call a consistent set of graphic methods and GDI, in conjunction with the Windows device drivers, outputs the image onto the device. Devices can include windows, printers, and metafiles (which consist of a recorded set of graphic commands that can be played back). Applications can draw to specific output resolutions and sizes or can define logical windows with a standard or user-defined coordinate system and rely on GDI to map the images to the specified device area.

The essential concept you must understand with regards to GDI is that of a device context (hDC). A device context represents the object that maps graphics commands to devices. You can obtain a device context for any output device. All GDI graphic commands draw to device contexts. This is illustrated in Figure 12-1.

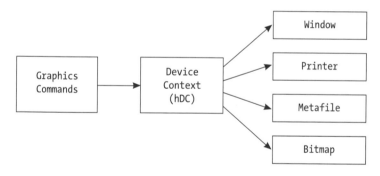

Figure 12-1. Operation of GDI.

The behavior of graphics commands under traditional Win32 API calls depends on objects such as pens, brushes, fonts, and bitmaps that are "selected" into the device context. This means that under Win32, device contexts are stateful—their state is dependent on the currently selected set of objects. You must be careful to set the state of the device context before drawing and, more important, to restore the state of a device context that is being used elsewhere in the program so that you don't interfere with its behavior. This is especially important when calling GDI API functions with Visual Basic 6. If your API code modifies the device context in a

---

10. DOS era, circa late '70s through early '90s.

way that VB6 does not expect, your regular VB6 graphic commands will no longer work correctly.

The .NET Framework introduces the successor to GDI called GDI+.

The biggest difference between GDI and GDI+ is that graphic output is now stateless. The System.Drawing.Graphics object is the GDI+ equivalent to a device context, as shown in Figure 12-2. Every graphic command specifies the pen, brush, or font to use—you no longer need to worry about graphic routines interfering with each other.

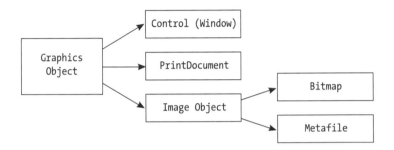

Figure 12-2. Operation of GDI+.

The following code from the GraphicsDemo sample project illustrates use of the Graphics, Brush, Pen, and Font objects:

```
Private Sub cmdDraw_Click(ByVal sender As System.Object, ByVal e As _
System.EventArgs) Handles cmdDraw.Click
    Dim g As Graphics
    ' Can also draw from library of stock brushes
    Dim b As SolidBrush = New SolidBrush(color.Beige)
    g = pictureBox1().CreateGraphics() ' Get the graphics object
    g.FillRectangle(b, pictureBox1().ClientRectangle)
    ' Constructor that allows quick modification of existing font
    Dim f As Font = New Font(Me.Font, FontStyle.Bold)
    g.DrawString("Some Text", f, brushes.Black, 10, 10)
    g.DrawRectangle(pens.Blue, 50, 50, 50, 50)
    g.DrawLine(pens.Red, 50, 50, 150, 150)
    g.Dispose() ' Don't forget to dispose!
    b.Dispose()
    f.Dispose()
End Sub
```

The System.Windows.Forms.Control object defines the CreateGraphics method that retrieves a Graphics object configured to draw onto the control. All Windows-based controls (including forms) are derived from System.Windows.Forms.Control so they all have this method available.

The System.Drawing.Brush object is the base class for different types of brushes from textured to solid. In this example, we use a solid brush created from one of the standard colors defined in the System.Drawing.Colors class. The example creates a new font using a constructor that bases this new font on an existing font but allows changing the font style. There are many font constructors available.

The System.Drawing.Graphics object has many graphics methods. Note how each one requires that you specify the font, pen, or brush needed to perform the graphic operation. The Graphics object itself does not maintain state.

The Brush, Font, Pen, Graphics, and other GDI+ objects are wrappers for underlying GDI objects and there needs to be a way to release those underlying objects. All of these objects implement the IDisposable interface so you should call the Dispose method when you are finished drawing. It's not the end of the world if you forget because the Finalize method of these objects does perform cleanup of the underlying objects. But it's more efficient for you to do so yourself.

GDI+ offers additional advantages over GDI besides being stateless. It implements drawing techniques such as blending and anti-aliasing and it has sophisticated algorithms for stretching bitmaps. Many of these are found in the System.Drawing.Drawing2D. Here's some sample code that fills a form with a gradient image:

```
Private Sub cmdGradient_Click(ByVal sender As System.Object, ByVal e As _
System.EventArgs) Handles cmdGradient.Click
    Dim lb As New Drawing2D.LinearGradientBrush(Me.DisplayRectangle, color.Blue, _
    color.Red, Drawing2D.LinearGradientMode.Horizontal)
    Dim g As Graphics = Me.CreateGraphics()
    g.FillRectangle(lb, Me.DisplayRectangle)
    lb.Dispose()
    g.Dispose()
End Sub
```

Bitmaps

The System.Drawing.Bitmap object makes it easy to load bitmap images in a variety of formats from a variety of sources. You can obtain a Graphics object for a bitmap that makes it easy to draw into the bitmap. The Bitmap object also allows you to set pixel values (replacing the VB6 PSet command) as you can see in Listing 12-5, which contains code from the GraphicsDemo sample application.

Listing 12-5. Bitmap operations.

```
Private Sub cmdBitmap_Click(ByVal sender As System.Object, _
ByVal e As System.EventArgs) Handles cmdBitmap.Click
    Dim g, g2 As Graphics
    g = pictureBox1().CreateGraphics()
    Dim bm As New Bitmap(pictureBox1().ClientRectangle.Width, _
    pictureBox1().ClientRectangle.Height, g)

    g2 = graphics.FromImage(bm)
    dwgraphics.CopyImage(g, g2, pictureBox1().ClientRectangle.Width, _
    pictureBox1().ClientRectangle.Height)

    g2.DrawLine(pens.Green, 60, 50, 160, 150)
    bm.SetPixel(1, 1, color.Red)
    bm.SetPixel(1, 2, color.Blue)
    bm.SetPixel(1, 3, color.Green)

    g = graphics.FromHwnd(pictureBox2().Handle)
    ' Another way to get a graphics object
    Dim g3 As Graphics = graphics.FromHwnd(pictureBox2().Handle)
    g3.DrawImage(bm, 0, 0, pictureBox2().DisplayRectangle.Width, _
    pictureBox2().DisplayRectangle.Height)
    g.Dispose()
    g2.Dispose()
    g3.Dispose()
    bm.Dispose()
End Sub
```

In what I can only imagine to be an amazing oversight, GDI+ does not provide an easy way to copy a bitmap image from an existing window. I created the simple class shown in Listing 12-6, which uses API functions to use an old fashioned BitBlt operation to copy the current contents of a window to a Graphics object representing a bitmap or other window.

Listing 12-6. Using BitBlt to copy an image from a window.

```
Private Module APIDeclarations
 Friend Const SRCCOPY As Integer = &HCC0020&
 Friend Declare Ansi Function BitBlt Lib "gdi32" (ByVal hDestDC As IntPtr, ByVal x As _
 Integer, ByVal y As Integer, ByVal nWidth As Integer, ByVal nHeight As Integer, _
 ByVal hSrcDC As IntPtr, ByVal xSrc As Integer, ByVal ySrc As Integer, ByVal dwRop _
 As Integer) As Integer
End Module

   Public Class dwGraphics
      Shared Sub CopyImage(ByVal Source As System.Drawing.Graphics, ByVal Dest As
_
      System.Drawing.Graphics, ByVal Width As Integer, ByVal Height As Integer)
          Dim dhdc, shdc As IntPtr
          dhdc = Dest.GetHdc
          shdc = Source.GetHdc
          BitBlt(dhdc, 0, 0, Width, Height, shdc, 0, 0, SRCCOPY)
          Dest.ReleaseHdc(dhdc)
          Source.ReleaseHdc(shdc)
      End Sub
   End Class
```

I can only assume that they will come up with a better way to do this since
Win32 API functions should be avoided (for reasons that will become apparent in
Chapter 15). Check Desaware's Web site at `http://www.desaware.com` for updates
I'll post more information on this subject as soon as I hear about it.[11]

Strategies for Approaching GDI+

As I mentioned earlier in this section, GDI+ is a subject that deserves a book of its
own. Yet, the basic concepts are simple:

- If you want to draw, obtain a System.Drawing.Graphics object for the surface to which you want to draw.

- Create additional pens, brushes, fonts, etc. that are needed by the drawing
  commands.

- Use the drawing methods of the Graphics object to draw to the surface.

---

11. With my luck it will turn out that there is some subtle way to do this that I missed while
    exploring the namespaces. If so, that will show up on the Web site as well. Meanwhile, you've
    had a nice preview of how API calls can still be used from VB.NET

- Dispose of all of your objects when you are through with them.

My suggestion is that you sit down with the documentation and just read through the class descriptions for the following namespaces:

- System.Drawing—All the base GDI+ classes.

- System.Drawing.Design—Contains dialog box classes you can use to load bitmaps, edit fonts, and perform other typical user-interface tasks relating to drawing and imaging.

- System.Drawing.Drawing2D—Contains classes for more complex drawing operations such as blends and gradients.

- System.Drawing.Imaging—Contains classes that support metafiles and more complex image-related operations such as color space translations.

- System.Drawing.Printing—Contains classes that support printing, a subject I will discuss further in the next section.

Remember to use the Derivation2 tool to gain insight into the organization of objects in these namespaces. For example, a check of the System.Drawing.Brush class determines that the following objects derive from this class:

System.Drawing.Drawing2D.HatchBrush

System.Drawing.Drawing2D.LinearGradientBrush

System.Drawing.Drawing2D.PathGradientBrush

System.Drawing.SolidBrush

System.Drawing.TextureBrush

Printing

The name of the printing namespace, System.Drawing.Printing, gives an early hint of what is to come. You have just read how GDI+ requires VB6 programmers to switch from the old VB style of graphics to a variation of the kind of graphic programming familiar to Win32 API programmers. It probably won't be too much of a surprise to learn that printing requires the same kind of transition.

The transition can be described in five words:

The Printer object is gone.

And no, it hasn't been renamed. The whole concept of an object that you can simply print to is gone.

But don't panic.

The good news is that the .NET approach to printing is incredibly easy to use once you understand a few simple concepts. And it is very, very powerful.

My goal in this section is to guide you through the mental shift needed to understand printing under .NET. Once you have that down, you'll be able to learn the rest from the namespace documentation.

Printing under VB6 uses a simple model shown in Figure 12-3.

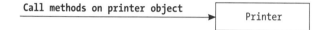

Figure 12-3. Printing under VB6.

You simply send commands to the printer—commands to start printing, commands to draw graphics and text, commands to switch pages, and commands to actually print.

Printing under .NET uses a more complex model shown in Figure 12-4.

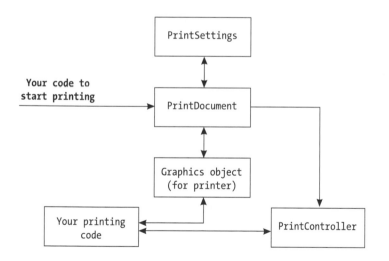

Figure 12-4. Printing on .NET.

Whoa!!! This is simple?

Actually it is. Look closely.

The idea is this: instead of printing each page in a single function, you use one function to tell .NET that you want to start printing. Then, the .NET Framework raises an event whenever it is ready to print a page. You then draw into that page during the event.

To look at it another way: printing three pages in VB6 can be described using the following pseudocode:

```
Sub Print
Print page 1
Print page 2
Print page 3
End Sub
```

Printing three pages in VB.NET can be described using pseudocode as follows:

```
Sub Print
        Print The Document
End Sub

Sub PrintDocument_PrintPage Handles Document's PrintPage event
        Print a page
Return value that tells system whether you want to print another page or not
End Sub
```

Let's look how this translates into real code in the PrintingDemo sample project.

The sample project contains a text box that will hold a line of text to print. In this project, we cheat by using the font specified by the text box to print to the printer. You can, of course, use any Font object (including one you configure using the System.Windows.Form.FontDialog common dialog box). The project also includes a PictureBox that contains an image to print.

You begin the process of printing by creating a new System.Drawing.Printing.PrintDocument object as shown next. This object has two other objects associated with it: a PrinterSettings object and a PrintController object. The PrinterSettings object determines the printer and print settings to use. The Print-Controller object actually handles the printing operation. In most cases, you'll use the standard PrintController object but you can derive a new one if you wish to perform specialized operations such as displaying a status window during printing.

In this example, the PrinterSettings object is set using the common dialog for printer settings that every Windows user is familiar with. This dialog is accessed using the PrintDialog objects. When this code returns from the prDialog.ShowDialog method, the PrinterSettings object for the document has been set to the selected printer.

That's right—in VB.NET it is trivial to print to any accessible printer—you don't have to worry about which is the default printer. Naturally, you can select printers and change their settings for a specific print job without using a dialog box just by using the appropriate objects in the System.Drawing.Printing namespace.

The command to start the print job is the prDoc.Print method. But before calling it, you must specify the event that is to be raised for each page. Fortunately, you've already read Chapter 10 so you know that an event is actually a delegate and it's trivial to use the AddHandler command to connect the event to any method— in this case, the PagePrintFunction method:

```
Private Sub cmdPrint_Click(ByVal sender As System.Object, _
ByVal e As System.EventArgs) Handles cmdPrint.Click
    Dim prDialog As New PrintDialog()
    Dim prDoc As New Drawing.Printing.PrintDocument()
    prDoc.DocumentName = "My new printed document"
    prDialog.Document = prDoc
    prDialog.ShowDialog()

    ' Wire up the event to be called for each page
    AddHandler prDoc.PrintPage, AddressOf Me.PagePrintFunction
    prDoc.Print()
    prDoc.Dispose()
    prDialog.Dispose()
End Sub
```

The PagePrintFunction method (which is the handler for the PrintDocument.PrintPage event) receives two parameters: a reference to the PrintDocument object (the sender) and a reference to a PrintPageEventArgs object, which contains many properties you can read to obtain information about the printed page.

The most important of these properties is the Graphics object. That's right, the same Graphics object you learned about in the previous section. This example prints two lines of text: the bounding rectangle (so you can see the coordinates used by the page) and a line of text from the text box. Note the use of the Font object's GetHeight method to determine the height of a line of text on the current graphics surface. The DrawImage method expands the bitmap image to fill the rest of the page (when you run this demo, expect it to take a long time to print— especially on a Postscript printer). You can set the PrintPageEventArgs.HasMorePages property to tell the printer controller whether there are additional pages or not:[12]

```
Public Sub PagePrintFunction(ByVal sender As Object, ByVal e As _
Printing.PrintPageEventArgs)
    Dim LineHeight, LineNumber As Single
    LineHeight = txtText().Font.GetHeight(e.Graphics)
```

---

12. A feature not shown in this example.

```
        Dim TextRect As New RectangleF(0, LineHeight * LineNumber, _
        e.PageBounds.Width, e.PageBounds.Height - LineHeight * LineNumber)
        Dim SF As New StringFormat(StringFormatFlags.LineLimit)

        e.Graphics.DrawString(e.PageSettings.Margins.ToString, txtText().Font, _
        brushes.Black, TextRect)
        LineNumber += 2
        e.Graphics.DrawString(txtText().Text, txtText().Font, Brushes.Black, 0, _
        LineHeight * LineNumber)
        LineNumber += 1
        e.Graphics.DrawImage(pictureBox1().Image, 0, LineNumber * LineHeight, _
        e.PageBounds.Width, e.PageBounds.Height - LineNumber * LineHeight)
    End Sub
```

Before going on, there are two insights that you should consider:

- Delegates define the PagePrintFunction and other PrintDocument and
  PrintController event handlers. Delegates, as you recall, can attach to a specific
  instance of an object. This means that if you have an application that handles
  multiple documents, you can tie the delegates to a specific instance of your
  document class and use class fields to keep track of information between
  pages (such as the page count).

- Because all drawing is to a Graphics object (regardless of device), you can
  define generic output routines that take Graphics objects as parameters
  and use them for both printing and drawing to windows.

One application of this can be seen in the PrintingDemo example in the
cmdPreview_Click method shown here:

```
Private Sub cmdPreview_Click(ByVal sender As System.Object, ByVal e As _
System.EventArgs) Handles cmdPreview.Click
    Dim previewDialog As New PrintPreviewDialog()
    Dim prDoc As New Drawing.Printing.PrintDocument()
    prDoc.DocumentName = "My new printed document"
    ' Wire up the event to be called for each page
```

```
    AddHandler prDoc.PrintPage, AddressOf Me.PagePrintFunction
    previewDialog.Document = prDoc
    previewDialog.ShowDialog()
    prDoc.Dispose()
    previewDialog.Dispose()
End Sub
```

This example creates a PrintDocument object just as you saw earlier. It skips the PrintDialog dialog box (though you should use it to target the print preview to a specific printer). It creates a PrintPreviewDialog object that provides a standard print-preview dialog box and sets the PrintDocument object as the object to print. The PrintDocument object is connected to the same PagePrintFunction method as before.

When the PrintPreviewDialog box is shown, you'll see a print preview of your document that uses the exact same code as will be used with the actual print job!

Take that, VB6!

It just doesn't get any easier than this.

So you see, you do need to understand the change to the printing architecture—but once you understand the new concepts, printing is easy. Plus, you get to take advantage of all the new features of .NET in terms of printer setting, configuration, and sophisticated graphic output.

I encourage you to review the objects in the System.Drawing.Printing namespace for further information on printing in .NET.

I/O

You already know that VB.NET continues to support traditional BASIC file I/O commands such as Get, Put, Print#, etc. The VB.NET language also continues to support traditional file I/O commands such as CurDir, ChDir, Kill, etc. These are all part of the Microsoft.VisualBasic namespace.

While you can certainly continue to use the VB commands if you are comfortable with them, it's a good idea to be familiar with the System.IO namespace. It contains objects that perform all of the traditional VB file operations—but more important, it contains objects that are useful for other types of I/O operations. You'll run into some of the System.IO objects in applications ranging from serialization to cryptography to network data transfers. So, you might as well invest a few minutes and learn about them here.

There is just one catch to using the System.IO namespace—one that, by now, you are probably familiar with.[13] The .NET Framework has a new approach to I/O that will be unfamiliar to VB6 programmers (and C++ programmers, for that

---

13. Though some might prefer the term "sick and tired of" instead of "familiar with."

matter). My goal in the next few pages is to teach you the concepts behind I/O in .NET so that you will be able to see how the various objects fit together and learn to use them successfully on your own.

The critical concept to understand with regard to .NET I/O is actually quite simple: just as GDI provides a generic access layer for drawing on different image surfaces, the System.IO classes provide a generic access layer for reading and writing to different I/O devices.

Most objects that represent I/O devices derive from the System.IO.Stream object. This object views a device as providing access to a stream of bytes (either to read or as a destination for writing) and provides the base functionality that allows you to do the following:

- Read one or more bytes of data.

- Write one or more bytes of data.

- Perform an asynchronous read or write operation (with optional notification when the operation is complete).

- Flush written data to the device.

- Seek to a position in the stream.

- Close the stream (device) when it is no longer needed.

Naturally, not all of these operations are supported for every device but you can determine that as well.

Each device that inherits from the Stream object may define its own additional methods. For example, you can lock access to all or part of a FileStream object to prevent simultaneous access to that part of the file by more than one process.

Some of the objects representing devices that provide streams are shown in Figure 12-5.

As you can see, there are streams for files, blocks of memory, encrypted data, network sockets, HTTP network transfers, XML data, and more. Use the Derivation2 project and check out the list of objects that inherit from System.IO.Stream for a complete list.

Each stream can also be attached to a BufferedStream object. The BufferStream object can improve performance in cases where you are performing many short I/O operations—say, reading one character at a time from a device. The BufferedStream object acts as a cache to reduce the number of calls to the actual device, buffering data according to a buffer size you specify.

While you can read and write data directly to the streams, you can also use one of the specialized objects that inherit from the TextReader class. This class is

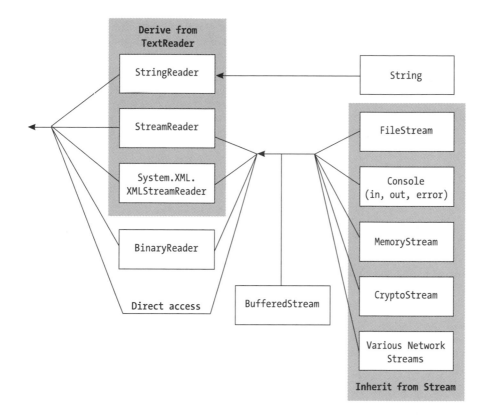

Figure 12-5. I/O under .NET.

optimized for handling text. The StreamReader object, for example, has the ability to read lines of text (up until the next crlf pair). The StringReader allows you to treat a String variable as if it were a stream. The XMLTextReader allows you to treat the stream as XML data.

You can derive your own classes from the TextReader class to implement specialized objects for accessing streams.

The System.IO.Stream class lets you read one or more bytes into Byte variables or arrays. The BinaryReader object is useful for reading arbitrary variables from a stream. The BinaryReader allows you to treat the stream as a source of any primitive data type. Thus, you can read data directly into Boolean, Integer, Long, String, and other primitive object types.

Finally, it should go without saying that while the entire discussion here has to do with reading streams, everything works identically in the other direction with objects such as TextWriter, StringWriter, BinaryWriter, StreamWriter, etc.

The IODemo sample project in Listing 12-7 offers a very simple illustration of these concepts, depicting how the common ShowTheStream function can be implemented to process data from two completely different types of streams.

Listing 12-7. IODemo sample application.

```vb
' I/O Demo
' Copyright ©2001 by Desaware Inc.
Imports System.IO

Module Module1
    Const StringToReadFrom As String = "This is a string to read with a string
reader"

    Private Sub ShowTheStream(ByVal tr As TextReader)
        Dim i As Integer
        Do
            i = tr.Read()
            If i >= 0 Then
                Console.Write(Chr(i))
            End If

        Loop While i >= 0

    End Sub


    Sub Main()
        Dim sr As New StringReader(StringToReadFrom)
        Dim i As Integer
        ShowTheStream(sr)
        Console.WriteLine()

        Dim fs As New FileStream("..\demo.txt", FileMode.Open)
        Dim strread As New StreamReader(fs)
        ShowTheStream(strread)
        fs.Close()
        strread.Close()

        Console.Readline()
    End Sub

End Module
```

Other System.IO Classes

Here are a few other classes in the System.IO namespace that may be of interest.

System.IO.Directory and System.IO.DirectoryInfo

These classes perform a variety of directory operations, including creating, deleting, and moving directories. You can get or set the directory modification and access times.

System.IO.File and System.IO.FileInfo

These classes perform a variety of file operations including creating, deleting, copying, and moving files. Use these classes to test for a file's existence. You can also use these classes to open files (functions that open files return System.IO.FileStream objects you can use to read or write the files).

System.IO.FileSystemInfo

This is the base class for the System.IO.DirectoryInfo and System.IO.FileInfo classes. It is used when navigating a directory hierarchy to obtain information about the directories and files on a system.

System.IO.FileSystemWatcher

Use this class to watch for file system events such as the creation, deletion, or modification of files.

System.IO.IsolatedStorage (Namespace)

The objects in this namespace allow you to allocate a directory unique to a given assembly and, optionally, to a given Application Domain. It is similar to the idea of storing information in the registry under a key that is unique for a particular application, except that you can store entire files.

Serialization and Data Management

Much of what VB programmers do consists of moving and organizing data. So, it's no surprise that the .NET Framework includes a great deal of support for data storage, management, and conversions. You have the System.Data namespace that implements ADO.NET—the latest incarnation of a data model called ADO (which is, of course, different from the ADO that is familiar to VB programmers). You have the System.XML namespaces that allow you to work with XML data —the new standard for describing and transmitting data. And you have the System.Runtime.Serialization namespaces that allow you to store the contents of objects in streams and restore them at will.

I know for a fact that Apress has authors working on books about ADO.NET. And we have authors working on books on XML using the .NET Framework. I don't think we have a book on serialization yet but we're open to volunteers.

My point is that it is completely futile for me to tackle these subjects here. My first reaction was to punt—just leave them out completely. But I found I couldn't leave them out without a few words. Think of this as the part of the tour when you're on a long, rather boring highway between two points of interest and the tour guide is telling you about other great tours available for cities you can just barely make out on the horizon but can't visit on this particular trip.

Serialization

You now know a bit about streams. The concept of serialization is actually quite simple. When you serialize an object, it stores its state in a stream of data. When you deserialize it, you create an object based on data stored in a data stream. It is up to an object to know how to serialize and deserialize itself.

VB6 component developers are familiar with the concept of serialization through property bags. COM developers know that internally, COM serialization is implemented using interfaces such as IPeristStream and IPersistStorage. VB.NET works in a very similar manner from a developer's perspective, although, internally it is completely different.

Object serialization is important in many situations. It can be used to store object state in stateless Web applications and services. It can be used to store and restore object state so the objects themselves can otherwise be pooled. It can be used to convert objects into data that is easily transmitted across a network— since serialized data does not include references.

The Serialization sample program in Listing 12-8 shows a simple, self-persisting class called SerializationTest. The class has two Public variables: m_MyString and m_MyInteger. The class is given the ability to serialize itself by giving it the Serializable attribute. This attribute tells .NET to automatically serialize any fields and properties of the class that are not explicitly marked with the <NonSerialized> attribute.

The class also includes two methods, one to serialize the object to a SOAP stream, the other a shared method to create a new SerializationTest object from a SOAP stream. Keep in mind that these methods do not need to be part of the class—they are in the class in this example for convenience.

Listing 12-8. Serialization example.

```
' Simple serialization example
' Copyright ©2001 by Desaware Inc. All Rights Reserved
Imports System.Runtime.Serialization

<Serializable()> Public Class SerializationTest

    Public m_MyString As String
    Public m_MyInteger As Integer

    Public Function DumpToSoap(ByVal sc As SerializationTest) As String
        Dim ms As New System.IO.MemoryStream()
        Dim sf As New Formatters.Soap.SoapFormatter()
        ' Serialize the class into the memory stream
        sf.Serialize(ms, sc)
        ms.Flush()
        ' Read the stream out into a string
        ms.Seek(0, IO.SeekOrigin.Begin)
        Dim tr As New System.IO.StreamReader(ms)
        Dim res As String
        res = tr.ReadToEnd()
        ms.Close()
        Return res
    End Function
```

```
    Public Shared Function GetFromSoap(ByVal soapstring As String) As
SerializationTest
        Dim ms As New System.IO.MemoryStream()
        Dim sw As New System.IO.StreamWriter(ms)
        ' Write the string into a memorystream
        sw.Write(soapstring)
        sw.Flush()
        ms.Flush()
        ms.Seek(0, IO.SeekOrigin.Begin)
        Dim sc As SerializationTest
        ' Load the object from the Soap description
        Dim sf As New Formatters.Soap.SoapFormatter()
        sc = CType(sf.Deserialize(ms), SerializationTest)
        ms.Close()
        Return (sc)
    End Function

End Class


Module Module1

    Sub Main()
        Dim st As New SerializationTest()
        st.m_MyInteger = 5
        st.m_MyString = "A test string"

        Dim soapstring As String
        soapstring = st.DumpToSoap(st)
        Console.WriteLine(soapstring)
        st = serializationtest.GetFromSoap(soapstring)
        console.WriteLine("Results after object is loaded")
        console.WriteLine(st.m_MyString & "   " & CStr(st.m_MyInteger))
        console.ReadLine()

    End Sub

End Module
```

The serialization takes place in two parts. A serialization formatter of type System.Runtime.Serialization.Formatters.Soap.SoapFormatter can serialize an object into any Stream type. In this case, we use a memory stream, then immediately read the contents of the stream into a text string using a StreamReader object. The .NET Framework also includes a BinaryFormatter object that serializes the object into a compact binary stream. The process is reversed when the object is created: a string is written into a memory stream, and then deserialized using the SoapFormatter object. You can, of course, create your own serialization objects. You can also customize the serialization of your objects by implementing the ISerializable interface.

SOAP, for those of you who have avoided the latest "objects and the Internet" hype, refers to the Simple Object Access Protocol—a standard way of describing objects, their contents, and their methods using XML (extensible markup language). The SOAP serialized version of this object appears as follows:

```
<SOAP-ENV:Envelope xmlns:xsi="http://www.w3.org/2000/10/XMLSchema-instance"
xmlns:xsd="http://www.w3.org/2000/10/XMLSchema"
xmlns:SOAP-ENV="http://schemas.xmlsoap.org/soap/envelope/"
SOAP-ENV:encodingStyle=http://schemas.xmlsoap.org/soap/encoding/
xmlns:a1="http://schemas.microsoft.com/urt/NSAssem/Serialization/Serialization">
<SOAP-ENV:Body>
<a1:SerializationTest id="ref-1">
<m_MyString id="ref-3">A test string</m_MyString>
<m_MyInteger>5</m_MyInteger>
</a1:SerializationTest>
</SOAP-ENV:Body>
</SOAP-ENV:Envelope>
```

SOAP, being a text-based protocol, can be transported using HTTP and can thus be sent through firewalls (assuming those firewalls allow access to HTTP—the primary protocol for the World Wide Web). Since it is a standard, objects defined by SOAP can be called from any operating system or software environment.

Well, that's the theory, at least. In reality, SOAP is still in the process of being standardized and considerable debate is still going on regarding the standards that will exist and whose custom extensions will or will not become part of the standard. In other words, it is still too early to say whether there will truly be a SOAP-based object standard or whether SOAP, too, will degenerate into an array of barely compatible protocols as HTML and DHTML have become.

We can only hope.[14]

---

14. My technical editor pointed out that it's not clear which of these outcomes we should actually hope for. Personally, I'd vote for a successful and thoroughly compatible, cross-platform, industry-wide standard.

ADO.NET and XML

If you plan to use database access from VB.NET (which is the case for most developers), I encourage you to read Microsoft's documentation, then go out and find a good book on ADO.NET.[15]

Meanwhile, I'll just share a few things you should know about ADO.NET.

- You don't have to use it. You can still access COM ADO using Interop.

- ADO.NET is designed to be stateless. You access data through a DataSet object that holds an in-memory copy of the data you are working with. You can then make your changes and they are written back out to the data source.

- ADO.NET can connect to a variety of data sources. However, one of its most intriguing features is its ability to work on XML data. In fact, ADO.NET uses XML to communicate with the data source (thus, again, avoiding some of the security and firewall issues that make remote data connections so much fun in the world of COM).

The TVListing sample program illustrates a simple application of ADO.NET. The TVListing.vb module is shown in Listing 12-9. The TVListingDB class wraps an ADO.NET Table object. The table is created on the fly by defining two columns, one with the name of a TV show, the other with its time (in string format, to keep things simple). The DataColumn objects that are used to define columns have a variety of properties to control the behavior of the database column.

The LoadInitialData method loads the table with some initial data. The Debug statements show how the state of each row changes. When you first create a DataRow object and load it with data, it is disconnected (not yet in the table). After you use the DataRow.Add method, the DataRow is considered "New"—but is not yet accepted into the table. After you call the DataTable.AcceptChanges method, the DataRow is considered "Unchanged" and remains in that state until you edit it, at which point it becomes "Modified" until you accept the changes. The GetDataSet method shows you one way to retrieve a DataSet that contains the table. In many cases, you will load the DataSet by executing an SQL query or applying a filter to the table.

---

15. Preferably one published by Apress (http://www.apress.com) but I'm sure there will be other good ones as well.

Listing 12-9. Module TVListing.vb from the TVListing sample project.

```vb
Imports System.Data
Public Class TVListingDB
    Public TVTable As New DataTable("TVListing")

    Public Sub New()
        Dim showcol As New DataColumn("Name", GetType(String))
        Dim showtime As New DataColumn("Time", GetType(String))
        ' Don't allow null values
        showcol.AllowDBNull = False
        showtime.AllowDBNull = False

        TVTable.Columns.Add(showcol)
        TVTable.Columns.Add(showtime)
    End Sub

    Public Sub LoadInitialData()
        Dim newRow As DataRow

        newRow = TVTable.NewRow()
        newRow.Item(0) = "Star Trek"
        newRow.Item(1) = "13:00"
        TVTable.Rows.Add(newRow)
        newRow = TVTable.NewRow()
        newRow.Item("Name") = "Babylon 5"
        newRow.Item("Time") = "14:00"
        TVTable.Rows.Add(newRow)
        newRow = TVTable.NewRow()
        newRow("Name") = "BattleStar Galactica"
        newRow("Time") = "15:00"
        Debug.WriteLine("Before adding, Row is: " & newRow.RowState.ToString)
        TVTable.Rows.Add(newRow)
        Debug.WriteLine("Before accepting to table, Row is: " & _
        newRow.RowState.ToString)
        TVTable.AcceptChanges()
      Debug.WriteLine("Before modification, Row is: " & newRow.RowState.ToString)
        newRow("Time") = "15:30"
        Debug.WriteLine("Before accepting changes, Row is: " & _
        newRow.RowState.ToString)
        newRow.AcceptChanges()
        debug.WriteLine(TVTable.Rows.Count)
    End Sub
```

```
Public Function GetDataSet() As DataSet
    Dim ds As New DataSet()
    ds.Tables.Add(TVTable)
    Return ds
End Function


End Class
```

A DataSet object can contain multiple tables and objects that define relationships between the tables.

The cmdCreateDB_Click method shown here demonstrates the creation of the TVListingDB object and how you can set the table to be a source for a DataGrid control.

```
Private Sub cmdCreateDB_Click(ByVal sender As System.Object, ByVal e As _
System.EventArgs) Handles cmdCreateDB.Click
    Dim tv As New TVListingDB()
    tv.LoadInitialData()
    dataGrid1().DataSource = tv.TVTable
    dataGrid1().PreferredColumnWidth = -1
End Sub
```

The cmdXML_Click and cmdXML2_Click methods shown in Listing 12-10 illustrate how you can use the DataSet.WriteXmlSchema and DataSet.WriteXml methods to output data in XML format.

Listing 12-10. XML output in the TVListing sample project.

```
Private Sub cmdXML_Click(ByVal sender As System.Object, ByVal e As _
System.EventArgs) Handles cmdXML.Click
    Dim tv As New TVListingDB()
    Dim sr As New StringWriter()
    tv.LoadInitialData()
    txtResult().Text = ""
    tv.GetDataSet.WriteXmlSchema(sr)
    txtResult().Text = sr.ToString
End Sub
```

```
Private Sub cmdXML2_Click(ByVal sender As System.Object, ByVal e As _
System.EventArgs) Handles cmdXML2.Click
    Dim tv As New TVListingDB()
    Dim sr As New StringWriter()
    tv.LoadInitialData()
    txtResult().Text = ""
    tv.GetDataSet.WriteXml(sr)
    txtResult().Text = sr.ToString

End Sub
```

The XML data is shown in Listing 12-11. One of the nice things about ADO.NET (which isn't shown here) is its ability to transport only changes when writing data back to the data store. This helps minimize traffic on the network.

Listing 12-11. XML Data from the TVListing sample project.

```
<NewDataSet>
  <xsd:schema id="NewDataSet" targetNamespace="" xmlns="" xmlns:xsd="http://
www.w3.org/2000/10/XMLSchema" xmlns:msdata="urn:schemas-microsoft-com:xml-
msdata">
    <xsd:element name="TVListing">
      <xsd:complexType>
        <xsd:all>
          <xsd:element name="Name" type="xsd:string"/>
          <xsd:element name="Time" minOccurs="0" type="xsd:string"/>
        </xsd:all>
      </xsd:complexType>
    </xsd:element>
    <xsd:element name="NewDataSet" msdata:IsDataSet="true">
      <xsd:complexType>
        <xsd:choice maxOccurs="unbounded">
          <xsd:element ref="TVListing"/>
        </xsd:choice>
      </xsd:complexType>
    </xsd:element>
  </xsd:schema>
```

```
<TVListing>
  <Name>Star Trek</Name>
  <Time>13:00</Time>
</TVListing>
<TVListing>
  <Name>Babylon 5</Name>
  <Time>14:00</Time>
</TVListing>
<TVListing>
  <Name>BattleStar Galactica</Name>
  <Time>15:30</Time>
</TVListing>
</NewDataSet>
```

The .NET Framework also includes the System.XML namespace, which allows you to parse and manipulate XML data streams as well.

Recap

This concludes our brief guided tour of some of the more important namespaces. You might be wondering what's been left out—I assure you that I have left out far more than I have included. The entire realm of enterprise services and component development hasn't even been touched. There are namespaces to cover everything from resources to globalization to parsing of HTML and XML files.

You did, however, see the high points of certain fundamental namespaces that are key to many programming tasks—especially those relating to features no longer supported directly in Visual Basic.NET. You learned about the system objects and how they relate to each other. You learned about Collections, I/O, Drawing and Printing, and the concepts behind those namespaces and how they differ from the approaches used by Visual Basic 6. Finally, you saw a quick introduction to serialization and ADO.NET (two other subjects deserving an entire book of their own).

One reminder, most classes in the System namespace are not thread safe. Use care when accessing them in multithreaded applications (in other words, don't share .NET Framework objects among threads unless the documentation explicitly says that they are thread safe). Many of the classes have features built-in to help you synchronize access—check for those in the documentation as well.

Though you have finished the short tour, your visit to the world of VB.NET is not yet complete. In the next three chapters, we'll pay a visit to the System.Windows.Forms namespace used for Windows applications and those namespaces that deal with network operations and COM interop. These, again, will not go into nearly enough depth but will hopefully cover the concepts necessary to get you started off right.

CHAPTER 13

Windows Applications

FALSE START #1

Visual Basic.NET offers developers the same visual, rapid-application development tools proven successful by Visual Basic developers. Creating a user interface is a simple matter of selecting a control from a toolbox and dropping it onto a form. You can set the properties for controls either programmatically or by using a Property Browser window. You then add code to respond to the various events raised by the control.

Here is a simple walkthrough of how to create a "Hello World" application with Visual Basic.NET...

Well, that's the traditional approach for introducing Windows applications. It suffers from two failings. First, it is a complete rehash of the existing documentation and thus boring to read and to write. Second, if you don't understand the concepts covered in such an introduction, you probably aren't experienced enough to be reading this book in the first place.

The fact is, most VB.NET programmers won't take more than half an hour to become familiar with the Visual Studio IDE without my help (and probably without reading the Visual Studio documentation).

False Start #2

As an intermediate or experienced VB6 programmer approaching VB.NET Windows's application programming, you already know what you want to do. The trick is to figure out the correct selection of properties, methods, and events to do it. VB.NET forms and controls support almost all of the features of VB6 (along with some new ones) but it's not always clear how they match up. Even with the "What's New in VB.NET" section in Microsoft's documentation, you'll be spending a fair amount of time at first experimenting with the new forms package and getting it to do what you want.

This is absolutely true. Much of your time will be spent getting acquainted with the new Object properties and events. And no, I won't try to summarize them all here. There are more than enough controls, methods, and properties in the System.Windows.Forms namespace to fill a book—far more than will fit in this chapter.

Which leaves me with a dilemma. What is there for me to write about?

A Whole New Forms Package

My intent in this chapter is to provide a context to the changes in the forms package. Hopefully, I can offer some insights that will help you get up to speed more quickly than you would otherwise.

The first thing you must realize (which you probably realize already) is that the forms package under .NET is not the same one used by VB6. It is a completely different, written-from-scratch forms package.[1]

This means, first and foremost, that you should make no assumptions beyond what you find in the documentation, in VB.NET books, or that you learn through your own experimentation. I'm not really referring to the big things here—things like properties and events that work in more or less the same way. I'm referring rather to the hard-learned experience you have—little details such as the right way to validate fields or the order in which events occur or how data binding works. You'll gradually gain this information and experience but it won't happen overnight and this chapter will only get you started in that direction.

Most of the changes you'll be dealing with are small—there are a myriad of small changes and their implications that you'll gradually become familiar with.

There are, however, several huge, fundamental changes that you must be aware of from the beginning

Recreatable Windows

There are many properties in VB6 controls that can only be set at design time. For example, you can't change a listbox from single to multiple select at runtime. This may seem like a careless omission to some but to those familiar with how Windows works, the reason for this limitation is clear: these properties correspond to Windows styles that cannot be changed once a window is created.

In VB6, once a form is created or a control is sited on a form, a window exists for that form or control. The only way you can change those styles is to destroy the window and recreate it—which would cause any data in the window to be lost.

However, in VB.NET, you can change these properties as shown in the following code sample from the Recreate project:

---

1. While it is true that the Form and UserControl classes and those they are built on are completely new, many of the common controls like the RichTextBox control are just wrappers over the standard Windows common controls or their COM counterparts. This means they are still subject to the potential distribution problems (DLL Hell) as any other component based on the underlying common control DLLs.

```
Private Sub Form1_Load(ByVal sender As System.Object, _
ByVal e As System.EventArgs) Handles MyBase.Load
    Dim x As Integer
    For x = 1 To 20
        listBox1().Items.Add("Entry # " & CStr(x))
    Next
    lblWindow().Text = "hWnd = " & listBox1().Handle.ToString
End Sub

Private Sub chkMulti_CheckedChanged(ByVal sender As System.Object, _
ByVal e As System.EventArgs) Handles chkMulti.CheckedChanged
    If chkMulti().CheckState = CheckState.Checked Then
        listBox1().SelectionMode = SelectionMode.MultiExtended
    Else
        listBox1().SelectionMode = SelectionMode.One
    End If
    lblWindow().Text = "hWnd = " & listBox1().Handle.ToString
```

As you can see, the checkbox on the form switches the listbox from single to multiple selections. Feel free to experiment and verify that the listbox changes its behavior to match the new SelectionMode property setting.

Now, watch the Label control as you change Listbox modes. As you will see, the window's handle changes.

Each time you change the Listbox mode, all of the data in the listbox is serialized into a temporary buffer; the Listbox window is recreated under the new style; and the data is restored.

Which brings us to the first lesson, which will be especially important to those using Win32 API functions: window handles in .NET are subject to change.

Graphical Controls

Visual Basic 4 introduced a kind of control called a "lightweight" or "graphical" control. These are controls that do not actually have windows. You can think of them as instructions for the control's container to draw certain information. Graphical controls were added to OLE because they used fewer resources and offered better performance.

Under .NET, all controls are Windows-based. This is nice in that it provides a more consistent model for programmers—you no longer have to deal with some of the quirks relating to the differing behavior of windowed and windowless controls. The disadvantage is that now all controls enjoy the overhead of having windows associated with them.

If you were accustomed to using Line and Shape controls (two of the most commonly used lightweight controls, neither of which are supported in VB.NET), it's now time to switch to the approach you probably should have been using all along—drawing the images you want during the form's Paint event.

Consistent Hosts

As an experienced ActiveX control developer, I can tell you the worst thing about ActiveX controls—you can never be sure they'll work on any given container. Subtle differences between hosts result in subtle (or major) changes in the behavior of ActiveX controls. Thus, a control tested on VB6 may not work correctly when hosted in Visual C++ or Microsoft Word or Excel. The reason for these incompatibilities is because each host provides its own container implementation. Inconsistency develops based on each host developer's interpretation of the (occasionally vague) COM specifications and the inevitable bugs present in any complex piece of software.

This means, in practical terms, that control vendors create and test controls for VB6 (and perhaps one or two other hosts) where there is a known market and essentially abandon the other platforms because the costs to test and support the controls on those hosts cannot be justified. The lack of controls on those platforms impedes the growth of a real market for controls for those platforms, reducing further the incentive to develop those controls—a vicious cycle. These same issues apply for in-house control development as well, albeit to a lesser degree.

On .NET, components all run in hosts provided by the .NET Framework. Once your control or component works correctly, it should work consistently across all .NET containers (or even COM containers as you'll learn in Chapter 15).

Patterns and System.Windows.Forms

There's a lot of talk about using design patterns to improve software development. This means, in a nutshell, to spot how a generally established solution for common software problems can be adapted to specific software problems.

Your ability to quickly learn the Windows.Forms namespace will depend on your ability to spot the patterns of methods and properties used by the many controls in the namespace. Think of it this way, you can try to learn each control independently with all its methods and properties or first learn the methods and properties that are common to all controls, then focus on the relatively few methods and properties unique to each control.

I'll take the latter approach.

The most important thing to realize is that the forms package is based on inheritance. In fact, any time you create a form, you are actually creating a class that inherits from the System.Windows.Forms.Form class.

Figure 13-1 illustrates part of the class hierarchy for the .NET forms package. The figure does not include every object but is sufficient to give you a sense of how the package is built via inheritance.

Let's review the key classes.

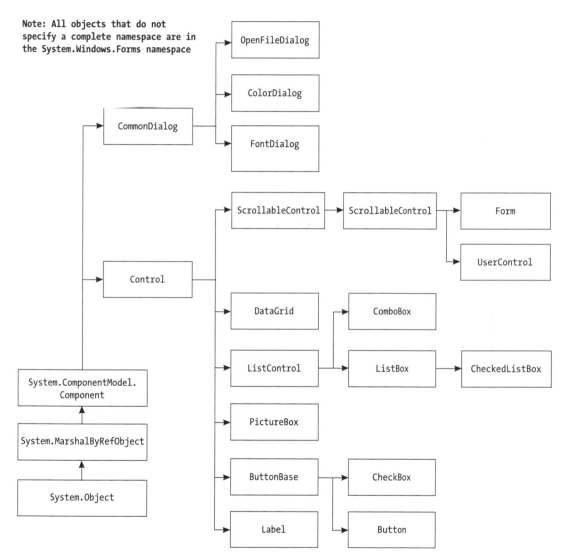

Figure 13-1. A portion of the Windows.Forms package.

System.ComponentModel.Component

The System.ComponentModel namespace contains objects that manage components and their relationships.

- A component can be hosted inside a container and may serve as a container for other components as well.

- A component keeps track of contained components and calls the Dispose method on each contained component when the component's Dispose method is called.

- Components can be marshaled across application domains.

- Components can have associated designers. This means that they can be represented on the Visual Studio toolbar and work with the Visual Studio Property Browser window.

- Components and their properties can be serialized. They can work with type converters to represent property values as text in the Visual Studio Property window. Or, you can create your own property editors that work within the Property window.

System.Windows.Forms.Control

To understand the hierarchy of a form, let's take a look at a series of sample programs that illustrate the functionality added by each object along the derivation chain. The first project is the ControlOnly project. We'll look at this one in-depth in order to also understand how the form itself works.

The first thing you will notice is that the form inherits from System.Windows.Forms.Form as shown here:

```
Public Class Form1
    Inherits System.Windows.Forms.Form
```

In VB6, when you create a new application, the programming element "Form1" has two meanings. It represents both the type of form and the global name of the first form of that type. You can have code such as this:

```
Dim f2 As New Form1
Form1.Caption = "First form 1"
f2.Show
f2.Caption = "Second form 1"
```

…which creates two forms of type Form1, one named Form1, the other named f2.

This concept does not exist in VB.NET. Here, Form1 refers to a new Object type that derives from the Form type. You reference that object using the keyword Me.

The VB.NET form has a default constructor that first calls the base constructor (as usual), then calls InitializeComponent:

```
#Region " Windows Form Designer generated code "

    Public Sub New()
        MyBase.New()

        'This call is required by the Windows Form Designer.
        InitializeComponent()

        'Add any initialization after the InitializeComponent() call
    End Sub
```

Forms also implement the IDisposable interface. Like other components that can contain other components, the form maintains a list of contained components in a System.ComponentModel.Container object, which has the ability to dispose of all of those contained objects:[2]

```
    'Required by the Windows Form Designer
    Private components As System.ComponentModel.Container

    'Form overrides dispose to clean up the component list.
    Public Overloads Overrides Sub Dispose()
        MyBase.Dispose()
        If Not (components Is Nothing) Then
            components.Dispose()
        End If
    End Sub
```

This sample program includes three controls. The first is of the most interest in this example—it is a generic Control type. You are unlikely to ever create controls of this type in practice but it serves the purpose here to help you understand the functionality of the different objects upon which forms are based:

```
    Private WithEvents ctl1 As System.Windows.Forms.Control
    Private WithEvents textBox1 As System.Windows.Forms.TextBox
    Private WithEvents textBox2 As System.Windows.Forms.TextBox
```

---

2.   Some code elements have been rearranged here to improve readability.

The really interesting thing about the InitializeComponent function is that it clearly illustrates a major difference between VB6 and VB.NET. In VB6, properties are stored and retrieved almost magically behind the scenes. In VB.NET, properties are set via code at runtime. The Property window in the Visual Studio environment is just a different type of code editor.

The ctl1 control (of type Control) is added to the form's Control collection. The textBox1 control is actually contained in ctl1—not the form. How can you tell? Because it is added to ctl1.Controls (the ctl1 control collection) instead of the form's control collection. The form's initialization is shown in Listing 13-1.

Listing 13-1. Form Initialization for the ControlOnly sample project.

```
'NOTE: The following procedure is required by the Windows Form Designer
'It can be modified using the Windows Form Designer.
'Do not modify it using the code editor.
<System.Diagnostics.DebuggerStepThrough()> Private _
Sub InitializeComponent()
    Me.ctl1 = New System.Windows.Forms.Control()
    Me.textBox1 = New System.Windows.Forms.TextBox()
    Me.textBox2 = New System.Windows.Forms.TextBox()
    Me.ctl1.SuspendLayout()sp
    Me.SuspendLayout()
    '
    'ctl1
    '
    Me.ctl1.BackColor = System.Drawing.Color.Bisque
    Me.ctl1.Controls.AddRange(New System.Windows.Forms.Control() _
    {Me.textBox1})
    Me.ctl1.Name = "ctl1"
    Me.ctl1.Size = New System.Drawing.Size(128, 112)
    Me.ctl1.TabIndex = 0
    '
    'textBox1
    '
    Me.textBox1.Location = New System.Drawing.Point(32, 48)
    Me.textBox1.Name = "textBox1"
    Me.textBox1.Size = New System.Drawing.Size(72, 20)
    Me.textBox1.TabIndex = 1
    Me.textBox1.Text = "textBox1"
    '
    'textBox2
    '
```

```
Me.textBox2.Location = New System.Drawing.Point(24, 128)
Me.textBox2.Name = "textBox2"
Me.textBox2.Size = New System.Drawing.Size(96, 20)
Me.textBox2.TabIndex = 1
Me.textBox2.Text = "textBox2"
'
'Form1
'
Me.AutoScaleBaseSize = New System.Drawing.Size(5, 13)
Me.ClientSize = New System.Drawing.Size(292, 273)
Me.Controls.AddRange(New System.Windows.Forms.Control() _
{Me.textBox2, Me.ctl1})
Me.Name = "Form1"
Me.Text = "Form1"
Me.ctl1.ResumeLayout(False)
Me.ResumeLayout(False)

End Sub
```

The fact that textBox1 is contained within ctl1 results in some rather bizarre behavior. The Visual Studio designer is not able to select the text box directly. When you tab between the two text boxes, you'll find that the ctl1 control also receives the focus. These problems occur because a Control object is not itself designed to directly host other controls—at least, Visual Studio is not designed for this scenario.

Even so, you'll find that the ctl1 Control object includes most of the properties that you would expect to see in a control, including: BackColor, ForeColor, BackgroundImage, ClientRectangle, ContextMenu, Cursor, Enabled, Font, Top, Left, Width, Height, Parent, Visible, etc. Once an object inherits from the Control class, it automatically inherits all of these properties. Standard controls such as the TextBox, Label, and DataGrid inherit directly from this class.

Clearly then, one of the first steps you should take when studying the Windows.Forms namespace is to explore the properties and methods of the Control class.

Now, let's look further at the objects on which a form is based.

System.Windows.Forms.ScrollableControl

The ScrollableOnly project is similar to the ControlOnly project except that the ctl1 object derives from the ScrollableControl classes (which itself derives from Control). In the following example, several text boxes and a label are also created:

```
Private WithEvents ctl1 As System.Windows.Forms.ScrollableControl
Private WithEvents label1 As System.Windows.Forms.Label
Private WithEvents textBox2 As System.Windows.Forms.TextBox
Private WithEvents textBox1 As System.Windows.Forms.TextBox
Private WithEvents textBox3 As System.Windows.Forms.TextBox
```

The InitializeComponent function shown in Listing 13-2 sets the properties of these controls as shown here (only some of the properties are shown to conserve space).

Listing 13-2. Form Initialization for the ScrollableOnly sample project.

```
<System.Diagnostics.DebuggerStepThrough()> Private _
Sub InitializeComponent()
    Me.textBox2 = New System.Windows.Forms.TextBox()
    Me.textBox1 = New System.Windows.Forms.TextBox()
    Me.ctl1 = New System.Windows.Forms.ScrollableControl()
    Me.label1 = New System.Windows.Forms.Label()
    Me.textBox3 = New System.Windows.Forms.TextBox()
    '
    'ctl1
    '
    Me.ctl1.AutoScroll = True
    Me.ctl1.BackColor = System.Drawing.Color.Crimson
    Me.ctl1.Controls.AddRange(New System.Windows.Forms.Control() _
    {Me.textBox2, Me.textBox1, Me.label1})
    Me.ctl1.Location = New System.Drawing.Point(40, 16)
    Me.ctl1.Size = New System.Drawing.Size(200, 136)
    Me.ctl1.TabIndex = 0
    '
    'label1
    '
    Me.label1.BackColor = System.Drawing.Color.FromArgb(0, 192, 0)

    Me.AutoScaleBaseSize = New System.Drawing.Size(5, 13)
    Me.ClientSize = New System.Drawing.Size(292, 273)
    Me.Controls.AddRange(New System.Windows.Forms.Control() _
    {Me.textBox3, Me.ctl1})
    Me.Name = "Form1"
    Me.Text = "Form1"

End Sub
```

The textBox2, textBox1, and label1 controls are contained in the ctl1 control. The textBox3 control is contained in the form itself. The ctl1 control's AutoScroll property is set to True. This is one of the properties added by the Scrollable Control class that allows the control to not only contain controls logically but to do so visibly as well. When a contained control is outside of the visible boundaries of the ScrollableControl, scrollbars appear allowing the user to scroll those contained controls into view.

When you experiment with this project, you will see this scrolling in action. In Design mode, you will see that it is now possible to select contained controls and to drop new controls onto the ctl1 control.

However, when you tab among the controls, you will still see odd behavior. The ctl1 control still receives the focus.

Containers, Forms, and UserControls

The ContainerControl project is virtually identical to the ScrollableOnly project. The only difference is that the ctl1 object now derives from the ContainerControl. The ContainerControl derives from the ScrollableControl class but includes the focus management features needed to properly handle contained controls. For example, it automatically passes focus to the first contained control when an attempt is made to set the focus to the container. Try running the program and tabbing among the controls to see this in action.

Both Forms and UserControls derive from the ContainerControl class. Forms add properties and methods to control borders and top-level captions, MDI support, and other features relating to being a top-level window. The UserControl object adds few new members to the ContainerControl class. But it does have attributes that tell the Visual Studio runtime to use the UserControl designer to provide the expected rich development environment.

Navigating the System.Windows.Forms Namespace

When you look in the online documentation for classes in the Forms namespace, you'll see that all of the members supported for each class are listed in the documentation for that class. The documentation also shows which members are implemented (or overloaded) by the class and which are derived from other classes. While this provides an easy way to determine the members of a class, it makes it difficult to tell, at a glance, which members are implemented or overloaded directly—to do so, you must search through the entire list.

The DirectMembers sample project provides a tool to quickly find which members are implemented directly by a class. It also offers a look at features common to many controls.

The project form contains a single TreeView control whose Sorted property is set to True. During form initialization, the LoadTreeview function is called. Let's look at this function step-by-step:

```
Private Sub LoadTreeview()
    Dim asm As [Assembly]
    Dim asmtypes() As Type
    Dim ThisType As Type
    asm = Reflection.Assembly.GetAssembly( _
        GetType(System.Windows.Forms.Form))
```

Retrieving assembly information should be routine by now. In this case, we're explicitly asking for the assembly that contains the forms package:

```
asmtypes = asm.GetTypes()
For Each ThisType In asmtypes
    If ThisType.IsClass And ThisType.IsPublic Then
```

The asmtypes variable is loaded with an array of all of the types in the assembly. We're only interested in Public classes:

```
Dim tn As New TreeNode(ThisType.Name)
```

The root-level nodes of the TreeView control will contain the class names. A TreeView control contains a TreeNodeCollection containing TreeNode objects. Each TreeNode object can, in turn, contain its own TreeNodeCollection—which is how the tree is built.

The interesting thing about this approach is that it is used virtually everywhere that a control contains a list of items. For example, the ListBox control no longer exposes methods to directly add and remove entries. Instead, you perform those operations using the ListBox's Items property, which accesses a collection. Even though this represents a big change from VB6, the shift is largely intuitive since you already know how to work with a collection. Even more intriguing, the items in a listbox can be any object. The listbox simply calls the ToString method to display the string representation for the object. This eliminates the need to manage extra information using an ItemData property. To store complex information in a listbox, you simply define a class, load all the data you wish into the class, and override the ToString property to display what you wish in the listbox.

Those VB6 programmers who complain about the incompatibility of the .NET listbox with the VB6 listbox miss the point. The .NET approach is actually more intuitive and because it is used in every case where a control manages a list, the approach offers a more consistent programming environment. Consistency results in a shorter learning curve for new controls and code that is easier to read and support in the long run.

But I digress.[3] Back to the DirectMembers project. Remember, the following takes place for each class in the System.Windows.Forms namespace:

```
Dim members(), mi As MemberInfo
treeView1().Nodes.Add(tn)
members = ThisType.GetMembers(BindingFlags.DeclaredOnly _
        Or BindingFlags.Public Or _
        BindingFlags.Instance Or BindingFlags.Static)
```

The Members array is loaded with all public and shared members that are declared at this level (which includes overloaded implementations but not those derived unchanged from base classes). The code then loops through each element in the array as follows:

```
For Each mi In members
    Dim methinfo As MethodInfo
    Select Case mi.MemberType
        Case MemberTypes.Method
            methinfo = CType(mi, MethodInfo)
            If Not methinfo.IsSpecialName Then
                tn.Nodes.Add(StripType(mi.ToString))
            End If
        Case MemberTypes.Event
            tn.Nodes.Add(StripType(mi.ToString) & " event")
        Case Else
            tn.Nodes.Add(StripType(mi.ToString))
    End Select
    Next
End If
Next
End Sub
```

The MemberInfo class's ToString method displays the complete signature of each member. This includes the return value (specified with complete namespace) and special accessor methods such as get_xxx for property xxx. If the member is a method, we check for and ignore it if it is one of these special accessor

---

3. For those of you who are wondering, this particular digression is not as casual as it may seem. This is an important point and one of the main reasons that I am taking the time to walk through this sample so closely.

methods. If it is an event, the word "event" is added for clarity. Properties are added directly. The StripType method shown here simply removes the return type to promote readability. You can always check the documentation to determine the return type:

```
Private Function StripType(ByVal s As String) As String
    Dim spacepos As Integer
    spacepos = InStr(s, " ")
    If spacepos > 0 Then Return Mid$(s, spacepos + 1)
    Return (s)
End Function
```

This utility offers a quick method of determining which members were added to a class. Figure 13-2 clearly shows that the UserControl class adds little to the ContainerControl class from which it derives.

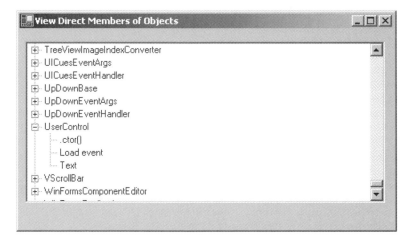

Figure 13-2. The DirectMember project in action.

Exploring Further

I will keep my earlier promise not to attempt to cover all of the changes to the forms package. Nevertheless, there are a few other important classes and changes that are deserving of further attention.

AutoRedraw—Plus, Events versus Overrides

I don't like the VB6 AutoRedraw property. To offer some historical perspective, back in the days of VB1, the designers of Visual Basic decided that event-driven programming was going to be difficult for programmers to handle when it came to drawing. It was bad enough that VB programmers had to redesign their DOS-based applications to handle events; asking them to respond to a Paint event and redraw their graphics each time was just too much to ask.

In this, they were probably correct.

Only those of us who've been around for a long time remember how extremely difficult event-driven programming was for those developers coming from the world of DOS programs.[4]

So, Microsoft created a background bitmap for each Form and Picture control. All drawing operations to those objects actually drew the graphics onto the background bitmap, which was then automatically transferred to the form or control. The use of this bitmap depended on the setting of the AutoRedraw property, which defaulted to True (indicating the background bitmap should be used). While this did make life easier for ex-DOS programmers, it was very costly in terms of resources—especially on the 16-bit operating systems of the day.

In later editions of Visual Basic, the default value of this property was set to False, enabling the Paint event for drawing.

Today it is probably safe to say that most VB developers do not set AutoRedraw to True. The one case where there is value in doing so is when a control's graphics are complex and reducing the time to render the graphic is worth the memory cost of holding a background bitmap (which is much less costly on today's more powerful systems).

The AutoRedraw sample project illustrates how you can add AutoRedraw style functionality to your application.

The background bitmap object is defined and the Paint event overridden as shown here:

```
Dim backgroundbitmap As Bitmap

Protected Overrides Sub OnPaint(ByVal _
e As System.Windows.Forms.PaintEventArgs)
    ' MyBase.OnPaint(e) ' What happens if you leave this out?
    If backgroundbitmap Is Nothing Then
        ' May get bitmap before Resize - especially first time
        backgroundbitmap = New Bitmap(Me.ClientSize.Width, _
        Me.ClientSize.Height)
    End If
    e.Graphics.DrawImage(backgroundbitmap, 0, 0)
End Sub
```

---

4. One of my most successful early-published articles was one that taught the principals of event-driven programming at an introductory to intermediate level.

As you can see, the bitmap is created if it does not yet exist. Otherwise, the content of the background bitmap is simply drawn onto the form.

One thing you might find puzzling about this code is that unlike the case with VB6, this is not actually an event!

Well, think about it. What is an event? It is a way for an object to signal clients of the object that something has occurred. So, a form would raise an event to some code outside of the form to indicate that something occurred in the form.

Let me stress this: **an event is a way for an object to signal to code outside of the object that something has occurred.**

However, in this code, you are not *using* the form. You are implementing the form. In VB6, your code is effectively a "client" that is using a standard Form object. Thus, you need to respond to events from that Form object. In VB.NET, you are creating your own unique class that derives from the standard form class. Rather than handling events from the base class, you will typically override base class implementations to provide your own unique functionality.

But how will your class raise Paint events?

The AutoRedraw application contains the cmdOtherForm_Click method that creates a new instance of the Form1 class. In other words, the first form is now acting as a true client to another instance of the class. As a client, it can detect events of that object as shown here:

```
Private Sub OtherFormPaint(ByVal sender As Object, _
ByVal args As PaintEventArgs)
    Debug.WriteLine("Other paint arrived")
End Sub

Private Sub cmdOtherForm_Click(ByVal sender As System.Object, _
ByVal e As System.EventArgs) Handles cmdOtherForm.Click
    Dim f As New Form1()
    f.Visible = True
    AddHandler f.Paint, AddressOf Me.OtherFormPaint
End Sub
```

I don't have to worry about holding on to the f variable that declares the form because the CLR considers top-level forms to be root-level objects themselves. Try running the sample and clicking on the Other Form button twice: once with the Mybase.OnPaint commented out (currently shown in the OnPaint method) and once with it enabled. You'll find that the Paint event is only raised if the MyBase.OnPaint method is called. Clearly the base class (derived from the Control class) raises the Paint event.

You should almost always call the base implementation when you override methods or you might end up causing side effects like this.

What if you wanted your form to have its own Paint event, perhaps with its own unique signature? No problem. Just create your own event that shadows the base event:

```
Shadows Event Paint(ByVal sender As Object, ByVal args As PaintEventArgs)
```

You can then use the RaiseEvent command to raise the new event when you wish.

The difference between implementing and using a form or control is a subtle one and will take some getting used to for most VB6 programmers. Fortunately, it is a case where there are several ways to accomplish the task at hand and no one way is clearly better than the others.

Back to the project. Two other Command buttons are included in the sample project: one that invalidates the surface of the form (thus forcing a redraw and ultimately a Paint event), the other just draws a large X on the form and invalidates the form as shown here:

```
Private Sub cmdInvalidate_Click(ByVal sender As System.Object, _
ByVal e As System.EventArgs) Handles cmdInvalidate.Click
    Me.Invalidate()
End Sub

Private Sub cmdDrawStuff_Click(ByVal sender As System.Object, _
ByVal e As System.EventArgs) Handles cmdDrawStuff.Click
    Dim g As Graphics = graphics.FromImage(backgroundbitmap)
    g.DrawLine(pens.Black, 0, 0, 200, 200)
    g.DrawLine(pens.Red, 0, 200, 200, 0)
    cmdInvalidate_Click(Me, Nothing)
End Sub
```

The interesting part of the background image implementation is in the handling of the Resize event:

```
Protected Overrides Sub OnResize(ByVal e As System.EventArgs)
    If Not Me.ClientRectangle.IsEmpty Then
        If Not Me.ClientSize.Equals(New Size( _
            backgroundbitmap.Width, backgroundbitmap.Height)) Then
            Dim newbitmap As Bitmap
            newbitmap = New Bitmap(Me.ClientSize.Width, _
                    Me.ClientSize.Height)
```

```
                    If Not backgroundbitmap Is Nothing Then
                        Dim g As Graphics = graphics.FromImage(newbitmap)
                        g.DrawImage(backgroundbitmap, 0, 0)
                    End If
                    backgroundbitmap = newbitmap
                End If
            End If
        End Sub
```

When a resize occurs, the function first checks to make sure that the form is not minimized (in which case, the ClientRectangle structure is empty). If the new size of the form is equal to the current bitmap size (which happens anytime a form is restored), there is no need to do anything. Otherwise, a new bitmap is created with the correct size and the contents of the current bitmap are drawn into the new bitmap.

Try resizing the form while the program is running to see the consequences of this approach. Be sure to minimize the form to be smaller than the drawn X and then resize it outward again.

One other small change of note: all calculations and coordinates are in pixels. The drawing package does allow you to work in other units; however, basic windows management is all in pixels. Frankly, I never could understand why Visual Basic 6 and earlier uses twips. Twips are a unit that few people ever use[5] and one that leads to the possibility of round-off errors during drawing and rectangle calculations.

The best reason to use pixels is that they are simply far more efficient. Windows uses pixels and integer values throughout the internal windows system. The use of twips and floating-point coordinates only served to slow Visual Basic's performance with no benefit in functionality.

MDI Forms, Parenting, and Ownership

VB6 programmers constantly struggle to manage the relationships between forms. They use the SetParent API to try to move controls from one form to another or otherwise move them among containers. They struggle with owner relations—all owned windows are minimized with the parent. This is important for applications

---

5. Be honest, did your elementary school teacher cover inches, feet, yards, and twips? In high school, you probably learned hexadecimal and metric but I'll bet your teacher (who probably barely understood metric) would have choked on twips. Note for readers from most of the world: both your elementary and high school teachers probably would have found inches, feet, and yards as mysterious as twips. And you're probably having a good laugh at being reminded that we Americans still afflict our children with those units. As for me, one of my favorite teachers had us calculate speed in units of angstroms per micro-century, which probably explains a great deal.

that have multiple top-level forms on the screen at once—it's a pain to detect when one form is minimized and then have to manually minimize all the others.

And they struggled to create robust MDI frameworks where child forms could be implemented in separate DLL files. One of my most popular articles described a dynamic MDI framework that showed how to use dynamically created VB6 UserControls to solve this problem but even it had subtle quirks and licensing issues when used with many commercial controls.

Watch this.

To establish an ownership relation between windows, create an application with two forms. In the first form, create an instance of the second form:

```
Dim f2 As New Form2()
```

Then, anywhere you wish to establish that relationship, add the second form to the OwnedForms collection of the first form as follows:

```
Me.AddOwnedForm(f2)
```

How cool is this? Very cool because changing ownership after a form is created is not only impossible in VB6, it's impossible in Windows! Ownership in Windows must be established when a window is created. How does the .NET Framework accomplish this? The same way it allows you to change style properties on Windows—it tears down the existing window and recreates it with the new ownership style.

Like that? It gets better.

Make your main form an MDI form. You do this by setting the IsMDIContainer property as follows:

```
Me.IsMdiContainer = True
```

That's it, no separate MDIform class. Now, let's say you have another form, even one implemented in a separate assembly. It need only set its MdiParent property to the MDI form and bang—it is instantly an MDI Child window.

```
Me.MdiParent = parent
```

It simply doesn't get any easier. Check out the FormInForm example application to see these techniques in action.

And while you're at it, try the Parenting example application to watch a Button control transport itself from one form to another in a single line of code.

Until VB6, controls were generally static—they had to be created at design time. The only way to dynamically create controls was by using control arrays.

VB6 has the ability to create controls dynamically but it is a bit awkward, especially when it comes to event handling.

In VB.NET, all controls and forms are created dynamically. There is no such thing as a static "Design Time" control. When you draw a control on a form at design time, you're just telling the Designer Wizard to write code to dynamically create the control. No wonder they work!

For those of you who still miss control arrays, refer to the EventExample project in Chapter 10 for an example of how to implement similar functionality in VB.NET.

Subclassing and the Application Object

Subclassing refers to the ability to intercept Windows messages going to a form or control, typically in order to provide functionality not exposed through standard Visual Basic events.

My company, Desaware, built it's reputation on having the best and most powerful subclassing component back in the days before VB5 when you could not do subclassing in Visual Basic at all.[6] Once it was possible to do subclassing in VB5, we created a VB component that showed VB programmers how to do it correctly and shipped it with source code as part of SpyWorks.

The Messages sample application shows how it's done in VB.NET:

```
Private Sub button1_Click(ByVal sender As System.Object, _
    ByVal e As System.EventArgs) Handles button1.Click
    listBox1().Items.Clear()
End Sub


Protected Overrides Sub wndproc(ByRef m As Message)
    Select Case m.Msg

        Case &H20, &H84
            ' Ignore WM_SETCURSOR, WM_NCHITTEST
            ' Because there are so many of them
        Case Else
            listBox1().Items.Add(m.ToString)

    End Select
    MyBase.WndProc(m)
End Sub
```

The form has a listbox loaded with all of the messages received by the form, except from the WM_SETCURSOR and WM_NCHITTEST (because there are so

---

6. That was our original SpyWorks-VB package. SpyWorks then continued to grow far beyond its subclassing roots.

many of them). All you need to do is override the Control base class wndproc function and handle the messages that you are interested in. Be sure to call MyBase.WndProc, however, or you will cause the form to seriously malfunction. TheMyBase.WndProc method performs the default message processing that gives every window its characteristic behavior.

True, you can't use this approach on contained controls—only on those classes you are creating yourself. But many VB6 subclassing techniques consist of subclassing your own form in order to detect top system messages sent to top-level windows. This solution performs that task handily.

You can also install a message pretranslation filter by overriding the PreProcessMessage function. This allows you to perform special handling of certain keystrokes such as tabs and arrows.

You can also use the System.Windows.Forms.Application object to add a thread message filter using the Application.AddMessageFilter method. This adds a thread-specific hook to detect messages being retrieved from the message queue for a thread. Be careful if you use this approach as it can impair performance.

I encourage you to explore the Application object further. It contains a number of useful properties and methods relating to applications including the notorious DoEvents method (which you should avoid, especially now that VB.NET supports multithreading).

In fact, our next example shows you how the Application object is used behind the scenes to make your application run.

For those of you who wish to create applications that have the ability to subclass across processes, intercept messages by hooking other processes or the entire system, or detect all keystrokes system wide, VB.NET offers no more answers than did VB6. But SpyWorks 6.5 (which should be shipping by the time you read this) has been enhanced to perform these tasks for Visual Basic.NET applications. Visit http://www.desaware.com for details.[7]

Forms and Threads

By now, I hope you've recovered from the terror I instilled in Chapter 7 about multithreading, at least to the point where you're willing to consider its use again. It's time for me to scare you again.

Just kidding.

But it is important to understand how to work with forms and controls in a multithreaded application.

---

7. Occasionally, readers are upset that I mention my software company and products in the book. Most understand that the economics of publishing are such that if I did not use the books to help promote our products, I'd never be able to afford to write in the first place.

The Threading sample project shows how to create a form in a separate thread. As usual, the code omits most of the designer generated code. During the Form1_Load event, a Label control is set to display the current thread ID for the form as shown here:

```
Private Sub Form1_Load(ByVal sender As System.Object, _
ByVal e As System.EventArgs) Handles MyBase.Load
    label1.Text = "Thread ID: " & CStr(appdomain.GetCurrentThreadId)
End Sub
```

The OtherThread variable defines a Thread object that references the OtherThreadEntryPoint in a module. When this thread is started (when button1 is clicked), a new instance of the form is created.[8] The Application.Run method is called with that form as a parameter. The Application.Run method causes the thread to enter a message-processing loop. The form is shown and messages are processed until the form is closed. The CLR automatically does this for you behind the scenes for the startup form in your application. The OtherForm1 variable holds a reference to this new form:

```
Dim OtherThread As New Thread(AddressOf OtherThreadEntryPoint)

Module UsedByThread
    Public OtherForm1 As Form1
    Public Sub OtherThreadEntryPoint()
        OtherForm1 = New Form1()
        Application.Run(OtherForm1)
    End Sub
End Module

    Private Sub button1_Click(ByVal sender As System.Object, _
        ByVal e As System.EventArgs) Handles button1.Click
        OtherThread.Start()
    End Sub
```

The ThreadIdInLabel2 method for the form displays the current thread in the label2 control:

```
Public Sub ThreadIdInLabel2()
    label2.Text = "Current Thread" & CStr(appdomain.GetCurrentThreadId)
End Sub
```

---

8. Don't click Button1 a second time. This is a simple demo and has no built-in error checking.

When button2 is clicked, the ThreadIdInLabel2 method of the OtherForm1 form is called using the following code:

```
Private Sub button2_Click(ByVal sender As System.Object, _
ByVal e As System.EventArgs) Handles button2.Click
    If Not OtherForm1 Is Nothing Then
        OtherForm1.ThreadIdInLabel2()
    End If
End Sub
```

As you will see, the new form displays the thread of the original form, not the thread for the new form.

This is bad.

The reason being that the forms package itself is not documented as being thread safe. In fact, Microsoft specifically states that you should call all methods of a form or control on the thread that created it.

Fortunately, there is an easy way to accomplish this. The Invoke method of the Control class (which is, as you recall, the base class for all forms as well as controls), correctly marshals method and subroutine calls to the control's thread. The button3 click routine shown here illustrates how you can correctly call the method. You'll see that the new form displays its own thread number when you take this approach:

```
Delegate Sub NoParams()

Private Sub button3_Click(ByVal sender As System.Object, _
ByVal e As System.EventArgs) Handles button3.Click
    If Not OtherForm1 Is Nothing Then
        Dim usedel As NoParams = AddressOf OtherForm1.ThreadIdInLabel2
        OtherForm1.Invoke(usedel)
    End If
End Sub
```

```
End Class
```

It is safe to raise events from objects in other threads. Events use invocation through delegates and will also marshal method calls to the correct thread.

You should also avoid using the SyncLock or other thread-waiting functions on threads that are managing controls or other user-interface elements. Not only does this potentially interfere with the operation of the user interface but you also run the risk of deadlock situations arising because these objects are often reentrant (for example, method calls in these objects often cause additional events or method calls to occur in the object).

Finally, you really should avoid creating forms in different threads in the first place. Very few applications benefit from a multithreaded user interface—only those where each form behaves as if it were a separate application (for example, Web browser windows typically belong in different threads, document windows do not). However, the principles shown here do apply directly to the more common case of creating a component or class in a background thread where the component needs to interact with the user interface (typically through events).

Recap

No simple lists of VB6 versus VB.NET features here—in this chapter we took a look at the architecture and, dare I say it, philosophy of the new forms package offered by the .NET Framework. You learned about the hierarchy of key objects in the System.Windows.Forms namespace and how the Control object forms the basis of all controls and forms in .NET. You saw a sample application that can help you quickly figure out which members are defined directly by any object in the namespace.

We then explored a number of changes from VB6 that represent not only feature changes but also architectural changes. You saw a way to mimic the VB6 AutoRedraw property and through it, the difference between using a form (VB6) and implementing a new Form type (VB.NET). You saw an example of form and control relationships and how they are a natural consequence of the fact that all controls in .NET are created dynamically. You saw how to implement message processing easily and how to handle threads properly when using the forms package.

Internet Applications and Services

I'D LIKE TO PAUSE FROM the normal narrative of this book to address a certain subset of readers—those who have not read the previous chapters but have instead turned directly to this chapter to find out what this book has to say about Web applications and services and why the subject is barely mentioned until near the end of the book.[1]

Yeah, I mean you—the one browsing through the book at a bookstore trying to decide whether this is a serious professional book on VB.NET or a quick shovel-ware book thrown together by some publisher trying to make a quick buck.

To answer this question, allow me to ask you one.

What Is Microsoft .NET?

The answer is simple: it depends on whom you ask.

It's just like asking someone what ActiveX is, or what COM is—or better yet, what is Windows DNA? There are lots of definitions for these, many depending on whom you ask.

Microsoft. NET suffers from the same flood of marketing white papers, technical-strategy briefing papers, media interpretations, and confusion as other Microsoft initiatives. And don't think that asking someone from Microsoft will solve the problem—their answers depend very much on whom you talk to and which PowerPoint slide deck they happen to be using at the moment.

For example, I recently got into an argument with a Microsoft marketing person who believes that Biztalk 2000 is an essential, inseparable part of Microsoft .NET.

Oh please...

Sure, it's a key part of the overall strategy that is Microsoft .NET, as are the .NET Enterprise Services (some of which are Windows DNA under a new name) and the elusive Hailstorm project. But if you're not careful, you might get the

---

1. To those of you who have stuck with me through the previous chapters, don't look at this as an excuse to skip this part. I think you'll find it entertaining and you're more likely than the others to understand it.

impression that you need all of those pieces and services in order to work with .NET—and that simply isn't true.

The way I see it, anyone reading this book is either a software developer or a manager of software developers. And from our perspective, .NET was defined in Chapter 4. It's a new virtual machine that we can program against.[2]

But what about the Internet?

From a strategic and marketing viewpoint, Microsoft .NET is an expression of Microsoft's vision of the future of the Internet—and it looks like anything they have that even remotely works with the Internet is going to have the .NET label slapped on it in one way or another. From a developer's perspective, Microsoft .NET represents a virtual machine designed to make programming the Internet as easy as traditional Windows programming.

I won't waste anymore time trying to define Microsoft .NET—even if I succeeded, I have no doubt the definition (or at least emphasis) will change by tomorrow. For us, .NET is about software development tools and architectures. Internet development is a large part of that.

The reason I haven't mentioned it until now is simple: virtually everything you have read so far in this book, with the exception of Chapter 13, applies to Internet development in VB.NET.

So, if you are a casual browser wondering why Internet development waited until now, you should, I hope, understand why you really need to go back and read the entire book—so that you'll understand the concepts that every VB.NET programmer needs to know, whether it is for the Internet or for traditional Windows programming.

Programming the Internet

Earlier in the book, I used the term "programming the Internet." How does one program the Internet?

To understand this term, you need to understand something fundamental about Microsoft's vision of the Internet. But before I explain that vision, let me stress one thing: that vision is not an inseparable part of .NET. Microsoft .NET is a tool designed to implement that vision but it will prove equally effective in implementing other visions (including, probably, some of your own).

Microsoft's vision of the Internet is actually quite simple and is based on one fundamental idea (though they would never express it this way):

The Web today sucks.

Yes, I know that sounds like blasphemy but hear me out.

---

2. I mean virtual machine in the classic computer science sense—one that describes the target for a software development environment as compared to the other usage where virtual machine describes a specific machine emulator(as is the case with the Java Virtual Machine).

Back when the Web was created, there were several document file formats that did an excellent job of rendering text and images. For example, rich-text format (RTF) was supported by most word processors and Adobe PDF could render complex documents identically on any machine. So, what did we get? HTML—a standard that can't get two pages to render exactly the same way on different browsers not to mention different versions of the same browser.[3]

Worse yet, information on Web pages is mixed up with formatting commands. If you look at a page that displays, say, stock quotes, it might be easy for you to figure out what the stock price is but it's extraordinarily difficult for a program to do so since it must parse through a morass of formatting tags to extract the information it needs. And since Web sites can change their look any time, it's virtually impossible to create a program that can read data from a Web page reliably.

Now look at programming. If you've ever seen an ASP script (Active Server Pages) up close, you'll find the most insane mishmash of data you can imagine. There's HTML ready to be served up to the client, client-scripting commands, and server-scripting commands, all mixed up in virtually any order. I've seen ASP scripts so like Spaghetti code it almost made you want to bring back the Goto command. What happened to good object-oriented programming? What happened to separating the user interface from the code so that maybe you can have graphic designers modify pages without requiring programmers to get into the act and vice versa?

Recent trends in Web development (including Microsoft .NET) are finally moving us in the right direction.

XML

XML.[4] Just say the word out loud—X-M-L. Sounds intimidating doesn't it? Sounds like something you should go out and by a big fat book on, right? In fact, you probably already have.

You may need a big book to understand all the subtleties of XML (although, I doubt it) but you surely don't need one to understand it enough to work with it. XML is simply a file format for holding data. It uses tags, much like HTML tags, except that the tags specify names of data items that you can define at will and the element between the start tag and close tag represents the value of the data.

Here's a simple example of an XML database from the SimpleXML sample directory:

---

3. I exaggerate—but only slightly.
4. Extensible Markup Language—but everybody just calls it XML.

```
<?xml version="1.0" encoding="utf-8" ?> <?xml-stylesheet type="text/xsl"
href="BillingExample.xslt"?>
<BillingTable>
    <Heading>Billing records</Heading>
    <data>
        <record>
            <name>Dan</name>
            <hours>5</hours>
            <description>First job</description>
        </record>
        <record>
            <name>Jill</name>
            <hours>3.2</hours>
            <description>Second job</description>
        </record>
    </data>
</BillingTable>
```

Does this even require an explanation? XML lets you organize data in a hierarchical manner using tags that you define to identify the data elements in the file.
This file describes billing records for individuals in a firm and could be applied
equally well to consulting firms, law firms, or any other company that bills according
to time.

XML describes the data. A special form of an XML file called an XSL[5] file
describes how that data can be viewed.

An XSL file is used to transform XML data into another form—in this case, into
HTML.[6] The BillingExample.xslt file is listed in the BillingExample.XML file as the
style sheet for the file—the file that describes how the XML file should be displayed.
Listing 14-1 shows the BillingExample.xslt file.

---

5. Extensible Stylesheet Language, or XSLT (for XSL Transform)—but everybody just calls it XSL
    or XSLT.
6. XSL can also be used to transform XML to other formats. In fact, Biztalk is based around the
    idea of using XML as an intermediate format to convert data in most any format to most any
    other format.

Listing 14-1. The BillingExample.xslt file.

```
<?xml version="1.0" encoding="UTF-8" ?>
<xsl:stylesheet version="1.0" xmlns:xsl="http://www.w3.org/1999/XSL/Transform">
    <xsl:output method="html" />
    <xsl:template match="/">
        <HTML>
            <Head>
                <Body>
                    <h1>
                        <xsl:value-of select="//BillingTable/Heading" />
                    </h1>
                    <table border="1" width="100%">
                        <xsl:for-each select="//data/record">
                            <tr>
                                <td>
                                    <xsl:value-of select="name" />
                                </td>
                                <td>
                                    <xsl:value-of select="hours" />
                                </td>
                                <td>
                                    <xsl:value-of select="description" />
                                </td>
                            </tr>
                        </xsl:for-each>
                    </table>
                </Body>
            </Head>
        </HTML>
    </xsl:template>
</xsl:stylesheet>
```

Tags that begin with the prefix xsl: represent XSL commands that are inter-preted during the transform process according to the XSL specification. All of the other tags represent HTML that is output directly. The xsl:value-of tag performs a substitution—reading data indicated by a tag from the XML file and writing it as part of the HTML output.

When you view the XML file as a Web page using Internet Explorer you get the following display:

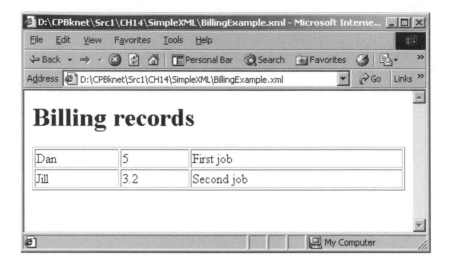

The XSL file provided the formatting tags necessary to display the XML file in the desired format.

XML is an industry standard meaning that Microsoft may influence its development but does not actually own it. Microsoft's decision to embrace and integrate XML is quite impressive considering its tradition of preferring proprietary solutions.

XML addresses the problem of separating data on the Internet from its visual presentation.

Later in this chapter, you'll learn how ASP.NET addresses the problem of separating the appearance from the functionality of a Web site as well.

Distributed Applications

Throughout this book, I've tried to focus on concepts before code. If you understand the concepts underlying the tools and languages you are using, it's relatively easy to pick up implementation details from Microsoft's documentation. When I first started thinking about this chapter, I was somewhat overwhelmed. Here again is a subject deserving of an entire book (I'm sure numerous books are being written on ASP.NET and Internet programming with VB.NET even as you read this). And here again is a subject on which I don't want to rehash material that you can (and should) read in Microsoft's documentation.

What's an author to do?

The answer came to me as I started writing sample programs. The real story of Internet programming with .NET is not in Web services or ASP.NET or XML or any specific technology—it's in the way you should be thinking about writing applications.

Consider the ways people have thought about applications in the past. Once upon a time, a program was a program—a single executable file (maybe with DLLs or overlays). Later, the buzzword was "client-server" programming—separating the user interface from the database layer of an application. Then came "three-tier client server" where you have a user-interface tier, a middle tier containing business logic, and a database tier. Naturally, you have both thick clients and thin clients, where a thick client provides a rich user interface that is sometimes difficult to deploy and distribute, and a thin client provides a poor user interface but is relatively easy to distribute.[7]

The funny thing is that each time one of these new buzzwords comes out, everyone gravitates to it as the newest and best solution for all possible problems. Publishers write dozens of tomes on the latest architecture and developers become even more confused as to how this new architecture applies to their own situations.

I finally realized that what I can really offer here—which isn't readily found in Microsoft's documentation—is a solid introduction to distributed applications as they apply to the .NET Framework.

To do so, let's explore a scenario introduced earlier in this chapter.

A fictional company needs to track hourly billing of employees. They would like to accurately and quickly track hours spent by their employees.

The following section describes how a .NET programmer might address that situation.

The .NET Way of Designing Applications

Because the focus of this chapter will be on concepts and architecture, I will keep the samples as simple as possible, focusing on the principals of each technology. We'll begin with the lowest, or database, tier.

The Database Tier

Let's assume the company has a database somewhere in which it stores the billing information. I won't even begin to discuss the implementation of the database side—that is far beyond the scope of this book. For this example, we'll model the database using a simple XML storage from a dataset.

All access to the database for billing applications will be through a component found in the BillingComponent sample directory. This particular component will

---

7. I've always found it ironic that the so-called "thin client" requires use of a browser application that is "thicker" in terms of system impact and often installation challenges than almost any traditional thick-client application.

store the data in an XML file based on a schema defined in the BillingSet.xsd file shown in Listing 14-2.

Listing 14-2. The BillingSet.xsd file.

```xml
<?xml version="1.0" encoding="utf-8" ?>
<xsd:schema id="BillingSet" targetNamespace=http://tempuri.org/BillingSet.xsd
elementFormDefault="qualified" xmlns=http://tempuri.org/BillingSet.xsd
xmlns:xsd="http://www.w3.org/2001/XMLSchema">
            <xsd:element name="BillingTable">
                <xsd:complexType>
                    <xsd:sequence>
                        <xsd:element name="Name" type="xsd:string" />
                        <xsd:element name="Hours" type="xsd:integer" />
                        <xsd:element name="Description" type="xsd:string" />
                    </xsd:sequence>
                </xsd:complexType>
            </xsd:element>
</xsd:schema>
```

An XML schema file is a file that defines the structure of a data but does not include the data itself. Each data element is strongly typed making it easy to store and retrieve data correctly from an XML file based on the schema. In this case, the schema defines three fields, the name of the employee, the number of hours worked, and a description of the project.

The BillingComponent class shown in Listing 14-3 is used for all access to the billing database. In a real application, you can use other objects to provide access to the database for different purposes. For example, you might have one object dedicated only to recording information in the database—that's the one you'll distribute to applications and components used by your employees. A second object might be used to read information from the database—your accounting department would use that one.

> **NOTE** *Modify the BillingXMLLocation constant for your sample application to define the location to store the XML file. Be sure you copy the BillingSet.xsd file to that directory before you try running any of the sample programs.*

Listing 14-3. The BillingComponent.vb file.

```vb
' Billing Component
' Copyright ©2001 by Desaware Inc. All Rights Reserved

Public Class BillingComponent

    Inherits System.ComponentModel.Component

    ' Modify this for your system
    Private Const BillingXMLLocation As String = "d:\cpbknet\src1\ch14\"

#Region " Component Designer generated code "

    Public Sub New(ByVal Container As _
    System.ComponentModel.IContainer)
        MyClass.New()

        'Required for Windows.Forms Class Composition Designer support
        Container.Add(Me)
    End Sub

    Public Sub New()
        MyBase.New()

        'This call is required by the Component Designer.
        InitializeComponent()

        'Add any initialization after the InitializeComponent() call
        OpenXML()

    End Sub

    'Required by the Component Designer
    Private components As System.ComponentModel.Container
```

```
        'NOTE: The following procedure is required by the Component Designer
        'It can be modified using the Component Designer.
        'Do not modify it using the code editor.
        <System.Diagnostics.DebuggerStepThrough()> Private Sub _
         InitializeComponent()
            '
            'BillingComponent
            '
        End Sub
    #End Region

        Private myds As New DataSet()
        Private xmllocation As String

        Public Sub OpenXML()
            Dim loc As String
            xmllocation = BillingXMLLocation
            myds.ReadXmlSchema(xmllocation & "billingset.xsd")
            Try
                myds.ReadXml(xmllocation & "BillingData.xml")
            Catch e As Exception
            End Try
            Dim t As DataTable
        End Sub

        Public Sub AddRecord(ByVal Name As String, ByVal Hours As Double, _
        ByVal Description As String)
            Dim dr As DataRow
            dr = myds.Tables(0).NewRow
            dr.Item(0) = Name
            dr.Item(1) = Hours
            dr.Item(2) = Description
            myds.Tables(0).Rows.Add(dr)
            ' We want the dataset to be up to date
            myds.AcceptChanges()
        End Sub

        Public Overloads Overrides Sub Dispose()
            MyBase.Dispose()
            myds.AcceptChanges()
            myds.WriteXml(xmllocation & "BillingData.xml", _
            XmlWriteMode.IgnoreSchema)
            myds.Dispose()
        End Sub
```

```
Public ReadOnly Property Info() As DataSet
    Get
        Return myds
    End Get
End Property
```

```
End Class
```

Let's review the important methods of this class.

The first thing the component does when it is created is to read the XML schema file and load the current database file (if one exists). The data is loaded into an ADO.NET Dataset object. This object can be retrieved using the Info property. The Dataset objects in ADO are disconnected—they contain a snapshot to the data. This may not be obvious when working with a database but it is certainly obvious here. The XML database will not be updated until it is written during the object's Dispose method. The XML database is written without the schema because the schema is already available in the XSD file.

The AddRecord method is used to add new billing records into the database.

There are two things to keep in mind with regards to this component. First, this is a simple example that represents the entire class of database access solutions for the lowest-level tier. Obviously, an XML store of this type would suffer serious synchronization problems if multiple users used it simultaneously. But it could be useful in a scenario where each person had his or her own data store (since it is unlikely one person would access the same data store from multiple applications at once).

Second, remember that all access will be through this component. This means that it is no longer necessary for the various clients of this component to be aware of the details of how the component actually stores the data or how it connects to the data store. The clients just need to know how to access the component wherever it may be located.

The BillingComponent in .NET would probably be located either on the same system as the database or on a server that is tightly coupled to the database on a local network.[8] In either case, it can be accessed by a locally installed, traditional "thick-client" application. This is the scenario we will consider next.

A Traditional Windows Application

The BillingWinApp sample application illustrates the scenario in which you distribute a thick-client application to employees on a local network. They would

---

8. You can configure the BillingComponent itself to be remotable but doing so involves a more in-depth discussion of .NET remoting than I can manage here. Besides, you'll soon see that there are better ways to accomplish the same thing.

run this application to enter billing information. The BillingWinApp sample application references the BillingComponent component directly (open the BillingWinApp solution that references both the component and the Windows application). In this example, it is on the same system—presumably, you would modify the BillingComponent to reference the database correctly wherever it may be (or you might redesign the BillingComponent to itself be remotable).

The code for this Windows application is very simple. It simply sets the dataset to be the data source for a DataGrid control as shown here:

```
Private BillingInfo As New MovingToVBNet.Billing.BillingComponent()

Private Sub Form1_Load(ByVal sender As Object, ByVal e As _
System.EventArgs) Handles MyBase.Load
    If components Is Nothing Then components = New _
    System.ComponentModel.Container()
    components.Add(BillingInfo)
    DataGrid1.DataSource = BillingInfo.Info
    DataGrid1.NavigateTo(0, "BillingTable")
    DataGrid1.CurrentRowIndex = 0
End Sub
```

The only subtle point is making sure to add the BillingInfo component to the form's components collection. Because the component does not have a designer associated with it, the Visual Studio designer doesn't manage it so the designer doesn't automatically add it to the list of components.[9] The reason you must add it to the components collection is to make sure its Dispose property is called when the form is Disposed. This is important because it is during the Dispose method that the BillingInfo component writes the updated XML file.

You can view the current contents of the database and add new entries to the database directly using the DataGrid control as shown in Figure 14-1.

So far what you've seen is analogous to a traditional, three-tier thick-client solution.

But we've only just begun.

---

9. The subject of creating .NET components is itself vast and one that will be covered thoroughly in a book being written by a good friend of mine—however, it hasn't yet been publicly announced.

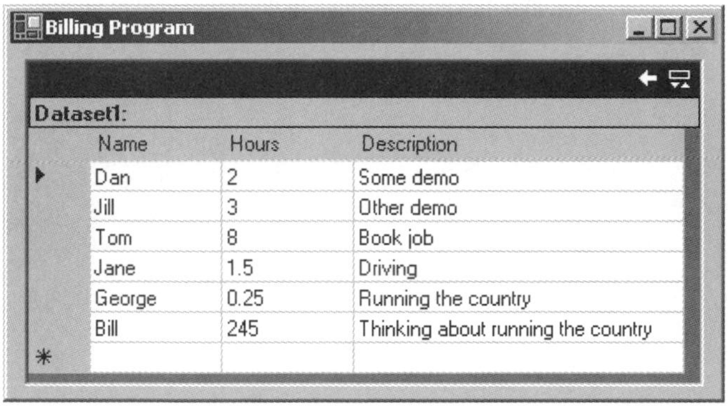

Figure 14-1. The traditional Windows version of the billing application.

A Web Application-Based Solution

Web applications represent one of the major innovations of Microsoft .NET and are based on a new version of ASP (Active Server Pages) called ASP.NET. While there are many differences between ASP and ASP.NET, perhaps the most important is that ASP.NET applications are scripted using any .NET language. In other words, you no longer use VBScript or JavaScript to write ASP.NET scripts. Actually, the terms "scripting" and "scripts" are not completely applicable. ASP.NET does not use scripting at all—it runs true .NET-compiled managed code. ASP.NET, in fact, supports full VB.NET, C#, or any other .NET language.

Whether you are an experienced ASP developer or this is the first time you've used ASP, the most important thing to remember about the .NET Internet story is this:

Visual Studio.NET is designed to make Web applications as easy to develop as traditional Windows applications.

In other words, the goal is to allow you to take all of the knowledge that you already have related to traditional, Windows VB programming and apply it directly to Internet programming.

Guess what? They largely succeeded.

When you create a Web application, you see a designer that looks very much like a Windows form. You drop controls on the form. You set properties on the controls. You double-click on the controls to add code that responds to the control's events. When you run the application, it runs just like a VB application would except that the user interface is implemented by sending HTML to a browser. Sure, the controls aren't quite as powerful as traditional Windows controls since they are mapped into the limited capabilities of HTML but, overall, the development process is identical to that of a Windows application.

Wow.

The ch14SimpleWebApp sample program offers a simple illustration of this technology.

> **NOTE** *All of the Web application and Web service samples can be found in the Webs directory on the source tree. Each directory represents a virtual directory on a server. To deploy, you'll need to create new subWebs on your server and copy the necessary files onto the virtual directories you created. It may be easiest for you to create new Web applications or Web services for each project, then simply copy the sample files provided over the default ones created in your new project (I've used this solution with success). Full deployment files (installations scripts or programs) are not provided at this time because I prefer not to risk anything that could interfere with the normal operation of your system, in view of the pre-release nature of this software.*

A Simple Web Application

Create a new Web application and place two Button controls on the form. The first one should be a Webform Button control, the other an HTML Button control (the different types of controls can be found on different tabs on the toolbar).

Right click on the HTML Button control and use the context menu to set it to run on the server.

This results in two files being created. The WebForm1.aspx file is the ASP.NET file that is referenced from a browser using the Web application. The WebForm1.aspx.vb file is the "code-behind" file—a file containing VB.NET code that processes the page.

Remember how I complained at the start of the chapter that ASP files mix client script, server script, and HTML code haphazardly? ASP.NET still allows you to do so but those using Visual Studio will find it easy to separate their user-interface HTML code from server-side code because the server code mostly exists in the code-behind file. The ASPX file containing the visual components is usually edited by dragging controls onto the designer surface and modifying their properties. You may never need to edit the ASPX file's source code manually at all.

In fact, one of the great advantages of Visual Studio (over manual coding techniques) is that you can remain largely ignorant of the tags and HTML generated—allowing Visual Studio to do all the work of connecting events and properties to the controls.

Nevertheless, let's take a quick look at the Webform1.aspx file shown in Listing 14-4.

Listing 14-4. The Webform1.aspx file.

```
<%@ Page Language="vb" AutoEventWireup="false" Codebehind="WebForm1.aspx.vb"
Inherits="ch14SimpleWebApp.WebForm1"%>
<!DOCTYPE HTML PUBLIC "-//W3C//DTD HTML 4.0 Transitional//EN">
<HTML>
  <HEAD>
    <meta name="GENERATOR" content="Microsoft Visual Studio.NET 7.0">
    <meta name="CODE_LANGUAGE" content="Visual Basic 7.0">
    <meta name=vs_defaultClientScript content="JavaScript">
    <meta name=vs_targetSchema content="http://schemas.microsoft.com/intellisense/ie5">
    </HEAD>
    <body>
        <form id="Form1" method="post" runat="server">
            <P>
                <INPUT type=button value=HtmlButton
                        id=HTMLButton name=Button1 runat="server">
            </P>
            <asp:Button id=WebControlButton runat="server"
                  Text="WebControlButton">
            </asp:Button>
        </form>
  </body>
</HTML>
```

As you can see, the ASPX file consists mostly of regular HTML along with some server-side tags prefixed with asp.

Listing 14-5 shows the code-behind module, Webform1.aspx.vb.

Listing 14-5. The Webform1.aspx.vb file.

```
Public Class WebForm1
    Inherits System.Web.UI.Page
    Protected WithEvents HTMLButton As _
    System.Web.UI.HtmlControls.HtmlInputButton
    Protected WithEvents WebControlButton As System.Web.UI.WebControls.Button

#Region " Web Form Designer Generated Code "

    'This call is required by the Web Form Designer.
    <System.Diagnostics.DebuggerStepThrough()> Private Sub _
    InitializeComponent()

    End Sub
```

```
    Protected Sub Page_Init(ByVal Sender As System.Object, _
    ByVal e As System.EventArgs) Handles MyBase.Init
        'CODEGEN: This method call is required by the Web Form Designer
        'Do not modify it using the code editor.
        InitializeComponent()
    End Sub

#End Region

    Private Sub Page_Load(ByVal sender As System.Object, _
    ByVal e As System.EventArgs) Handles MyBase.Load
        'Put user code to initialize the page here
    End Sub

    Private Sub HTMLButton_ServerClick(ByVal sender As System.Object, _
    ByVal e As System.EventArgs) Handles HtmlButton.ServerClick
        Page.Response.Write("HTML Button was clicked")
    End Sub

    Private Sub WebControlButton_Click(ByVal sender As Object, _
    ByVal e As System.EventArgs) Handles WebControlButton.Click
        Page.Response.Write("Web control button was clicked")
    End Sub
End Class
```

The remarkable thing about this code is that it is virtually identical to a VB.NET Windows application form. The biggest difference is that it inherits from System.Web.UI.Page instead of System.Windows.Forms.Form. Otherwise, controls are defined in a similar manner.

When the browser requests a Web page, ASP.NET takes care of creating the WebForm1 class. ASP.NET calls the Page_Init and Page_Load methods and any others you choose to override in your implementation. It raises events based on the information received during the Page event.[10] It sets all of the properties of objects (such as the controls you use) and, in fact, takes care of storing those properties so that they remain valid as long as a session is valid even across multiple page requests.

How does it do this?

I don't care and neither should you. That's the magic that ASP.NET does for you and the reason .NET makes Web application programming easy.

One of the nice things about Web controls is that they can be designed to take into account the browser being used. The HTML code they generate can be basic

---

10. Events are not raised until the user takes an action that submits a request to the Web application. Then they are raised as defined in the online documentation with the event that caused the submission raised last.

platform-independent HTML—so that even though you are using Microsoft technology on the server, you can create HTML that is compatible with any browser.

At the beginning of this section, I had you drop two different button controls on the ASP.NET designer, one from the HTML group in the Toolbox window and one from the Web Forms group in the Toolbox window. These represent two different types of controls you can use with ASP.NET applications. There are a number of differences documented between HTML controls and Web controls. HTML controls map directly to HTML elements while Web controls provide a higher level of abstraction and functionality. But the main difference between them can be seen if you open the aspx page in a traditional Web page editor like Microsoft FrontPage.[11]

You'll only see the HTML button.

You see, standard HTML tags describe HTML controls. Web controls like the Button control are defined by special tags (in this case, the asp:Button tag) that aren't recognized by other HTML editors. The Visual Studio Web form editor recognizes these tags and correctly renders Web controls on the form.

If you make use of outside designers who prefer to use their own HTML editors, you will probably want to stick with HTML controls most of the time. When you use Web controls, you'll need to provide them with the tags to use so they can enter them manually. You'll need to coordinate the space needed by the Web control with the designers so they can take it into account.

This actually brings up a potentially important aspect of Web application development with Visual Studio.

Web applications with Visual Studio are clearly designed for programmers. They make it possible to quickly program complex Web applications with minimal training (once you know .NET programming in general—which is a substantial task as you well know). But the vast number of Web designers who rely on traditional client-side tools will not welcome this approach quickly. Many Web developers have little or no programming background and are accustomed to using non-Microsoft tools like Dreamweaver.[12] You can bet that they have no interest in doing their development in the Visual Studio Web page editor, which is, frankly, functional but not spectacular. At this time, none of the non-Microsoft HTML editors (that I know of) have announced integration with Visual Studio.

It will be fascinating to see how things develop. Will Web designers learn Visual Studio? Will Web application developers truly separate their UI and code development? It is far too soon to anticipate the best way to integrate the two approaches. However, I would be thrilled to hear of your success stories (or failures) in this regard.[13]

---

11. You'll need to rename the Webform1.aspx file to Webform1.asp in order to open it in FrontPage and possibly other Web page editors as well.

12. Many of them truly despise FrontPage.

13. Please email me at dan@apress.com if you'd care to share your own war stories.

The BillingInfo Web Application

The CH14WebBilling sample directory contains the WebBilling Web application. This Web application demonstrates the case where our fictional service company wants to allow employees to record their time using a Web browser across the Internet.

Figure 14-2 shows the layout of the form in the Visual Studio Webform Designer window. There are three Text controls for entering the billing information. There is a Validator control to make sure the number of hours is between 0.1 and 200 (the message you see on the screen will only appear if an attempt is made to enter an invalid value).

There are two Label controls that display the most recent entry and the one before it—the example actually uses this to demonstrate how you can store additional data in the Session object. A DataGrid control displays the current content of the billing database but unlike the Windows forms version, does not permit editing the database in the control.

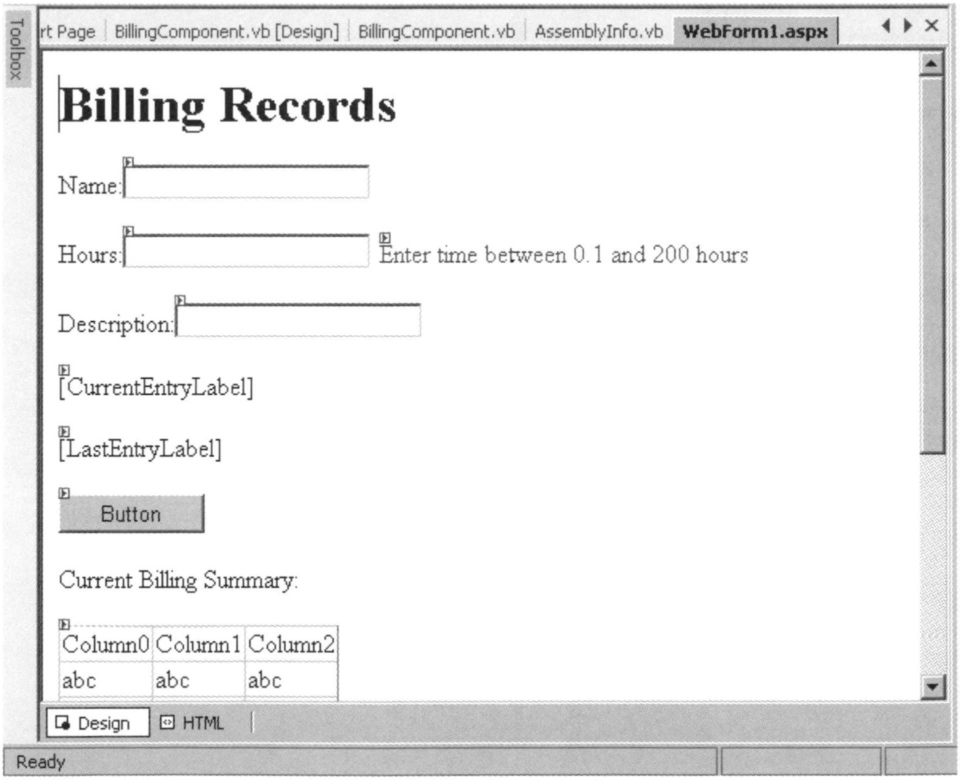

Figure 14-2. Visual Studio designer view of the WebBilling form.

Listing 14-6 shows the Visual Basic code behind the .aspx file.

Listing 14-6. The code behind the VB module for the WebBilling application.

```vb
Public Class WebForm1
    Inherits System.Web.UI.Page
    Protected WithEvents txtName As System.Web.UI.WebControls.TextBox
    Protected WithEvents txtHours As System.Web.UI.WebControls.TextBox
    Protected WithEvents txtDescription As System.Web.UI.WebControls.TextBox
    Protected WithEvents DataGrid1 As System.Web.UI.WebControls.DataGrid
    Protected WithEvents LastEntryLabel As System.Web.UI.WebControls.Label
    Protected WithEvents CurrentEntryLabel As System.Web.UI.WebControls.Label
    Protected WithEvents RangeValidator1 As _
    System.Web.UI.WebControls.RangeValidator
    Protected WithEvents cmdAddEntry As System.Web.UI.WebControls.Button


#Region " Web Form Designer Generated Code "

    'This call is required by the Web Form Designer.
    <System.Diagnostics.DebuggerStepThrough()> Private Sub _
     InitializeComponent()

    End Sub

    Protected Sub Page_Init(ByVal Sender As System.Object, _
    ByVal e As System.EventArgs) Handles MyBase.Init
        'CODEGEN: This method call is required by the Web Form Designer
        'Do not modify it using the code editor.
        InitializeComponent()
    End Sub

#End Region

    Private BillingInfo As MovingToVBNet.Billing.BillingComponent

    Private LastEntryInfo As String
```

```vbnet
Private Sub Page_Load(ByVal sender As System.Object, _
ByVal e As System.EventArgs) Handles MyBase.Load
    BillingInfo = New MovingToVBNet.Billing.BillingComponent()
    Dim dv As New DataView(BillingInfo.Info.Tables(0))
    DataGrid1.DataSource = dv
    DataGrid1.DataBind()
    If Page.IsPostBack Then
        LastEntryInfo = Ctype(Session("LastEntry"),String)
        LastEntryLabel.Text = "Prior entry: " & LastEntryInfo
    End If
End Sub

Private Sub cmdAddEntry_Click(ByVal sender As System.Object, _
ByVal e As System.EventArgs) Handles cmdAddEntry.Click
    BillingInfo.AddRecord(txtName.Text, Cint(txtHours.Text), _
    txtDescription.Text)
    Session("LastEntry") = txtName.Text & ": " & txtHours.Text & _
    " hours - " & txtDescription.Text
    CurrentEntryLabel.Text = "Current entry: " & txtName.Text & _
    ": " & txtHours.Text & " hours - " & txtDescription.Text
    txtHours.Text = ""
    txtDescription.Text = ""

    ' Update grid
    Dim dv As New DataView(BillingInfo.Info.Tables(0))
    DataGrid1.DataSource = dv
    DataGrid1.DataBind()
End Sub

Protected Overrides Sub Render(ByVal writer As _
System.Web.UI.HtmlTextWriter)
    MyBase.Render(writer)
    writer.WriteLine("Here is some extra text ")
End Sub

Private Sub WebForm1_Unload(ByVal sender As Object, _
ByVal e As System.EventArgs) Handles MyBase.Unload
    BillingInfo.Dispose()
End Sub

End Class
```

There are a number of interesting aspects to this code:

- Control objects are defined just as they are within traditional Windows applications.

- During the Page_Load event, an instance of the BillingComponent class is created. An ADO DataView is created for the BillingTable table and set as the data source for the DataGrid control. This control requires that the DataBind method be called to bind the control to the data.

- The Page.IsPostBack property lets you determine if the page has been loaded due to a form submission or if it is the first call to the page.

- The Session variable can be used to store session information for the page or to share among pages in the same application.

- You can override the Render method to generate additional HTML to the page.

The Web application approach offers our fictional service company a great tool for helping employees keep record of their hours as long as they have Web access. But this still remains only a first step in considering the possibilities offered by .NET.

A WebService-Based Solution

Say that our fictional service company decided to also implement the billing solution as a Web service. A Web service is essentially a way of exposing an object through the Web. Unlike a Web application, it has no associated user interface—just methods and properties.

The WebBillingService solution in the CH14WebBillingService directory illustrates how the methods of the original BillingComponent are exposed through a Web service.

The code for the WebBillingService class is shown in Listing 14-7. It is so trivial as to be hardly worth mentioning. The only difference between it and a regular Windows component is that it inherits from System.Web.Services.WebService and some of its methods have the attribute WebMethod().

Listing 14-7. The WebBillingService class.

```vb
Imports System.Web.Services

Public Class WebBillingService
    Inherits System.Web.Services.WebService

#Region " Web Services Designer Generated Code "

    Public Sub New()
        MyBase.New()

        'This call is required by the Web Services Designer.
        InitializeComponent()

        'Add your own initialization code after the _
         InitializeComponent() call

    End Sub

    'Required by the Web Services Designer
    Private components As System.ComponentModel.Container

    'NOTE: The following procedure is required by the Web Services Designer
    'It can be modified using the Web Services Designer.
    'Do not modify it using the code editor.
    <System.Diagnostics.DebuggerStepThroughAttribute()> _
    Private Sub InitializeComponent()
        components = New System.ComponentModel.Container()
    End Sub

    Overloads Overrides Sub Dispose()
        'CODEGEN: This procedure is required by the Web Services Designer
        'Do not modify it using the code editor.
    End Sub
```

```
#End Region

    Dim BillInfo As MovingToVBNet.Billing.BillingComponent

    <WebMethod()> Public Sub AddBillingRecord(ByVal Name As String, _
    ByVal hours As Double, ByVal Description As String)
        BillInfo = New MovingToVBNet.Billing.BillingComponent()
        BillInfo.AddRecord(Name, hours, Description)
        BillInfo.Dispose()
    End Sub

    <WebMethod()> Public Function GetBillingInfo() As DataSet
        BillInfo = New MovingToVBNet.Billing.BillingComponent()
        Return (BillInfo.Info)
    End Function

End Class
```

If you run this service in the Visual Studio environment, you will obtain a browser view of the Web service that provides you with a great deal of information about the service[14]. It will list all of the methods and properties exposed by the Web service. It will show you sample syntax of how you can invoke any of the methods or properties of the Web service using SOAP, HTTP Get, or HTTP Post commands. It will even allow you to invoke methods or properties directly as long as they are simple enough to invoke using a simple HTTP Get command.

Because the requests ride on the HTTP protocol, these services can be hosted on any IIS-based Web server that permits it. Since most firewalls have openings for HTTP requests (all public Web servers must have that opening), one of the biggest problems relating to remote access is solved.

This gives you the information you'll need to use the Web service from any application or component that can make an HTTP request. If you are using the Web service from within a Visual Studio application, the process is even easier.

Thinking Distributed

Client-Server, Three Tier, Distributed—all are terms for solution architectures. Microsoft .NET does not add a new term to this array, rather it suggests a new way to look at distributed applications. Current approaches suggest the need to choose a single architecture for your solution. This actually puts quite a bit of pressure on the solution architect since an error can result in poor performance and lost time

---

14. Running the service in Visual Studio simply views the ASMX file in a browser. You can also right click on the ASMX file in the Solution window and select "View in Browser".

and money. The .NET approach represents a different way of looking at architectures. Instead of choosing and committing to a particular architecture, you create components, then deploy them in various ways to find not one but possibly many optimal solutions.

In our billing example, the key decision was to create a BillingComponent that would handle the database connection. With this component, it became trivial to create a thick client for use on the local network. It also became easy to create a Web application for remote access through a browser.

The BillingWinAppWeb sample directory shows how a thick-client application can consume a Web service simply by adding a Web reference to the project. Doing so immediately makes all of the objects and their members available to the Windows application as if it were a component on the local machine. All of the work needed to serialize objects and marshal method and property calls to and from the Web service are handled automatically. Thus, we have come full circle, with Web services enabling the use of remote, thick-client applications without the complexities of DCOM or concern about firewalls.

But that's not all.

Consider some of the applications that are made possible by the existence of Web services:

- You can create a wireless application for PDAs or cell phones, which allows you to enter billing information quickly and using a simple HTTP request, send that information by invoking a method on the Web service.

- You can create a Word macro that keeps track of how long a document is open. Before you close it, the macro prompts you for a description, then sends the amount of time the file was open to the database by accessing the Web service.

- If your cell phone software was sophisticated enough, it could record the length of each phone call and, using a Web service, record the length of the call and the phone number called into the database.

- You can take the Web form defined for the billing Web application and turn it into a Web control. This control can be dropped onto other Web pages so that employees can record time spent even as they browse through other parts of the corporate Web site.

- You can create a Windows form-based control and deploy it as a thick client in a browser (just as you would host ActiveX controls in COM). This control would use the Web service to provide a rich user interface within a browser while still using the same Web service.

In other words, the service company can largely automate the previously tedious and inaccurate process of collecting work statistics to provide accurate billing information automatically.[15]

Microsoft has a vision of the Web changing from its current form—in which Web sites primarily serve up information in humanly readable form—to one where Web sites serve up functionality. The Web, in their eyes, will become a network of computers providing objects that offer defined functionality.

It is far too early to know if this vision is an accurate one. Surely there are some cases where it will make sense. A company such as Federal Express would be highly motivated to offer a Web service that performs a tracking function so that other Web sites can integrate tracking into their site without requiring their users jump to the FedEx Web site. But it's not clear where the other business models will be or how widespread they will become.

Regardless of whether public Web services become the wave of the future, there is no doubt that Web services will provide a valuable tool for many enterprise applications as a foundation for distributed applications.

Perhaps that is the real Internet story for .NET: instead of choosing one architecture for your solution, you can choose them all—deploying multiple solutions simultaneously with Web services acting as the glue that binds the various components together.

When you design a .NET solution to a problem, your focus should be less on the architecture you will end up using and more on how you will componentize your solution. If you define a flexible set of components to solve your application, you will find that you end up with enormous flexibility in how they are ultimately deployed. For example, if you find that network bandwidth is a problem between the database and a Business object, you can easily reposition it to the server or try different remoting channels that might be more efficient.

A Quick Aside with Winsock

There is more to the .NET Internet story than the higher-level Web applications and Web services. .NET provides a nice class for working directly with Winsock.

Listing 14-8 shows a simple application designed to probe the ports of a computer. Both hackers and security experts often use this kind of tool to try to find vulnerabilities on a computer.

---

15. Whether employees would be pleased to have "big brother" recording their actions to this degree is another issue entirely. Remember, just because you *can* do something doesn't necessarily mean you *should*.

Listing 14-8. The Probe sample application.

```
Imports System.Net
Public Class ProbeForm
    Inherits System.Windows.Forms.Form

#Region " Windows Form Designer generated code "

    Public Sub New()
        MyBase.New()

        'This call is required by the Windows Form Designer.
        InitializeComponent()

        'Add any initialization after the InitializeComponent() call
    End Sub

    'Form overrides dispose to clean up the component list.
    Public Overloads Overrides Sub Dispose()
        MyBase.Dispose()
        If Not (components Is Nothing) Then
            components.Dispose()
        End If
    End Sub
    ' Allow access to UI elements from other thread.
    Friend WithEvents listBox1 As System.Windows.Forms.ListBox
    Friend WithEvents txtIP As System.Windows.Forms.TextBox
    Private WithEvents cmdProbe As System.Windows.Forms.Button
    Private WithEvents label1 As System.Windows.Forms.Label
    Friend WithEvents statusBar1 As System.Windows.Forms.StatusBar

    'Required by the Windows Form Designer
    Private components As System.ComponentModel.Container

    'NOTE: The following procedure is required by the Windows Form Designer
    'It can be modified using the Windows Form Designer.
    'Do not modify it using the code editor.
    <System.Diagnostics.DebuggerStepThrough()> Private Sub InitializeComponent()
        Me.txtIP = New System.Windows.Forms.TextBox()
        Me.cmdProbe = New System.Windows.Forms.Button()
        Me.label1 = New System.Windows.Forms.Label()
        Me.listBox1 = New System.Windows.Forms.ListBox()
        Me.statusBar1 = New System.Windows.Forms.StatusBar()
        Me.SuspendLayout()
        '
```

```
'txtIP
'
Me.txtIP.Location = New System.Drawing.Point(88, 16)
Me.txtIP.Name = "txtIP"
Me.txtIP.Size = New System.Drawing.Size(184, 20)
Me.txtIP.TabIndex = 1
Me.txtIP.Text = ""
'
'cmdProbe
'
Me.cmdProbe.Location = New System.Drawing.Point(112, 48)
Me.cmdProbe.Name = "cmdProbe"
Me.cmdProbe.Size = New System.Drawing.Size(64, 24)
Me.cmdProbe.TabIndex = 3
Me.cmdProbe.Text = "Probe"
'
'label1
'
Me.label1.Location = New System.Drawing.Point(32, 16)
Me.label1.Name = "label1"
Me.label1.Size = New System.Drawing.Size(56, 23)
Me.label1.TabIndex = 2
Me.label1.Text = "IP:"
Me.label1.TextAlign = System.Drawing.ContentAlignment.MiddleRight
'
'listBox1
'
Me.listBox1.Location = New System.Drawing.Point(16, 88)
Me.listBox1.Name = "listBox1"
Me.listBox1.Size = New System.Drawing.Size(256, 160)
Me.listBox1.TabIndex = 0
'
'statusBar1
'
Me.statusBar1.BackColor = System.Drawing.SystemColors.Control
Me.statusBar1.Location = New System.Drawing.Point(0, 253)
Me.statusBar1.Name = "statusBar1"
Me.statusBar1.Size = New System.Drawing.Size(292, 20)
Me.statusBar1.TabIndex = 5
Me.statusBar1.Text = "statusBar1"
'
'ProbeForm
'
```

```
            Me.AutoScaleBaseSize = New System.Drawing.Size(5, 13)
            Me.ClientSize = New System.Drawing.Size(292, 273)
            Me.Controls.AddRange(New System.Windows.Forms.Control() _
            {Me.statusBar1, Me.cmdProbe, Me.label1, Me.txtIP, Me.listBox1})
            Me.Name = "ProbeForm"
            Me.Text = "port prober"
            Me.ResumeLayout(False)

        End Sub



#End Region
        Private ProbingThread As Threading.Thread
        Private ProberClass As SocketProber


        Private Sub cmdProbe_Click(ByVal sender As System.Object, _
        ByVal e As System.EventArgs) Handles cmdProbe.Click
            If cmdProbe().Text = "Stop" Then
                ProberClass.StopTheThread = True
                ProbingThread.Join()
                cmdProbe().Text = "Probe"
                ProbingThread = Nothing
                ProberClass = Nothing
                Exit Sub
            End If
            ProberClass = New SocketProber()
            ProberClass.TheForm = Me
            ProbingThread = New System.Threading.Thread(New _
            Threading.ThreadStart(AddressOf ProberClass.SubThreadEntry))
            cmdProbe().Text = "Stop"
            ProbingThread.Start()
        End Sub

    Friend Function GetIP() As String
            Return txtIP.Text
        End Function

    Friend Sub SetStatus(ByVal s As String)
            Me.statusBar1.Text = s
        End Sub
```

```
      Friend Sub AddToList(ByVal s As String)
          listBox1.Items.Add(s)
      End Sub
End Class


Delegate Function fNoParams() As String
Delegate Sub fSetString(ByVal s As String)


Class SocketProber
      Friend TheForm As ProbeForm
      Friend StopTheThread As Boolean
      Public Sub SubThreadEntry()
          Dim s As Sockets.Socket
          Dim ip As IPAddress
          Dim ep As IPEndPoint
          Dim textfp As fNoParams = AddressOf TheForm.GetIP

          ip = IPAddress.Parse(CStr(TheForm.Invoke(textfp)))
          Dim portnumber As Integer
          For portnumber = 1 To &H7FFF
              Dim fpstat As fSetString = AddressOf TheForm.SetStatus
              TheForm.Invoke(fpstat, New String() {"Checking port: " & _
              Str(portnumber)})
              ep = New IPEndPoint(ip, portnumber)
              s = New Sockets.Socket(Sockets.AddressFamily.InterNetwork, _
              Sockets.SockelType.Stream, Sockets.ProtocolType.Tcp)
              Try
                  s.Connect(ep)
                  Dim plist As fSetString = AddressOf TheForm.AddToList
                  TheForm.Invoke(plist, New String() {"Connected to port " & _
                  Str(portnumber)})
              Catch ex As Exception
                  debug.WriteLine("Failed port " & Str(portnumber) & " - " & _
                  ex.Message)
              End Try

              s.Close()
              If StopTheThread Then Exit Sub ' Request to terminate
          Next
      End Sub


End Class
```

The sample performs the probing on a separate thread to avoid interfering with the performance of the user interface. Some of the interesting features of this application include:

- The ipaddress.Parse method offers a great way to convert a text form IP address into an IPAddress structure.

- Note how access to the form from the background thread is correctly called using the Invoke method rather than through direct access. Remember what you learned in Chapter 13—forms are not thread safe.

A Guest Commentary

Occasionally, believe it or not, people ask me whether I actually write my own books. Rest assured, I do indeed write my books—I even draw every illustration (though a professional graphic artist is usually needed to make them look clean and nice).

However, I do occasionally welcome additional contributions. I have been fortunate for this book to have a fantastic technical editor by the name of Scott Stabbert. Scott works at Microsoft and is currently involved working closely with the development team to generate .NET training material and sample code (the kind of things you see when Microsoft people do their presentations or training). He is especially focused on the .NET Web story so I asked him to share a few words about his perception of .NET on the Web. Here it is with only minor editing.

> Web controls are very, very important for one big reason. But to appreciate it, you'll first have to get into the Way-Back machine and revisit the launch of VB3. Why did VB become so popular? There were a few good reasons but the VBX was the biggie. The third-party control market coming out with widgets and gadgets seemingly every week was enough to make a VB programmer giddy with delight with every issue of *Visual Basic Programmers Journal*. Now, some of those controls were great—"insanely great" (as our friend Mr. Jobs likes to say). And some, well, sucked. People bought the good ones and the bad ones went away.[16]
>
> Now pop forward a few decades (seems like that long, at least) to the mid to late '90s when tools like Visual InterDev with its Design Time Controls, FrontPage, and other tools appeared. These tools write

---

16. A quick aside here (this is Dan again)—my company, Desaware, launched our first product in the days of VB1, and while I'm far too modest to mention the quality of controls at this point, allow me to point out that *we're still here!*

code for you. The code works—but just try changing it to do what *you* want. Wizard generated code never does exactly what you want. Often, tool-generated sites have the look of a cookie cutter site—they are nice and fast to generate, but you can tell. Strict professionals generally write every line of code by hand because their requirements cannot be kicked out by a tool. In many cases, the code generated by these tools and others are not maintainable, editable, and, in some cases, usable. But I digress.

Now, step into the twenty-first century. Web controls are the Internet's equivalent to the VBX/OCX control. There will be insanely great ones written—maybe you'll write one. And there will be bad ones. Largely, the quality will be judged by the quality of the HTML/DHTML and client script that they produce. Do they intelligently change their output based on the make of browser hitting the site or based on the fact that it's a cell phone using WAP (Wireless Application Protocol) that is requesting the page?

Web Control architecture is designed to promote "lookless" output that can then be given a look and feel by the developer using the control. Web controls can use templates that get around the problems of cookie cutter HTML output. This is another level where the interface has been separated from the implementation. The control writer defines the control's functionality but the developer using the control can manage the look and feel of the HTML outputted by the control.

Web controls can (like any other .NET control) be inherited by controls you create and their behavior modified if needed.

Web Controls, like their VBX/OCX cousins, will hopefully generate a very robust third-party market, which is great for those companies and especially great for every VB programmer who wants to write cool Web applications.

There are quite a number of control developers that are feverishly working on their controls so they will be ready when .NET hits the streets and *you*, as a part of the VB developer community, are going to benefit from it. The marketplace will reward the good controls and punish the bad ones (or so we can only hope) and the ASP.NET Framework will become more powerful and easier to use with every control published.

Thank you, Scott.

Frankly, I'm not sure he's right about this. Oh, I fully agree with the power of Web controls. But the business case is too soon to say—though I don't doubt that many component vendors will offer Web controls and some will certainly be successful. Of course, Desaware has long since left the business of generic user-interface widgets— we prefer to solve trickier and less obvious problems. But who knows? Maybe we'll do a few Web controls as well. Stay tuned…

Recap

This chapter focused more on architecture and concepts than on specific implementations. You learned that XML and XSL are actually remarkably simple
concepts—and that all the fuss over them is not due to their complexity but rather
to their very simplicity and elegance. You then saw how proper componentization
of a solution enabled the creation of a truly distributed application. You saw how
the components could be deployed in many different ways, from traditional,
single system, thick applications to Web applications and Web services. You also
saw that this distributed approach along with the consistent .NET architecture
that applies to all of these approaches offers long-term flexibility to integrate different systems and technologies as they become available—even technologies
offered by companies other that Microsoft.

COM Interop and Accessing the Win32 API

ONCE UPON A TIME there was a programmer. This programmer had written many programs over the years and they worked rather well. One day, the spirit of the great OS appeared before him and presented a brand new way of programming—one that would allow the programmer to write many more programs that would work even better than before.

But the poor programmer looked at the new OS and realized that it would take many years for him to convert his previous programs (which worked rather well) to the new OS (besides, he was really more interested in cashing out what was left of his options and going sailing for a few years than in spending the next two decades porting code). And he saw there were still a few things the new OS couldn't do that he would still have to do the old way.

However, the great OS spirit appeared before him and gave him a magic lamp. He rubbed the magic lamp and a giant blue genie appeared who sang very funny songs to Disney music. The genie magically ported all of the existing code to the new OS. The genie also gave the programmer a magic ring that would cause new classes to spontaneously appear anytime the programmer needed some functionality that was missing from the OS.

The programmer went home at promptly 5:00 P.M., cashed in his remaining stock options, and went to Disney World (having been given some free tickets by the giant blue genie).

And he lived happily ever after.

Alas, if only it were so....

Unfortunately, Disney holds the copyright on giant blue genies so Microsoft was unable to provide us with a way to port all of our existing COM-based applications and components to .NET. All of the magic rings have been allocated to the upcoming Lord of the Rings movie.[1] So, vast as the .NET class library is, there still remain tasks it cannot accomplish. Fortunately, Microsoft did the next best thing. They invested a huge effort to make sure that new .NET programs can continue to use COM components and that they can call the underlying Win32 API calls. The former is accomplished through a feature called COM Interoperability (interop,

---

1. With which I have no connection whatsoever but am eagerly awaiting.

for short). The latter, through a feature called Platform Invoke (P-Invoke). Most of the objects and attributes I'll be referring to in this chapter can be found in the System.Runtime.InteropServices namespace.

Though these are really two different features, they are nevertheless closely related because both involve leaving the .NET Framework to work with unmanaged code.[2]

COM Interop

COM interop is the part of the .NET Framework that has to do with interoperability of existing COM components and applications with .NET components and applications. When thinking about COM interop, there are two key ideas to keep in mind:

- .NET components can only work directly with other .NET components. The .NET components all exist in memory that is managed by the CLR and are all garbage collected when they are no longer referenced by root-level variables.

- COM components can only work directly with other COM components. They all work with a specific low-level implementation that involves the use of tables of virtual pointers. COM components are reference counted— every reference to a COM object must increment a reference count. When the reference is freed, it must decrement the reference count. When the reference count reaches zero, the object is freed.

The .NET interop system acts as a gateway between .NET components and COM components. It makes a COM component look like a .NET component to other .NET objects. It makes .NET components look like COM components to other COM objects. This is illustrated in Figure 15-1.

When a .NET object wishes to use a COM object, it uses a Runtime Callable Wrapper (RCW). This is a .NET assembly that makes a COM object look like a regular .NET object.

When a COM object wishes to use a .NET object, the runtime creates a COM Callable Wrapper (CCW) that looks and works just like a COM object.

COM interop works in both directions. Yet, it seems clear that the direction of .NET objects calling COM objects is the most important one given that there are a vast array of COM objects in existence and very few .NET objects. Obviously, new .NET objects will have to work with COM but how often are people likely to create .NET objects that are used by existing COM objects? My suspicion is that this will be a relatively rare occurrence except, perhaps, for transactional components that

---

2. Code that is not managed by the .NET Framework.

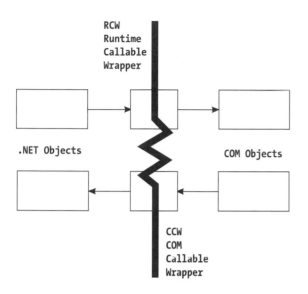

Figure 15-1. Illustration of COM interop.

are meant to work out of process (most components will just inherit from System.EnterpriseServices.ServicedComponent). Nevertheless, it is important for COM objects to be able to call into .NET objects because .NET applications will regularly need to expose their own objects to be used by COM-based systems.

I won't try to cover all of the intricacies of COM interop here. For one thing, it's not really necessary. While the COM interop documentation goes into a great deal of detail of every possible situation, most of you will only need to be concerned with interop scenarios that meet both of the following criteria:

- You'll be using Visual Studio rather than all of the framework tools whenever possible.

- Virtually all of the COM objects you'll be using are the same ones you are accustomed to using—those that are VB6-compatible. This means that all of the objects you'll be working with are automation-compatible and have dual interfaces (a direct interface and an IDispatch-based automation interface).[3]

I will be ignoring issues that fall outside of the scope of this scenario since it probably covers 95% (or more) of the situations you'll face.

Let's begin by looking at the .NET to COM direction.

---

3. Unfortunately, a tutorial of COM is beyond the scope of this book. If you are unfamiliar with COM, you can still follow the discussion—just ignore COM-based terms such as automation and IDispatch that you don't understand. If you really want to learn about COM from a VB perspective, consider my book *Developing COM/ActiveX Components with Visual Basic 6: A Guide to the Perplexed* (Que, 1998).

Calling COM Objects from .NET

Accessing COM objects from Visual Basic.NET is remarkably easy. All you need to do is the following:

1. Make sure the COM object you wish to use is registered.

2. Select Add-References in the Project menu or Solution Explorer window.

3. Select the COM tab, then select the desired object.

When you add a reference to a COM component from Visual Studio, it will prompt you to create a Primary Assembly (RCW) for the COM component based on the component's type library. This occurs when an RCW assembly is not already registered for a COM component in the global assembly cache. When you answer yes to the prompt, Visual Studio will create the RCW and place it in the build directory where it can be accessed by your project.[4]

The VB6 COM sample project contains a simple VB6 ActiveX DLL defined using the following code:

```
' Sample of component accessed from .NET
' Copyright ©2001 by Desaware Inc. All Rights Reserved
Option Explicit

Private Declare Function GetCurrentThreadId Lib "kernel32" () As Long

Public Function TimesTwo(ByVal x As Long) As Long
    TimesTwo = x * 2
End Function

Public Function TrimString(ByVal s As String) As String
    TrimString = Trim(s)
End Function

Public Function GetThisThreadId() As Long
    GetThisThreadId = GetCurrentThreadId()
End Function
```

You'll need to register the dwComFromDotNet.dll component to call it from VB.NET. Rebuilding the DLL or using the RegSvr32 program can also accomplish this.

---

4. This discussion will focus on local assemblies only. If you wish to create an RCW assembly to be deployed in the global assembly cache, use the TLBImp utility described in the framework documentation to create a signed RCW. You'll read more about deployment issues in Chapter 16.

Once the RCW assembly is created, it is accessed from the UsesCOM1 project as shown in Listing 15-1.

Listing 15-1. The UsesCOM1 sample project.

```
' Example of calling COM from VB.NET
' Copyright ©2001 by Desaware Inc. All Rights Reserved
Imports System.Threading
Module Module1
    ' The name of the component exposed to .NET includes the component name and
    '   type library version number
    Dim ComObject As New dwComFromDotnet.SampleClass1

    Sub FromAlternateThread()
        Dim tid As Long
        tid = ComObject.GetThisThreadId()
        Console.WriteLine("From other thread, TID = " & Str(tid))
    End Sub


    Sub Main()
        Dim newThread As New Thread(AddressOf FromAlternateThread)
        Dim tid As Long
        newThread.Start()
        tid = ComObject.GetThisThreadId()
        Console.WriteLine("From main thread, TID = " & Str(tid))
        Console.WriteLine(ComObject.TimesTwo(5))
        Console.WriteLine(ComObject.TrimString("    to trim    "))
        newThread.Join()
        Console.ReadLine()

    End Sub

End Module
```

As you can see, the COM object is created just as if it were a .NET object. The result when you run the program is as follows:[5]

```
From main thread, TID =  1692
10
to trim
From other thread, TID =  1692
```

---

5. The thread number will, of course, vary. The line "From other thread" may appear at different locations in the results depending on the interaction between threads.

It is interesting to note here that the framework automatically sees to it that the correct threading rules are supported for the COM object. Even though the UsesCOM1 program calls methods on the object from two different threads, both calls are marshaled into the correct thread for the object so that it can be used safely.

Error Handling

COM objects raise errors by returning 32-bit HRESULT values. The RCW automatically raises exceptions when it sees a failure HRESULT value. HRESULT values are mapped into the closest corresponding Exception type and are stored in the Exception object as well.

Object Release

The RCW creates a proxy object for each COM object that it wraps. This means that your .NET program deals with a real .NET object that does the work of marshaling method and property calls to the COM object. It holds a reference to the COM object, releasing the COM object when it is no longer needed. But when is that?

As you know, .NET objects are garbage collected and you can't be sure when they'll be finalized. This means that when you use COM objects from .NET, you can't be sure when they will actually be released once you no longer reference the proxy. If the COM object holds resources, you may wish to force a release before you clear your last reference to the object. This can be accomplished using the System.Runtime.InteropServices.Marshal.ReleaseComObject method to decrement the reference count to the COM object. The Marshal class also has an AddRef method to add a reference so you can, in effect, do your own reference counting on the object. Be careful though—incorrect use of these methods can lead to memory leaks or exceptions.

Versioning

You've already read that .NET solves DLL Hell problems by binding assemblies tightly to specific versions of dependent assemblies. Unfortunately, there is no magical way to extend this capability to COM. This means that COM objects called from .NET still potentially suffer from all of the versioning problems that VB programmers have come to know and love. Consider this a reminder to continue your versioning and compatibility discipline even in the unlikely event that your COM objects are only going to be used from .NET assemblies.

Late Binding

The COM interop layer allows for late binding to COM objects. The Type object includes methods GetTypeFromProgID and GetTypeFromCLSID that allow you to obtain a Type object for a COM object and which you can then invoke in a late bound manner as described in Chapter 11.

Marshaling Structures and Other Parameter Types

Most VB programmers are not accustomed to exposing structures (VB6 User types) from ActiveX DLL objects. That's because it was a new feature in VB6 and is both incompatible with older versions of VB (and other platforms) and one of the more unreliable features in the language.[6] It turns out that marshaling structures to unmanaged code is a rather complex proposition. Other than structures, marshaling of COM parameters and data types to .NET is fairly straightforward, with the exception of variants (which are marshaled into the .NET Object type). Marshaling does potentially become more complex when dealing with non-automation-compatible interfaces but that is a subject (as I mentioned earlier) I won't be covering in this chapter, as VB programmers will rarely face it.

Rather than discuss the problem of structures and other marshaling issues here, I'll cover them in depth later in this chapter when I discuss calling Win32 API functions from .NET. Unlike COM interop where the marshaling process is largely defined by importing and exporting type libraries, with Win32 API calls, you are responsible for defining the marshaling yourself. Once you understand Win32 API marshaling, you'll have no trouble handling any COM marshaling scenarios that may occur.

Further Thoughts

Visual Studio does a lot behind the scenes to make COM interop work well from within .NET. It even does an excellent job hosting today's ActiveX controls in .NET containers. C++ developers who are accustomed to creating more complex objects by directly working with IDL (Interface Description Language) files will need to refer to the interop specification for further details on how to handle various parameter types and other elements defined in IDL files. However, this is one situation where the fact that VB6 only supports the automation-compatible subset of COM is an advantage. Your VB6-authored COM objects will prove very

---

6. I was burned several times using public structures in VB6 and while it's possible they solved the problems in later service packs, I never felt the need to go back to using them.

compatible with .NET,[7] as will other COM subsystems that are compatible with VB6 COM objects.

Accessing .NET Objects from COM

Creating .NET objects that work well with COM is a somewhat trickier proposition. Not that there is any real difficulty—just that there are a few more issues to consider when going in this direction.

There are a number of issues, or shall we say—approaches, that are presented in the .NET documentation as optional. Rather than show you all of the possibilities, I'm going to limit myself to showing you the correct way to expose objects from VB.NET. This approach is applicable to objects that are automation-compatible and can be used reliably from VB6 or COM+ services. VB.NET is perfectly capable of allowing you to create non-automation-compatible objects, objects that are not VB6 compatible, and objects that do not version correctly with COM. But anyone who wants to create those types of objects can read how to do so in Microsoft's VB documentation.

There are a few things you need to know about how VB6 exposes COM objects in order to understand the requirements and reasons for the approach I'm about to show you. As I mentioned earlier, it's impossible for me to cover here in a few paragraphs what took entire chapters in my *Developing COM/ActiveX Components* book, so those of you without a strong COM background will have to take some of this on faith.

Every VB6 object supports two interfaces.[8] One is the direct interface for the class. This interface is, by convention, preceded with an underscore character and is used for early binding. A second interface is IDispatch, the interface that allows late binding using automation. Listing 15-2 shows the type library for the dwComFromDotNet.dll file created in the Listing 15-1.

> **NOTE** *The actual UUID and ID values of the samples provided will differ from the values shown in Listing 15-2.*

---

7. The degree to which .NET will host VB6 authored ActiveX controls is unclear at the time of publication. Keep in mind that ActiveX controls are much more complex than ActiveX DLL and ActiveX EXE components and are more likely to exhibit subtle differences in behavior in the .NET environment. Microsoft has invested a huge effort in interop but if there are imperfections, ActiveX controls are where they are most likely to appear.

8. Actually, more, but those perform standard COM tasks such as handling events and do not implement the methods you define.

Listing 15-2. Type library file from dwComFromDotNet.dll (VB6 ActiveX DLL).

```
// Generated .IDL file (by the OLE/COM Object Viewer)
//
// typelib filename: dwComFromDotNet.dll

[
  uuid(7CFFA0A5-388D-48DC-8C3F-A3F7206CFC86),
  version(6.0),
  helpstring("MovingToVB.NET: Example of calling COM component from .NET")
]
library dwComFromDotNet
{
    // TLib :      // TLib : OLE Automation : {00020430-0000-0000-C000-000000000046}
    importlib("stdole2.tlb");

    // Forward declare all types defined in this typelib
    interface _SampleClass1;

    [
      odl,
      uuid(F75159CA-A859-4B9A-864C-10596313D0E1),
      version(1.0),
      hidden,
      dual,
      nonextensible,
      oleautomation
    ]
    interface _SampleClass1 : IDispatch {
        [id(0x60030000)]
        HRESULT TimesTwo(
                    [in] long x,
                    [out, retval] long* );
        [id(0x60030001)]
        HRESULT TrimString(
                    [in] BSTR s,
                    [out, retval] BSTR* );
        [id(0x60030002)]
        HRESULT GetThisThreadId([out, retval] long* );
    };
```

```
[
  uuid(47B953CE-7E05-4408-95AA-2A79D739F237),
  version(1.0)
]
coclass SampleClass1 {
    [default] interface _SampleClass1;
};
};
```

What do you see in this type library listing?

- You can see an interface defined named _SampleClass1 that defines the methods and properties of the class. Each one returns an HRESULT value indicating whether the call succeeded.

- You can see that the interface is marked as "dual" and "oleautomation," indicating that it is automation compatible and that the methods on the interface are intended to be callable through IDispatch as well as the direct interface. This is also known by the fact that the interface inherits from IDispatch.

- You can see that the interface has a UUID assigned. UUID refers to a universally unique identifier, also referred to as an IID (interface identifier) or GUID (globally unique identifier) or CLSID (class identifier). These are all terms for a 16-byte value guaranteed to uniquely identify an object, interface, or class. The term used varies by the context in which it is used but always refers to a unique 16-byte identifier.

- Each method in the interface has a Dispid (dispatch identifier), a number used to identify the method when accessed via automation. The id(…) field indicates the dispatch identifier.

- The coclass entry identifies the object itself. Its UUID is the class identifier (CLSID) under which the object is registered.

I've already referred several times to DLL Hell. Now let's look at it from a COM perspective. In order for a new version of the dwComFromDotNet.dll component to be backward compatible with an existing version, the following must apply:

1. All of the UUID values in the new component must match the existing component.[9]

---

9. I will not go into typelib versioning issues at this time—it's unimportant for our purposes here.

2. All of the method names and parameters in the new component must match those in the existing component (you can add interface members even though it is not recommended but then you get into multiple type-library versions and things get more complicated).

3. The functional behavior of the methods and properties of the new component must be identical to that in the previous component.

Creating the CalledViaCOM Component—First Attempt

In building a .NET component intended to be accessed from COM, you can simply check the "Register for COM interop" checkbox on the project setting dialog box. However, doing so will result in a component that only supports late binding. VB.NET will not automatically create the private dual interface for a class that allows both early and late binding.

The correct way to create a component to be used by COM applications is to explicitly define the Class interface as shown in Listing 15-3.

Listing 15-3. Demonstration of the explicit creation of an interface.

```
Imports System.Runtime.InteropServices
Public Interface _CallFromCOM
    Function TimesTwo(ByVal i As Integer) As Integer

End Interface
Public Class CallFromCOM
    Implements _CallFromCOM

    Public Function TimesTwo(ByVal i As Integer) As Integer Implements _
    _CallFromCOM.TimesTwo
        Return i * 2
    End Function

    <ComRegisterFunction()> Public Shared Sub OnRegistration(ByVal T As Type)
        MsgBox("I'm being registered!!! :" & T.FullName)
    End Sub
End Class
```

The OnRegistration function is also interesting. It uses the ComRegisterFunction attribute to indicate that it should be called when the component is being registered. There is also a ComUnregisterFunction attribute that can be called when a component is unregistered.

It is also necessary to instruct the VB.NET compiler that COM objects can use this component. This is accomplished by setting the ComVisible attribute for the assembly in the AssemblyInfo.vb file as shown in Listing 15-4.

Listing 15-4. AssemblyInfo.vb file for the COM callable assembly.

```
Imports System.Reflection
Imports System.Runtime.InteropServices


' General Information about an assembly is controlled through the following
' set of attributes. Change these attribute values to modify the information
' associated with an assembly.

' Review the values of the assembly attributes

<Assembly: AssemblyTitle("CalledViaCOM")>
' This one will show up in VB6 references dialog!!
<Assembly: AssemblyDescription("MovingToVB.NET Example called via COM")>
<Assembly: AssemblyCompany("Desaware Inc.")>
<Assembly: AssemblyProduct("MovingToVB.NET")>
<Assembly: AssemblyCopyright("Copyright ©2001 by Desaware Inc.")>
<Assembly: AssemblyTrademark("")>
'The following GUID is for the ID of the typelib if this project is exposed to COM

<Assembly: Guid("6431f4c9-b2f9-40fb-9420-301b96e2fc8e")>

' Version information for an assembly consists of the following four values:
'
'       Major Version
'       Minor Version
'       Revision
'       Build Number
'
' You can specify all the values or you can default the Build and Revision Numbers
' by using the '*' as shown below:

<Assembly: AssemblyVersion("1.0.*")>

<Assembly: ComVisible(True)>
<Assembly: ClassInterface(ClassInterfaceType.None)>
```

The AssemblyDescription attribute is also important. This will be the description of the type library that will appear in the Project References list for Visual Basic 6.

When you set the ComVisible attribute to True, all of the public objects and class members in the assembly will be visible when the assembly is registered for use with COM. You can, however, control the visibility of individual elements in the assembly using the ComVisible attribute. If, for example, you specified the ComVisible(False) attribute for a Class method, that method would not be callable from COM. You'll see this in the CalledViaCOM2 example.

Specifying the ClassInterfaceType attribute to None prevents the type library exporter from automatically generating an IDispatch interface as the default interface, which allows the interface you've defined to be the default interface for all objects in the assembly. Don't worry, you'll still have late binding, as the interface you define will be a Dual interface (that's the default).

Creating and Registering the Component

Registering a VB.NET component for use with COM is extremely easy. Once you've created a class library (the only type of .NET component callable from COM), simply check the Register for COM Interop checkbox on the Configuration Properties Build page of the Project Properties dialog box. When you do this, VB.NET will notify you that only projects with strong names can be accessed from COM and will ask if you'd like to create a strong name for the assembly. Answer yes to the prompt—you'll learn all about strong names in Chapter 16.

After you build the assembly, it will be registered for access by COM objects. In fact, a number of tasks occur behind the scenes during this registration process:

- The name of the object (in this case, CalledViaCOM.CallFromCOM) is entered in the registry under the HKEY_LOCAL_MACHINE/Software/CLASSES key. An entry for the CLSID of the object is entered as well.

- An entry is made for the CLSID in the registry under the HKEY_LOCAL_MACHINE/Software/CLASSES/CLSID key. There's an InProcServer32 subkey that contains the following additional information:

  - The default value specifies the DLL that implements this object. It is, believe it or not, the .NET runtime DLL mscoree.dll! The .NET runtime creates the CCW that wraps the assembly so that it implements the DLL.

  - The Assembly value contains the strong name of the assembly including the version and public key that uniquely identifies the assembly (you'll read more about this in Chapter 16).

  - The CodeBase value contains the location of the assembly DLL file, eliminating the need to install the assembly in the global assembly cache or application directory of the calling component.

- The RuntimeVersion value contains the version of the .NET runtime needed to run this assembly.

- There are also entries for the class name (as it will be seen by the COM application) and the threading model.

- A type library is created for the assembly and it is registered in the HKEY_LOCAL_MACHINE/Software/Classes/TypeLib key.

The .NET Framework includes the TlbExp tool, which allows you to manually export a type library, and the RegAsm tool, which registers an assembly for use with COM. You may find yourself using RegAsm to register assemblies when deploying assemblies (the RegAsm tool, for example, can create a .REG file that can be used to easily register assemblies that you are distributing) but most developers will use the built-in Visual Studio registration during development.

The VB6NetTest sample VB6 project in the CalledViaCom project directory shows both a late bound and early bound call into the .NET objects:

```
Private Sub cmdLate_Click()
    Dim c As Object
    Set c = CreateObject("CalledViaCOM.CallFromCOM")
    MsgBox c.TimesTwo(5), vbInformation, "Result from .NET componet"
End Sub

Private Sub cmdEarly_Click()
    Dim c As New CallFromCOM
    MsgBox c.TimesTwo(5), vbInformation, "Result from .NET componet"
End Sub
```

Rebuilding the Component

Once you have this working, try the following:

1. Build the VB6NetTest sample program and make sure it works

2. Close VB6.

3. Rebuild the CalledViaCom assembly.

4. Try running the VB6NetTest executable (you must run the compiled VB6 executable—do not use the VB6 environment).

You'll see that late binding continues to work but the early bound call fails. Why is this?

Compare the type library produced the *first* time the assembly is registered (shown in Listing 15-5) with the type library produced the *next* time it is registered as shown in Listing 15-6.

> **NOTE** *The actual UUID and ID values of the samples provided will differ from the values shown in Listings 15-5 and 15-6.*

Listing 15-5. Original type library for the CalledViaCom assembly.

```
// Generated .IDL file (by the OLE/COM Object Viewer)
//
// typelib filename: CalledViaCOM.tlb

[
  uuid(6431F4C9-B2F9-40FB-9420-301B96E2FC8E),
  version(1.0),
  helpstring("MovingToVB.NET Example called via COM")
]
library CalledViaCOM
{
    // TLib :     // TLib : Common Language Runtime Library :
    {BED7F4EA-1A96-11D2-8F08-00A0C9A6186D}
    importlib("mscorlib.tlb");
    // TLib : OLE Automation : {00020430-0000-0000-C000-000000000046}
    importlib("stdole2.tlb");

    // Forward declare all types defined in this typelib
    interface _CallFromCOM;

    [
      odl,
      uuid(340729AC-2E20-3909-A94A-15EF27ED5F04),
      version(1.0),
      dual,
      oleautomation,
        custom({0F21F359-AB84-41E8-9A78-36D110E6D2F9},
        "CalledViaCOM._CallFromCOM")
    ]
```

```
    interface _CallFromCOM : IDispatch {
        [id(0x60020000)]
        HRESULT TimesTwo(
                        [in] long i,
                        [out, retval] long* pRetVal);
    };

    [
      uuid(541F4403-04F3-39B8-83AE-35AD26964015),
      version(1.0),
        custom({0F21F359-AB84-41E8-9A78-36D110E6D2F9},
        "CalledViaCOM.CallFromCOM")
    ]
    coclass CallFromCOM {
        interface _Object;
        [default] interface _CallFromCOM;
    };
};
```

Listing 15-6 Type library for the CalledViaCom assembly after rebuild.

```
// Generated .IDL file (by the OLE/COM Object Viewer)
//
// typelib filename: CalledViaCOM.tlb

[
  uuid(6431F4C9-B2F9-40FB-9420-301B96E2FC8E),
  version(1.0),
  helpstring("MovingToVB.NET Example called via COM")
]
library CalledViaCOM
{
    // TLib :      // TLib : Common Language Runtime Library :
    {BED7F4EA-1A96-11D2-8F08-00A0C9A6186D}
    importlib("mscorlib.tlb");
    // TLib : OLE Automation : {00020430-0000-0000-C000-000000000046}
    importlib("stdole2.tlb");

    // Forward declare all types defined in this typelib
    interface _CallFromCOM;
```

```
[
  odl,
  uuid(340729AC-2E20-3909-A94A-15EF27ED5F04),
  version(1.0),
  dual,
  oleautomation,
    custom({0F21F359-AB84-41E8-9A78-36D110E6D2F9},
    "CalledViaCOM._CallFromCOM")

]
interface _CallFromCOM : IDispatch {
    [id(0x60020000)]
    HRESULT TimesTwo(
                    [in] long i,
                    [out, retval] long* pRetVal);
};

[
  uuid(D54C0514-33B9-351F-BF11-923397721F88),
  version(1.0),
    custom({0F21F359-AB84-41E8-9A78-36D110E6D2F9},
    "CalledViaCOM.CallFromCOM")
]
coclass CallFromCOM {
    interface _Object;
    [default] interface _CallFromCOM;
};
};
```

As you can see in Listing 15-6, the resulting type library is very similar to that exposed by a Visual Basic component. However, the UUID of the CalledViaCOM.CallFromCOM object (as specified by the coclass field) has changed.

The only reason the UUID of the type library is the same is because Visual Studio.NET by default sets the type library UUID in the assembly info using the line:

```
<Assembly: Guid("6431f4c9-b2f9-40fb-9420-301b96e2fc8e")>
```

You can see that the UUID value of the type library in both Listings 15-5 and 15-6 match that specified in the Assembly:GUID attribute, although (of course), each assembly will have a different GUID value.

Curiously enough, the interface UUID will only change if you actually change the interface. This suggests that VB.NET itself is maintaining interface IIDs whenever possible—doing its own internal compatibility testing.

Late binding only needs the name of the object and method to work so it's not surprising that the late bound call continues to work with the rebuilt assembly. However, VB.NET is free to change all of the internal object UUID values, interface IID values, and Dispatch ID values on a rebuild. Thus, early bound access to the assembly is likely to fail each time the assembly is rebuilt.

Fortunately, you can handle this problem easily.

Creating the CalledViaCOM Component—Second Attempt

The trick is to assign your own UUID and Dispid values to the various parts of your assembly.

> **CAUTION**   *All UUID values that follow are for illustrative purposes only. Do not use these numbers in your own applications.*

The assemblyinfo.vb in the CallFromCom2 project has the UUID for the type library set as follows:

```
<Assembly: Guid("c392d911-7806-43e2-a61d-ad3cd3e2a8f3")>
```

Listing 15-7 shows the modified Class1.vb file.

Listing 15-7. The Class1.vb file from the CallFromCom2 assembly.

```
Imports System.Runtime.InteropServices
<Guid("fda97dca-bb0b-4987-961b-8383741cfa8f")> Interface _CallFromCOM2
    <DispId(1)> Function TimesTwo(ByVal i As Integer) As Integer
    <DispId(2)> Function BadWay(ByVal i As Integer) As Object
End Interface

<Guid("72d7e45a-3b76-4a12-bb7e-c096cd97709a")> Public Class CallFromCOM2
    Implements _CallFromCOM2

    <DispId(1)> Public Function TimesTwo(ByVal i As Integer) As Integer _
    Implements _CallFromCOM2.TimesTwo
        Return i * 2
    End Function
```

```
<DispId(2)> Public Function BadWay(ByVal i As Integer) As Object _
Implements _CallFromCOM2.BadWay
    Return i * 2
End Function


<ComVisible(False), DispId(3)> Public Function TimesThree(ByVal i As Integer) _
As Integer
    Return i * 3
End Function

<ComRegisterFunction()> Public Shared Sub OnRegistration(ByVal T As Type)
    MsgBox("I'm being registered!!! :" & T.FullName)
End Sub
End Class
```

The GUID attribute before the class becomes the object's UUID value. The interface UUID value and Dispatch IDs are maintained within the assembly.

You can obtain values to use with the GUID attribute using the uuidgen.exe utility found in the Visual Studio tools directory.[10]

Now try the same sequence as before:

1. Build the VB6NetTest sample program from the CalledViaCom2 sample directory and make sure it works.

2. Close VB6.

3. Rebuild the CalledViaCom2 assembly.

4. Try running the VB6NetTest executable.

This time the program will work.

Using this approach, you've effectively enforced binary compatibility on the assembly.

---

10. Installed in <drive>:\program files\Microsoft Visual Studio.NET\Common7\Tools" by default.

There's just one catch.

> **CAUTION** *WARNING—DANGER Since you are enforcing binary compatibility, be sure you do it correctly. Unlike VB6, VB.NET does not enforce binary compatibility or warn you if you are about to break compatibility!*

If you make a change to an interface that breaks binary compatibility, you will cause serious problems including Memory exceptions in every application using your component.

This is not a flaw or limitation in VB.NET. It is the nature of COM—and VB.NET does give you the tools to provide binary compatibility in the same manner as C++ programmers have been providing it for years. But this discipline is new to VB programmers. Remember though, you only need to worry about this if you're creating components designed to be used from COM.

If you are not prepared to follow this discipline, you can avoid problems relating to early binding by simply using late binding. To do so, perform the following:

- Don't add the line `<Assembly: ClassInterface(ClassInterfaceType.None)>` to your assemblyinfo.vb file.

- Don't create a separate interface for your class.

- Don't specify GUID attributes or Dispid attributes.

In this case, Visual Studio.NET will export a type library that always uses late binding. You must still make sure, though, that all of your method parameters remain unchanged between versions or you will see runtime errors.

Given that most VB programmers will rarely create .NET components for use with COM, this will be a viable strategy for many.

Additional Issues

There are some additional issues you should be aware of when it comes to calling .NET objects from COM:

- Only default constructors are used when objects are called from COM. Parameterized constructors are ignored.

- Shared members are not exposed to COM.

- Only the first two parts of an assembly version number are transferred to the type library version number.

- The program ID (ProgID) of a .NET object in COM is the namespace combined with the object name. This can be changed using the ProgID attribute.

- Parameters and return types defined "As Object" are marshaled into COM Variant types. Try to avoid using them.

- When a COM object releases your object, it will be garbage collected (in due course) like any other .NET object.

- The same structure and marshaling issues that I didn't cover when discussing accessing COM components from .NET also apply in this direction. I'll be discussing those in the "Accessing the Win32 API" section that follows.

Advanced COM programmers or those with special needs should explore the .NET Framework documentation further. Developers creating transactional components will want to further explore how to apply these techniques to components that will be usable via COM+. However, the information provided here should be sufficient for the vast majority of Visual Basic programmers.

Accessing the Win32 API

If you look at the history of Visual Basic, you'll see that in the days of Visual Basic 1, some access to the Win32 API was almost required to write any sort of reasonably professional looking application. As VB evolved, developers continued to access the Win32 API to perform many tasks. Some used API calls to take advantage of operating system features that were not otherwise accessible. Others used them to improve performance with, for example, complex graphic or drawing operations. Even as Microsoft exposed more and more functionality through COM components and wrappers, Win32 API calls remained a key part of the programming toolkit for any serious Visual Basic programmer.

Those days are over.

Oh, don't get me wrong—there are some things that are not yet supported by the .NET Framework classes so you will need to know how to call API functions. But your goal should be to avoid them as much as possible.

Some programmers have asked me if I'll be revising my *Visual Basic Programmer's Guide to the Win32 API*. The truth is, a *VB.NET Programmer's Guide to the Win32 API* would be largely a waste of time. I'll cover most of what you need to know about calling Win32 API functions here. As to whether there will be any sort of "successor" to my Win32 API book, you'll be able to read about my plans on my Web site at http://www.desaware.com sometime after this book is published.[11]

There are several reasons to avoid calling Win32 API functions:

- Win32 API calls require permission to run unmanaged code. You'll learn about .NET security in the next chapter. Suffice to say that as soon as you make a Win32 API call, your assembly instantly requires the highest possible level of permission that an assembly can have. This means that it will be much harder to distribute your assembly for any but the most trusted distribution scenarios.

- Win32 API calls are more prone to errors. Because they run in unmanaged code, you again open the door to the potential for Memory exceptions, memory and resource leaks, and all of the typical bugs that API programmers in any language are accustomed to.

- It's harder to call Win32 API calls than to use equivalent framework calls.

If you must use Win32 API calls, you should encapsulate them in their own classes rather than calling them throughout your code. You might also consider putting all the classes you create that used unmanaged code into their own assemblies. If you are absolutely certain that your objects cannot be used in a malicious manner, you can consider asserting to the .NET system that they are safe. This does not solve the distribution issue (performing such an assert itself requires a high level of trust), but once you do have your assembly deployed, it will be able to be used safely by less trusted code. I realize that this is rather confusing (relying, as it does, on issues relating to .NET security that you haven't learned yet) but fear not—this will become clear in the next chapter.

The Declare Statement Evolved

Anytime a .NET object communicates to unmanaged code, it needs to know several things:

- How to find the component (DLL or EXE) that contains the code and create an instance of that component, if necessary.

- How to find the correct code in the component (whether a method name or entry point).

- How to marshal method parameters to the unmanaged component.

---

11. And when I figure out what those plans actually are.

When dealing with COM objects, most of the information needed to perform these three tasks is communicated using type libraries. When dealing with API or DLL function calls, you must define all of this information using the Declare statement.

It is important that you understand the difference between a DLL component that exposes functionality through COM and one that uses traditional function exports. DLLs can expose functionality in three ways:

1. By implementing .NET assemblies. To use the functionality, you must load the assembly and access the objects and methods of the assembly using the .NET CLR.

2. By implementing COM objects. To use the functionality, you must ask the DLL to create an object of a specified type, and then invoke methods on that object.

3. By exporting functions. This is the original way that DLLs exported functionality. The Win32 API consists of thousands of these exported functions implemented by the core DLLs that make up Windows itself.

Some Visual Basic programmers do not clearly understand the differences between these approaches. Visual Basic.NET and C# assemblies cannot export functions in the traditional sense. They can only expose objects and their methods by way of the .NET CLR. Visual Basic 6 ActiveX DLLs cannot export functions unless you use a third-party component like Desaware's SpyWorks—the capability is not built into the language.

However, Visual Basic.NET, C#, and Visual Basic 6 can all access exported functions in DLLs. When we talk about calling Win32 API functions, we're still referring to calling exported functions—only the exported functions are those implemented by the operating system DLLs.

The Declare statement syntax is described in the .NET documentation as follows:

```
[Public | Private | Protected | Friend | Protected Friend] Declare [Ansi |_
 Unicode | Auto] [Sub] name Lib "libname" [Alias "aliasname"] [([arglist])]
```

Or

```
[Public | Private | Protected | Friend | Protected Friend] Declare [Ansi |_
 Unicode | Auto] [Function] name Lib "libname" [Alias "aliasname"]_
 [([arglist])] [As type]
```

The first part (`[Public | Private | Protected | Friend | Protected Friend]`) simply describes the scope in which the API call can be used.

You should never define Public declarations—there is no reason why those outside your assembly should ever call a DLL function through your assembly.

You should always define declarations with the minimal scope possible. If you expect it to be used within your entire assembly, use Friend scope. Your best bet, though, is to wrap any API calls you use inside a class. Aside from minimizing the chances of bugs due to errors in API calls, this approach will allow you much more control over the security configuration of your assembly as you will learn in Chapter 16.

The [Ansi | Unicode | Auto] section provides information to the CLR that defines how strings are handled.

Windows NT/2000/XP are based on NT technology that uses Unicode internally (as does both VB6 and VB.NET). However, Windows 95/98/ME are based on older technology[12] and use ANSI internally. In order to allow both ANSI and Unicode-based programs to work, Unicode-based operating systems actually export two versions of most API functions that use strings. For example, the GetWindowText API function is actually exported twice: once as GetWindowTextA (for ANSI), once as GetWindowTextW (for wide).

Visual Basic 6 always uses the ANSI entry point so that applications you create are compatible with both ANSI and Unicode-based operating systems.[13] You typically use the Alias field (which I'll be discussing in a moment) to specify the 'A'-suffixed entry point. This results in a rather peculiar phenomena on Unicode-based operating systems: in order to call an API function, VB6 first converts all string parameters to ANSI, then calls the ANSI entry point in the operating system DLL, which promptly converts the strings into Unicode for processing by the operating system!

Visual Basic.NET avoids this inefficiency by allowing you to specify the specific entry point to use. If you wish to force use of the ANSI entry point, you can specify ANSI and use the Alias command to specify the name of the ANSI entry point. If you wish to force use of the Unicode entry point, you can specify Unicode and use the Alias command to specify the name of the Unicode entry point. If there are no strings involved, you can simply leave off any of the three options and specify the exact entry point name (either in the name or aliasname fields of the Declare statement).

---

12. They still contain 16-bit code, believe it or not.

13. You can access the Unicode entry point when using VB6 if you are willing to handle the string access yourself. My book *Dan Appleman's Win32 API Puzzle Book and Tutorial for Visual Basic programmers* (Apress, 1999) covers this subject in nearly excruciating depth.

But most of the time, you will specify the Auto options. When Auto is specified, the CLR does a number of things for you:

- It checks to see if the entry point you specified exists.

- If the entry point isn't found, it tries an entry point with a suffix based on the operating system. If you're using a Unicode-based system, it will append a W to the name and see if the entry point exists. For ANSI-based systems, it will append an A and do the same.

- Once it finds the correct entry point, it will automatically marshal all strings according to the entry point found.

The Auto option will work for most API functions. There are some API functions (such as OLE API functions) where the function uses Unicode or ANSI strings regardless of operating system and thus has only one entry point. In this case, you should specify ANSI or Unicode as specified by the function documentation.

The aliasname field allows you to specify the entry point in cases where you wish the name you use in your application to be different from that of the entry point name. This is frequently used in cases where the exported API name conflicts with a Visual Basic language keyword.

I'll discuss the parameter arguments list shortly.

There are several other improvements to the Declare statement from Visual Basic 6:

- Visual Basic.NET requires you declare a return type to functions. This eliminates one of the most common errors that occurs in VB6: programmers forget to specify a return type, which results in a "Bad DLL Calling Convention" error when the API function returns a 32-bit value while VB6 expects a Variant.

- The vast majority of API functions use the traditional Win32 API calling convention (also called PASCAL). This is the default used for functions called through the Declare statement. However, you can use the Calling-Convention attribute in the Declare statement to specify the 'C' calling convention (Cdecl). The most common situation in which you would need this is when using a third-party DLL where the programmers did not understand how to specify the calling convention and inadvertently left the default C calling convention in place.

- Visual Basic.NET, in the current beta, does not detect bad DLL calling conventions as effectively as Visual Basic 6.

- Visual Basic.NET does not support "As Any" parameters.

The Three Most Important Things to Remember When Making API Calls from VB.NET

If you learn nothing else in this section, remember these three facts:

Even in Visual Basic.NET, API Calls Can Be Dangerous

An error in a declaration can lead to Memory exceptions.

Remember the ByVal Keyword

API calls are intolerant of errors (either missing ByVal keywords when one is expected or using a ByVal keyword for a variable that is expected to be called by reference).

Remember to Use Integer Parameters Instead of Long Parameters

In VB.NET, the Long data type is 64-bits. Using Longs within your VB.NET applications just results in inefficiency. Using Longs in your API declarations will cause errors and even Memory exceptions.

Platform Invocation

A surprising number of VB6 programmers have been complaining long and loud that Microsoft removed the hidden operators VarPtr, StrPtr, and ObjPtr from VB.NET. What they fail to realize is that those operators are unnecessary. The functionality that they represent isn't really gone—it's just been moved into the .NET Framework. In fact, the entire process of calling the Win32 API isn't part of the VB.NET language at all—the Declare statement is just a wrapper to the .NET Framework subsystem called P-Invoke (short for Platform Invocation).

The P-Invoke subsystem is controlled by methods in the System.Runtime.InteropServices namespace. This can be confusing because it's not always clear which of the objects and methods of this namespace are applicable to COM interop, which are applicable to P-Invoke, and which are applicable to both. This is especially true because the attributes that control marshaling of Win32 API calls can also control marshaling of COM method calls!

That's why I didn't bother discussing method parameters in the COM interop part of this chapter—they work the same way as method parameters to Win32 API calls. Because the COM interop default handling is excellent, you're far more likely to use the techniques shown here with Win32 API calls than with COM interop.

Which brings me back to why the lack of VarPtr, StrPtr, and ObjPtr doesn't matter. All the hack techniques that are typically implemented using those functions can be implemented in a far cleaner and more sophisticated manner using P-Invoke. Think about it—all of the .NET objects that need to use operating system features, from Windows forms to Winsock, must use P-Invoke. It should be no surprise that not only does P-Invoke handle any API-related task but it's also quite stable (since the whole framework is built on it).

That doesn't mean, of course, that it's easy to understand.

Marshaling Attributes

There are a few objects that can be used in front of parameters (and the return type) in API declarations. The trick to correctly handling complex API calls is to understand how to use these objects:

- MarshalAs—This attribute allows you to specify how the CLR should marshal data. For example, should a string be passed as a pointer to a Null-terminated string or as an OLE BSTR string?

- UnmanagedType—This enumeration is used in conjunction with the MarshalAs attribute to specify how a parameter should be marshaled.

- Marshal—This object has a huge number of shared methods to perform a remarkable variety of tasks related to unmanaged memory. For example, you can allocate a block of unmanaged memory and manually marshal data into that memory using any of the marshaling attributes.

- GCHandle—This object lets you freeze the location of an object in managed memory and obtain a pointer to that object that can be accessed from unmanaged memory. As exciting as this may sound, you'll find that you rarely, if ever, need it.

Learning P-Invoke

In writing this chapter, I found that I faced two separate dilemmas:

- With over nine thousand API functions in the Win32 API, I can't possibly anticipate how to handle every possible Win32 API call.[14] Nor can I teach it in this limited space.

- I can't possibly anticipate your current skill level. If I wrote this chapter for complete Win32 API beginners, it would probably take me about one hundred pages to cover the fundamental concepts.

So, I'm going to assume two things. First, that you've already had some experience calling API functions from VB.NET—enough for me to say that something is "just like VB6" and have confidence that you can take it from there. Second, that you'll be willing to read the documentation and do your own research when you run into complex function declarations.[15]

Based on these assumptions, I'm going to start out by showing you how to figure out what actually gets passed as a parameter when you make API calls. The approach I'm about to show you is the one I use to puzzle out what the various marshaling attributes actually do when you use them with a parameter.

The VBInterface Project

Open the solution in the VBInterface directory (don't worry that there are a bunch of .cpp files in that directory). You'll find that you opened two projects: VBInterface and VBInterfaceTest.

VBInterfaceTest is a VB.NET program that demonstrates how to call DLL function calls with various parameters. The VBInterface program is a C++ unmanaged DLL that exports functions.[16]

Both projects are loaded at the same time with the VBInterfaceTest project set as the startup project. The only other magic needed for debugging them together is to go to the Project properties dialog for the VBInterfaceTest project, select the Configuration Properties—Debugging entry in the left pane, and make sure the Unmanaged Code Debugging checkbox is checked.

---

14. For one thing, I don't know how to handle every one of those functions—oh, I'm sure I can figure them all out but the fact is, I don't have code demonstrating using P-Invoke to call nine thousand plus functions and I doubt anyone else does either.

15. If not, I occasionally do this kind of thing on a consulting basis—but it ain't cheap.

16. If you want to learn more about using C++ in this way, check out Jonathan Morrison's book *C++ for VB Programmers* (Apress, 2000). It's a good way for VB6 programmers who know no C++ to start out with the language.

Let's start with a simple example.

The ReceivesShort DLL call is defined as follows in VBInterface.cpp:

```
STDAPI_(short) ReceivesShort(short x)
{
  _itoa(x, tbuf, 10);   /* Place value in temporary buffer */
  MessageBox(GetFocus(), (LPSTR)tbuf, (LPSTR)"ReceivesShort", MB_OK);
  return(x);
}
```

When this function is called, it displays a message box showing the 16-bit value that it receives, and then returns the same value. The declaration in the VBInterface file is as follows:

```
Public Declare Auto Function ReceivesShort Lib _
"..\..\VBInterface\Debug\VBInterface.dll" (ByVal s As Short) As Short
```

It is used in the VBInterfaceTest Numbers function with the following code:

```
i = ReceivesShort(4)
Console.WriteLine(i)
```

When this code executes, you first see the number four displayed in a message box, then on the console.

Try setting a breakpoint on one of these lines and then single stepping. You'll find you can single step right into the C++ program. When in the C++ program, you can examine the contents of the parameters that it receives.

Here, then, is the trick:

Anytime you're having trouble coming up with the correct declaration and marshaling for an API call, simply create a function in the VBInterface.cpp file that exactly matches the C declaration for the API call you wish to call. Then try calling that function from your VB program. This allows you to see exactly what is getting passed to the API function

Solving the Marshaling Puzzle

On a simple level, most of the data types you use as parameters are fairly easily. If you are familiar with calling API functions from VB6, the only thing you'll need to remember (aside from the special handling of structures that I'll cover shortly) is to change Long parameters to Integers. Table 15-1 illustrates the most common

Win32 API parameter types (as described in the Win32 API documentation) and how you should define them in a VB.NET Declare statement.

Table 15-1. Passing Simple Parameters to API Function

PARAMETER TYPE	DECLARATION
BYTE	ByVal As Byte
CHAR, Char	ByVal As Char
SHORT, USHORT, WORD	ByVal As Short
int, INT, long, DWORD, ULONG, etc.	ByVal As Integer
LPBYTE	ByRef As Byte
LPCHAR	ByRef As Char
LPSTR	ByVal As String
LPSHORT, LPWORD	ByRef As Short
LPDWORD, LPLONG	ByRef As Integer
LPxxxPROC (function pointer)	ByVal As Delegate (specify Delegate type). Refer to the Delegates sample project in Chapter 10.

A Closer Look at Longs

As I've mentioned, I expect the most common mistake VB.NET programmers will make when accessing the Win32 API is to use 64-bit Long parameters instead of 32-bit parameters. The VBInterface project can show what happens when you pass a Long value-by-value.

In VBInterface.cpp:

```
STDAPI_(__int64) ReceivesLong(__int64 y)
{
    DumpValues((LPVOID)&y, 8);
    return(y+0x1000200030004000);
}
```

In Module1.vb from the VBInterfaceTest project:

```
Public Declare Auto Function ReceivesLong Lib _
"..\..\VBInterface\Debug\VBInterface.dll" (ByVal a As Long) As Long

    l = ReceivesLong(&H1000200030004000)
    Console.WriteLine(Hex$(l))
```

The message box displays: 00 40 00 30 00 20 00 10

The return value is: 2000400060008000

The message box might be a bit confusing. It uses the DumpValues routine that does a binary dump of memory. On PCs, memory is organized so that the lowest part of a numeric value appears in low memory. Thus, 00 40 corresponds to &H4000. When you display a number as it is stored in memory, it effectively appears backwards—but that's just an illusion.

Anyway, this example should serve to reinforce the importance of using Integers instead of Longs in API declarations. Clearly, if you pass a .NET Long parameter (64 bits) to a Win32 API function that expects a C++ "long" parameter (32 bits), a serious error is likely to occur.

Marshaling Strings

In virtually every case where you call Win32 API functions that take string parameters, you'll declare the string ByVal As String.

Now, you might recall everything I said in Chapter 9 about the way objects can be modified when passed by value and that strings would be as well except for the fact that they are immutable. Well, VB.NET pulls a fast one on the Declare statement. Even though you have ByVal specified in the Declare statement, VB.NET assigns the String variable used as the parameter to a new string value created from the value of the string after the DLL call returns.

In other words, this is one place where VB.NET remains syntax compatible with VB6. I find this rather odd considering that it was a clear example of terribly inconsistent syntax in VB6. You'd think that they would have found some way to clean this up. Oh well, you can modify the behavior of string parameters using attributes anyway.

Let's first look at some DLL functions that do not modify strings.

The ReceivesANSIString and ReceivesUnicodeString functions are intended to receive strings in ANSI or Unicode and display them. The ReceivesAutoString function does a dump of the buffer received so you can see what format is received under different operating systems:

```
/* Method used for most API calls.  VB passes a null terminated string
*/
STDAPI_(VOID) ReceivesANSIString(LPSTR tptr)
{
    /* Warning - it's not a copy despite the byval part in the declaration */
    MessageBox(GetFocus(), (LPSTR)tptr, (LPSTR)"ReceivesANSIString", MB_OK);
}
```

```
STDAPI_(VOID) ReceivesUnicodeString(LPWSTR tptr)
{
   MessageBoxW(GetFocus(), tptr, L"ReceivesUnicodeString", MB_OK);
}


STDAPI_(VOID) ReceivesAutoString(LPSTR tptr, int count)
{
   DumpValues(tptr, count);
}
```

Listing 15-8 shows how the functions are declared and called in the
VBInterfaceTest project.

Listing 15-8. String examples from the VBInterfaceTest project.

```
Public Declare Ansi Sub ReceivesANSIString Lib _
"..\..\VBInterface\Debug\VBInterface.dll" (ByVal s As String)
Public Declare Unicode Sub ReceivesUnicodeString Lib _
"..\..\VBInterface\Debug\VBInterface.dll" (ByVal s As String)
Public Declare Auto Sub ReceivesAutoString Lib _
"..\..\VBInterface\Debug\VBInterface.dll" (ByVal s As String, ByVal chars As _
Integer)
Public Declare Sub ReceivesNoInfoString Lib __
"..\..\VBInterface\Debug\VBInterface.dll" _
Alias "ReceivesAutoString" (ByVal s As String, ByVal chars As Integer)

    Dim s As String = "Test string"
    Dim s2 As String
    console.WriteLine("Strings examples")
    ReceivesANSIString(s)
    ReceivesUnicodeString(s)
    s2 = s
    ReceivesAutoString(s, Len(s))
    If Not s2 Is s Then
        Console.WriteLine(_
        "s and s2 are no longer the same after after ReceivesAutoString")
    End If
    ReceivesNoInfoString(s, Len(s))
```

Let's consider the results.

ReceivesAnsiString correctly receives and displays "Test String." So does
ReceivesUnicodeString. These prove that the Ansi and Unicode attributes do
marshal the string parameters as instructed.

ReceivesAutoString displays 54 00 65 00 73 00 74 00 20 00 73—clearly a Unicode string (since the example is running on Windows 2000—a Unicode-based operating system). It is truncated because the number of bytes is actually twice the number of characters in Unicode but it's enough to see clearly that it is Unicode.

It's fascinating to note that even though the string is passed ByVal, the message will be displayed indicating that the string has been changed. Again, this is something VB.NET does for you that is inconsistent with the normal behavior of the ByVal attribute.

When no option is specified, 54 65 73 74 20 73 74 72 69 6e 67 is displayed, indicating clearly that VB.NET uses ANSI as a default. This makes sense in that it maintains compatibility with VB6. Nevertheless, you should always specify an attribute.

Now let's look Listing 15-9, which modifies strings. From the VBInterface.cpp file you have the following.

Listing 15-9. String examples from the VBInterfaceTest project—continued.

```
/* This example shows how a string can be modified - as long as you don't
   go beyond the space allocated */

STDAPI_(VOID) ChangesStringA(LPSTR tptr)
{
   if (*tptr) *tptr = 'A';
}

STDAPI_(VOID) ChangesStringW(LPWSTR tptr)
{
            if(*tptr) *tptr = 'W';
}



STDAPI_(VOID) ChangesByRefStringW(LPWSTR *ptr)
{
            lstrcpyW(*ptr, L"New String");
}

STDAPI_(VOID) ChangesByRefStringA(LPSTR *ptr)
{
            lstrcpyA(*ptr, "New String");
}

STDAPI_(VOID) ChangesBSTRString(BSTR *sptr)
{
```

```
    if(!sptr) return;              // Should never happen - just being paranoid
    if(*sptr) SysFreeString(*sptr);
    *sptr = SysAllocString(L"Any Length Ok");
}



/* This example shows how you can return a string from a DLL. */
STDAPI_(BSTR) ReturnsVBString()
{
    return(SysAllocString(L"Here's a return string"));
}
```

And in the VBInterfaceTest project, you have the following code:

```
Public Declare Auto Sub ChangesString Lib _
"..\..\VBInterface\Debug\VBInterface.dll" (ByVal s As String)
Public Declare Auto Sub ChangesByRefString Lib _
"..\..\VBInterface\Debug\VBInterface.dll" (ByRef s As String)
Public Declare Unicode Sub ChangesBSTRString Lib _
"..\..\VBInterface\Debug\VBInterface.dll" _
(<MarshalAs(UnmanagedType.BStr)> ByRef s As String)
Public Declare Unicode Function ReturnsVBString Lib _
"..\..\VBInterface\Debug\VBInterface.dll" () As _
<MarshalAs(UnmanagedType.BStr)> String


    s2 = s
    ChangesString(s)
    If Not s2 Is s Then
        Console.WriteLine("s and s2 are no longer the same after ChangesString")
    End If
    Console.WriteLine("Changed String: " & s)
    ChangesByRefString(s)
    Console.WriteLine("Changed ByRef String: " & s)
    ChangesBSTRString(s)
    Console.WriteLine("Changed BSTR String: " & s)
    s = ReturnsVBString()
    Console.WriteLine("Returned String: " & s)
```

The results are as follows:

```
s and s2 are no longer the same after ChangesString
Changed String: West string
Changed ByRef String: New String
Changed BSTR String: Any Length Ok
Returned String: Here's a return string
```

Let's again consider the results one at a time.

The ChangesString function modifies a single character in a string passed by value. As with VB6, you must be very careful not to change data past the end of the string. Failing to initialize the string to a length sufficient to hold any returned data in the string parameter is a sure road to a Memory exception.

The fun thing about the ChangesString function is that it clearly illustrates how the Auto attribute on the declaration works. The ChangesString declaration does not specify an alias to ChangesStringA or ChangesStringW. Yet, from the result, you can clearly see that it found the ChangesStringW entry point in the DLL (assuming you are running the program on a Unicode-based operating system).

When you pass a string ByRef, the function receives a pointer to a variable containing a pointer to the string buffer. Do *not* try to assign a value to that variable. Changing it will only cause the program to fail. The rules about preallocating strings apply to this approach as well. Few Win32 API functions use this type of parameter (it would appear as LPLPSTR). Those that do can be handled by declaring the parameter ByRef As Integer, then using the Marshal object to retrieve the string from the pointer provided by the API call.[17] By the way, this differs from VB6 where a ByRef As String parameter passes a pointer to a BSTR (OLE String) type.

You can use BSTR types with API calls, though Win32 API functions do not use them (only those that are part of the OLE subsystem use BSTR types). This is demonstrated in the ChangesBSTRString and ReturnsVBString types. Note how the declaration uses the MarshalAs(UnmanagedType.BStr) attribute to tell the CLR that you wish to treat the strings as BSTR types. BSTR types have the advantage of being able to modify the length of the string or define an arbitrary return-string length.

While you won't be using the BSTR type for Win32 API calls, it should be no surprise that this marshal type is used extensively behind the scenes with COM interop.

Marshaling Arrays

Arrays can get tricky. Listing 15-10 shows the sample code from the VBInterface.cpp file that receives arrays. The ReceivesShortArray function receives a pointer to a

---

17. The Marshal.PtrToStringAnsi, Marshal.PtrToStringAuto and Marshal.PtrToStringUni methods allow you to obtain a .NET String given a pointer to the unmanaged heap. They work similarly to the Marshal.PtrToStructure method that you'll see later in this chapter.

short—the first in a sequence of values. The ReceivesShortRefArray receives a pointer to a variable that contains the address of an array. Both of these functions increment the first two entries in the array (so you can tell if the data is copied back to the original array). The ReturnsSafeArray function shows how a DLL function can completely redefine an array.

Listing 15-10. C++ code to reference arrays.

```
/* Array of integers - Be careful not to exceed the limit of the array!
   This technique can be used on all numeric data types.
   Note the special calling sequence in the VB example.
   It will not work on strings.
*/

STDAPI_(VOID) ReceivesShortArray(short FAR *iptr)
{
    wsprintf((LPSTR)tbuf, (LPSTR)"1st 4 entries are %d %d %d %d",
             *(iptr), *(iptr+1), *(iptr+2), *(iptr+3));
    MessageBox(GetFocus(), (LPSTR)tbuf, (LPSTR)"ReceivesShortArray", MB_OK);
    (*iptr)++; // Increment the int array for to verify the by reference features
    // (that way you  can tell if you are using a temporary copy
    (*(iptr+1))++;
}


short newArrayBuffer[4] = { 5, 4, 3, 2};

STDAPI_(VOID) ReceivesShortRefArray(short FAR **piptr)
{
    short *iptr;
    iptr = *piptr;
    wsprintf((LPSTR)tbuf, (LPSTR)"1st 4 entries are %d %d %d %d",
    *(iptr), *(iptr+1), *(iptr+2), *(iptr+3));
    MessageBox(GetFocus(), (LPSTR)tbuf, (LPSTR)"ReceivesShortArray", MB_OK);
    (*iptr)++; // Increment the int array for to verify the by reference features
    // (that way you  can tell if you are using a temporary copy
    (*(iptr+1))++;
    *piptr = newArrayBuffer;
}
```

```
STDAPI_(VOID) ReturnsSafeArray(SAFEARRAY **psa)
{
    short *pdata;
    pdata = (short *)((*psa)->pvData);
    wsprintf((LPSTR)tbuf,
    (LPSTR)"Array of %d dimensions, %ld bytes per element\n First int entry is %d",
    (*psa)->cDims, (*psa)->cbElements, *pdata);

    MessageBox(GetFocus(), (LPSTR)tbuf, (LPSTR)"ReturnsArray", MB_OK);
    SAFEARRAYBOUND bounds[1];
    long l;
    bounds[0].lLbound = 0;
    bounds[0].cElements = 4;
    *psa = SafeArrayCreate(VT_I2, 1, bounds);
    short storeval;
    for(l = 0; l<4; l++) {
                    storeval = (short)l * 5;
                    SafeArrayPutElement(*psa, &l, &storeval);
                    }
}
```

Let's start with ReceivesShortArray. This is a DLL function that expects to see a pointer to an array of 16-bit Short values. We call it through two different declarations, one that passes the first item in the array, and the other that passes the entire array by value as shown in Listing 15-11.

Listing 15-11. Array examples from the VBInterfaceTest sample project.

```
Public Declare Sub ReceivesShortArray1 Lib _
"..\..\VBInterface\Debug\VBInterface.dll" Alias _
"ReceivesShortArray" (ByRef i As Short)
Public Declare Sub ReceivesShortArray2 Lib _
"..\..\VBInterface\Debug\VBInterface.dll" Alias _
"ReceivesShortArray" (ByVal i() As Short)
```

```
Dim i() As Short = {1, 2, 3, 4}
Dim x As Integer

ReceivesShortArray1(i(0))
For x = 0 To 3
    Console.Write(Str(i(x)) & ", ")
Next x
console.WriteLine()

ReceivesShortArray2(i)
For x = 0 To 3
    Console.Write(Str(i(x)) & ", ")
Next x
console.WriteLine()
```

The first call to ReceivesShortArray displays 1, 2, 3, 4 in the message box indicating that even though we are passing the first element in an array, VB.NET is, in fact, marshaling the entire array into unmanaged memory. Logically, there is no reason to expect any but the first item to be marshaled into unmanaged memory so it looks like this is a feature added to VB.NET to support an approach frequently used by VB6 programmers to pass arrays to API functions. On return, 2, 3, 3, 4 is displayed, indicating that all of the elements of the array are marshaled back into the .NET array.

The same occurs when passing the array by value as shown in the second declaration, suggesting that both of these calls are identical.

The ReceivesShortRefArray does correctly receive the array (currently 3, 4, 3, 4) but on return, you'll find that the array's upper bound is now zero! What happened? There is no way for the Interop system to guess how long the modified array might be. So, it only copies back the first element of the array! Don't worry, though. As you will soon see, it is possible to define fixed-length arrays that let the Interop system know how long the array should be on return:

```
Public Declare Sub ReceivesShortRefArray Lib _
"..\..\VBInterface\Debug\VBInterface.dll" (ByRef i() As Short)

    ReceivesShortRefArray(i)
    Console.WriteLine("Array bound is now: " & UBound(i))
    console.WriteLine()
```

The ReturnsSafeArray function shown here illustrates how you can marshal an array by reference as an OLE SAFEARRY type:

```
Public Declare Sub ReturnsSafeArray Lib _
"..\..\VBInterface\Debug\VBInterface.dll" _
(<MarshalAs(UnmanagedType.SafeArray)> ByRef i() As Short)

    ReturnsSafeArray(i)
    For x = 0 To UBound(i)
        Console.Write(Str(i(x)) & ", ")
    Next
    console.WriteLine()
```

As with BSTR strings, you won't be using these for Win32 API functions except perhaps the OLE API functions. But COM Interop uses them extensively.

Structures

It is very common to pass structures to Win32 API functions. It is also common for Win32 API functions to need to modify the content of those structures. Thus, it is not only important to be able to correctly marshal structures to unmanaged memory, it is also important that it be possible to marshal the data back.

There are, however, several details that add quite a bit of complexity to this task:

- Structures in .NET do not work like structures you are familiar with. For example, fields in structures can actually be stored in any order in the structure.

- .NET does not support fixed-length strings—an essential part of many Win32 API structures.

- .NET does not support fixed-length arrays—another essential part of many Win32 API structures.

This means that part of the process of marshaling structures must include instructions on how the structure is laid out and how to handle string and array fields.

Structure Layout

The first thing you need to know about structure layout is that all API functions expect the fields in the structure to be in order. This much is obvious. But API functions don't always follow the same alignment rules. Most API functions use single-byte packing, meaning that all fields appear immediately after each other with no gaps. VB6 passes structures using natural alignment, meaning that each field aligns itself on a multiple of its size. Thus, bytes can appear anywhere, 16-bit values are on even-byte boundaries and 32-bit values are on 4-byte boundaries. Consider the following C++ structure:

```
typedef struct usertypestruct {
    BYTE a;                    // Matches VB Byte type
    short b;
    long c;
    BYTE d[4];
    char e[16];
} usertype;
```

With natural alignment, the ANSI version of this structure would appear as the following series of bytes (where each letter indicates the location of a byte from that field and zero indicates extra padding inserted by the compiler):

```
a 0 b b c c c c d d d d e e e e e e e e e e e e e e e e  = 28 bytes
```

With single-byte packing, the array would appear as follows:

```
a b b c c c c d d d d e e e e e e e e e e e e e e e e = 27 bytes
```

The compiler in the VBInterface project is set to single-byte packing, which means that in this case, VB6 would not be able to pass this structure successfully to the DLL function![18] Fortunately, most API functions include explicit padding bytes. So, even though they use single-byte packing, they still work correctly with VB6.

With VB.NET, you can specify the packing directly using the StructLayout attribute shown in Listing 15-12.

Listing 15-12. The StructLayout attribute.

```
<StructLayout(LayoutKind.Sequential, Pack:=1)> Public Structure GoodStruct
    Public A As Byte
    Public B As Short
    Public C As Integer
    <MarshalAs(UnmanagedType.ByValArray, SizeConst:=4)> Public D() As Byte
    <MarshalAs(UnmanagedType.ByValTStr, SizeConst:=16)> Public E As String
```

---

18. Desaware's SpyWorks includes a user-defined type byte-packing and unpacking component to help in cases like this.

```
        Public Sub InitStruct()
            A = 1
            B = 2
            C = 3
            ReDim D(3)
            D(0) = 4
            D(1) = 5
            D(2) = 6
            D(3) = 7
            E = "16 char string "    ' with null
        End Sub
    End Structure
```

You will almost always use sequential structure layout (LayoutKind.Sequential) as shown and will almost always specify single-byte packing as well. The StructLayout attribute even allows for explicit layout of fields where you can specify the exact offset of each field from the start of the structure. No more alignment problems!

The Byte array and string are defined as regular .NET array and String objects. The array must be initialized to the correct length in a Structure method (you can't override a structure's default constructor so be sure to call this method before you use the structure). The array is marshaled as an array that is passed ByVal (which you already know is the correct way to pass arrays to API functions from the array examples earlier). The length of the array is specified, allowing the fixed-length array to be marshaled both ways.

The string is a ByValTStr type—a TStr is a string whose type depends on the operating system in use. In other words, on a Unicode system, this will actually be a 32-byte Unicode string. Most structures used by the API are, in fact, TSTR strings whose type varies depending on the entry point used. Using the ByValTStr type for a structure is effectively the equivalent of using the Auto attribute on a Declare statement.

The ReceivesUserType DLL function is defined as an ANSI entry point as follows:

```
/* Call by reference only */
STDAPI_(VOID) ReceivesUserType(usertype FAR *u)
{
    DumpValues(u, 30);
    wsprintf((LPSTR)tbuf, (LPSTR)"usertype contains %d %d %d (%d %d %d %d) %s",
    u->a, u->b, u->c, u->d[0], u->d[1], u->d[2], u->d[3], u->e);
    MessageBox(GetFocus(), (LPSTR)tbuf, (LPSTR)"ReceivesUserType1", MB_OK);
    if(u->c == 3) {
            lstrcpy(u->e, "New Data");
            u->d[0] = 99;
            }
}
```

When called, it displays the data in the user-defined type as follows:

```
01 02 00 03 00 00 00 04 05 06 07 31 36 20 63 68 61 72 20 73 74 72 69 6e 67 20
```

This clearly matches the single-byte packing scenario shown earlier.

The DLL function copies the string New Data into the string. The data is marshaled back as shown by displaying the string when the function returns. The contents of the array are also marshaled back, as you can see from the 99 displayed on the Console window.

Advanced Win32 API Calls

Assuming you started out with a basic familiarity in calling API functions from VB6, the material you've just read should be enough to allow you to cover most of the API calls you'll need to call (keeping in mind that given the size of the .NET class library, you'll rarely need to call API functions anyway).

Before concluding this chapter, I thought I'd present a couple of examples of complex Win32 API calls.

Obtaining Dialup Entries Using the RasEnumEntries API

The RasEnumEntries API call loads a buffer with an array of RASENTRYNAME structures, one for each entry in your dialup networking phone book (you should add at least a couple of dialup or VPN entries onto your system before trying this program).

> **NOTE** *The RasEntries as RasGetEntry examples that are described in the remainder of this section demonstrate very advanced techniques that presume a good understanding of general computer science concepts, such as pointers and how data is organized in memory, and some understanding of advanced API techniques as they are used from VB6. I include them here for advanced users knowing that some readers will probably be unable to follow them in their entirety.*

The RASENTRYNAME structure is defined as follows:[19]

```
typedef struct _RASENTRYNAME {
  DWORD  dwSize;
  TCHAR  szEntryName[RAS_MaxEntryName + 1];
} RASENTRYNAME;
```

Where RAS_MaxEntryName is 256.

Listing 15-13 shows the RASENTRYNAME structure in the RasEntries sample project.

Listing 15-13. The RASENTRYNAME structure.

```
' RasEntries example
' Copyright ©2001 by Desaware Inc. All Rights Reserved

Imports System.Runtime.InteropServices
Module Module1
    ' szEntryName is 256 characters, or a 257 character buffer
    <StructLayout(LayoutKind.Sequential, Pack:=4, CharSet:=Charset.Auto)> _
       Structure RASENTRYNAME
         Public dwSize As Integer
         <MarshalAs(UnmanagedType.ByValTStr, sizeConst:=257)> Public szEntryName _
         As String
         Public Sub Init()
             dwSize = Marshal.SizeOf(Me)
         End Sub
    End Structure
End Structure
```

This structure uses a packing size of 4. This can be determined by examining the rasapi.h header file, where you'll find the line, `#include <pshpack4.h>`, which indicates that the structures in this header file use a packing size of four instead of the typical one.

It's also possible to specify the use of the Auto character set for structures as shown in Listing 15-13. This is just like using the Auto attribute on a Declare statement except that it applies to strings inside of structures.

The szEntryName field is marshaled as a fixed-width, 257-character string.

The dwSize field of this structure is supposed to be set to the size in bytes of the structure. While you can calculate this by hand, the Marshal object contains a shared method, SizeOf, which returns the size of the structure as it will be when marshaled to unmanaged memory. It is thus far more accurate even than VB6's

---

19. Windows 2000 additions to the structure have been left out to reduce complexity. Windows determines which version of the structure you are using based on the dwSize field.

LenB function and can be used as a tool to verify that you have set the correct attributes on structure fields. There is no need to initialize the szEntryName field because the MarshalAs attribute specifies the size of the string and will always marshal that length of data.

The RasEnumEntries API call is defined as follows in the MSDN documentation:

```
DWORD RasEnumEntries (
    LPCTSTR reserved,                  // reserved, must be NULL
    LPTCSTR lpszPhonebook,             // pointer to full path and
                                       //  file name of phone-book file
    LPRASENTRYNAME lprasentryname,     // buffer to receive
                                       //   phone-book entries
    LPDWORD lpcb,                      // size in bytes of buffer
    LPDWORD lpcEntries                 // number of entries written
                                       //  to buffer
);
```

We use the following Declare statement:

```
Public Declare Auto Function RasEnumEntries Lib "rasapi32.dll" (ByVal reserved _
    As Integer, ByVal lpszPhoneBook As String, ByVal rasentries As IntPtr, _
    ByRef lpcb As Integer, ByRef lpcEntries As Integer) As Integer
```

The rasentries parameter is passed as an address to a block of unmanaged memory. You'll see shortly how this block of memory is created and managed.

The RasEnumEntries function is called twice: once to retrieve both the number of entries in the array and size of the array, and again to retrieve the actual data.

The function begins by calculating the size of each RASENTRYNAME structure and allocating a block of unmanaged memory to hold a single structure. This allocation is done using the Marshal.AllocHGlobal method.

```
Sub Main()
    Dim res As Integer
    Dim cb, cbentries As Integer
    Dim idx As Integer
    Dim iptr As IntPtr
    Dim SizePerStruct As Integer
    SizePerStruct = Marshal.SizeOf(GetType(RASENTRYNAME))    _
    ' Get size needed for each structure
    iptr = Marshal.AllocHGlobal(SizePerStruct)
```

Next, we create a single RASENTRYNAME structure in an array, initialize it, and explicitly marshal it into the memory buffer using the Marshal.StructureToPtr method. Then we call the RasEnumEntries method and marshal the structure data back into the Structure variable using the Marshal.PtrToStructure method. Note how the unmanaged memory buffer is freed using the Marshal.FreeHGlobal method.

```
Dim rasentries(0) As RASENTRYNAME
rasentries(0).Init()
cb = rasentries(0).dwSize
cbentries = 1
Marshal.StructureToPtr(rasentries(0), iptr, False)

' First time through get the count
res = RasEnumEntries(0, Nothing, iptr, cb, cbentries)

rasentries(0) = CType(Marshal.PtrToStructure(iptr, _
        GetType(RASENTRYNAME)), RASENTRYNAME)
Marshal.FreeHGlobal(iptr)
```

If the function returns 603, this indicates that there are additional entries in the phone book. If that is the case, we ReDim the rasentries array to be large enough to hold all of the phone book entries, then manually marshal all of those entries into a newly allocated unmanaged memory buffer of the right size. You can also see how the IntPtr constructor used to create unmanaged memory pointers can be allocated based on a calculated memory address:

```
If res = 603 Then
    ReDim rasentries(cbentries - 1)
    cb = 0
    iptr = Marshal.AllocHGlobal(cbentries * SizePerStruct)

    For idx = 0 To cbentries - 1
        rasentries(idx).Init()
        Marshal.StructureToPtr(rasentries(idx), New IntPtr(iptr.ToInt32 + _
        cb), False)
        cb = cb + rasentries(idx).dwSize
    Next
    res = RasEnumEntries(0, Nothing, iptr, cb, cbentries)
End If
```

```
        If res = 0 Then
            cb = 0
            For idx = 0 To cbentries - 1
                rasentries(idx) = CType(Marshal.PtrToStructure( _
                New IntPtr(iptr.ToInt32 + cb), GetType(RASENTRYNAME)), RASENTRYNAME)
                cb = cb + rasentries(idx).dwSize
                console.WriteLine(rasentries(idx).szEntryName)
            Next
        End If
        Marshal.FreeHGlobal(iptr)

        console.ReadLine()
    End Sub

End Module
```

As you can see, Visual Basic.NET has no problem allocating unmanaged memory, and copying data to and from unmanaged memory. In fact, VB.NET is much more powerful than VB6 in that it is not limited to simply direct memory copies using the RtlMoveMemory API (which is frequently used in such cases with VB6). The Marshal.StructureToPtr and Marshal.PtrToStructure methods allow you to perform smart copy operations that take alignment into account and allow control of the marshaling of each field in the structure.[20]

It turns out that knowing how to marshal to and from memory buffers is important anyway because, as you will see next, sometimes API functions return variable-length buffers.

Obtaining Information about a Single Dialup Entry Using the RasGetEntryProperties API

Our goal is to load a RASENTRY structure with information about a specific phone book entry. This is a rather complex structure as you can see in Listing 15-14.[21]

---

20. You might be wondering why I didn't try to marshal the entire array of RASENTRYNAME structures at once. The answer is simple: I couldn't find a way to make it work. Marshaling the array data to the API function was no problem but I had no success marshaling the data back. The P-Invoke system knows how to handle arrays of simple types but the documentation does not state how it handles arrays of structures and at this time, they do not seem to be marshaled back. Whether this is normal behavior or a bug in the beta is not clear. Watch the Web site for updates.

21. Again, we are not using the latest version of the structure with Windows 2000 additions.

Listing 15-14. The RASENTRY structure (C++).

```cpp
typedef struct tagRASENTRY {
  DWORD       dwSize;
  DWORD       dwfOptions;
  //
  // Location/phone number.
  //
  DWORD       dwCountryID;
  DWORD       dwCountryCode;
  TCHAR       szAreaCode[ RAS_MaxAreaCode + 1 ];
  TCHAR       szLocalPhoneNumber[ RAS_MaxPhoneNumber + 1 ];
  DWORD       dwAlternateOffset;
  //
  // PPP/Ip
  //
  RASIPADDR   ipaddr;
  RASIPADDR   ipaddrDns;
  RASIPADDR   ipaddrDnsAlt;
  RASIPADDR   ipaddrWins;
  RASIPADDR   ipaddrWinsAlt;
  //
  // Framing
  //
  DWORD       dwFrameSize;
  DWORD       dwfNetProtocols;
  DWORD       dwFramingProtocol;
  //
  // Scripting
  //
  TCHAR       szScript[ MAX_PATH ];
  //
  // AutoDial
  //
  TCHAR       szAutodialDll[ MAX_PATH ];
  TCHAR       szAutodialFunc[ MAX_PATH ];
  //
  // Device
  //
  TCHAR       szDeviceType[ RAS_MaxDeviceType + 1 ];
  TCHAR       szDeviceName[ RAS_MaxDeviceName + 1 ];
  //
  // X.25
  //
```

```
    TCHAR       szX25PadType[ RAS_MaxPadType + 1 ];
    TCHAR       szX25Address[ RAS_MaxX25Address + 1 ];
    TCHAR       szX25Facilities[ RAS_MaxFacilities + 1 ];
    TCHAR       szX25UserData[ RAS_MaxUserData + 1 ];
    DWORD       dwChannels;
    //
    // Reserved
    //
    DWORD       dwReserved1;
    DWORD       dwReserved2;
} RASENTRY;
```

The trick to converting this structure to VB.NET is to be sure to get all the string lengths correct. The marshaling settings shown in Listing 15-15 are very similar to what you saw in the previous example (Listing 15-14).

Listing 15-15. The RASENTRY structure (VB.NET).

```
' RasGetEntry example
' Copyright ©2001 by Desaware Inc. All Rights Reserved
Imports System.Runtime.InteropServices

Module Module1

    <StructLayout(LayoutKind.Sequential, Pack:=4, CharSet:=charset.Auto)> _
    Structure RASENTRY
        Public dwSize As Integer
        Public dwfOptions As Integer
        Public dwCountryID As Integer
        Public dwCountryCode As Integer
        <MarshalAs(UnmanagedType.ByValTStr, SizeConst:=11)> _
          Public szAreayCode As String      '11 chars
        <MarshalAs(UnmanagedType.ByValTStr, SizeConst:=129)> _
          Public szLocalPhoneNumber As String
        Public dwAlternateOffset As Integer
        Public ipaddr As Integer
        Public ipaddrDns As Integer
        Public ipaddrDnsAlt As Integer
        Public ipaddrWins As Integer
        Public ipaddrWinsAlt As Integer
```

```
        Public dwFrameSize As Integer
        Public dwfNetProtocols As Integer
        Public dwFramingProtocol As Integer

        <MarshalAs(UnmanagedType.ByValTStr, SizeConst:=260)> _
          Public szScript As String

        <MarshalAs(UnmanagedType.ByValTStr, SizeConst:=260)> _
          Public szAutodialDll As String
        <MarshalAs(UnmanagedType.ByValTStr, SizeConst:=260)> _
          Public szAutodialFunc As String

        <MarshalAs(UnmanagedType.ByValTStr, SizeConst:=17)> _
          Public szDeviceType As String
        <MarshalAs(UnmanagedType.ByValTStr, SizeConst:=129)> _
          Public szDeviceName As String

        <MarshalAs(UnmanagedType.ByValTStr, SizeConst:=33)> _
          Public szX25PadType As String
        <MarshalAs(UnmanagedType.ByValTStr, SizeConst:=201)> _
          Public szX25Address As String
        <MarshalAs(UnmanagedType.ByValTStr, SizeConst:=201)> _
          Public szFacilities As String
        <MarshalAs(UnmanagedType.ByValTStr, SizeConst:=201)> _
          Public szUserData As String
        Public dwChannels As Integer

        Public dwReserved1 As Integer
        Public dwReserved2 As Integer
    End Structure
```

The RasGetEntryProperties function is defined in the MSDN documentation as follows:

```
DWORD RasGetEntryProperties(
  LPCTSTR lpszPhonebook,       // pointer to full path and
                               //  file name of phone-book file
  LPCTSTR lpszEntry,           // pointer to an entry name
  LPRASENTRY lpRasEntry,       // buffer that receives entry information
  LPDWORD lpdwEntryInfoSize,   // size, in bytes, of the
                               //  lpRasEntry buffer
  LPBYTE lpbDeviceInfo,        // buffer that receives
                               //  device-specific configuration information
  LPDWORD lpdwDeviceInfoSize   // size, in bytes, of the
                               //  lpbDeviceInfo buffer
);
```

We create two declarations for the RasGetEntryProperties function. One takes a single RASENTRY structure as a parameter; the other, a pointer to a block of unmanaged memory. You'll see why this is necessary shortly. The declarations are as follows:

```
Public Declare Auto Function RasGetEntryProperties Lib "rasapi32.dll" (ByVal _
lpszPhoneBook As String, ByVal lpszEntry As String, ByRef lpRasEntry As _
RASENTRY, ByRef lpdwEntryInfoSize As Integer, _
ByVal devinfo As Integer, ByVal devinfosize As Integer) As Integer

Public Declare Auto Function RasGetEntryProperties2 Lib "rasapi32.dll" Alias _
"RasGetEntryProperties" (ByVal lpszPhoneBook As String, ByVal lpszEntry As _
String, ByVal lpRasEntry As IntPtr, ByRef lpdwEntryInfoSize As Integer, _
ByVal devinfo As Integer, ByVal devinfosize As Integer) As Integer
```

The Win32 documentation states that if you don't want to use the devinfo and devinfosize parameters, you can simply pass Null for both parameters. Thus, in this example, both are declared to be passed ByVal As Integer and the sample will set both parameters to zero when the function is called.

You should begin by setting the PhoneBookEntryToGet constant to the name of an entry in your own default phone book. It is unlikely that you'll have an entry named DesawareModem. The function begins by setting the dwSize field in the structure to the correct length, setting the bufsize to the same size, and calling the RasGetEntryProperties function:

```
Const PhoneBookEntryToGet As String = "Your Phonebook Entry"


Sub Main()
    Dim res As Integer
    Dim re As RASENTRY
    Dim bufsize As Integer
    re.dwSize = Marshal.SizeOf(re)
    bufsize = re.dwSize
    res = RasGetEntryProperties(Nothing, PhoneBookEntryToGet, re, bufsize, 0, 0)

    If res = 623 Then
        Console.WriteLine("Can't find specified dial-up entry")
    End If
```

Why might this call fail? One obvious reason is if the specified phone book entry does not exist. If you see error 623 at this point, it's probably because you forgot to modify the PhoneBookEntryToGet constant to match the name of a phone book entry on your system.

But even if your modem entry is correct, you are still likely to see an error because the RasGetEntryProperties has the ability to return additional, device-specific information beyond the length of the structure. This is actually very common with complex API calls. In some cases, the extra space holds string data that is referenced by pointers within the structure (which are also easily extracted using P-Invoke marshaling). The solution in each case is to allocate an unmanaged memory block of the length expected by the function, marshal the structure to the memory block, call the API function, then marshal the data back as shown here:

```
If res = 603 Then
  Dim iptr As IntPtr
  iptr = Marshal.AllocHGlobal(bufsize)
  Marshal.StructureToPtr(re, iptr, False)
  res = RasGetEntryProperties2(Nothing, PhoneBookEntryToGet, iptr, bufsize, 0, 0)
  re = CType(Marshal.PtrToStructure(iptr, GetType(RASENTRY)), RASENTRY)
  Marshal.FreeHGlobal(iptr)
End If
Console.WriteLine(re.szLocalPhoneNumber)
Console.ReadLine()
End Sub

End Module
```

Recap

The .NET platform might be a better way of programming but the transition to that platform will be slow—very slow. Existing components don't magically switch over. Neither do Microsoft's own services such as Transaction Server and Microsoft Message Queue (by whatever names they refer to them at any given time). So, interoperability with both COM and the underlying system calls is an essential part of the .NET Framework.

In this chapter, you learned that it is remarkably easy to use COM components in .NET assemblies. Visual Studio magically handles most of the work for you. It is only a little more difficult to use .NET components in COM services. As long as you limit yourself to automation-compatible interfaces such as those used by VB6, you can avoid almost all of the potential complexity that comes into play with other data types. The most important issues to deal with when exposing .NET assemblies to COM relate to versioning—DLL Hell problems can occur if you are not careful.

Finally, we closed with one of my favorite subjects, calling API functions from Visual Basic.NET. You saw that VB.NET is even more powerful and flexible in this area than VB6. Most API calls can be handled as easily or more easily than with VB6 but handling complex API calls can still require advanced techniques and knowledge (which, by the way, are just as tricky to deal with in C#). The biggest problem most VB6 programmers will face when migrating to VB.NET is remembering to convert all those Long parameters to Integers and Integer parameters to Shorts.

CHAPTER 16

Living with .NET

THE TITLE OF THIS BOOK IS *Moving to VB.NET: Strategies, Concepts, and Code*. You've read about strategies for migrating to VB.NET. You've learned the key concepts that every VB.NET developer must know. You've seen not only the code changes in the VB.NET language but also sample code intended to teach the concepts behind some of the more important .NET namespaces you will be using.

The .NET Framework is vast. And while I've covered just a small part of it, I believe I've covered the fundamental concepts well enough to get you off to a good start.

There are, however, a few additional topics I want to cover that are essential parts of .NET, even though they represent a relatively small part of the software development process.

First, I would like to revisit the subject of DLL Hell one last time. That will be followed by a discussion of .NET security. I'll close with coverage of any final small topics that don't quite fit anywhere else.

Let me stress that this is an incredibly important chapter. These topics were not left to the end as afterthoughts. In fact, versioning and security were among the very first topics I listed on the original outline for this book—you cannot truly program in .NET without a good understanding of both. However, they are also concepts you will find far easier to understand now that you have a good familiarity with .NET—which you do if you've read to this point.

Versioning and .NET

> **NOTE** *Throughout this chapter, I will refer to applications that reference dependent components or assemblies. For the purposes of this chapter, every situation that involves applications referencing components or assemblies also applies to assemblies or components that reference other assemblies or components.*

In Chapter 11, you learned how .NET languages use just-in-time compilation to avoid many of the component conflicts that afflict COM-based applications. The ability of the JIT compiler to bind method names in dependent assemblies anytime those assemblies are rebuilt and to detect incompatible changes during the JIT compilation process solves a part of the class of DLL compatibility problems we affectionately refer to as DLL Hell.

But DLL Hell is a stubborn problem and the JIT compilation process does not address other important scenarios.

Nightmare Scenarios

Say that you've distributed application A, which uses COM DLL D version 1.0 (Dv1.0). You then ship application B, which uses a new version of COM DLL D version 2.0 (Dv2.0).

Unfortunately, even though the developer of Dv2.0 was careful to version the DLL using VB6's binary compatibility mode and all of the internal GUID values and method and parameters are fully compatible, an error crept in. Dv1.0 had a property named Value that, when set to a negative number, would automatically set the value to zero but would not return an error (since this property did not allow negative numbers). This was considered a bug and was fixed in Dv2.0—setting the Value property to a negative number *would* raise an error.

Application A also had a small bug in which it set the Value property to –1. This didn't impair the functionality because Dv1.0 simply set the property to zero and the application ran as expected.

When application B was distributed with Dv2.0, application B, of course, worked perfectly. However, as soon as Dv2.0 was installed on the system, application A would fail. Where before it would set the Value property to –1 without problem, now a runtime error would occur. And the programmer for application A did not include runtime error-checking at that point.

This is a true story.[1]

The reason this is a big problem under Windows is that generally speaking you can only have a single version of a component on a system at a time. Once a new component has been installed in the System directory or registered (depending

---

1. The component was called the "Animated Button" control—a subset of Desaware's Custom Control Factory product licensed to Microsoft to be included in Visual Basic. Application B was Visual Basic itself. During their testing process, Microsoft discovered the bug in the control's Value property and insisted that an error result be returned if a negative value was used. I told them that this would be a serious error due to potential compatibility problems but they insisted that it was a bug and anyone who was setting the property to –1 in their code would just fix their code. Since Microsoft was paying the bills, I changed the code and, sure enough, Application A broke—it was setting the Animated Button's Value property to –1 in error.

    Oh yes, application A was an early version of Microsoft Encarta.

    To this day, the Custom Control Factory (on which the Animated button was based) will accept a negative number in its Value property and quietly set it to zero. We at Desaware take backward compatibility *seriously* to the point that we'll add a new property to a component rather than fix a bug that could change the behavior of one of our components.

on whether it is a DLL that exports functions or a COM DLL that exposes objects), that component will be retrieved by any application that requests it.

This presents a whole series of potential problems. For example:

You install a new version of a component over an older version and the new version is not backwards compatible.

Someone installs an older version of a component over a newer version and an application depends on features present in the newer version.

Someone registers and older or newer version of a COM component so even though you have the correct version on your system, your application loads the other component based on the registry entries.

In short, you are in DLL Hell.

As you see, even if you maintain perfect binary compatibility, the possibility of functional incompatibilities always exists. As long as only one version of a component can be running on a system, the potential for DLL Hell cannot be eliminated.

Windows 98 and 2000 did add two features to the operating system that have the potential of addressing these to a degree. These operating systems support features called side-by-side execution and DLL indirection that make it possible for an application to load a DLL located in a local directory instead of one in the System directory. DLL indirection involves adding a file with the extension .local to a directory in order to force an application to load a local copy of a component even if another version exists on a system. Side-by-side execution requires specific design considerations when the component is written.

Unfortunately, these approaches suffer from a number of practical problems:

Since most software components were not designed to support side-by-side execution, there is no guarantee that the components will work properly when using DLL indirection.

Neither of these techniques works on versions of Windows before Windows 98 and Windows 2000, yet few component vendors can ignore those operating systems for commercial components.

VB6 components can work with DLL indirection but because you have no control over the registration process of a VB6 component, it is not possible to create side-by-side components in VB6.

It doesn't make much sense to invest heavily in designing your components for side-by-side execution in COM when .NET handles the problem very nicely (as you will soon see).

Paranoid Scenarios

I've recently been exchanging e-mail with a developer who is so concerned about someone reverse engineering his application that he wants to know how he can encrypt one executable within another, decrypt it when the first one is run, and prevent anyone from debugging it and even viewing it in the process list.[2]

I can't help but wonder what piece of software is so critical that it requires such a level of security.[3]

But as long as we're being paranoid, consider the following scenario:

Application A uses COM DLL Dv1. This component is very safe and could not possibly harm the system. A nefarious programmer hatches an evil scheme. He takes a copy of Dv1 and reverse engineers it. He doesn't need to figure out all of the component's functionality—most of the functions he doesn't change at all (he uses a disassembler and just reassembles those functions). But he modifies a few key methods to do terrible things, such as erasing the hard drive, sending out the corrupt DLL to everyone on a system's e-mail list, and so on. He then builds the DLL giving it the same name (we'll call it Dv1bad) and incrementing the revision number to 1.01 so it will install over any existing DLL of that name. Dv1bad has the same type library information, the same version properties, and so on. The evil programmer then ships the corrupted DLL with application B, which seems very innocent.

This is called *spoofing* and while not a common problem, can be very serious—especially if someone spoofs a system file.

Unfortunately there is nothing built into Windows to detect these kinds of problems. When one is discovered, it is typically (and correctly) treated as a virus and the file signature is added to the virus definition files of the various antivirus software products. However, by then, it may be too late for you.

.NET and Versioning

Microsoft .NET supports two different types of versioning based on how you name your assembly.

Name? What does versioning have to do with names?

As it turns out, a great deal.

Assemblies in .NET can be given a simple name or a strong name. A simple name consists of the name of the assembly as defined in the project properties for the assembly. This is typically also the name of the assembly file itself. A strong name includes the simple name, the version number, the culture, the public key, and a digital signature for the assembly.

---

2. No, I have not researched whether these are possible.

3. And no, I did not ask.

Every assembly we've built so far has used simple names. This is because the assemblies you've seen are simple programs created for educational purposes. As such, I don't particularly care about versioning or dependencies. I don't care about spoofing—you have the source code anyway.

But most of the assemblies you ship should use strong names.

Here's why:

Simple names are designed for the case where all of the assemblies are loaded from the local application directory.

Simple-named assemblies do not use versioning. When the CLR binds to an assembly with a simple name, it will load whatever assembly it finds with the specified name in the current directory without regards to the version number.

Simple-named assemblies provide no protection from spoofing.

The .NET runtime will detect if a simple-named assembly is missing from the local directory. If you break compatibility between versions of a dependent assembly that uses a simple name, the error will be detected at runtime and an exception will be raised—so at least you won't get a memory exception. Of course, if you don't handle the runtime error, your program will crash anyway.

The UnsignedApp1 and UnsignedDLL1 sample projects are designed to allow you to experiment with dependencies of simple assemblies. Try changing the version number of UnsignedDLL1 and then running UnsignedApp1. Also try changing the parameters of the Class1.MyVersion function in UnsignedDLL1 and see what happens when you run UnsignedApp1.

In other words, while .NET will protect you from the worst system crashes if you use simple-named assemblies, DLL Hell with simple-named assemblies is still a very real problem.

Are there any cases where simple-named assemblies should be used?

Only two come to mind:

1. When you simply don't care about versioning or dependencies. This might be the case if you are writing sample programs for a book or article.

2. When you have total control over the contents of the directory. Even simple-named assemblies benefit from the side-by-side execution that is a natural consequence of the fact that .NET always tries to load simple-named assemblies from the application's local directory first. But even in this case, there is no disadvantage to using strong-named assemblies other than a bit of extra hassle involved in the building phase (which is virtually automatic when you use Visual Studio).

Suffice to say that you should use strong names for all assemblies that you actually plan to deploy, even if it is within your own organization.

Strong Names

Try creating a simple VB6 application in which you use the CreateObject function to create an object with the name Project1.Class1.

If you've been developing with VB6 on your system for any length of time, this operation will succeed. You will get an object for whatever trivial throwaway ActiveX EXE or DLL you last created.

Under COM, there is nothing to prevent two people from creating objects that use the same name. COM addresses the problem of duplicate names by using GUID values—globally unique values that are the "true" names of an object, class, or interface.

Microsoft .NET addresses the problem of duplicate names by combining various pieces of information that together uniquely identify an assembly. These include:

The simple name of the assembly

The version number of the assembly

The culture (or locale) of the assembly (optional).

The public key of the assembly author.

A hash value for the assembly.

Together, these elements uniquely identify an assembly. Individually, they each serve a different purpose:

The simple name provides the humanly readable form of the assembly name.

The version number identifies the exact version of an assembly, making it possible for an assembly to request and load a specific version of an assembly.

The culture makes it possible to differentiate between editions of an assembly localized for different languages or otherwise supporting different cultures.

The public key makes it possible to determine if spoofing has occurred and if someone other than the original author has created a dependent assembly.

A hash value makes it possible to determine if an assembly has been modified.

Strong naming is the feature that makes it possible for .NET to eliminate DLL Hell for .NET components.[4]

---

4. Remember, this feature does nothing to prevent DLL Hell from occurring with COM components you are using via COM Interop.

Strong Names and Versioning

Consider how an application loads a COM component:

1. The application has the name or GUID of the object it needs to load.

2. The application searches the registry for the location of the object.

3. The application loads the object.

Since the registry only holds a single entry for each component, there is no mechanism for identifying, finding and loading different versions of the same component.[5]

Components in .NET don't use the registry at all. The central repository for shared assemblies is the global assembly cache (GAC). But only strong-named assemblies can be stored in the GAC, which stores assemblies by their strong name. In other words, the GAC is perfectly happy storing as many different versions of an assembly as you would care to install.

A .NET application loads a .NET component in a process called binding. This process is radically different from that of COM:[6]

- The application figures out the strong name of the assembly it needs to load based on the application, publisher, and system configuration files (which will be described shortly).

- If the assembly is already loaded, the application binds to the loaded assembly.

- The CLR checks to see if the assembly is in the GAC and, if present, loads it from there.

- The CLR performs a series of probes based on the configuration files. Locations searched include the location specified by the Codebase option (if present), the application directory, and any other subdirectories specified in the configuration files.

The binding process is based on the strong name. Since the strong name includes the version number, this means that every application has an exact list of the versions of all its dependent assemblies and, by default, will only work with that exact version.

Strong Name Example

The StrongApp1 and StrongDLL1 sample projects are intended to help you experiment with versioning.

---

5. With the exception of the infrequently used, COM-based side-by-side execution described earlier in this chapter.

6. This is a slight simplification. Refer to the online documentation under "How the Runtime Locates Assemblies" for an in-depth description of the loading sequence.

The StrongDLL1 sample project contains a single class with a method that returns the full version name of the component:

```
Imports System.Reflection
Public Class Class1
    Public Function MyVersion() As String
        Return Reflection.Assembly.GetExecutingAssembly.FullName()
    End Function

End Class
```

The exact version number should be set in the Assemblyinfo.vb file as shown here:

```
<Assembly: AssemblyVersion ("1.0.0.1")>
```

The StrongDLL1 project is configured to create a strong name by specifying a key file in the project settings (under the Sharing tab). The key file, named TestKeys.snk, is created using the sn.exe (strongname) tool with the –k parameter (though you can also create a new key set using Visual Studio when you set the strong name). The Testkeys.snk file can be found in the CH16 directory (it is used by several of the Chapter 16 projects). You should not use this key file in your own applications.[7]

In most cases, you will not actually have access to the key file—most enterprises prefer to keep their private keys secure on a floppy disk or secure server and do not release them to developers. To handle this situation, you'll actually check the Delay sign checkbox. This causes the public key to be embedded into the assembly—which is sufficient (as you will see) for applications to reference the assembly, and reserves space in the executable file for the full strong name to be added later. You can use the sn.exe program to extract the public key and distribute it to your developers. The sn.exe program can be used to re-sign the assembly using the private key, inserting the strong name into the assembly before it is released.

The StrongApp1 project references the StrongDLL1 assembly. It is a console application that displays the version of that assembly by calling its public MyVersion function as shown here:

---

7. This key file was generated specifically for these examples. You should assume that both the public and private key are known publicly and should not use this file for any purpose besides experimenting with these sample programs.

```
Imports strongDLL1
Module Module1

    Sub Main()
        Dim c As New strongDLL1.Class1()
        Console.WriteLine(c.MyVersion)
        Console.ReadLine()
    End Sub

End Module
```

When the program runs, you will see this result:

```
strongDLL1, Version=1.0.0.0, Culture=neutral, PublicKeyToken=4139a2c451ef76d7
```

The PublicKeyToken is a hashed version of the public key. I'll have more to say about this shortly. If you disassemble the StrongApp1 application, you will find the following code:

```
.assembly extern strongDLL1
{
  .publickeytoken = (41 39 A2 C4 51 EF 76 D7 )     // A9..Q.v.
  .ver 1:0:0:0
}
```

The application will only bind to version 1.0.0.0 of strongDLL1 that has the public key specified. This means that the default behavior of every strong-named assembly is that it must have exactly the right versions of each dependent assembly in order to work. This eliminates the possibility of version-based incompatibilities.

Of course, this default behavior also eliminates the possibility of upgrading components

Upgrading Strong-Named Components

At first glance, it looks as if anytime you distribute any upgraded component, you will also have to rebuild and redistribute any applications that use that component (otherwise those applications will continue to reference the existing version of the component). This might solve DLL Hell but would likely result in Distribution Hell.

Fortunately, .NET provides a configuration mechanism to control the binding of assemblies so that applications can load upgraded versions of dependent assemblies. This consists of not one, not two, but three XML-based configuration files. Configuration files provide control over the security, versioning, and remoting of an application.

The first of these is the application configuration file. This file specifies the default configuration for an application. The publisher configuration file is a file that is added when an application is updated to override default settings including those relating to versioning. Finally, there is the machine configuration file. Set by the system administrator, this file controls the behavior of all assemblies on the system (overriding the values in the application and publisher configuration file).

The application configuration file uses the name of the application with the suffix .config, for example, Myapp.exe.config. The publisher configuration file has the format policy.major.minor.myassembly.dll—major and minor are the major and minor numbers of the assembly to which the policy applies and myassembly is the name of the assembly to which the policy applies. The policy for versions 2.1.0.0 through 2.1.x.x of assembly strongdll1 would be in a policy file named policy.2.1.strongdll1.dll. Policy files only apply to assemblies stored in the GAC. Refer to the online documentation for instructions on building policy files. The system configuration is generally set using the Microsoft Management Console.

The top-level tag for each configuration file is <Configuration> (so the file opens with the tag <Configuration> and closes with </Configuration>).

Consider the following sample configuration file:

```
<configuration>
    <runtime>
        <assemblyBinding  xmlns="urn:schemas-microsoft-com:asm.v1">
            <dependentAssembly>
             <assemblyIdentity name="strongDLL1"
             PublicKeyToken="4139a2c451ef76d7" culture="" />
             <bindingRedirect oldVersion="1.0.0.0-1.0.0.1"
             newVersion="1.0.0.2" />
            </dependentAssembly>
        </assemblyBinding>
    </runtime>
</configuration>
```

There is a <dependentAssembly> block for each dependent assembly whose behavior you wish to modify. This block includes an <assemblyIdentity> tag, which contains tags that identify the assembly by its strong name (including the name, version, culture, and public key with which it is signed).

The <codebase> tag can be used to indicate from where to load the assembly if it is not located in the global assembly cache or local directory.

The <bindingRedirect> tag can be used to specify that the runtime should load an updated assembly. In this case, applications that are built with versions 1.0.0.0 through 1.0.0.1 of the strongDLL1 assembly will load version 1.0.0.2. The assumption is that you'll test out the compatibility of the newer assembly before you set this.

The <publisherPolicy> tag (not shown here) determines whether the publisher's configuration file should be used (it represents the assembly publisher's view of the which version should be bound). In other words, even if a component publisher releases an updated assembly with a policy file that permits automatic upgrading, you have the option to override that policy file and force the application to use the previous version of the component.

The `<probing>` tag (which appears under the `<assemblyBinding>` tag) allows you to specify which application subdirectories to search for assemblies. This allows you to organize assemblies more effectively if you have many assemblies in a project.

Versioning the .NET Runtime

Consider the following sample configuration file:

```
<configuration>
   <startup>
      <requiredRuntime version="1.0.0.0" safeMode="false"/>
   </startup>
</configuration>
```

This allows an application to specify that it requires a specific version of the .NET runtime in order to run.

So far in this chapter, you've heard about .NET's ability to eliminate DLL Hell by allowing an assembly to specify exact versions of dependent assemblies. It is good that Microsoft recognized the fact that this applies to the .NET runtime itself—given that Microsoft itself has caused more DLL Hell problems through incompatible components than any other company (nothing against Microsoft—it's a simple reflection of the fact that they've shipped more DLLs than anyone else). You can, in fact, have multiple versions of the .NET runtime installed on a system and running simultaneously.

The only limitation to this flag is that it doesn't necessarily help you with applications (such as Web controls) that are hosted in Internet Explorer since Internet Explorer may already be running an instance of the runtime and you can't have two different versions of the .NET runtime working with the same process simultaneously.

Strong Names and Spoofing

You've seen how strong names deal with versioning problems by incorporating the version number into the assembly name. Now let's explore how they solve the problem of assembly spoofing or modification.

As you've seen, the StrongApp1 application contains the public key token of the StrongDLL1 assembly. This token is a hash of the actual public key. The idea here is that there is no need to store the entire public key in your application—you only need to ensure that the public key contained in the dependent assembly is the same one that was there when your application was built. A hash value does this nicely because it is virtually impossible for two different public keys to generate the same hash value (just as it is virtually impossible to generate the public key given the hash value).

At load time, the CLR loader looks at the dependent assembly and hashes its public key. It compares this with the public key token in the calling application. If they match, the CLR knows that the public key in the calling application is valid for further tests.

The nature of public key encryption is such that only a public key can be used to decrypt information encrypted with a corresponding private key. When an assembly is signed with the private key (during build or release), a hash is made of the entire assembly, which creates a digital signature. This signature can be encrypted using the private key and decrypted with the public key.

As long as the private key is uncompromised, it is impossible for anyone to modify an assembly undetected. At load time, a hash is made of the entire assembly as it actually exists. The public key can be used to decrypt the signature that was placed in the assembly when it was created. If the new hash value does not match the digital signature in the file, the CLR knows the file has been modified and it will not load.

It's impossible to modify the stored signature because a private key encrypts it. It is impossible to modify the public key because the token will not match the one stored in the application.

Thus, strong names nicely solve the problem of assembly spoofing.

Strong Names versus Signcode

Strong names do not, however, solve the problem of accurately identifying the source of an assembly. In other words, say you are given a component from a company called hcwrecords.com. You can reference it and use it without any problem but how do you know that it actually came from hcwrecords.com? Simply put, strong names are anonymous. Hackers can give their component strong names too.

That's where code signing comes in. This is familiar to ActiveX control authors who use Authenticode to sign their controls. Code signing uses a trusted third party to provide you with the public key of the component vendor. Assuming you trust the third party to perform their verification correctly, you can be sure that a component from hcwrecords.com really comes from them and not someone else pretending to be them.[8]

Strong names and code signing are complimentary—you can use both with an assembly. If you choose to use both, you must apply the strong name first.

Namespace Conflicts

It is easy to confuse assembly naming with namespaces. I encourage you to review Chapter 10 where this subject is discussed in depth. Remember, it is important that you make any namespaces of shared assemblies (those you plan to install in the global assembly cache) unique. The best way to do this is to use your company name as the root of your namespace. That's why all of the .NET Framework namespaces provided by Microsoft begin with either System or Microsoft.

It is a good practice to use this naming convention even for assemblies you do not plan to install in the global assembly cache.

.NET and Side-by-Side Execution

The Microsoft .NET runtime is designed to support two types of side-by-side execution: one on the same machine and one within the same process. However, the current version of the runtime does not support side-by-side execution in the same process. The documentation suggests that this will be a feature in a future release.

This means that two different versions of an assembly can be run by two different applications at once. However, at this time, a single process cannot load two versions of an assembly. If you examine the StrongDLL2A, StrongDLL2B, and StrongApp2 projects, you'll see a demonstration of this fact.

StrongDLL2B references version 1.0 of the StrongDLL2A assembly. StrongApp2 references version 1.0.0.1 of StrongDLL2A and references StrongDLL2B directly. This means that in order to run, both version 1.0.0.0 and 1.0.0.1 would need to be loaded into memory at once. Since this is not possible, loading fails unless the policy file StrongApp2.exe.config specifies that it accepts version 1.0.0.1 as an upgrade to 1.0.0.0.

Because your assemblies have machine side-by-side execution enabled, you must keep this in mind when designing your assemblies. For example, if your assembly has hard-coded file paths, or uses named mutexes, you must keep in mind that those objects may be accessed by two different versions of your components simultaneously.

---

8. I'm not going to go into further detail of code signing at this point since it will probably be used less frequently than it was with ActiveX controls now that strong names provide the protection from modification that was one of the features of Authenticode.

Security

Security means different things to different people:

It means the ability to authenticate users, either locally or over the Internet.

It means the ability to protect your computer or server from various types of attacks.

It means the ability to allow or prevent applications from running.

It means the ability to prevent malicious software from doing harm to your system.

It means the ability to keep information private or maintain private communication channels.

That's right—security is also a subject deserving of an entire book.[9] But you're used to that by now. At the same time, you're probably familiar with at least some of these aspects of security. You can start out by assuming that the types of security features you have controlled programmatically in VB6 can still be coded using .NET, in many cases using related .NET namespaces such as System.Security or System.DirectoryServices.

In this section, I'd like to focus primarily on one aspect of security, the ability to prevent malicious software from doing harm to your system. This is an area where the .NET Framework provides new features that are incredibly exciting and of which you must become familiar.

Goodbye Crashes, Goodbye Viruses?

The .NET Framework has, as one of its goals, nothing less than the elimination of unrecoverable application crashes and the ability to protect your system from viruses and other malicious code.

I can see you shaking your head. "Yeah, right—I've heard that before…"

I don't blame you for being skeptical. Every time Microsoft announces a new security scheme, it seems to be inevitably followed by a series of news report of security holes and patches from Microsoft. And every time we hear about a new operating system that is even more stable than the previous one, we still run into all sorts of quirks that require rebooting (whether voluntarily or not).

It is too early to know how truly secure .NET will be or whether it will really be more stable but I think after you read this section, you'll agree that the security architecture of .NET shows that they are taking these subjects very seriously. At the very least, it is a huge step in the right direction.

---

9.   Still looking for authors here. ☺

On Crashes and Pointers

If you think back to the days of 16-bit Windows (assuming you were around back then), you may recall the joys of the UAE (Unrecoverable Application Error), which was replaced with the GPF (Global Protection Fault). Nowadays, while you will still experience application crashes (indicated by either a "Memory exception has occurred" error or the sudden disappearance of the application), you rarely experience a true system crash, such as a total freeze on Windows 98/ME or the BSD (blue screen of death) on NT/2000.

Why do these things happen?

Because most applications are written in languages like C++ that use pointers. And any time you have a pointer, there is the possibility that it will somehow be assigned an incorrect value. It might be an uninitialized pointer that points to nonexistent memory. It might point to code segments in your application and accidentally erase your code.[10] It might point to your application's data but not the correct data and cause some of your data structures (including other pointers) to be corrupted. Or, you may accidentally use a pointer to write past the end of the destination buffer, again corrupting the next variable in memory.

Yes, there are other causes for applications to crash, such as dividing a number by zero. And many applications raise runtime errors (sometimes intentionally and sometimes unintentionally). But pointer errors are the source of most unexpected crashes.

Microsoft's 32-bit operating system eliminated most system crashes through the simple expedient of isolating processes from each other and from the operating system.[11] However, this kind of process isolation is not sufficient for .NET. As you learned in Chapter 10, .NET focuses on Application Domains rather than processes. Yes, an Application Domain might correspond to a single process but in hosts such as ASP.NET, hundreds or thousands of Application Domains might be hosted in the ASP.NET process.

If it were possible for a pointer in one of these Application Domains to somehow corrupt other Application Domains (or ASP.NET itself), it would be very difficult to achieve any sort of stability.

Your first thought might be that this problem was solved by removing pointers from the .NET languages (such as VB.NET and C#), yet you saw in Chapter 15 that even VB.NET could use Int32Ptr pointer variables to work with unmanaged code.

The answer has to do with type safety. Think about what you learned in Chapter 15 about how to work with unmanaged code. Access to unmanaged code uses the Marshal object in which each transfer to and from unmanaged code is through a clearly defined data structure. In other words, even though you are copying

---

10. Depending on the OS and Pointer type, trying to write to code will either modify your code or cause a memory exception.

11. This is not *entirely* accurate for Windows 95/98/ME but close enough for our purposes.

memory, you are doing so by specifying the exact layout of data in memory using strongly typed variables. Assuming your function and structure declarations are correct, the CLR can guarantee that the transfer will occur correctly—there will be no mysterious buffer overruns or data corruption.

As for other access to managed memory, since all access is through strongly typed objects (as discussed in Chapter 10), you can accomplish *verifiable* isolation between Application Domains. An application that meets this requirement is called *verifiably type safe*. The CLR has the ability to scan the code and verify type safety. Not every .NET language creates verifiably type safe code (it's possible for code to be type safe but not verifiable—C++ can generate this type of code) but VB.NET code should always pass this test. You can check an assembly's type safety using the Preverify.exe tool. With C# you have a choice but there is little benefit (if any) to using unsafe code.

There is, however, one serious disadvantage to using unsafe code: it requires a higher degree of trust to run. I'll explain what that means shortly.

On Malicious Code and Viruses

Code arrives on your system from many different sources. There is, of course, code you install using a CD or floppy. At one time, that was all you had to worry about. But now you have controls and components downloaded with Web pages, scripts that run on Web pages, software uploads brought in from Web and FTP sites, files attached to e-mail messages—even macros hidden in text or spreadsheet documents.

And every one of those pieces of code can cause total havoc on your system.

Why? Because with the exception of certain scripting languages, every one of those programs has full permission to do anything on your system once given the opportunity to run.

The operating system security on Windows NT/2000 is very limited in its ability to secure applications. It can prevent a particular user or group from running a particular application but once that application runs, it can do anything. Some scripting languages run in what's called a sandbox—a virtual machine that severely restricts what the languages are able to do. This prevents the scripts from causing harm but also denies them the ability to do many useful tasks.

The .NET Framework takes a radically different approach to application security. In addition to the role-based security with which you are familiar (permissions based on who the user is), .NET adds *code access* security.[12]

---

12. Role-based security in .NET is actually quite flexible. In addition to allowing identity based on system security accounts and groups, you can define custom roles. You could, for example, create a database of user identities and roles independent of those built into the operating system and use those to base security decisions. Role-based security is, nevertheless, similar in concept to the role-based security with which you are probably familiar. Thus, I will not go into great detail on the subject in this chapter.

The basic idea is as follows.

Every assembly runs in its own security context based on information about the assembly and the security policies set on the system.

When an assembly is verifiably type safe, the CLR can accurately track what code is running and what it is doing (there's no way to somehow jump to some location in code without the knowledge of the CLR). That means the CLR can be sure when the code is accessing a particular method in a namespace. That, in turn, means it is possible to reliably impose security constraints on an object or method level.

The CLR has the ability to perform a stack walk—checking the security not only of the code that is running but also of every assembly that has called it. This makes it difficult for a malicious piece of code to use another assembly to do its dirty work.

That's the quick summary. Now let's take a closer look at .NET security and how it works in practice.

Assemblies and Security Policies

The first thing you need to know about code access security is that .NET bases security decisions on evidence—information it knows about an assembly.

Evidence

What kinds of things can .NET know about an assembly? In other words, what kind of evidence can it store about an assembly?

- The publisher of the assembly if the assembly has a digital certificate.

- The Web site that is trying to execute the assembly (when called through a Web page access).

- The strong name of the assembly (identifies a unique assembly).

- The URL (Web site or FTP site) from which the code was downloaded.

- The Internet zone from which the code was downloaded. Zones are based on the traditional Internet Explorer settings and include the Internet, private Intranet, any sites marked specifically as trusted or restricted, and the local machine itself.

- Whether or not an assembly is in the same directory as the launching application or in its subdirectory.

Consider some possible scenarios:

Your ASP.NET components can be effectively secured based on the site that originates the call because the CLR can use the site identity as evidence.

When browsing, the CLR knows exactly where any downloaded code comes from. Say you trust assemblies from both your local Intranet and those from Microsoft.com, you can specify that assemblies from those sources are trusted.

You can fine tune permission even to the point of prohibiting all code on a specific Web site from modifying your registry or writing to disk.

When an assembly is installed on your system, .NET will store any of this evidence if it is available and use it when evaluating the security policies for that assembly.

Permissions

The System.Security.Permissions namespace contains objects that define permissions. Permission objects represent the right to access a protected resource or operation. You can define your own as well but that's a subject beyond the scope of this book.

Table 15–1. The Permission Classes

PERMISSION OBJECT	OPERATION SECURED
DirectoryServicesPermission	Objects in the System.DirectoryServices namespace.
DnsPermission	DNS operations.
EnvironmentPermission	Environment variables.
EventLogPermission	The event log.
FileDialogPermission	Files selected using the File Open common dialog box.
FileIOPermission	File and directory access.
IsolatedStorageFilePermission	Private virtual file systems.
IsolatedStoragePermission	Isolated storage—a new type of storage in .NET associated with the identity of the code.
MessageQueuePermission	Microsoft Message Queue (MSMQ).
OleDbPermission	OLE DB operations.

Table 15–1. The Permission Classes (Continued)

PERMISSION OBJECT	OPERATION SECURED
PerformanceCounterPermission	Performance counters.
PrintingPermission	Printer operations.
ReflectionPermission	.NET reflection operations.
RegistryPermission	System registry operations.
SecurityPermission	A variety of code access permissions.
ServiceControllerPermission	Windows services.
SocketPermission	Socket operations.
SQLClientPermission	SQL database operations.
UIPermission	User-interface functions.
WebPermission	Web operations (send or accept).

Each of these Permission objects has methods that allow you to control the way the CLR secures the operation in question. You'll read more about those shortly.

Permission Sets

A permission set is a set of possible permissions. It's just a way of taking various settings of these Permission objects (and others you define), placing them in a group, and giving it a label. For example, the Internet permission set defines the permissions that you wish to typically use for code downloaded from the Internet. The Full trust permission set allows code permission to perform any operation.

Remember, permission sets are just a group of permissions. You can assign any permission set to any code group. You can define new permission sets. You can even change the permissions in a default permission set.

Policies

All code under .NET can be associated with one or more code groups based on evidence available for the code. For example, all code belongs to the "All code" group. Code with a digital signature from Microsoft would belong to the "Published by Microsoft" group. A code group can even consist of a single assembly specified by its strong name. Code groups are defined in a hierarchy with the "All code" group at the top.

Every system has up to three different policies in effect: that of the entire enterprise, that of the machine, and that of the individual user.

Consider, for example, an assembly running in a browser downloaded from BadCodeSite.bad. Based on evidence available, it belongs to two code groups:

- All Code

- Internet Zone

The machine policy for the Internet zone would most likely deny permission to write to disk, access your local e-mail folders, access the registry, or perform other Internet operations. As a result, if the assembly tried to do anything dangerous, a Runtime exception would occur.

But what if that code had a digital signature from HCWrecords.com, a trusted site? In this case, it might be part of the HCWRecords code group. If that code group allowed permission to write to disk or perform other secured operations, the assembly would be granted those rights.

In other words, within a policy level, rights are additive. If a right is granted due to the presence of code in any code group, the assembly will have that right. You can also configure the security search to stop at a particular code group or policy level, as you will soon see.

The actual permissions granted are the least among the three policy levels. Thus, in this example, if the Enterprise policy were set to deny a certain permission to the HCWRecords code group, that would take precedence even if the machine and user policy permitted it.

Policy groups are applied in order: Enterprise, then User, and then Machine.

In addition to these three groups, every assembly is also checked against the security settings for the Application Domain.

I realize this is somewhat confusing. I encourage you to read the Microsoft documentation as well—look in the .NET Framework SDK under the hierarchy, "Programming with the .NET Framework\Securing your Application." Their explanation is more thorough than mine but I found it to be more than a little confusing. My hope is that between this chapter and the documentation, you will gain a real understanding of .NET security.

Meanwhile, let's look at a specific example that will help you see how this works in practice.

Security Examples

There's nothing like a practical example to make a complex subject more clear. I think you'll find the ones that follow intriguing.

Configuration and Stack Traces

The CallUnmanaged1 solution opens two projects, CallUnmanaged1 and UnmanagedClass. The UnmanagedClass object is defined as follows:

```
Public Class Class1
    Private Declare Auto Function GetTickCount Lib "kernel32" () As Integer
    Public Function Ticks() As Integer
        Return GetTickCount()
    End Function
End Class
```

As you can see, this is a simple example of an API call wrapped into an object. You and I know this is a completely harmless API call—but the CLR does not. Because API calls can perform many dangerous operations and bypass the .NET Framework (and thus the standard Permission objects you read about earlier), permission to run unmanaged code is one that requires a great deal of trust.

For instance, you would never want to grant unmanaged code permission to execute code downloaded from the Internet unless you had some very strong evidence that you could trust it.

This is one of the major reasons why you should avoid using Win32 API calls in VB.NET—it makes your code much less mobile. For example, you can't use API calls in controls that you want people to be able to run in their browsers through the Internet because chances are good that they will fail.

Now, this particular assembly is created and installed on the system—and since it belongs to the local system code group, it is fully trusted. So, this code will work if called from a Windows application but what would happen if it were called from an assembly downloaded from the Internet?

The public Ticks function does not itself use unmanaged code. Could an assembly without unmanaged code permission use the Ticks function to trick the UnmanagedClass.Class1 object into calling an API function in its behalf?

Let's see.

The CallsUnmanaged1 console application creates a Class1 object and calls its Ticks method as shown here:

```
' Calling unmanaged class
' Copyright ©2001 by Desaware Inc. All Rights Reserved
Imports UnmanagedClass
Module Module1

    Sub Main()
        Dim c As New Class1()
        Dim x As Integer
        For x = 0 To 100
            Console.WriteLine(c.Ticks)
        Next
        Console.ReadLine()
    End Sub

End Module
```

If you just build the object and run it, the code will work because the CallsUnmanaged1 application also belongs to the local system code group. To test the security system, you need to change the permission set for this application. To do this, use the .NET configuration tool. Start by running mmc.exe (the Microsoft Management Console) and add the .NET configuration snap-in using the Add/ Remove snap-in command.[13]

Figure 16-1 shows the runtime security policy for a system. In this case, the machine policy is expanded. You can see that the machine defines a number of code groups. It also defines a number of permission sets that can be assigned to specific code groups. In this figure, you can see the permission allowed by the Internet permission set.

What we're going to do is add the CallsUnmanaged1 application to a new code group. This is done by right-clicking on the My_Computer_Zone group (since this assembly is a subset of that group) and defining a new subgroup.

The wizard will prompt you for a name and description of the code group. Enter any name you wish.

Next, you'll be asked for the membership condition. This is where you specify the type of evidence that is used to identify assemblies belonging to this code group. Choose Strong-Name.

Then you'll be asked for the public key, name, and version information that identifies the assembly. The easiest way to handle this is to click the Import button and import the information from the CallsUnmanaged1.exe executable file. Be sure to check the Name and Version checkboxes or you'll change security for every assembly that uses your public key!

---

13. You can also use the caspol utility program to configure security. In fact, you can even hand edit the system configuration files using a text editor—they are just XML.

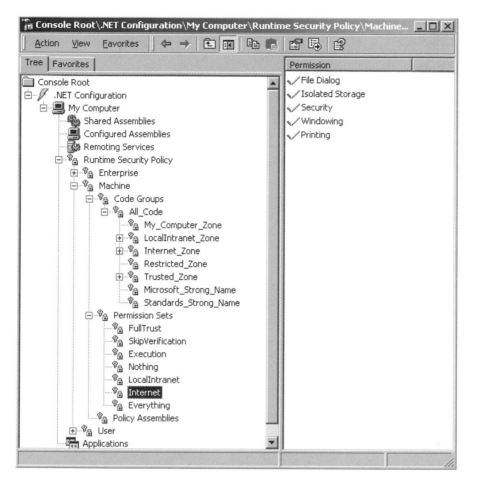

Figure 16-1. The MMC snap-in runtime security policy.

Next, the wizard will ask you for the permission set to use. Choose the Internet permission set.

After you have finished this step, you will need to go back and right-click on your newly created code group and select the Properties option. Check the check box labeled "This policy level will only have the permissions from the permission set associated with this code group." This is important in this case because the code (being local) might exist in other code groups as well, and permissions are additive within the level. This tells the security system that you wish to apply the permission set for this code group to all assemblies in this code group regardless of whether or not they are in another group. The other checkbox indicates that this is the last policy level you want to check. In this case, if you check it, the User policy level won't be searched.

Right-click on the Runtime Security Policy node and select Save All to save the settings you've changed.

If you've followed this sequence correctly, as far as the CLR is concerned, the CallsUnmanaged1 application has permissions typical of a downloaded Internet application.

So, what happens when you try to run the application?

If you call it from a command prompt, you'll see the following:[14]

```
Unhandled Exception:
System.Security.SecurityException:
Request for permission of type "System.Security.Permissions.SecurityPermission,
mscorlib, Version=1.0.?.?, Culture=neutral, PublicKeyToken=b77a5c561934e089"
failed.   at System.Security.CodeAccessSecurityEngine.CheckHelper(PermissionSet
grantedSet, PermissionSet deniedSet, CodeAccessPermission demand, PermissionToken
permToken) at UnmanagedClass.Class1.GetTickCount() at Unmanaged-
Class.Class1.Ticks() in D:\CPBknet\Src1\CH16\UnmanagedClass\Class1.vb:line 4 at
CallsUnmanaged1.Module1.Main() in D:\CPBk-
net\Src1\CH16\CallsUnmanaged1\Module1.vb:line 10


The state of the failed permission was:
<IPermission class="System.Security.Permissions.SecurityPermission, mscorlib, Ver-
sion=1.0.?.?, Culture=neutral, PublicKeyToken=b77a5c561934e089"
            version="1"
            Flags="UnmanagedCode"/>
```

Now, here's the question: the security configuration was set to deny unmanaged code permission to the CallsUnmanaged1 console application. But the GetTickCount call was in the UnmanagedCall.dll assembly.

How did the CLR know to deny permission to the code?

The answer is simple. Any time a securable operation takes place, the CLR performs a stack trace. It goes up the call stack checking the securable operation against the security settings for every function. Before the GetTickCount API is called, the CLR checks to see if it is allowed at that level. It is because the assembly is part of the local machine group (My_Computer_Zone). It then checks the Ticks method. That passes as well because it is part of the same assembly. It then tries the Main subroutine in the CallsUnmanaged1 application. Here, it fails because that assembly does not have unmanaged code permission.

As you can see, the CLR does a very good job of identifying and securing code. Code security can be set according to the degree of trust you have in the code. Not only that but from a programmer's point of view, you can degrade your code gracefully by trapping security runtime errors and disabling functionality in less secure environments.

---

14. The version numbers, tokens, and message details may differ on your system.

But what about cases where you can guarantee that an operation is safe and want less secure assemblies to be able to perform the operation, assuming your component is itself trusted?

Security Demands and Assertions

The CallsUnmanaged2 solution opens two projects, CallsUnmanaged2 and UnmanagedClass2.

Before continuing, you should first build both project, then use the mmc configuration program to set the CallsUnmanaged2 application to use the Internet permission set as you did earlier for the CallsUnmanaged1 program.

The UnmanagedClass2 object defines GetTickCount as before but the Ticks function has been modified as shown here:

```
Imports System.Security.Permissions
Imports System.Security.Principal
Imports System.Security

Public Class Class1
    Private Declare Auto Function GetTickCount Lib "kernel32" () _
    As Integer

    <SecurityPermission(SecurityAction.Demand, _
     Flags:=SecurityPermissionFlag.UnmanagedCode)> _
    Public Function Ticks() As Integer
        Return GetTickCount()
    End Function
```

The SecurityPermission attribute with the Demand action specified tells the CLR that this method must have the unmanaged code permission in order to run. The nice thing about demanding permission is that you no longer have to trap individual runtime errors inside the method. The caller must have unmanaged code permission in order to even call the method. When you use an attribute in this manner, it is called "Declarative Security" because you are declaring the security requirements as part of the method declaration.

You can even add the following line to the assemblyinfo.vb file for an assembly to prevent it from loading if certain minimum permissions are available:

```
<Assembly: SecurityPermission(SecurityAction.RequestMinimum, _
Flags:=SecurityPermissionFlag.UnmanagedCode)>
```

The UnmanagedClass2 assembly has a number of test routines that are called from the CallsUnmanaged2 program. The routines measure the time to perform fifty thousand calls and returns the duration in a TimeSpan object. The value in milliseconds is displayed on the console.

The Ticks2 function shown in Listing 16-1 shows how to create a SecurityPermission object at runtime for a specified permission.

Listing 16–1. The UnmanagedClass2.Class1.Ticks2 method.

```
Public Function Ticks2() As TimeSpan
    Dim x As Integer
    Dim l As Long
    Dim t As New DateTime()
    Dim ts As TimeSpan

    Dim sec As New _
    SecurityPermission(SecurityPermissionFlag.UnmanagedCode)

    sec.Assert()

    t = DateTime.Now
    For x = 0 To 50000
        l += Ticks()
    Next
    ts = DateTime.Now.Subtract(t)
    CodeAccessPermission.RevertAssert()
    Try
        Ticks()
    Catch e As Security.SecurityException
        MsgBox("Caught the security exception after revert!")
    End Try
    Return ts
End Function
```

The Assert method tells the CLR that this code should be allowed to call unmanaged code. Because this assembly is fully trusted, it is allowed to make such an assertion. When the CLR begins the stack walk to check security, it reaches the block in which the Assert has been called and stops the stack walk granting permission. Performing a security request at runtime in this manner is referred to as an "Imperative Security."

You should obviously be very careful when you use the Assert method. Only use it if you are sure there is no way your code can be used maliciously.

Assertions are removed as soon as the function returns. You can also explicitly cancel all assertions in effect for a function using the CodeAccessSecurity Revert-Assert shared method.

This function also demonstrates how you can catch a security error. When the Ticks function is called, it fails immediately because the Ticks method has a security demand attribute in its declaration (and the previous assertion had been revoked).

> **NOTE** *Depending on the speed of your system, it might take a minute or two for the message box to appear.*

Since the GetTickCount API is always safe to call, you can short circuit this process by applying the Assert in the API declaration itself as shown here:

```
<SecurityPermission(SecurityAction.Assert, _
  Flags:=SecurityPermissionFlag.UnmanagedCode)> _
  Private Declare Auto Function GetTickCountSpecial Lib "kernel32" _
  Alias "GetTickCount" () As Integer
```

Be sure to only use this if the API function is safe or if it is private and you only call it in ways that are absolutely safe.

The Ticks3 method shown in Listing 16-2 illustrates a common approach for using the Assert method. Rather than just doing an Assert, you first use a Demand for some other permission so that you stay as restrictive as possible. In this example, role-based security (as compared to code access security) is used to allow the unmanaged access to take place only when called by members of the local Administrators group.

Listing 16–2. The UnmanagedClass2.Class1.Ticks3 method.

```
Public Function Ticks3() As TimeSpan
    Dim x As Integer
    Dim l As Long
    Dim t As New DateTime()
    Dim ts As TimeSpan
```

```
' Only allow administrators to override here - _
  not really needed in this
' example, as you can read in the text
Dim sec2 As New _
SecurityPermission(SecurityPermissionFlag.ControlPrincipal)
sec2.Assert()
AppDomain.CurrentDomain.SetPrincipalPolicy(_
PrincipalPolicy.WindowsPrincipal)
Dim roleSec As New PrincipalPermission(Nothing, _
"BUILTIN\Administrators")
roleSec.Demand()

AppDomain.CurrentDomain.SetPrincipalPolicy(_
PrincipalPolicy.UnauthenticatedPrincipal)
CodeAccessPermission.RevertAssert()
t = DateTime.Now
For x = 0 To 50000
    l += GetTickCountSpecial()
Next
ts = DateTime.Now.Subtract(t)

Try
    GetTickCountSpecial()
Catch e As Security.SecurityException
    MsgBox("Caught the security exception after revert!")
End Try
Return ts
End Function
```

First, the routine asserts permission to control the principal settings for the
Application Domain. A Principal is an object that represents a role for a user. It
includes their identity, group membership, and whether the user is authenticated.
By default, you can't obtain the Principal identity of an Application Domain.
Doing so allows the code to determine the user ID of the person running the
code—a potential security breach.

Once permission is granted to change the principal settings, the PrincipalPolicy
for the current Application Domain is set to allow retrieval of the actual user
information.

Next, a PrincipalPermission object is created that specifies the built-in
Administrators group. The Demand method of this object will raise a runtime
error if the current user isn't an administrator.

The function then reverts the Assert, restoring the Application Domain settings
to the more secure state.

Finally, the function calls the GetTickCountSpecial function fifty thousand times. This function, as you recall, performs its own declarative Assert.

You'll notice that this function is much faster than the previous one. The earlier in the chain you can perform the Assert, the less time spent walking the stack.

You'll also find a Ticks4 method in the class. This class performs no assertions and would fail if called from the CallsUnmanaged2 application (which it isn't). The function is intended to be called from the CallsUnmanaged2b sample project, which is virtually identical to CallsUnmanaged2 except that you should leave it with the default (fully trusted) security settings. Use this project to get a sense of the impact of security checks on the speed of an application.

Security Techniques

There are a number of additional techniques you can use with regards to security. Here are some of the more important ones:

In addition to using Asserts, you can also Deny permission. Use this if you're unsure whether your code is perfectly safe and you want to ensure that it cannot perform certain operations.

You can restrict permissions to a certain set even if the assembly calling yours allows greater permission than you need.

You can request permissions at load time, setting minimum permissions needed for an assembly to run and optional permissions (which you'll use if available). You can even refuse permissions, preventing your assembly from being granted available permissions.

Let me stress just a few key points. Please take them seriously:

ASSERTS ARE DANGEROUS.

Do *not* assert a permission unless you are absolutely sure that your component cannot be misused.

Do *not* use Asserts unless absolutely necessary. If you do, use a Demand to restrict the Assert to the smallest possible set of callers.

Do use declarative demands to degrade gracefully if your code does not have sufficient permission to run.

Do write code that uses the least number of permissions possible. The result will be mobile code that can be easily distributed.

Bits and Pieces

This is the part of the book where I get to toss in all the final small topics that somehow don't quite fit anywhere else.

The Disassembly Dilemma

Imagine that one of your programmers has just created a truly sophisticated solution to a software problem, incorporating into the code information that you consider proprietary. The software ships and one day someone sends you the following e-mail: *Hi, I was looking at the assembly you shipped with your Emailer 2000 super application. It's pretty interesting. I was looking at your VerifyEmail algorithm shown in the following listing I obtained by disassembling your product:*

```
//  Microsoft (R) .NET Framework IL Disassembler.  Version 1.0.2914.16
//  Copyright (C) Microsoft Corp. 1998-2001. All rights reserved.


.namespace Disasm
{
  .class public auto ansi Emailer
        extends [mscorlib]System.Object
  {

    .method public instance bool
    VerifyEmail(string Email) cil managed
    {
      // Code size       20 (0x14)
      .maxstack  3
      .locals init (bool V_0)
      IL_0000:  ldarg.1
      IL_0001:  ldstr      "@" /* 70000001 */
      IL_0006:  ldc.i4.0
      IL_0007:  call       int32
      [Microsoft.VisualBasic]Microsoft.VisualBasic.Strings::
      InStr(string, string, valuetype
      [Microsoft.VisualBasic]Microsoft.VisualBasic.CompareMethod)
      IL_000c:  ldc.i4.0
      IL_000d:  ble.s      IL_0012

      IL_000f:  ldc.i4.1
      IL_0010:  br.s       IL_0013

      IL_0012:  ldloc.0
      IL_0013:  ret
    } // end of method Emailer::VerifyEmail
```

Anyway, it looks pretty obvious that the only thing you are doing here is checking to see if it has an @ sign in the e-mail address. It looks like someone didn't tell your programmers about your marketing material claiming to have a patented new algorithm for reliably checking e-mail.

And your reliable host verification routine:

```
.method string
        GetMyHost() cil managed
{
  // Code size       16 (0x10)
  .maxstack  1
  .locals init (string V_0)
  IL_0000:  ldarg.0
  IL_0001:  callvirt    instance object Disasm.Emailer
  IL_0006:  pop
  IL_0007:  call        string [System]
  IL_000c:  br.s        IL_000f

  IL_000e:  ldloc.0
  IL_000f:  ret
} // end of method Emailer::GetMyHost
```

...all it's doing is returning the value of the .NET Framework System.Net.Dns.GetHostName function.

And I looked inside your code and found this Delay function:

```
.method int32
        Delay() cil managed
{
  // Code size       48 (0x30)
  .maxstack  2
  .locals init (int32 V_0,
          int64 V_1,
          int64 V_2)
  IL_0000:  ldc.i8      0x1
  IL_0009:  stloc.1
  IL_000a:  ldloc.2
  IL_000b:  ldc.i8      0x1
  IL_0014:  add.ovf
  IL_0015:  stloc.2
  IL_0016:  ldloc.1
  IL_0017:  ldc.i8      0x1
  IL_0020:  add.ovf
  IL_0021:  stloc.1
```

```
    IL_0022:  ldloc.1
    IL_0023:  ldc.i8      0xf4240
    IL_002c:  ble.s       IL_000a

    IL_002e:  ldloc.0
    IL_002f:  ret
  } // end of method Emailer::Delay
 } // end of class Emailer


} // end of namespace Disasm


//*********** DISASSEMBLY COMPLETE **********************
// WARNING: Created Win32 resource file D:\CPBknet\Src1\CH16\Disasm\Disasm.res
```

A loop? You're delaying your code with a loop? Haven't you ever heard of wait-able timers? I'm not impressed. I think I'll post this on the Internet and see what people think.

Oh my.

There has been a fair amount of debate on this subject. Some developers have strongly criticized .NET as being easy to disassemble (the disassembly program used here, ildasm.exe, is included in the .NET Software Development Kit). Commercial component developers have been pressuring Microsoft to come up with some sort of obfuscator tool that can scramble data by doing things such as renaming variables, parameters, and private names and methods so it is harder to figure out what a particular assembly is doing.

I strongly encourage Microsoft to follow through with some sort of obfuscator tool but there are a few things you should consider before you get too excited about this issue.

This problem is not unique to .NET—other virtual machine-based platforms suffer the same problem (can you say Java?).

Some of the information people are concerned about is the same information .NET uses to prevent versioning conflicts. The JIT compiler needs class, method, and parameter information in order to work.

I once worked for a company that did semiconductor failure analysis. Some of our clients used our services to figure out how their competitor's chips worked. The truth is that any piece of hardware or software can be reverse engineered if you are willing to spend enough money.

Back when Visual Basic first came out, there was a lot of excitement because some German company came out with a VB disassembler. Ultimately, the issue was forgotten. Truthfully, disassembly isn't that big of a deal for most companies.

Remember, one thing a company cannot do is disassemble your code, then reassemble it with your company name and substitute it for one of yours. The strong name security described earlier in this chapter prevents this.

The relative ease of disassembling .NET applications is not, as I see it, a big problem. It won't be an issue at all for the vast majority of developers. The only reason I am writing about it here is because it is something you should be aware of. (And perhaps to give me one last opportunity to take a stand on a controversial issue).

Deployment

Time and space do not permit me to go into deployment issues in this book. While I doubt anyone will write an entire book on the issue, it certainly deserves a chapter of its own, which I'm afraid I'll have to pass on, at least for this edition.

However, I can't resist sharing one thought:

Windows has advanced greatly over the years growing more and more sophisticated. Along the way, installation programs have also grown in complexity and sophistication.

Now, with .NET, Windows has finally grown so sophisticated that it is actually possible to install an entire application by simply copying a program and its entire dependent files into a directory or directory structure using a simple Copy or XCopy operation.

Just like we used to do in MS-DOS.

Recap

This chapter focused on two critical subject areas that are essential for every VB.NET programmer to know. You first learned about versioning and how strong-names allow you to create assemblies that are bound closely to specific versions of dependent assemblies and prevent assembly spoofing and hacking. You learned how to use configuration files to allow selected assembly upgrades to occur.

Next, you learned about .NET security and how code access security is an essential innovation to allow increased code mobility without increased security vulnerability. You learned how to incorporate security into your application to perform privileged operations (if your assembly has sufficient permission to request them) and how to degrade gracefully when your caller does not have adequate permission to perform some of the operations required by your assembly. Don't forget, though, that the same capability .NET provides to control security down to the method level (or even within methods) can be applied to role access security and that roles can be whatever you define—not just user and group accounts defined by the operating system.

Finally, we discussed the disassembly dilemma and took a quick look at deployment.

Conclusion

THEY SAY THE BEST WAY to learn something is to teach it.

I think that is true.

I wrote this book for two reasons. First, because I had a clear vision of what today's VB6 programmers really need in order to learn .NET. I've been using some of these techniques (such as inheritance and multithreading) for years and knew right off they were the most likely to get people into trouble. I feel confident that this book is a good implementation of that vision and hope you now feel the same.

I also wrote this book because I knew it would force me to really dig into .NET and understand it myself. I'm the kind of software developer who likes to understand not just how to do something but how and why it works. I've found that understanding the concepts behind the language (and in this case, the framework) make me a better programmer. At the very least, the untold hours spent figuring out how to perform certain tasks (at times, uncertain whether the problem was a lack of understanding on my part or a bug in the framework or language) have given me exactly the kind of .NET background that I wanted to gain as quickly as possible.

And now you have that background as well.

I hope you enjoyed the journey as much as I enjoyed being your guide.

—Dan Appleman
May 2001

Index

Symbols

& (concatenation) operator, 205

+ (concatenation) operator, 205

= (Eqv) operator, 207

A

Active Server Pages, 423. *See also* ASP.NET

ActiveX, 6, 400

Adams, Scott, 30

AddHandler statement, 308

AddMessageFilter method, 417

AddressOf operator, 136, 308

ADO.NET, 388, 392–95

AndAlso operator, 203–5

And operator, 185, 203

ANSI-based operating systems, 476

API functions. *See* Win32 API functions

Append method, 58, 61, 69

application configuration files, 514, 515

Application Domains

    defined, 259

    deploying, 260

    illustrated, 259

    and security, 519–20

Application object, 417

applications. *See also* code examples

    client, 19–20

    deployment, 38, 267, 537

    distributed, 426–27

    role of Microsoft .NET in design, 427–31

    server-based, 18–19

    thick-client, 431–33

    traditional Windows, 431–33

    Web-based, 433–41

    WebService-based, 441–43

arrays

    ArrayExample code, 194–95

    control, 312–13

    marshaling, 487–91

    ObjectParams example, 222–23

    as objects, 222, 223

    passing as parameters, 222–23

    VBInterface example, 487–89

    VBInterfaceTest example, 489–91

    in VB.NET, 193–95

    zero-based, 193–94, 195

ASP (Active Server Pages), 423

ASP.NET

    and Button controls, 434, 437

    overview, 433

    and simple Web sample application, 436

assemblies

    default namespace, 263

    defining namespace, 263

    first mention, 36

    and manifests, 36

T

books for professionals by professionals™

About Apress

Apress, located in Berkeley, CA, is an innovative publishing company devoted to meeting the needs of existing and potential programming professionals. Simply put, the "A" in Apress stands for the "Author's Press™." Apress' unique author-centric approach to publishing grew from conversations between Dan Appleman and Gary Cornell, authors of best-selling, highly regarded computer books. In 1998, they set out to create a publishing company that emphasized quality above all else, a company with books that would be considered the best in their market. Dan and Gary's vision has resulted in over 30 widely acclaimed titles by some of the industry's leading software professionals.

Do You Have What It Takes to Write for Apress?

Apress is rapidly expanding its publishing program. If you can write and refuse to compromise on the quality of your work, if you believe in doing more then rehashing existing documentation, and if you're looking for opportunities and rewards that go far beyond those offered by traditional publishing houses, we want to hear from you!

Consider these innovations that we offer all of our authors:

- **Top royalties with *no* hidden switch statements**
  Authors typically only receive half of their normal royalty rate on foreign sales. In contrast, Apress' royalty rate remains the same for both foreign and domestic sales.

- **A mechanism for authors to obtain equity in Apress**
  Unlike the software industry, where stock options are essential to motivate and retain software professionals, the publishing industry has adhered to an outdated compensation model based on royalties alone. In the spirit of most software companies, Apress reserves a significant portion of its equity for authors.

- **Serious treatment of the technical review process**
  Each Apress book has a technical reviewing team whose remuneration depends in part on the success of the book since they too receive royalties.

Moreover, through a partnership with Springer-Verlag, one of the world's major publishing houses, Apress has significant venture capital behind it. Thus, we have the resources to produce the highest quality books *and* market them aggressively.

If you fit the model of the Apress author who can write a book that gives the "professional what he or she needs to know™," then please contact one of our Editorial Directors, Gary Cornell (gary_cornell@apress.com), Dan Appleman (dan_appleman@apress.com), Karen Watterson (karen_watterson@apress.com) or Jason Gilmore (jason_gilmore@apress.com) for more information.

Apress Titles

ISBN	LIST PRICE	AUTHOR	TITLE
1-893115-01-1	$39.95	Appleman	Appleman's Win32 API Puzzle Book and Tutorial for Visual Basic Programmers
1-893115-23-2	$29.95	Appleman	How Computer Programming Works
1-893115-97-6	$39.95	Appleman	Moving to VB.NET: Strategies, Concepts and Code
1-893115-09-7	$29.95	Baum	Dave Baum's Definitive Guide to LEGO MINDSTORMS
1-893115-84-4	$29.95	Baum, Gasperi, Hempel, and Villa	Extreme MINDSTORMS
1-893115-82-8	$59.95	Ben-Gan/Moreau	Advanced Transact-SQL for SQL Server 2000
1-893115-85-2	$34.95	Gilmore	A Programmer's Introduction to PHP 4.0
1-893115-17-8	$59.95	Gross	A Programmer's Introduction to Windows DNA
1-893115-62-3	$39.95	Gunnerson	A Programmer's Introduction to C#, Second Edition
1-893115-10-0	$34.95	Holub	Taming Java Threads
1-893115-04-6	$34.95	Hyman/Vaddadi	Mike and Phani's Essential C++ Techniques
1-893115-50-X	$34.95	Knudsen	Wireless Java: Developing with Java 2, Micro Edition
1-893115-79-8	$49.95	Kofler	Definitive Guide to Excel VBA
1-893115-56-9	$39.95	Kofler/Kramer	MySQL
1-893115-75-5	$44.95	Kurniawan	Internet Programming with VB
1-893115-19-4	$49.95	Macdonald	Serious ADO: Universal Data Access with Visual Basic
1-893115-06-2	$39.95	Marquis/Smith	A Visual Basic 6.0 Programmer's Toolkit
1-893115-22-4	$27.95	McCarter	David McCarter's VB Tips and Techniques
1-893115-76-3	$49.95	Morrison	C++ For VB Programmers
1-893115-80-1	$39.95	Newmarch	A Programmer's Guide to Jini Technology

ISBN	LIST PRICE	AUTHOR	TITLE
1-893115-81-X	$39.95	Pike	SQL Server: Common Problems, Tested Solutions
1-893115-20-8	$34.95	Rischpater	Wireless Web Development
1-893115-93-3	$34.95	Rischpater	Wireless Web Development with PHP and WAP
1-893115-24-0	$49.95	Sinclair	From Access to SQL Server
1-893115-94-1	$29.95	Spolsky	User Interface Design for Programmers
1-893115-53-4	$39.95	Sweeney	Visual Basic for Testers
1-893115-65-8	$39.95	Tiffany	Pocket PC Database Development with eMbedded Visual Basic
1-893115-59-3	$59.95	Troelsen	C# and the .NET Platform
1-893115-54-2	$49.95	Trueblood/Lovett	Data Mining and Statistical Analysis Using SQL
1-893115-16-X	$49.95	Vaughn	ADO Examples and Best Practices
1-893115-83-6	$44.95	Wells	Code Centric: T-SQL Programming with Stored Procedures and Triggers
1-893115-95-X	$49.95	Welschenbach	Cryptography in C and C++
1-893115-05-4	$39.95	Williamson	Writing Cross-Browser Dynamic HTML
1-893115-78-X	$49.95	Zukowski	Definitive Guide to Swing for Java 2, Second Edition
1-893115-92-5	$49.95	Zukowski	Java Collections

Available at bookstores nationwide or from Springer Verlag New York, Inc. at 1-800-777-4643; fax 1-212-533-3503. Contact us for more information at sales@apress.com.

Apress Titles Publishing SOON!

ISBN	AUTHOR	TITLE
1-893115-99-2	Cornell/Morrison	Programming VB.NET: A Guide for Experienced Programmers
1-893115-72-0	Curtin	Trust: Online Security for Developers
1-893115-55-0	Frenz	Visual Basic for Scientists
1-893115-96-8	Jorelid	J2EE FrontEnd Technologies: A Programmer's Guide to Servlets, JavaServer Pages, and Enterprise
1-893115-87-9	Kurata	Doing Web Development: Client-Side Techniques
1-893115-58-5	Oellerman	Fundamental Web Services with XML
1-893115-89-5	Shemitz	Kylix: The Professional Developer's Guide and Reference
1-893115-29-1	Thomsen	Database Programming with VB.NET

Available at bookstores nationwide or from Springer Verlag New York, Inc. at 1-800-777-4643; fax 1-212-533-3503. Contact us for more information at sales@apress.com.

Announcing *About VS.NET*—
the *free* Apress .NET e-newsletter with great .NET news, information, code—and attitude

We guarantee that this isn't going to be your typical boring e-newsletter with just a list of URLs (though it will have them as well).

Instead, *About VS.NET* will contain contributions from a whole slate of top .NET gurus, edited by award-winning, best-selling authors Gary Cornell and Dan Appleman. Upcoming issues will feature articles on:

- Best coding practices in ADO.NET

- The hidden "gotchas" in doing thread programming in VB.NET

- Why C# is (not) a better choice than VB.NET

- What Java can learn from C# and vice versa

About VS.NET will cover it all!

This *free* e-newsletter will be the easiest way for you to get up-to-date .NET information delivered to your Inbox every two weeks—more often if there's breaking news!

From Books to Software

A message from the author…

I hope you've enjoyed this book. I'd like to take this opportunity to tell you about some other books and software products I've been working on.

Is your company trying to decide between **C#** and **VB.NET**? Before you make any final decisions, be sure to read my PDF ebook "Visual Basic or C#: Which to Choose" available at `http://www.desaware.com/VBorCSharp.htm`.

I've often been asked by programmers to recommend books for beginners—something they could read with their kids (or show to their managers). I ended up writing one: *How Computer Programming Works* also available from Apress (ISBN 1-893115-23-2).

When not writing books, I am the president of **Desaware Inc.**—A leading vendor of software components. We're rapidly moving into products for .NET as well. Visit `http://www.desaware.com` for information on these products and more:

SpyWorks 6.3: Our best-selling low level toolkit for VB programmers now supports system hooks, cross-task subclassing and keyboard hooks for VB.NET and C#.

VersionStamper: The .NET framework does solve DLL Hell problems for .NET components, but what about the COM components you use from your .NET assemblies (something that will be common for quite a while). VersionStamper is being updated to be easily useable from VB.NET and C# to provide the auto-update and remote diagnostic capabilities that have made it an essential part of every VB6 project.

StorageTools: Microsoft's OLE Structured Storage is a powerful data storage mechanism that is actually better than databases for many types of data storage applications. We're updating StorageTools for use from VB.NET and C# as well.

NT Service Toolkit: Desaware's best-selling NT Service toolkit makes it so easy to create complex services for Windows NT and 2000 that we have C++ programmers switching to VB just to create services. Hard to believe? It's true. Visit `http://www.desaware.com/NTToolkitL2.htm` for details.

If you'd like to stay up to date with these projects and others not yet announced, the best way is to sign up for our listserve by sending an Email to `listserve@desaware.com` and including the word "Subscribe" in the subject line. Don't worry—we won't overwhelm you with spam—we'll often go months between messages, and we never sell or lend out our list.

Thank you for your support

Dan Appleman
dan@desaware.com, dan_appleman@apress.com